Radical Conduct

While the French Revolution drew immense attention to French radicals and their ideas, London also played host to a radical intellectual culture. Drawing on both original material and a range of interdisciplinary insights, *Radical Conduct* transforms our understanding of the literary radicalism of London at the time of the French Revolution. It offers new accounts of people's understanding of and relationship to politics, their sense of the boundaries of privacy, their practices of sociability, friendship, gossip and discussion, the relations between radical men and women, and their location in a wider world of sound and movement in the period. It reveals a series of tensions between many radicals' deliberative practices and aspirations and the conventions and practices in which their behaviour remained embedded. Exploring these relationships and pressures reveals the fractured world of London society and politics, dramatically illuminating both the changing fortunes of radical men and women and the intriguing uncertainties that drove some of the government's repressive policies.

MARK PHILP is Professor of History at the University of Warwick and an Emeritus Fellow of Oriel College. He has published widely on the history of ideas, late eighteenth and early nineteenth century European history and on political realism and ethics in public life. He is the author of *Political Conduct* (2007) and *Reforming Ideas in Britain* (2013).

T0364205

Radical Conduct

*Politics, Sociability and Equality
in London 1789–1815*

Mark Philp

University of Warwick

CAMBRIDGE
UNIVERSITY PRESS

CAMBRIDGE
UNIVERSITY PRESS

Shaftesbury Road, Cambridge CB2 8EA, United Kingdom

One Liberty Plaza, 20th Floor, New York, NY 10006, USA

477 Williamstown Road, Port Melbourne, VIC 3207, Australia

314–321, 3rd Floor, Plot 3, Splendor Forum, Jasola District Centre, New Delhi – 110025, India

103 Penang Road, #05–06/07, Visioncrest Commercial, Singapore 238467

Cambridge University Press is part of Cambridge University Press & Assessment, a department of the University of Cambridge.

We share the University's mission to contribute to society through the pursuit of education, learning and research at the highest international levels of excellence.

www.cambridge.org
Information on this title: www.cambridge.org/9781108820219

DOI: 10.1017/9781108898768

First published 2020
First paperback edition 2022

A catalogue record for this publication is available from the British Library

ISBN   978-1-108-84218-1   Hardback
ISBN   978-1-108-82021-9   Paperback

For the home team, with thanks: Sarah, Joe, Ruth, Hannah, Matthew and Ben

Contents

Figures and Tables

Acknowledgements

A much earlier version of Chapter 2 was published in *Enlightenment and Dissent* in 2014; Chapters 5 and 6 develop some material from my essay 'William Godwin' in Sandrine Bergès, Eileen Hunt Botting and Alan Coffee (eds.), *The Wollstonecraftian Mind* (London and New York: Routledge, 2019); Chapters 6 and 7 use material in 'Unconventional Norms' in Kevin Gilmartin (ed.), *Sociable Places* (Cambridge: Cambridge University Press, 2017); and Chapter 8 greatly expands and repurposes a line of argument and some material from a forthcoming short essay in the *Journal of British Studies*.

In writing this book I have relied heavily on primary sources – but have done so against the background of long immersion in the scholarly community and scholarship of those working in the eighteenth and early nineteenth centuries. I have sought to reference this work where specifically relevant, but it is difficult to do justice to the extensive coffee (and cake) discussions, the lunches, teas, dinners and late-night conversations I have been privileged to have had. Therefore, I am sure there are many unrecognised influences and assumptions in what follows. Nonetheless, I try here to acknowledge some of those who have been willing to indulge me.

Since moving to Warwick in 2013 I have benefitted greatly from the conviviality and stimulus provided by my History colleagues – especially Mark Knights, Maria Luddy, Dan Branch and Rebecca Earle, but also David Anderson, Maxine Berg, Michael Bycroft, Bernard Capp, Anne Gerritsen, Joachim Häberlen, Sarah Hodges, Laurence Klein, Imogen Peck, Naomi Pullin, Giorgio Riello, Sarah Richardson, Anna Ross, Carolyn Steedman and Mathew Thomson – together with colleagues in other departments, Kate Astbury, Katherine Hambridge (now Durham), James Hodkinson, Tina Lupton (now Copenhagen), Maria Roca Lizarazu (now Birmingham), Rebecca Probert (now Exeter), Johannes Roessler, John Snape and David F. Taylor (now Oxford), with whom I have collaborated in various projects. I have also had a stream of bright and energetic undergraduates working with me on related projects who have also made me think harder at getting my story straight – especially Tier Blunden, Ian Caistor-Parker, Clare Clarke, Charles Edwards, Sarah Gray, El Kerfoot, Amal Malik, Ewan McGowan, Isabelle Rieppe and Celine Romano.

I have continued to benefit hugely from the ongoing practice of debate and disagreement that I have shared with Jo Innes on the Re-imagining Democracy project over the past twenty years and from the generosity of all those associated with it – especially Maurizio Isabella and Eduardo Posada Carbo – but including so many others that we had to have a separate list in the most recent volume on *Re-Imagining Democracy in the Mediterranean* (2019), a great many of whom have remained actively in touch and have contributed to the web-project, barricades.ac.uk, that is exploring changing forms of protest and con-tention in Europe between 1815–1850 and that has informed some of my thinking here. My less institutional interlocutors are owed thanks for their ongoing intellectual engagement and friendship – John Barrell, Pam Clemit, Mary Ann Constantine, James Cummings, Kate Davison, Michael Drolet, Helen Edmundson, Mary Fairclough, Martin Fitzpa-trick, Alex Franklin, Kevin Gilmartin, James Grande, Harriet Guest, David Hopkin, Jane Huyg, Oskar Cox Jensen, David Kennerley, Sarah Lloyd, Jon Mee, Ian Newman, Eliza O'Brien, Eamonn O'Keefe, David O'Shaughnessy, Fred Rosen, Michael Rossington, Gillian Russell, Adam Swift, Georgios Varouxakis, Anne Verjus, David and Cathy Wells-Cole and Tim Whelan. Natalie Hanley Smith has been my doc-toral student over the last three years and proved admirably tolerant of me pressing my explanatory preoccupations on her while she was trying to remain focused on her thesis on *ménage à trois*. My family, having maintained an ironic detachment towards Godwin over the last thirty years came up trumps by reading sections and making me think harder about a range of topics: Ruth tutored me on politeness and sexual conduct in the early eighteenth century; Hannah did so in relation to elements of the chapter on music; and Joe pointed me to a range of literature in anthropology. The book has been written despite competi-tion for domestic computing equipment with the organisation Prison Reading Groups (http://prisonreadinggroups.org.uk/) – but given what it and its Director do, I claim it as an honour to have been so consist-ently sidelined.

In the later stages of the book I became involved in the Digitens Project (www.digitens.fr/1/accueil) funded by the European Union's Horizon 2020 research and innovation programme under the Marie Curie grant agreement No 823862, which gave me the opportunity to test out some ideas with people who know the field of sociability more intimately, especially Kimberley Page Jones, Annick Cossic and Valery Capdeville, and to work with and at the BNF Richelieu.

I have also benefitted greatly from Edward Pope's forensic work on Godwin's Diary (www.edpopehistory.co.uk/), especially from his expert knowledge of archival resources relating to births, deaths and marriages; I also had technical assistance on stats in relation to Chapter 1 from Henry Bradshaw and in Chapter 7 from Adam Obeng (both of whom helped me see more precisely what I wanted to ask them to do!); and Ragini Puri helped with the Index (on the History Department's research assistance scheme). Special thanks are due to the support of Sue Palmer and her colleagues at the Soane Museum and Library, Richard Ovenden and the staff of the Bodleian, An de Camp and the Ashmolean staff, Corinne Le Bitouze at the BNF, and staff at the National Archive, the manuscripts room of the British Library, The London Metropolitan Archive, The Lambeth Palace Archive, Barnsley Library, the New York Public Library and its Pforzheimer and Berg Collections and the Huntington Library.

I have given a number of papers on material related to this book, at The Huntington, Newcastle, Sheffield, Princeton, Queen Mary, Oxford, Brest, Warwick and on several occasions on different sections in York (more or less a home from home) and I am grateful to my hosts and the audiences' responses to what were often more like ruminations than clear and cogent arguments. Liz Friend-Smith has yet again shown Cambridge University Press's willingness to indulge me and was able to find two extremely helpful reviewers for me to respond to and largely agree with. And thanks are owed to the Cambridge University Press team, including Liz Steel, Tom Haynes, Shaheer Husanne and Atifa Jiwa.

Just over five years ago Peter Dahlman, Andreas Kyrris, Jonathan Hughes, Lisa Fraser and the staff of the Head and Neck Unit at the Churchill Hospital in Oxford saved my life. I am very grateful to them for doing that. I hope they approve of how I've used the time they gave me. For my part, it has been a great privilege and pleasure to have had the chance to do this.

Introduction

A New Era

In response to the French Revolution, a wave of enthusiasm for and optimism about social and political change swept Britain. The Dissenting minister Richard Price famously provoked Edmund Burke's ire in 1789 by preaching that, having shared in the benefits of the Glorious Revolution of 1688, and seen two other revolutions (American and French) he could see 'the ardour for liberty catching and spreading, a general amendment beginning in human affairs, the dominion of kings, changed for the dominion of laws, and the dominion of priests giving way to the dominion of reason and conscience.'[1] Other members of the middling and professional orders, especially those concentrated around the arts, literature and professions of London, also saw these events as heralding wider changes in the European order: from war to peace; from competition to harmonious and productive exchange; from force and fraud to a rational grounding of authority. Tom Paine felt sufficient confidence that the age of European wars was over that he designed a whole welfare system on the assumption that the taxation collected to fight wars could safely be repurposed to promote a better society.[2]

People brought to these expectations a legacy of enlightenment critiques of luxury and the waste and decadence of fashionable society, a scepticism about the legitimacy of monarchy, aristocracy and priest-craft and a set of aspirations for a more egalitarian and open world that would be based on talent and contribution. Above all, they wanted to think for themselves, to read about events and ideas, to discuss them with their associates and to be in the vanguard of change. And they acted: they met and talked; they established societies; they wrote tracts and texts; they

---

[1] Richard Price, 'A Discourse on the Love of our Country', in *Price, Political Writings* (Cambridge: Cambridge University Press, 2009), p. 194.
[2] Thomas Paine, 'Rights of Man: Part the Second' (1792), in Mark Philp (ed.), *Rights of Man, Common Sense, and other Political Writings* (Oxford: Oxford University Press, 1995), chapter 4.

1

abjured aristocratic manners and excess; they cut their hair and changed their clothes; they preached and practiced the improvability of human capacities; and they sought to practice equality. Theirs was not a passive response to events overseas, but an active attempt to be involved with, to embody, and thereby to further the changes they saw as immanent in the world unfolding around them. With the benefit of hindsight, Wordsworth's description of their French compatriots captured their ambition and his anxiety about their hubris.

> The inert
> Were roused, and lively natures rapt away!
> They who had fed their childhood upon dreams,
> The playfellows of fancy, who had made
> All powers of swiftness, subtilty, and strength
> Their ministers, – who in lordly wise had stirred
> Among the grandest objects of the sense,
> And dealt with whatsoever they found there
> As if they had within some lurking right
> To wield it; – they, too, who, of gentle mood,
> Had watched all gentle motions, and to these
> Had fitted their own thoughts, schemers more wild,
> And in the region of their peaceful selves; –
> Now was it that both found, the meek and lofty
> Did both find, helpers to their heart's desire,
> And stuff at hand, plastic as they could wish;
> Were called upon to exercise their skill,
> Not in Utopia, subterranean fields,
> Or some secreted island, Heaven knows where!
> But in the very world, which is the world
> Of all of us, – the place where in the end
> We find our happiness, or not at all![3]

This is a book about these members of the middling orders who championed reform, who believed in the importance of reason as a basis for equality and an authoritative guide for their own behaviour, and who challenged the conventions and practices of society. This includes Mary Wollstonecraft, William Godwin, Mary Hays, Thomas Holcroft, Elizabeth Inchbald, Amelia Alderson and many of their associates.[4]

---

[3] Wordsworth, 'The Prelude' (1805) Bk X, l. 711–731. In Stephen Gill, *William Wordsworth*, Oxford Authors series (Oxford: Oxford University Press, 1984), p. 550.

[4] Something needs to be said about the terminology of 'middle class' and the middling sort. There is evidence of the emergence of people engaged in a broad range of occupations and activities that involved little menial labour, that relied on some skills and some education and that generated an income that allowed people to maintain their families in a moderate style, with a developing range of entertainments, consumption patterns,

In the title, and in what follows, I emphasise 'conduct' because I am concerned less with what people said or wrote and more with how they conducted themselves. That is, with how they acted, what principles and aspirations they sought to embody, how they measured themselves in relation to those around them and how they read and responded to the conduct of others. Their conduct was for them a work in progress. They practised it through their relationships, in their writing and in their actions. Indeed, their lives were conducted through a range of activities or 'practices' – where that term denotes a combination of components that have an internal logic that delimits and enables agency and through that produces and reproduces the person's world of experience. Their conduct and commitments have to be understood in relation to the shared practices, networks and discourses that operated in their circles and in the wider society. And we can appreciate the distinctive character of some of their more radical relationships only by locating their conduct within the set of more widely shared conventions and activities that they partly took for granted. At the same time, it is clear that those involved often underestimated the influence that these wider conventions exerted on their individual choices and commitments.

Most of those on whom I focus welcomed the French Revolution and supported the cause of parliamentary reform in Britain in the following decade. William Godwin plays a key role, in part because of the resource that his diary offers to historians,[5] and in part because he epitomises

---

activities, etc. that they participated in and that partly emulated but were also often distinct from those of the aristocracy. Drawing objective boundaries for such a class is unlikely to be successful in this period, as would be searching for evidence of a strong subjective unitary identification as a class. There was a good deal of awareness of position, but it was on a complex, gradated ladder. As I argue in Chapter 8, we have to ask different questions about how particular groups and communities might come to have a sense of shared identity and commitments. With the people I examine here, I do not claim that middle class identity was what they fixed on, so much as that writers, professionals and those connected with arts and entertainment in London began to have a sense of themselves as something like a universal class – in the sense of it being in the vanguard of thinking and progress. They were not on the edge of precarity, nor working wholly at the behest of others, nor were they part of a wealthy and idle élite, and they came to see themselves as in some sense holding the balance and ensuring that society would be progressive – although these two impulses parted company in the 1790s under the pressure of political polarisation. Dror Wahrman makes a case for that emerging identity to be fundamentally about politics and ideas. If I disagree, it is because I think those are not 'natural kinds' and we are better looking at sets of shared and developing practices. But in either case – I want to argue that, seen from the inside of the group I am interested in exploring – there was a strong sense that in some respects their time had come. See Dror Wahrman, *Imagining the Middle Class: The Political Representation of Class in Britain 1780–1840* (Cambridge: Cambridge University Press, 1995).
[5] A digital edition which I edited with Victoria Myers and David O'Shaughnessy in 2012 with a grant from the Leverhulme Trust: *The Diary of William Godwin*, edited by

some of the distinctive features of this group of intellectuals of the middling and professional orders and their hopes and expectations. But, while some sections of the book are particularly devoted to Godwin and his immediate circles, my aim throughout is to draw on a wide range of primary resources so as to more fully understand the context for people's thinking and acting. I am also especially concerned to understand the ways in which women in these circles conducted themselves, the challenges and pitfalls they faced and the extent to which their actions were similar to or distinct from those of men and women of similar social status who did not share their political aspirations. More widely, I examine how the agency and understandings of this group fared as the world they inhabited faced the challenges of the developing war with France and the escalation of government repression. Dealing with often dramatic changes and sometimes traumatic experiences, how did people whose hopes and ideals were so positive cope with an increasingly dispiriting and oppressive reality? How did they explain these changes to themselves and how far did they adjust their actions to the more straitened circumstances in which they found themselves?

I have written previously about the political ideas of the period, about both loyalist and reform movements and about areas of literary activity, but this book tries to think more systematically about a range of practical and discursive tensions that emerged in the period between what these men and women aspired to and what they were able to achieve. It focuses in particular on the way that, for all their aspirations, their lives remained embedded in and profoundly shaped by often very conventional social expectations, practices and forms that often undermined or challenged their hopes and ambitions. There are ironies here, and in some cases tragedies, and many were not solely of their own making. But change brings challenges, and this book is an attempt to examine how the rhetoric and the ambitions for change, particularly in relation to inequality, were formulated and practised within a society of deeply engrained customs and conventions.

The multiple dimensions of people's lives and worlds, how they knitted together and with what degree of individual agency demands attention. There was for my subjects what we might think of as a 'Neurath's boat' problem.[6] Otto Neurath drew an analogy between how we make

---

Victoria Myers, David O'Shaughnessy and Mark Philp (Oxford: Oxford Digital Library, 2010), http://godwindiary.bodleian.ox.ac.uk.

[6] In his *Anti-Spengler* (München: Georg D. W. Callwey, Verlagsbuchhandlung, 1921): 'we are like sailors who on the open sea must reconstruct their ship but are never able to start afresh from the bottom'.

critical progress in relation to knowledge and how we might repair a boat at sea. We can take up any given plank, scrutinise and replace it or repair it; but we cannot take them all up simultaneously without drowning. So too my subjects conducted themselves and lived their lives through sets of practices replete with assumptions and categories, principles of exchange and equivalence, and forms of engagement with a material world that invoked categories of salience and value, permanence and instability. Some of this they took largely for granted; some they were acutely aware of and critically reflective about. In any context, trying to focus on all the moving parts simultaneously produces disorientation and confusion. For my subjects, their enthusiasm for France, their sense that they were participating in a new age, their beliefs in the remediability of the present and their optimism about the changes they saw as prefigured in events around them were accompanied by much that they barely attended to or assumed to be natural, inevitable or a task for the future.[7]

The period 1789–1815 has been the focus of extensive scholarly work because of the drama of events, the belief that it represents a turning point in the development of popular politics, and the wealth of literary and cultural material relating to the politics of the period.[8] This attention

---

[7] One question I cannot deal with here concerns the complex relationships between the reforming literary culture of the 1790s and the advocates for ending the slave trade. My sense is that here too there was considerable inattention and unexamined assumptions both of their own superiority and of the eventual emancipation from nature for those in chains. But serious questions as to the capital's dependence on slavery, how deeply the trade ran through its commercial and intellectual veins and the way in this inflected the lives and attitudes of those so connected seem rarely to have been asked. Slaves were used as a poignant image – but their embodied reality and their contribution to the wealth of the country and to the racial distortion of its culture was rarely the subject of sustained reflection. In Mary Hays, *Memoirs of Emma Courtney* (1796), edited by Eleanor Ty (Oxford: Oxford University Press, 1996), for example (as in Jane Austen's *Mansfield Park*), it is clear that our heroine's family is steeped in the trade. This raises questions for the modern reader about how far Emma's own disordered emotional world is in part an inflection of that deeper corruption and how far Mary Hays intended this or was relying on a commonplace understanding of the hazards of the trade. But these are not issues that the literary radicals dealt with directly for the most part – and if we look, for example, at women using the analogy between slavery and the position of women at the end of the eighteenth century, we do not find ourselves in contact with their most progressive thinking.

[8] There is a voluminous literature, detailed extremely well in Boyd Hilton's text and the bibliographical essay in his *A Mad, Bad, & Dangerous People* (Oxford: Clarendon Press, 2006), which should be accompanied by Arthur Burns and Joanna Innes, *Rethinking the Age of Reform: Britain 1780–1830* (Cambridge: Cambridge University Press/Past and Present, 2003), especially the essays by Burns and Innes. In relation to the rise of popular radicalism and the government response, see: John Barrell, *Imagining the King's Death: Figurative Treason, Fantasies of Regicide, 1793–1796* (Oxford: Oxford University Press, 2000) and *The Spirit of Despotism: Invasions of Privacy in the 1790s* (Oxford: Oxford University Press, 2006); Albert Goodwin, *The Friends of Liberty: The English Democratic*

is coupled with a powerful sense that this quarter of a century represents a peak of enlightenment optimism alongside the dawn of romanticism with its recognition of more subterranean forces in the human and natural world. And in that combination it includes an acknowledgement of the impact on men and women in Britain of wider events: the traumas of war; the mixed horror and intoxication of the Revolutionary Terror in France; the re-ordering of Europe under Napoleon; the challenge to Britain's trade and colonial activity following the American Revolution and subsequently the Napoleonic blockade; and the growing movement against the slave trade on which so much British wealth rested. Professional and literary men and women and more generally people of the middling sort were trying to exercise agency and realise their hopes in a world that was rapidly changing, both promising much and at times seeming on the brink of disaster.

London

In the 1790s the population of London stood at about one million people. It was then the biggest city in the world. Heinrich Heine wrote to his friend Friedrich Merckel, while visiting London in April 1827, 'London has surpassed all my expectations in respect of its vastness; but

Movement in the Age of the French Revolution (London: Hutchinson, 1979); Jenny Graham, *The Nation, the Law and the King: Reform Politics in England, 1789–1799* (Lanham, MD: University Press of America, 2000); J. Ann Hone, *For the Cause of Truth: Radicalism in London 1796–1821* (Oxford: Clarendon Press, 1982); Mark Philp, *Reforming Ideas in Britain: Politics and Language in the Shadow of the French Revolution 1789–1815* (Cambridge: Cambridge University Press, 2014); E. P. Thompson, *The Making of the English Working Class* (Harmondsworth: Penguin, 1963) and *Customs in Common* (Harmondsworth, Penguin, 1993). For print culture and the related literary world see: Kevin Gilmartin, *Print Politics: The Press and Radical Opposition in Early Nineteenth-Century England* (Cambridge: Cambridge University Press, 1996), *Writing against Revolution: Literary Conservatism in Britain, 1790–1832* (Cambridge: Cambridge University Press, 2007); Harriet Guest, *Unbounded Attachment: Sentiment and Politics in the Age of the French Revolution* (Oxford: Oxford University Press, 2013) and *Small Change: Women Learning, Patriotism, 1750–1810* (Chicago, IL: Chicago University Press, 2000); Jon Mee, *Conversable Worlds: Literature, Contention, and Community 1762 to 1830* (Oxford: Oxford University Press, 2011) and *Print, Publicity, and Popular Radicalism in the 1790s: the Laurel of Liberty* (Cambridge: Cambridge University Press, 2016); and Olivia Smith, *The Politics of Language 1791–1819* (Oxford: Oxford University Press, 1984). For war and its impact, see: John Cookson, *The British Armed Nation 1793–1815* (Oxford: Oxford University Press, 1997); Jenny Uglow, *In These Times: Living in Britain through Napoleon's Wars, 1793–1815* (London: Faber and Faber, 2014). And for the wider cultural and social changes of the period, see: Dror Wahrman, *The Making of the Modern Self: Identity and Culture in Eighteenth Century England* (New Haven, CT: Yale University Press, 2006) and his *Imagining the Middle Class*.

I have lost myself' – nicely capturing the spatial *and* personal disorientation produced by the sheer size, and, implicitly, the sense that one maintains one's orientation only in more constrained circles.[9] The city grew significantly in the first half of the century, but it is still plausible to think that something of that experience would have been shared by visitors thirty years earlier. Despite this, there is a tendency to think of 1789–1815 as a period in which everyone knew everyone else (or at least, 'anyone who is anyone' would have done so). I previously thought something like this in relation to William Godwin, since his diary is such a cornucopia of reference for London between 1788 and 1836. Over time, however, I have become increasingly convinced that while he met a lot of people in his lifetime, we need to avoid overstating his and other people's connectedness and we need to reflect carefully on what this apparently dense sociability in fact meant to those involved. We should also not assume that his experience was a common one. Accordingly, I have tried to look much more closely at the bases on which people's core circles were formed and to assess the extent to which a relatively small group of associates played a dominant role in most people's sociability.[10]

The groups of reformers and literary radicals that I focus on are a particular slice of London's life. In exploring this world I also examine some of the assumptions often made about the period: that people were all equally in the know about scandals, fashions, literary disputes, and so on; that caricatures spoke to a wide general audience; that those in government understood a good deal about the nature or ambitions of the reform societies; and that the deliberative equality to which reformers aspired was widely reciprocated by those with whom they interacted in bookshops, at dinners or in meetings. To take one example, much of the extensive literature on the period sees the literary and political culture of London as a relatively unified domain, in which people knew each other and in which there was extensive engagement, often across gender boundaries and those of social class. In contrast, I argue that the worlds people inhabited may have been much more fractured and divided and that what held those worlds together might have varied considerably between men and women and between areas of cultural activity and profession. I suggest we might usefully think of a range of ways in which

[9] Celina Fox, *London: World City* (New Haven, CT: Yale University Press, 2002), p. 12.
[10] I have also been influenced (if not wholly persuaded) by the suggestion of the anthropologist Robin Dunbar that there might be an upper limit to the number of people we can know. R. I. M. Dunbar, 'Neocortex Size as a Constraint on Group Size in Primates', *Journal of Human Evolution* 22(6) (1992), 469–493.

people were known to each other: friendship, acquaintance and ties based on family and locality; and that we should reflect on the way that people's aspirations for certain types of exchange influenced the relationships they formed. To take one instance, it is clear that the egalitarian aspirations that fuelled many male relationships often raised substantially greater difficulties when people sought to extend them across gender boundaries.

The literary and political radicalism of the period was the culmination of decades of relative stability coupled with a growing optimism about the possibilities of progress and the development of knowledge. This did not equip people well to handle the pressures introduced by government repression and loyalist reaction during the long and exhausting war with France or to appreciate and develop responses to the stubborn resistances of their political and social worlds. Their eventual fragmentation under the pressures of repression involved some degree of failure to recognise the deep embeddedness of many of their contemporaries (and themselves) in an order and ways of seeing the world that undercut their aspirations. That most people fell back on older ways does not mean that things remained wholly unchanged – but their experience testifies to the fragility of their deliberative ambitions and conduct when these came into conflict with the conventional practices of the social world. This is not a story of radical hubris, nor it is one only of government repression, although there are elements of both. It offers instead an account of the complex world of late eighteenth and early nineteenth century London in which people developed aspirations for a different sort of future and sometimes experimented with approximations to that future, but found their pasts and their present encroaching in ways that further alienated the wider community they had hoped to take with them.

My concern here is to try and tell a more subtle and convincing story about how men and women of the middling orders, arts and professions of the 1790s and 1800s (predominantly in London, but drawing on other evidence where relevant) sought to live their lives and to assess the obstacles and opportunities they faced or could create and to set this analysis in the context of increasing government repression and intolerance towards unorthodox political views.

The Structure of the Book

The book is structured in three parts. The first two chapters explore people's understanding of 'politics' and the changes this undergoes in the first thirty years of the nineteenth century. This involves recognising that for most people politics was matter for discussion, but it was not thought about as something in which they were practically involved. This was partly because it was largely seen as a matter of private deliberation. In the 1790s, as John Barrell has shown, the traditional distinction between public and private was increasingly encroached on by government.[11] Over time the lines were re-drawn and a new understanding of political activity emerged. As part of this discussion I also contrast the idea that many radicals held, that deliberation would produce convergence with their ongoing experience of disagreement. Using Godwin, I examine how that played out, especially in cases in which the disagreement seemed to him to involve the apostacy of and betrayal by his friends. And I consider other dimensions of his radical conduct that generated further conflicts, especially in relation to debt, but also in relation to his relationship to Wollstonecraft and the publication of his *Memoirs ... of her*.

The middle section of the book (Chapters 3–7) turns to questions of sociability, friendship and acquaintance, particularly with respect to gender. In such relationships people argued and debated and did so in the belief that it was through deliberation that knowledge would expand and the world would change. As such, sociability was both the medium for their practice and the essential vehicle for societal change. The models we have of this world of sociability are often based on élite sources. In contrast I explore relatively middle class and professional circles and do so partly quantitatively, looking especially at differences between male and female circles and practices. To do that I begin by examining the diaries of Marianne Ayrton and Elizabeth Soane, before moving to look at the evidence for the existence of a radical sociability among some of the leading female proponents of reform. I will argue that male social circles were largely driven by ideas of disinterested friendship; female circles much less so. That leads me to a discussion of the problems that arose from attempts to practice that egalitarian model across the gender divide. In the final parts of this section I examine the changing character of Godwin's deliberative practice in relation to women and especially in relation to Amelia Alderson, Mary Wollstonecraft and Sarah Elwes. Here too, the conventional practices he encountered consistently complicated his attempts to establish more egalitarian and intellectually productive relationships.

In the final section (Chapter 8), I turn to examine music, dance and song, areas of activities that the more literary radicals were often resistant to and critical of. These practices deserve attention for the ways in which they embedded their participants in a particular narrative of the world,

---

[11] See Barrell, *The Spirit of Despotism*, chapter 2.

which consistently undercut the more rationalist aspirations of the radicals. This area should also encourage us to recognise that many of the earlier components of discussion, including ideas of public and private, the place of loyalist intervention in communities and the conventions of male/female conduct, were implicated in and reproduced in part through these more emotional and bodily practices.

Tools, Methods and Materials

This book is a work of history that draws on historical and literary materials and on the methods and the ideas of the social sciences. In that spirit, it is a set of inquiries that uses a range of ideas and tools from the social sciences to examine this particular historical period and to raise a series of issues that are historical – what happened?, how did this work?, why did this change? and in what way? – and methodological – how could we assess this?, what does it mean when people use particular words in certain ways?, how are what people say and what they mean related to what they would do?, what resources might we need from other disciplines to think about issues that strike us as surprising or discomfiting in certain ways? and how far might our picture of this world be too directed by our own certainties about what makes sense and what doesn't?

In making my case I rely on a number of tools and ideas that it is useful to set out briefly here. The first concerns the concept of politics; the second concerns sociability and the nature of acquaintance and friendship; and the third explores forms of talk that are not deliberative, but serve other functions, and here I am principally interested in practices of talking *about* others.

In considering 'politics' we need to consider the difference between, on the one hand, the exact character and local understanding of what was or was not 'political' in this period and, on the other, whether there are not components of this 'domain' that are invariable in various ways. The latter view sees a certain structure to the field of politics, involving attempts to establish authority and legitimacy in a context of conflict. It does not presume that every society has politics; but it does see politics as a domain that exists in many societies to order conflict through the exercise of authority and power that requires a degree of legitimation. Furthermore, political disagreement operates in at least two different dimensions – the substance of the differences and their claims and questions about the norms, rules and practices by which that difference is to be contested, negotiated and settled. Under what we might call 'normal politics' the second dimension is largely taken for granted; in less settled times, it too becomes a focus for contention. In so far as it does, government may begin to lose its grip on political authority and may resort increasingly to force and violence. In the period covered in this book, this latter dimension can be seen to be increasingly contested in and through conceptions of loyal opposition, patriotism, justified resistance, sedition and repression, with people developing and further challenging what was within and what was beyond the pale and for whom. It was also in evidence in the government resorting to increasingly blunt forms of repression that sought effectively to deny its accountability to a wider public and its responsibility to protect the liberty and interests of all its citizens. On the account I give, many radicals did not start the last decade of the eighteenth century thinking that they were participating in politics and many might have been uncertain as to how they might do that. Forty years later, I shall suggest, that situation had changed radically.

In the 1790s, however, people deliberated about both ideas and matters of substance: they discussed how they should think and argue and they sought to identify (often to stipulate) lines between public and private and political and non-political. They did this in company, as well as in print, in settings of domestic sociability as well as in public meetings or dinners for reform. Their conduct was shaped by the social settings in which these deliberations took place and by the reactions they encountered there. While the chapters separately discuss issues of language and disagreement from matters of sociability, I do want to emphasise that these are dimensions of the same worlds and, because it is not possible to say everything at once, I have focused on different elements in different parts.

My second area of concern is with sociability and involves networks and numbers. The mapping of people's networks has become widespread but I argue that it is worth doing some more qualitative thinking about the basis, structure and significance of social networks.[12] I explore how people's relationships actually operated, examining the tensions between theory and practice and assessing how far their deliberative ambitions were often undermined and challenged by the deep inequalities that existed in the period. This is especially salient for conduct in relations between the sexes where the use of both qualitative and quantitative sources for people's conduct helps map this complex terrain on which emotion, rationality and the conventions and norms in the wider

---

[12] See the critical review by Kate Davison, 'Early Modern Social Networks: Antecedents, Opportunities, and Challenges', *American Historical Review* 124(2) (April 2019), 456–482; and Joanna Innes, 'Networks in British History', *East Asian Journal of British History* 5 (2016), 51–72.

society collided. Many of these personal relationships had wider significance, especially for those who sought to promote or to question and challenge traditional conceptions of the social world and of sexual relationships, in which deep structured inequality was a potent denominator. This was a period of a slowly declining élite libertine culture, together with the bordellos and bagnios that served it, which saw the rise of a more moralistic and prudish culture in respect of sexual conduct. At the same time, there were members of the more middling and professional orders who engaged in a degree of sexual experimentation as a form of resistance to the more customary and restrictive norms of their social milieu. In the process of this experimentation, many discovered anew quite how powerful wider expectations of behaviour were and how difficult they were to challenge successfully.

One dimension of people's networks concerns whom they know; another concerns whom they know about. In our own time we know a lot about a lot of people whom we don't know – a common feature of celebrity culture. In this earlier period there was a degree of name recognition and some narrative about, for example, kings and queens, murderers and adulterers and performers and entertainers. These people had a public reputation, relayed in part through the press, prints and caricatures and through second-hand (or third or even less direct) information, whose circulation was a common feature of social interaction and more general public gossip.[13] Something of this sort clearly existed to a degree in this period – perhaps especially around the Royal Family, politicians, military heroes and particularly egregious criminals or scandalous conduct. Nonetheless, we should not overstate the size and spread of this particular universe or the degree of familiarity that most people had with the details of the lives they in some sense felt they were cognizant of. It is especially important to reflect on exactly what kind of information actually achieved wide circulation. The reporting of particularly grotesque murders and trials was commonplace; but a lot of scandal circulated much less widely.[14] This was partly because at least some newspapers were still in the business of being willing to sell their silence

---

[13] One area for reflection concerns how far prints and caricatures were often representing people who were known in only relatively restricted circles. From our overwhelmingly visual world, it can be difficult to grasp how complex a process identification of the subjects of caricatures might be.

[14] The coverage of the case of Lady Worsley is an interesting example of the restraint shown in the newspaper press – which would reach a wide audience (and may have had concerns about losing readers of a puritanical bent) – in comparison to the caricatures that circulated amongst the élite and the pamphlets, whose pricing would also have restricted their circulation. See Hallie Rubenhold, *Lady Worsley's Whim* (London: Chatto and Windus, 2008).

rather than print a story; but it was also because most scandals and indiscretions were practically salient for only a relatively small group of people. To take an élite example: Lady Bessborough was deeply distressed by a series of reports in the press about her and her sister Georgiana, Duchess of Devonshire, and the conduct of their friends – the reporting 'sometimes cuts at a display of melancholy, but usually [gives] accounts of violent dissipation and gaiety'.[15] More tellingly, the paragraphs being submitted to the paper were in a hand that Lady Bessborough thought she recognised. She managed to get Dr Foster not to print them in the *Morning Post* and they did not appear elsewhere. This suggests that this was a very internal affair, relevant to a restricted group of people (possibly with a degree of blackmail from the editor). The stories were embarrassing for their victims, because they were hurtful and shaming within their circles rather than because they were subjected to wide public perceptions of frivolity and misconduct.

Similarly, with respect to 'public celebrity', exactly what was known by whom about Sir William Hamilton, Emma Hamilton (and her past) and Lord Nelson is a complex question. In relation to Hamilton's infatuation with Emma, there was much reluctance to acknowledge her among Hamilton's own family and in court circles, in part because of Sir William's formal position as Ambassador. Most newspaper stories were extremely discrete (by modern standards) and it is entirely possible that relatively few people had much sense of her past or of the character of the relationship that developed subsequently with Nelson. Certainly some knew, but they were primarily concerned after the trio's return to Britain with the injury to Lady Nelson. Emma's reception in London was widely spoken of in élite letters and there were some characteristically sharp prints drawn by Gillray and others, but there is little sense of a scandal very widely shared. The caricatures of Hamilton and the couple are best read as speaking to a restricted audience 'in the know'.[16] The trio's tour round the country was very successful and does not seem to have raised problems for people in the provinces about how to respond to her – and

---

[15] Lord Granville Leveson Gower (first earl Granville). *Private Correspondence, 1781 to 1821*, edited by Castalia, countess Granville (London: J. Murray, 1916), vol. ii, pp. 7–8.

[16] See for example George Cruikshank's *A Mansion House Treat – or Smoking Attitudes* (S. Fores, 1800, BMS 9550); Gillray's *Dido in Despair* (H. Humphrey, 1801, BMS 9752) and *A Cognocenti contemplating the Beauties of ye Antique* (H. Humphrey, 1801, BMS 9753); and Thomas Rowlandson's *Modern Antiques* (T. Tegg, 1811, BMS 11819). See Vic Gattrell, *City of Laughter, Sex and Satire in Eighteenth Century London* (London: Atlantic Books, 2006), pp. 318–322; and my 'Politics and Memory: Nelson and Popular Song' in my *Reforming Ideas in Britain*, pp. 322–359.

most people would simply not have faced the problem of how to receive her.

We also need to consider the exact nature of the ties that people had in their networks. For many people family remained an extremely important set of relationship; and families remained normative for the vast majority of young people. Certainly they sought to do so, especially with respect to their daughters and to their eldest sons through the control of their inheritance. Also, while many commercial and professional relationships look very like the transactional relationships that we associate with a free-market economy, if we scratch the surface of these we can often identify underlying structures of family connections and embeddedness in localities, suggesting that many such activities remained underpinned by strong ties.

By contrast, there were the kinds of relationships that Godwin sought to develop in his interaction with others. His diary demonstrates that he saw an immense number of people. At the same time, he had his own concerns about the superficiality of many social relationships (and in this he was deeply influenced by Rousseau's *Discourse on the Origin of Inequality*). Moreover, his correspondence and his behaviour towards a number of key individuals make unequivocally clear that he was especially concerned with developing deep, deliberative relationships with particular others. These relationships rested wholly on the disinterested evaluation of the worth of the other involved and were based essentially on mutual esteem and the ongoing practise of intensive debate and discussion.

One way of clarifying some of these differences is to consider Mark Granovetter's distinction between strong and weak ties. 'Strong ties' involve relations of duration, emotional intensity, intimacy and reciprocal services. They are distinguished from 'weak ties', which are contingent, rely on balanced reciprocity (across the whole of a social network) and are superficial and transient.[17] Granovetter's claim is that whereas strong ties serve to absorb information and rumour and tend to form silos, weak ties provide means by which information can flow freely across a large population. His account should encourage us to focus on exactly what types of relationship operated in London in our period. Above all, it should underline the distinctiveness of the kind of relationship that Godwin was seeking out in his circles. While these were not weak ties (which the proliferation of names in the diary might suggest), nor were they the traditional form of strong tie arising out of family or

---

[17] See Mark Granovetter, 'The Strength of Weak Ties', *American Journal of Sociology* 78 (1973), 1360–1380, and his subsequent *Society and Economy: Framework and Principles* (Cambridge MA: Belknap/Harvard University Press, 2017).

locality, although they shared some of the features of these ties – such as duration, intensity, intimacy and reciprocal services.

In 'Friendship in Commercial Society', Allan Silver identifies a line of thinking in writers of the Scottish Enlightenment that saw commerce as helping to set people free from familial, embedded and unchosen sets of relationships (i.e., traditional 'strong ties') by which one's interests were defined and in which friendship and interest were both very closely connected but also potentially fragile. They were fragile because, where friendship was entangled in interest, it had sometimes to give way to it. Thus Adam Ferguson mused on the maxim 'Live with your friend as with one who may become your enemy'.[18] The Scots saw the paradoxical development of an interested commercial society serving to free friendships from interest, thereby enabling the formation of friendships based on mutual sympathy and one's judgment of people's virtues and talents – and the development of wider aspirations for an openness to universal sociability, benevolence and the free communication between persons.

This sense of a space emerging for disinterested friendships, unconnected to family or patronage networks, seems especially pertinent in the 1790s when activity and debate around the French Revolution and the reform of Parliament brought people together in a range of venues to discuss political and more widely philosophical issues. Many of the relationships among supporters of reform and those who saw themselves as a part of a literary and philosophical vanguard were understood as disinterested and mutual. Indeed, in addition to their more general sense of the character of their friendship and acquaintance, there was also, for many radicals, a sense that this very disinterestedness was key to the development of a culture in which progress was to be made through the circulation and further development of ideas.

Granovetter and Silver's distinctions are certainly suggestive for aspects of the period 1790–1815.[19] There is a tendency among commentators of the period to assume that this is a period of the blossoming of the public sphere and the engagement of more and more members of the middling orders with that sphere, meeting each other as equals, forming friendships based on their perceptions of other people's qualities and displacing concerns with interests and practicing a benevolence rooted in mutual sympathy, while relying implicitly on a balanced reciprocity over

---

[18] Allan Silver, 'Friendship in Commercial Society: Eighteenth-Century Social Theory and Modern Sociology', *American Journal of Sociology* 95(6) (May 1990), 1486.

[19] Granovetter's later discussion of Silver's piece in his *Society and Economy* (2017), pp. 83–84, rightly raises some doubts about the sharpness of the separation of commercial interests and non-market relations.

time. On this picture, strong ties, based on family and relationships that locked together interests and friendship, were displaced or set aside (for many in London, these were literally 'left with their relations' in the provinces) by a wider acquaintance made up of weak ties. Nonetheless, some of these 'weak ties' were relationships that developed into much more intensive if untraditional forms of strong ties, through the practice of deliberation and the exchange of ideas.

One key historical question is what it was that enabled these disinterested friendships and relationships among the radicals to emerge and survive. That is, what material and social preconditions were required and under what conditions might these relationships flourish or founder? We might also ask about the level of independence these ties actually had from people's interests: if the routeing of interests into commercial relationships left men (and it was men that Ferguson was discussing) free to develop relationships with others independent from those interests, were those friendships wholly severed from more interested ties and from ties of family or did those more traditional ties provide an underpinning security that then left them free to develop other (non-commercial) interests? How far could those disinterested friendships serve as a bulwark against intrusive forms of government and loyalist pressures? And at what point might interests come back into play to condition people's sense of where their loyalties lay?

The disinterested benevolence that Godwin and his associates preached and their aspirations for a deliberative culture focused around the exercise of private judgement and the pursuit of truth and justice looks like a particularly demanding form of disinterested friendship. It clearly was one such form, not tied to interests, interpolating others as equals and exploring together beliefs and ideas to the end of social progress and enlightenment. As such, it clearly resonates with the idea of an emergent public sphere that has had a deep influence on eighteenth century historiography, although it is a particular and especially demanding conception of the nature of authentic public communication. It also suggests that, rather than there being a single public sphere, there were a variety of intensive friendship groups operating on a variety of bases, which nurtured various deliberative practices.[20] With others, my sense is that we need to look at what kinds of relations people aspired to

---

[20] See Jurgen Habermas, *The Structural Transformation of the Public Sphere*, trans. T. Berger and F. Lawrence (Cambridge: Polity Press, 1989); his 'The Public Sphere: An Encyclopedia Article', *New German Critique* 3 (1974, orig. 1964), 49–55; and 'Further Reflections on the Public Sphere', in C. Calhoun (ed.), *Habermas and the Public Sphere* (Cambridge, MA: MIT Press, 1992). There has been a veritable industry responding to the idea in communication studies and history more widely – see especially Gillian

construct through their conversations and meetings with each other and how far these might have shared similar standards and expectations with groups from across different sectors in society. There is also something to be said about exactly how people conceived of and practiced deliberation and conversation, and about how those in power interpreted this activity. Moreover, as I will argue, even if Godwin and his compatriots thought of their deliberative friendship as a form of free-standing philosophical discourse, that did not necessarily make it so. It was a discourse anchored in and enabled by a particular social setting and, as people reacted to the pressures of events and the incursions of public scrutiny and intervention in these private relations, so too did tensions develop between these relations and people's other stronger ties and between them and their more particular interests

Male friendships might well look like (and sometimes be) a case of 'disinterested relations', linked by a general sympathy and not dominated by calculation or seeking advantage and taking place across class and status divisions. But they might also mask differences that, under other circumstances, might become salient and could undermine their independence from instrumental concerns, professional connections and familial relations. Where Ferguson seems to have thought of this as a relatively robust realm of disinterested sociability, we can see that in the form in which Godwin and his associates pursued it, it might be vulnerable to political pressure, to disillusion and betrayal, to disagreements about the requirements for a secure and progressive society and to rumbling social and status differentials which could be triggered into effect when lesser men demonstrated too much presumption. Disinterested friendship might work in a relatively egalitarian society, even when placed under various forms of duress, but this was not an egalitarian society. It was strongly marked by class and status divisions, and these had powerful effects on the extent to which relationships were really equal or entirely disinterested.

A third area of sociability concerns the way that people's social circles functioned in a variety of implicit ways to respond to and attempt to mould the conduct of others. To understand how that worked we need some sense of the nature of the relationship between sociability and talk in London in this period. The ideal form of Godwinian discourse was

Russell and Clara Tuite's edited collection *Romantic Sociability: Social Networks and Literary Culture in Britain 1770–1840* (Cambridge: Cambridge University Press, 2006); Jane Rendall's 'Women and the Public Sphere', *Gender & History* 11 (1999), 475–488; and Amanda Vickery, 'Golden Age to Separate Spheres? A Review of the Categories and Chronologies of English Women's History', *Historical Journal* 36 (1993), 383–414.

disinterested, orientated to truth and concerned to explore exhaustively a topic and appropriate principles, which makes it seem very much like a Habermasian form of free communicative action. But it is also clear that talk within Godwin's circles, as in all others, also included the exchange of information about the behaviour of others.

This sort of talk is much more obvious in the detailed discursive diaries of men like Joseph Farington and Henry Crabbe Robinson. Some talk might have served purely instrumental purposes: Farington, for example, was an information gatherer, a mapper of the wider world and in some cases it seems clear he was using his sources to influence decisions about membership of the Royal Academy. But in most instances his recording of information about other men (and often about women) seems to have had few implications for his behaviour toward them. More widely, there appears to be a difference between the way in which male and female circles operated, with male talk seeming to lack much sense of urgency and exhibiting little reaction to how others acted, while female talk adhered more closely to older models of strong ties of interest and family (and family connections, most saliently through husbands) in which talk – indeed gossip – played a major social role in shaping conduct. The insight that 'gossip centers on areas where the cultural ideal is demanding and creates stress'[21] gives us some purchase on why gossip may have been systematically more important in women's circles in this period. Moreover, the practices of gossip also indicate that it takes place in relationships that have strong rather than weak ties.

Certainly, many women's social relationships do seem to have been rather different from Silver's model of disinterested friendship. For example, for women from outside of the aristocracy, acceptance within such élite circles was extremely fragile. Actresses, singers and entertainers might find some conditional acceptance – occasionally aristocrats made actresses their wives, only for them subsequently to be consigned to the country estate.[22] For the most part, women were defined by their rank and their social lives were restricted to social circles appropriate to

---

[21] Sally Engel Merry, 'Rethinking Gossip and Scandal', in Donald Black (ed.), *Toward a General Theory of Social Control*, v. 1 (New York: Academic Press, Inc., 1984), p. 279.

[22] Lord Derby and Elizabeth Farren were exceptional in that his first wife was unfaithful and the couple were careful to present a perfect picture of modest and chaste mutual affection under the watchful eye of her duenna mother until the death of Derby's wife, which then allowed them to marry and for her to be received at court. That did not, of course, prevent their caricaturing – See James Gillray's *A Peep at Christies* (H. Humphrey, 1796, BMS 8888); *Contemplations on a Coronet* (H. Humphrey, 1797, BMS 9074); and *The Marriage of Cupid & Psyche* (H. Humphrey, 1797, BMS 9076) (this last being especially brilliant); nor did it stop James Sayer from depicting her naked in *A Peep Behind the Curtain at Widow Belmour* (no publisher (n.p.), 1790, BMS 7736).

that status. When they left it, they found only limited tolerance. Even within one's own status group, acceptance could be fragile. Status denoted but did not wholly determine how one was responded to; that was also affected by those with whom you mixed. Mix low and you would be treated as such; mix high and, while increasingly vulnerable to predatory and exploitative behaviour from your new (especially male) friends, you might also lose ready acceptance within your own milieu – and the issue of with whom you were associating was very much a matter of gossip. Here women policed women, still more than did their husbands. Smith describes Mrs Nollekens as noted for the fact that her 'female acquaintances were not all equally well or wisely selected; some of them having been opera-singers, and others servants to their husbands, and in some instances worse'. Her friend, Mrs Carter berated her for her laxity, and warned of the consequences: 'You can clearly see', she observed one day during a sale of choice china at Christie's, that

that duck-footed woman, your 'dear friend', as you have just been pleased to call her, is not at all noticed by the wives of those gentlemen to whom her husband is known. They all shun her as they would a wife who has been made over to her husband with what her former possessor considered a *handsome consideration*. Indeed, my old friend, you should at all events be a little more cautious in your epithets, or you will at last, like her, pass unnoticed.[23]

This type of gossip is intimate, and would have been extremely salient for Mrs Nollekens, who was being encouraged to consider her position. In this form of gossip, you gossip about people you know, to people who know them, and the likelihood is that the people who are being gossiped about know that they are being talked about. Functionalist accounts in anthropology tend to stress the place of gossip as a form of collective policing of intimate social groups, with strangers being excluded through their lacking knowledge of the principals (and, more crucially, lacking

---

For a more comprehensive discussion of representations see Gattrell, *City of Laughter*, esp. chapters 11–14, and Katrina O'Loughlin '"Strolling Roxanas": Sexual Transgression and Social Satire in the Eighteenth Century', in Susan Broomhall (ed.), *Spaces for Feeling: Emotions and Sociabilities in Britain 1650–1850* (London: Routledge, 2015), pp. 112–136. Later, and similarly, Catherine Stephens who married the 5th Earl of Essex found a reception in Queen Victoria's Court. But the standard result was largely exclusion or very incomplete inclusion: Louisa Brunton, who married the Earl of Craven in 1807; Harriot Mellon, who married Henry Beauclerk in 1827; Maria Foote, who married Charles Stanhope in 1831, never attained the same degree of acceptance by their marriages. See for example Kimberly F. Schutte, *Marrying by the Numbers: Marriage Patterns of Aristocratic British Women, 1485–2000*, Phd. Thesis, University of Kansas, 2011, and her subsequent *Women, Rank, and Marriage in the British Aristocracy, 1485–2000: An Open Elite?* (London: Palgrave, 2014).

[23] John Thomas Smith, *Nollekens and His Times* (Oxford: Oxford University Press, 1929 [first published in 2 vols 1828]), p. 215.

any social relation with them).[24] This underlines the intimacy required for participation and is in sharp contrast to 'celebrity gossip'. Even this form of gossip might vary, from the passing of social information with little moral judgement, through to talk which has major consequences for one's interaction with the subject, ranging from destabilising a person's position within a group to resulting in their social exclusion. It may also play an important role in signalling to one's closest connections (especially one's family) areas of their vulnerability to social reaction or condemnation and in imposing conduct on (or in disguising the conduct of) members of one's most intimate circles.[25]

I have no wish to resurrect a separate spheres picture in relation to gender.[26] My case here is grist to the mill of those who want a more complex picture – who recognise women's participation in publishing, campaigning and organising but who also recognise that there were more barriers and costs to such participation than for many men and who also acknowledge that men's worlds might be more complex and multiple than that older thesis proposed. My concern is to try and tell a more subtle and convincing story about how men and women of the middling orders, arts and professions of the 1790s and 1800s (predominantly in London, but drawing on other evidence where relevant) sought to live their lives, to assess the obstacles and opportunities they faced or could create and to regulate their relationships with those whom they knew and to set this in the context of increasing government repression and intolerance towards unorthodox political views.

Godwin is a frequent participant in the discussions of this book. It is not a book about him, but it does focus recurrently on the circles in which he moves in London and it makes extensive use of his diary. But I have also sought out other diaries and journals, letters and memoirs of the period (several of which have not been explored by scholars of the period) as a way of engaging in a more detailed (occasionally quantitative) analysis of how people conducted their lives and how more broadly social circles in London worked. In doing so, I aim to help us appreciate

---

[24] Such as Max Gluckman's 'Gossip and Scandal', *Current Anthropology* 4(3) (June 1963), 307–316.

[25] As is often pointed out – gossip is most intense in exclusive groups – See Gluckman, 'Gossip and Scandal', p. 315; Diego Gambetta, 'Grandfather's gossip', *Archives Européennes de Sociologie*, XXXV (1994), 199–223; Merry, 'Rethinking Gossip and Scandal'; and Patricia Meyer Spacks, 'In Praise of Gossip', *The Hudson Review* 35(1) (1982), 19–38.

[26] See the very useful review of literature by Vickery, 'Golden Age to Separate Spheres' for Britain (and the also useful North American discussion in Linda Kerber, 'Separate Spheres, Female Worlds, Woman's Place: The Rhetoric of Women's History', *Journal of American History* 75(1) (1988), 9–39.

how, in particular, the circles around those who responded warmly to the opening events of the French Revolution and who were enthusiastic for domestic reform and for the spread of education and enlightenment at home operated and responded to the government's commitment to war and its recourse to repression and to the wider societal reaction that emerged under loyalism.

In the final part of the book, I turn to questions of music and movement and make a case for the way that music moves people in this period, both emotionally and physically – sometimes emotionally because physically, sometimes physically because emotionally – and to think through the ways that this contributes to the maintenance and expression of a set of cultural and social commitments that complicate the processes of political dissent and protest. Here, too, the tapestry of sound and of the culture it contributed to and shaped was one that, even when it operated largely unawares, was not reducible to such elements. Indeed, neither element – whether sound or movement – is often wholly under people's conscious control. The best players of instruments have disciplined and habituated themselves to forge a relationship with their instrument and the medium of sound and music. They do so as much by 'inhabiting' it as by subjecting it to their will. And those who sing, dance or otherwise respond to them are similarly 'in' the medium. Understanding this, I believe, helps us to recognise how such performances in the period embedded a range of dispositions which often had significant political implications that my reformers attempted to resist.

In my discussion I refer to different forms of dance, music and song and will argue for their importance in understanding the texture of people's lives and for moulding people's worlds and their accompanying narratives. At the same time, I examine the question of how resources from the same domain might serve to assist people in standing against the status quo and with what limitations.

The approach I have taken has, I believe, wide implications for how we should understand the period as a whole. Much of the extensive literature on the period sees the literary and political culture of London as a relatively unified domain, in which people knew each other and in which there was extensive engagement, often across gender and class boundaries. In contrast, I want to suggest that the worlds people inhabited may have been much more fractured and divided and that the character of these worlds might have varied considerably between men and women and between areas of cultural activity and profession. I suggest we might usefully think of a range of ways in which people were known to each other – friendship, acquaintance and ties based on family and locality.

We should be concerned to distinguish strong and weak ties and should look carefully at the different forms that 'strong' ties might have taken; and that we should reflect on the way that people's aspirations for certain types of exchange might have influenced the types of relationships they formed. Some relationships became, in this period, fraught with difficulties when people sought to extend them across gender boundaries. Moreover, as the government challenged the claim that private discussion had no public or political implications, the character of people's relationships also began to be influenced and began to change. Out of those changes comes a different kind of oppositional political discourse and set of practices – if not immediately, at least in the period immediately following the end of the war.

The account I give also suggests that as the boundaries between the public and the private were challenged in various ways there was a brief flourishing of more egalitarian relations between the sexes, albeit rapidly politicised and contributing to the emerging censoriousness in relation to female conduct and reputation and to the remarginalisation of many literary and professional women in the romantic period.

Finally, my account is intended to help us see how difficult it was to question the established order at this particular time (with the war on France) and in the way that many of the most outspoken critics sought to do. The existence of these aspiring critics was the culmination of decades of relative stability coupled with a growing optimism about the possibilities of progress and the development of knowledge. Their failure was in part a failure of enlightenment thinking (with its heady optimism), in part a failure fully to appreciate the underlying dynamics of the political world (and its stubborn resistances) and in part a failure to acknowledge the deep embeddedness of many of their contemporaries (and themselves) in a taken for granted order that they found undercutting their aspirations. That most people fell back on older ways does not mean that things remained wholly unchanged – but their experience testifies to the fragility of people's deliberative ambitions and conduct when these came into conflict with the conventional practices of their social worlds. This is intended as an account of the complex world of late eighteenth and early nineteenth century London in which people developed aspirations for a different sort of future and sometimes experimented with approximations to that future, but found their present repeatedly encroaching in ways that further alienated and fragmented the wider community they had hoped to take with them.

1   Politics and Privacy

1.1   Politics

In 1950 Alfred Cobban famously noted of the 1790s in Britain that this was 'perhaps the last real discussion of the fundamentals of politics in this country ... Issues as great have been raised in our day, but it cannot be pretended that they have evoked a political discussion of the intellectual level of that inspired by the French Revolution'.[1] The rise of popular societies agitating for reform, which elicited widespread prosecutions for sedition and then the 1794 Treason Trials, followed shortly after by the 1795 Gagging Acts and by the repeated suspension of habeas corpus, seems to confirm Cobban's view and suggests that this was, indeed, one of the most political of decades. After 1800, and particularly after the return of the war with France and the long campaign against Napoleon, domestic discontent was stifled. There was a resurgence of activism only in the 1810s and early 1820s, especially around the Spa Fields meetings, the trials of Hone, the Peterloo Massacre, the Cato Street conspiracy and the Queen Caroline Affair. Once again, however, with government repression and some improvement in the economy, political activism was largely closed down until the development of chartism.

Is this how people at the time understood their activity? Did they think of themselves as discussing the fundamentals of politics? And did they see their doing so as itself 'political'? We are so used to thinking about this as an opening era for popular politics that we tend not to concern ourselves with how people used that term or with whether they saw themselves as practically engaged in the activity of politics. I will argue that when people talked about politics they mainly referred to matters of government, foreign policy and Parliamentary activity and the events associated with these, together with reference to a wider constitutional

---

[1] Alfred Cobban, *The Debate on the French Revolution 1789–1800* (London: A & C Black, 1950), p. 31. It is worth emphasising that this chapter partly responds to Cobban's emphasis on the 'discussion' of politics, since it has been read in very expansive ways.

order and an associated set of conventions.[2] In each case these was seen as something rather removed from the great majority of the people and were not activities or arenas that members of the more middling and lower orders saw themselves as actively and personally engaged in. Moreover, there was a powerful negative language of politics – hostile to 'politicians' who were seen as pursuing their own interests and to party politics, which was seen in terms of factional interests being pursued against the interests of the community at large.

On 19 November 1795, Thomas Gandy wrote a letter to his son, the artist Joseph Gandy, who was in Italy, in which he reported:

At this time politics are nearly put a stop to, a bill is passing through Parliament which seems to aim at the preventing of discussing on political topics by newspaper. You learn how our King was used going to and returning from Parliament for which etc. they seem determined to prevent the like or even to talk on Government. We must bridle our tongues, it may be very right, and at some time they may as well draw the teeth for every article of life is at an extravagant price, I wonder how the poor live, they do not, they are starving, witness a woman was detected stealing a loaf, she was followed home, she had five children, to each she gave a share, and when she was asked by the persons who followed if she did not make a practice of it, she declared it was the first time, that she had not a morsel in the house to give the children, they then searched the cupboards, and found nothing, but in one which was locked, and in which she was very unwilling they should enter, they broke open and to their surprise found part of a dog, the other part having been eaten, so that I conclude much worse things are done we hear not of, and I think an Englishman cannot see without endeavoring to remedy and search into the cause, [in] so plentiful a summer. I hope Government has it not to answer for, though it seems to be the general cry and are aiming to stop the tongue. Petitions are applying, the mobs are raising, the soldiers are parading, everything seems in preparation of some great event, a little time will decide. I hope God will avert his judgments on this nation.[3]

Gandy's letter reveals a mix of concerns: that 'politics are nearly put a stop to' seems essentially to concern the end of parliamentary debate and discussion; the bill passing through Parliament concerns the 'Gagging Acts' of 1795, shutting down political associations and public meetings; but there is also a sense that the government is acting so intrusively, especially on people's talk, and that economic unrest is so high that the

---

[2] I have been engaged in a long discussion with Jo Innes on this – and each of us has explored ngrams and other ways of formally assessing use through quantification. Some of our early thoughts can be found on the 'Reimagining Democracy' website, https://re-imaginingdemocracy.com/, under the Mediterranean section, linked to the partner meeting in Lisbon in the spring of 2015 on 'Conceptions of politics in Europe 1750–1860'.

[3] Soane Museum, *Diary of Joseph Gandy*, f.179.

political order is in real danger. Nonetheless, it is not clear that he thought the wider discussion of the issues of the day was part of 'politics', even if the discussion was about politics and even if the government was directing its energies to shutting down such talk as a threat to order.

In 1809, when John Spencer determined to undertake a 'political' journal he wrote: 'I this morning came to a resolution to commence a sort of political journal a thing which I had often resolved to undertake.'[4] The journal referred to the parlous state of international affairs, especially in relation to France and Austria, matters of military resource (as discussed in a published letter from the Earl of Chatham), the Spanish war, the resignation of the Duke of Portland and Mr Canning from government in September 1809, following a duel between Lord Castlereagh and Mr Canning, and the subsequent agitation of 'the Publick mind in London' concerning the uncertain state of the administration. Spencer's resolution to keep a journal rather quickly petered out, but the focus of his attention in relation to politics was clear: it concerned governmental and parliamentary activity and international affairs. The 'agitation of the Publick mind in London', however, was probably not itself thought of as political activity – although it might have been a problem that called for attention by the government.

In 1793, Daniel Isaac Eaton launched a series of 'Political Classics' – 'in weekly numbers, price 6d, containing Algernon Sydney, Rousseau, Milton, Harrington, More, Buchannan, Locke, Paine, Price, Burgh, Godwin &c &c., And every thing of what ever Country that can convey information, and may thereby promote the happiness of man'. Eaton claims that he was induced

to give these works to the world at as easy a rate as possible, as a certain means of destroying those weak and partial affections which the generality of my fellow-citizens entertain for the particular forms of government under which they live. And I sincerely hope, that every person who may peruse these pages, will apply dispassionately their reason and understanding, in reflecting on the beauties of a just and equitable form of government, in comparison with those profuse, venal, and corrupt systems, which now almost universally obtain through the globe … [These] judicious Philosophers, who, to their immortal honour, have united learning and Philanthropy with Patriotism; … have laid down such principles of government, as must flash conviction on the most despotic mind, and which have lived, and will live, to immortalise their names till time is no more.[5]

---

[4] Barnsley Record Office and Local Studies Department, SpSt/60644/11 (1809).
[5] The advertisement appears on the opening two pages of *The Measures of Ministry to Prevent a Revolution Are the Certain Means of Bringing It On*, 2nd ed. (London: D. I. Eaton, 1794).

Moreover, his *Politics for the People*[6] was similarly an attempt to introduce a mix of political classics, satire and commentary to a wider public audience. It is not clear that he initially conceived its purpose as political or that he saw it as 'political' in more than its subject matter, although the key commitment was to stimulating discussion as a process of enlightening the mind, which he clearly thought would have consequences for government. But his subsequent brushes with the law certainly brought home to him that his activities were being read as transgressive by those in politics.

Writing about philosophy and questions of the design of government was for most people clearly distinct from both popular activism within the constitution and practical activity to bring about a change in the constitution or in policy. Moreover, when people did think about philosophy as sufficiently enlightening to produce a change in society they did not usually think of this as political activity or as engaging in 'politics'. It was, rather, something that took place on a higher plane. For all his more scurrilous tendencies, Charles Pigott's analysis of the situation was very much in keeping with the view that change should be understood in terms of 'the approaching aera of light'. In the entry to his *Political Dictionary* on 'Truth' he wrote:

What kind of government, or rather what kind of tyranny must that be, where the noble and investigating mind of man dares not promulgate known truths, where the scrutinizing eye of the philosopher has penetrated, but where the eye can only see in secret? ... Truth in such a country is a stranger; she wanders up and down like a houseless pilgrim, not having where to lay her head; and if she chance to stray into some lowly cottage, she is driven out with unrelenting fury, by some loyal brute or other, in the person of an ignorant, hot-headed magistrate, or a bigoted intolerant priest! Thus persecuted, and thus driven from all society, she droops her head in piteous languishment, yet still struggles against the opposing tide, each struggle fainter than former, and her fate still tumbling in the balance, til at last she is overwhelmed at once by the strong arm of power, and plunged into the pitchy shades of everlasting night.[7]

Truth here is not a means of mobilising or marshalling support in politics; it is more an activity of a higher form – one that was increasingly becoming a fugitive form of thought.

Thomas Spence followed much the same route in distinguishing politics from the pursuit of knowledge: he quoted Harrington's examination by the Earl of Lauderdale when he was accused of 'being

---

[6] Daniel Isaac Eaton, *Politics for the People or a Salmagundi for Swine*, vol. 1 (London: D. I. Eaton, 1794).
[7] Charles Pigott, *Political Dictionary* (London: D. I. Eaton, 1795), pp. 27, 156.

eminent in principles, contrary to the king's government, and the laws of this nation. Some my Lord, have aggravated this, saying, that *I, being a private man have been so mad as to meddle with politics: what had a private man to do with government?*' – and Harrington went on to argue that 'there is not any public person, nor any magistrate, that has written in the politics worth a button' – which is to say that all writers of merit have been private men.[8]

In these accounts the activity of thought and philosophical reflection and speculation is seen as personal. It might be a process of reflection on 'politics', because it refers to the activities of government or parliament or the conduct of foreign affairs. That made it political in its subject matter, but this did not mean that those who engaged in such reflection and discussion saw themselves as engaged in political activity. As we will see, that people did not see themselves as actively political did not mean that the government shared that view; and being treated as if they were engaging in political activity would subsequently force people to reflect further on whether they had more practical aspirations. Early in the decade, that was not something they felt they had to do.

There are wider symptoms of this apparent distancing of politics from individual thought and the advancement of knowledge, even among those we treat as central to the 'politics' of the decade. Paine's *Rights of Man, Part the Second* (1792) effectively insisted that government was a residual activity in well-organised systems, so minor that it was effectively dispensed with by America during the Revolution.

Government is no farther necessary than to supply the few cases to which society and civilization are not conveniently competent ... Formal government makes but a small part of civilised life, and when even the best that human wisdom can devise is established, it is a thing more in name and idea, than in fact. It is on the great and fundamental principles of society and civilization ... infinitely more than to anything which even the best instituted government can perform, that the safety and prosperity of the individual and of the whole depends.[9]

For all the emphasis on 'political justice' in the title of his *Enquiry Concerning Political Justice* (1793), William Godwin effectively extended Paine by rejecting politics and government, in favour of an enlarged personal morality that would prove sufficient for the ordering of the whole.[10] Both developed further a discourse that was anti- or apolitical.

---

[8] Thomas Spence, *Pigs' Meat; or Lessons for the Swinish Multitude* (London: T. Spence, 1795), v. 1, p. 79.

[9] Paine, *Rights of Man*, pp. 215–216.

[10] William Godwin, *An Enquiry Concerning Political Justice* (1793), edited by Mark Philp (Oxford: Oxford University Press, 2013).

It was anti-political in the sense that it had an explanatory theory of the force and fraud that underlay contemporary political institutions and that explained why things were bad. It was apolitical in that it had a largely positive view of the individual's ability to step up and, through the development of rationality and virtue, carry the full weight of social order, so that government and politics would become redundant. That encouraged Godwin's own disavowal of associations and societies.[11] He referred to these as 'political associations', but he saw their tendency as one of encouraging faction and intemperance – their tendency was to 'give weight to the opinions of the persons so associated, of which the opinions of the unconfederated and insulated part of the community are destitute'.[12] And lest we think his position eccentric, we should recognise that his views won very wide support even within the societies – to the point that, in the first nine months of 1795, the LCS had a series of controversies over whether they in fact needed a constitution, or indeed any rules governing the conduct of their members, with a group, clearly allied to Godwin, suggesting that many members had become persuaded of the possibilities of free and open discussion in Godwinian mode, as against 'political organisation'.[13] What does seem clear is that many thought of general discussion as not intrinsically 'political' – and reserved that term for matters of international affairs, domestic government and, negatively, for the play of faction and interest.

Not everyone followed this course.[14] The veteran Parliamentary scourge, Horne Tooke purportedly dismissed Godwin's *Political Justice* by saying that 'the book was written with very good intentions, but to be sure nothing could be so foolish'.[15] Foolish for a practical and 'political' man like Horne Tooke who was steeped in the ways of parliamentary controversy. But for many other readers it represented a commitment to philosophy over politics and to the discussion of truth and the

---

[11] This did not mean Godwin was not interested in 'politics' – he attended a number of Parliamentary debates, had a backstory of close involvement with Whig political activity and for a brief period in 1796–1797 considered the possibility of entering Parliament – but not all interest in politics was seen as itself political.

[12] Godwin, *Enquiry Concerning Political Justice*, IV.II.iii, 114 (hereafter *Enquiry* – followed by Book, chapter (section where appropriate) and page – using for the page the 1793 edition, edited by Mark Philp (Oxford: Oxford University Press, 2013).

[13] See my *Reforming Ideas in Britain*, chapter 11.

[14] See, for example, Susan Thelwall's claim to having become 'a great politician' – although this seems to be a reference to her engagement in discussions about politics, rather than a claim about influencing the character of the politics of the day. See Jon Mee's *Print, Publicity, and Popular Radicalism*, p. 55.

[15] Charles Kegan Paul, *William Godwin: His Friends and Contemporaries*, 2 vols (London: H. S. King, 1876), I, p. 116; Don Locke, *A Fantasy of Reason: The Life and Thought of William Godwin* (London: Routledge and Kegan Paul, 1980), p. 62.

development of a fuller personal morality against, and as a superior alternative to and effective displacement of, partisan politics. Moreover, when Godwin's followers claimed more for politics they were largely concerned with people's rights to think for themselves – as when John Thelwall inveighed against those who wanted to restrict the right of discussion[16] or when Joseph Gerrald dismissed the pernicious view encapsulated in the thought – 'What have I to do with politics? Nothing!' – against which he argued:

Did you ever doubt what connection you had with morals and virtue? And yet, what are politics, but that wide system of duties which nation owes to nation? Politics are to nations what morals are to individuals ... It is upon a strict performance of these duties alone, that you can expect to be prosperous and happy as a people ... Parties are only a succession of birds of prey, for which the people are the banquet. Confide then in neither (party).[17]

The right to discuss is natural, the duty to do so is moral, the subject matter may indeed be 'politics', but the activity is rarely seen as precisely that.

Even if Gerrald's invective was un-Godwinian in its stridency, the lesson was not far removed from the master's – what mattered was the development of individual morality, not what was generally thought of as political activity. And Wollstonecraft equally identified the science of politics as having little to do with the practical politics of the period and she represented the alternative as one of intellectual development and the pursuit of truth – crucially, that science was not about the organisation and representation of distinct partisan interests:

The whole system of British politics, if system it may courteously be called, consisting in multiplying dependents and contriving taxes which grind the poor to pamper the rich; thus a war, or any wild goose chace is, as the vulgar use the phrase, a lucky turn-up of patronage for the minister, whose chief merit is the art of keeping himself in place.[18]

In his *Memoir* of the founding of the LCS Thomas Hardy recalled them debating whether we 'as treadesmen, mechanics and shopkeepers' had any right to seek Parliamentary reform? It was a question they debated for five successive nights – giving, in one sense, a performative answer – but it also testified eloquently to the sense that it was not

---

[16] John Thelwall, *Rights of Nature* (London: H. D. Symonds, 1796), p. 48.
[17] Joseph Gerrald, *A Convention the Only Means of Saving Us from Ruin*, 2nd ed. (London: np, 1794), pp. 3–4.
[18] Mary Wollstonecraft, *A Vindication of the Rights of Women* and *A Vindication of the Rights of Men*, edited by Janet Todd (Oxford: Oxford University Press, 1994), chapter ix, p. 224.

something they assumed.[19] We might also press the question of whether
that anxiety and uncertainty was compatible with Hardy's earlier comment in a letter to his geographically distant cousin expressing the hope
that they might converse by correspondence and mentioning that 'A dish
of chat about politicks, Foreign or Domestick I relish very well when
I have a leisure hour or two.'[20] He went on to venture the view that the
French Revolution is 'one of the greatest events that has taken place in
the history of the World; as to domestick politicks, there is a good deal of
talk here of societys forming/ in different parts of the Nation for a reform
of parliament that is to have an equal representation of the people and
shortening the duration of parliaments'. He mentioned one such society
in Sheffield, 'and another in London of which I am a member and
original projector'. He went on, but subsequently deleted: 'The people
are really so oppressed and borne down with taxes which makes them
associate together for the purpose of trying to get themselves eased a little
of the burden that they are groaning under.'[21]

Did Hardy think of this as all one activity or as different types of
activity? Was a 'dish of chat about politics' distinct from or continuous
with 'being a member and original projector' of a society for a reform of
parliament? The metaphor – from 'a dish of tea' – implies something to
be consumed in a convivial and sociable manner, which raises the
question as to whether the society he was forming was to be of that
character or whether he initially conceived of it as something radically
different. It also raises questions about how clear-sighted people were as
to the options and possibilities open to them in the initial stages and
how far these were thought of as *political* in character, as against government and loyalist reaction forcing them to reflect on their activity
because it was being understood by others in a light they did not
themselves recognise. When Hardy wrote to his uncle in Scotland, later
in the year, he noted:

---

[19] See Mary Thale (ed.), *Selections from the Papers of the London Corresponding Society:
1792–1799* (Cambridge: Cambridge University Press, 1983), pp. 6–7, in which Hardy
emphasises that the problem is the ignorance and prejudice of the bulk of the nation and
that their aim was 'to have a well regulated and orderly society formed for the purpose of
dispelling ignorance and prejudice as far as possible, and instill into their minds by
means of the press a sense of their rights as freemen, and of their duty to themselves, and
their posterity, as good citizens.'

[20] Hardy, in Add ms 27811, fol 4r. See also Amanda Vickery's William Ramsden, who took
over the delivery of London newspapers to Elizabeth Shackleton, promising her 'a Dish
of Politicks every Post-Day'. Amanda Vickery, *The Gentleman's Daughter: Women's Lives
in Georgian England* (London: Yale University Press, 1999), p. 259.

[21] BL Add ms 27811, fol 4r–v.

You are all petitioning for the abolition of that notorious traffick denominated the slave trade. So far you are in your duty but, that is not all, there are other evils existing in this country for which it is equally our duty to endeavour to remedy, and a principal way to remove those prevailing evils is to have a more equal representation of the people in parliament instead of an industrious class being burdened with heavy taxes to support a set of idle placemen and pensioners and haughty and imperious landlords ... There are many in England which we have corresponded with – our society began last Jan^{ry} with three or four meeting in one anothers houses in an evening consulting and condoling the low and even miserable condition of the people of this nation were reduced to by the avariciousness and extortion of the haughty, voluptuous, and luxurious class of beings who would have to possess no more knowledge than to believe all things were created for the use of that small group of worthless individuals.[22]

For Hardy and the other artisanal societies, the model (both in terms of an emphasis on restoring liberties and in seeking to correspond) was set by the SCI, and the SCI saw the progress of reform in terms of the spread of information, the discussion of politics in polite circles and the presentation of petitions. Moreover, its 'manifesto', the Duke of Richmond's *Letter to Lt Col Sharman*, initially written in 1783 but re-circulated widely in the 1790s, emphasised that it was *from* the reform of Parliament that he expected a change in the public to arise, rather than seeing the public as an originating and animating political force.[23] In a letter in March 1793, Hardy wrote:

The country associations goes on bravely, they are preparing petitions to parliament. Of course the subject of a reform in parliament will be repeatedly agitated in the House of Commons, the debates will be published in [...?] newspapers there circulated in different parts of the country, thousands of people will make it the subject of conversation and inquiry who never thought of it before.[24]

Even if there were groups of people driven to contemplate more active steps, the dominant meanings of politics were those associated with central government, parliament and with foreign policy – which provided material for discussion. And, for the most part, people did not see that discussion as in itself political; and they might well have thought of petitioning more as a formal representation of views contributing to the public interest than as an expressly political activity. At the same time, we can see that there is a potential collision course here: the language used to

---

[22] BL Add ms 27811, fol 12 r–v.
[23] *A Letter from His Grace the Duke of Portland to Lieutenant Colonel Sharman ... with Notes by a Member of the Society for Constitutional Information*, 3rd ed. (London: np, 1795; first published August 1783).
[24] BL Add ms 27811, fol 19r.

describe the 'haughty, voluptuous, and luxurious class of beings' and their activities conceives of the conflict as one between those outside politics and those inside and between those committed to truth and the public good against those committed to their own interests alone. In part, by not seeing themselves as a part of politics, those who then critiqued it brought to bear ideas and methods that were likely to go well beyond existing politics and in doing so challenged not so much the policies of government as the very ground of the political system as a source of order.

Underlying these questions lie two deeper issues. The first concerns the problems that those excluded from the political system faced when they agitated for reform, since it is easy to see how their demands could be seen as a challenge to that political system itself. The challenge was for those 'without' (the political system) to influence activity 'within', when that latter activity was premised on their exclusion. Hardy may have thought of himself as a free man – but whether he could be recognised as a political agent when he had no standing in that set of practices or would be seen as a fomenter of revolt against that system was uncertain. Indeed, the response to them – to accuse them of sedition and treason – was precisely to deny them political status and to brand them as evil and conspiring men.

The second issue concerns how people at the time understood the essential character of politics. I put this intentionally in general – indeed universal – terms, seeing 'politics' as a central sphere of human activity in most societies, that is differentiated from (even if implicated in) economic or social relations. This does not make it common to all societies, but it is common to most societies with any degree of complexity and division. Where there is conflict, or a need for coordination, we create and maintain forms of political authority. In such systems, some are accorded the right to rule others and they exercise that authority and command compliance by an appeal to their legitimacy. The practice of politics requires negotiation and compromise between different interests, authoritative interpretation of shared laws and rules and the imposition of order. In reasonably sophisticated political systems, a great deal of government is carried out through the use of validated procedures for decision, election, delegation and appointment. Where the process commands respect, outcomes are validated by the process. Where there is little trust in processes, the validity and effectiveness of outcomes depends more directly on whether they can command support or on the capacity of those who rule to impose them (or a combination of the two). On any moderately sophisticated understanding of the nature of complex societies, it seems plausible to claim that, in most cases, decisions will not be wholly consensual, but will involve the success of one proposal, one conception of the public good or one set of interests over others. Politics, as Bernard Williams points out, involves some people winning and some people losing.[25]

If we ask how far that was a widely accepted understanding of the nature of politics in Britain at the end of the eighteenth century, it is clear that it was not. Moreover, when the literary radical and reformers reflected on politics it is clear that they did not accept that it was a zero-sum game in which some would lose. This is not to say that they were unsophisticated in their understanding. There were a number of commitments that jostled together in people's discourse about politics that narrowed the field of what politics involved. There was the sheer resilience of the doctrine of a mixed constitution as the balancing mechanism for all legitimate interests.[26] There remained a degree of sanctification for royal authority and for political authority more widely through both the doctrine and the ritual invocations of the established church. There was a clear commitment to a specialisation of function, as in *Village Politics*, when Tom is reminded (biblically) that there are people better able to protect his interests ('How can he be wise whose talk is of oxen?').[27] There was the relative insulation of the parliamentary process from the people to underline its distance from their immediate concerns. And there was a range of local institutions and authorities who managed and effectively absorbed much of the local pressures and unrest of ordinary people. Indeed, there are parts of Burke's *Reflections* which can be read as hymning this beneficent system that accommodated and reconciled the concerns of all.[28] Less obviously, however, many of those observing politics drew on elements of a wider republican language, and a growing language of public utility, both of which, while often critical of the status quo, effectively denied that there had to be winners and losers and emphasised the common good or public interest as a way of reconciling all in a harmonious polity. By emphasising the possibility of a

---

[25] Bernard Williams, *In the Beginning Was the Deed* (Princeton, NJ: Princeton University Press, 2005), p. 13.

[26] Although see J. A. W. Gunn's shrewd analysis of the shifting sands for this debate, that gradually changed the doctrine into something more rooted in (and conforming of) the balance between political parties and delimiting royal influence, in J. A. W. Gunn, 'Influence, Parties and the Constitution: Changing Attitudes, 1783–1832', *Historical Journal* 17(2) (June 1974), 301–328.

[27] Hannah More, *Village Politics* (London: np, 1793) (see also Ecclesiasticus (Apocrypha) 38:25).

[28] Edmund Burke, 'Reflections on the Revolution in France (1790)', in Leslie Mitchell (ed.), *The Writings and Speeches of Edmund Burke*, General Editor Paul Langford, v.viii (Oxford: Clarendon Press, 1989).

common interest those perspectives served to fuel the deployment of a language of corruption whenever there seemed to be clear winners – how else could one explain the success of certain interests that were seen as clashing with the perceived good of the public? And this suggested both the desirability and the feasibility of an order in which all reasonable concerns would be met. Fundamental conflict of interests – a real zero-sum game between individuals or groups of equal rationality, was largely ignored as a possibility. Where government was bad, it could be fixed; where there was conflict, harmony could be introduced; where there was faction, the public interest could modify and ameliorate it. The appeal to reasonableness might sound unthreatening and plausible, but we should not underestimate the existential threat it posed to a system conducted on a very different conception of the political game.

The reformers' widely held commitments to free discussion, reason and progressive reform framed people's responses to the government and the politicians of the period. It helped to account for people's disdain for factional politics, place seeking and corrupt practices that distorted parliamentary debate and prevented the voice and interests of the ordinary person from informing debate; and it pointed to these things as remediable. In that sense it had rather a lot in common with the more Painite view of minimum government, or with Godwin's view of the gradual eradication of force and fraud and the exercise of authority over men of good judgement, as their understandings improved, since here too the expectation was of (in the long term) consensus. But its discursive logic entailed a very real threat to politics as it was conducted by turning political interests into deviations from collective concerns. Winners in the political game were thereby portrayed as forces for corruption, even though they (the winners) did not see themselves in that light. But because they did not see themselves in this light, they inevitably saw those extra-political forces as a fundamental challenge to the system and as illegitimate – because they were a corrosive threat to the established order, as radical in many ways as those occasionally smouldering suspicions of popery and the questioning of Anglican religious dominance.

George Canning's extensive 'Letter Journal' for 1793–1795 gives us some insight into the thinking of someone who was highly political, was deeply in William Pitt's debt (refusing a seat at the hands of the Duke of Portland and trusting to Pitt's offer to find him one), but who also had friendships among the opposition, to many of whom he was tied by family connections and amongst whom he had many admirers. What the Letter Journal gives us is a very clear picture of the nature of the 'political friend' who was understood to be one of the ministerial party, and private friends, with whom one might disagree heartily. Moreover, there were political enemies, who might be personal friends. As Canning pointed out, when trying to bring his friend Boringdon back into line in support of the war:

> With decided political friends one is of course easy and unembarrassed – with *decided* enemies one always knows one's ground exactly, and can get on very well, joking and abusing each other in perfect good humour – but with an ambiguous friend and *half* enemy, there is no knowing what tone to take ... for nothing is so violent in *abuse* as a *candid friend*.[29]

This does not, in fact, exhaust the possibilities. These were distinctions within the politically active. Canning's close friend from Christ Church, Oxford, the MP Charles Rose Ellis, explained to him that

> I do not *now*, nor do I mean *ever* to take an *active* part in the politicks of any party. But I give my full support to Ministry, and that, not only from conviction at the present juncture of affairs – but from party *attachment* also – attachment not indeed to *Ministers*, but to *people whom I love*, and *whose interests are connected with Ministry* ... *I should be sorry if* you *thought it* possible – that – *little* interested as *I* am myself in politicks, and *greatly* as *you* as well as *Jenkinson* and others – are interested – I could ever fail to support *that* party, with which *you* are connected. Though I do not like politicks particularly, I like Parliament – because it is an occupation – because it gives one a sort of situation and countenance – but for nothing so much as because it may enable me to be of service and support to those that I love.[30]

This does not mean that Canning and Ellis believed the same on all things. When there was to be a vote on the slave trade, which Canning wished to see ended, he recognised that Ellis, whose income derived from the West Indies, had opposite views. Because this was not a ministerial matter, they could disagree – and on the night of one vote on the issue, when Ellis asked him to dine after the debate, Canning gave him the choice of his (Canning) staying until the vote and voting (against Ellis) for abolition and subsequently going for dinner together or his leaving early (to go to dinner with Sir Ralph Payne) and not joining Ellis for dinner. Ellis chose the former – backing friendship and the pleasures of dining together above his interests.[31] Canning also had a very explicit discussion with Pitt about his views on the repeal of the Test Act initiated by Sheridan's motion for its repeal, which he thought unwise at the time

---

[29] George Canning, *The Letter Journal of George Canning 1793–1795*, edited by Peter Jupp (London: Royal Historical Society, 1991), p. 187. Ellis, as one 'within', clearly thought there was a line between 'party political' and the government as political – although that distinction was not much recognised 'without'.

[30] Ibid., p. 115.   [31] Ibid., pp. 63–64.

but ultimately desirable, and Pitt encouraged him to avoid the vote rather than making a principled statement of his position and then voting against the repeal (and with the government).[32] Pitt's handling of the matter was clearly very deft and politically astute, but it is easy to see that many of our reformers would have thought Canning irredeemably compromised by his lack of openness in the House – indeed, purloined by his place under Pitt. There is, then, a set of expectations from 'without' that fundamentally underappreciate the complexities of the insider's view of politics.

Parliamentary politics and the alignments of the élite were complex matters of political friendships, but that was little appreciated or understood by many of those advocating reform. For insiders, it was a select club (or group of select clubs) that clearly did not involve even all parliamentarians and that was closely tied to pressing matters of the day, the need to sustain majorities and the management of office. For those on the outside, it doubtless seemed less than transparent. That this was so, and that so much of the population was largely factored out of any practical engagement in this form of politics, helps explain the relative paucity of discussion of the term (and relative infrequency of its use) and their depiction of their own activity as essentially non-political – as mere reasonableness.[33]

1.2   Political Terminologies

There are a range of digital tools for counting what people talked about and how they did so, but many of them are flawed, either because of the restricted sources on which they are based or because of problems with character recognition. As such, we should avoid putting too much weight on them and I don't intend to encumber the reader with a succession of graphs. What the evidence suggests is that if we combine all the various uses of politics and political and set that figure against, for example, Parliament and Court, we can see that the talk of what we regard as the 'political world' has changed greatly, but that it did so largely in the second half of the twentieth century rather than earlier. In all the searches I have run, an essentially similar dominance of the parliamentary over the

---

[32] Ibid., pp. 97–100.

[33] Running n-grams of the use of politicks, politic, politics, political from 1600–today demonstrates clearly the extent to which the prominence of politics and cognate terms rises slowly from c.1750, but takes off only in the 1900s and still further in the period after the second World War. In the eighteenth century more significant and widely used terms are parliament, court and party. There is also a new search tool for Hansard that allows visualisation – available at https://hansard.hud.ac.uk/site/site.php.

political is a feature until at least the middle of the nineteenth century and more often later. People may have been *doing* a lot of what *we* think of as politics, but they were not writing about it as such, and that raises questions of how far they were thinking and talking about it in this way. If they were not, how might they have been conceptualising it? They referred much more to parliament and the crown and to a lesser extent the Lords and at a similar rate to the Commons. What we certainly don't find is any sudden 'peak' in the use of political terms in the 1790s.

There are changes in the use of words around the beginning of the nineteenth century, however, that I do want to highlight. Between the 1780s and the 1840s the popular voice became seen as a necessary component of the process of managing the political system. 'Opinion', on which all government is founded (as David Hume, and subsequently Godwin noted) became more extended and popular in character and this was something which the public presses and expansion of newspapers contributed to.[34] Moreover, it was something whose expression also began to take more organised forms. Although this begins in the 1780s and 1790s, sources of a more quantitative kind suggest that the major change in this aspect of the construction of politics and political activity was a feature less of the 1790s and more of the late teens and early 1820s. Moreover, the evidence suggests that many people in the 1790s expressly turned their backs on politics in the course of the decade: it was seen as an élite occupation, associated with faction and division and referring to the offices of the state, rather than being thought to be essentially linked with the expression of opinion, discussion and deliberation. It is also true that many turned their back on the first stirrings of popular activism because of their stronger commitment to a language of universal morality, and that failed to protect or guide them in the face of determined government repression and loyalist suspicion – while it also opened them to charges of backsliding. When Thomas Holcroft met the dissenting divine Joseph Towers at Debrett's bookshop in 1799 he noted:

Saw Dr Towers at Debrett's. His democracy still maintains its violence; I should scarcely exceed if I said its virulence. He asked me if the universal defection had not made me turn aristocrat. I answered that I supposed my principles to be founded in truth, that is, in experience and fact: that I continued to believe in the perfectibility of man, which the blunders and passions of ignorance might apparently delay, but could not prevent; and that the only change of opinion

---

[34] Hume's essay: 'It is therefore, on opinion only that government is founded'. David Hume, 'Of the First Principles of Government', in Eugene F. Miller (ed.), *Essays: Moral, Political and Literary* (Indianapolis, IN: Liberty Classics, 1987), p. 32; Godwin, *Enquiry*, II, iv, p. 65: 'All government is founded in opinion'.

I had undergone was, that political revolutions are not so well calculated to better man's condition as during a certain period I, with almost all thinking men in Europe, had been led to suppose.[35]

Holcroft had certainly not given up debate and discussion or his interest in public affairs, but he clearly sought to distance himself from any association with activism.

If the first reaction among many of those deliberating about progress and reform might have been to insist that their activity was not a challenge to the authority of the state, it remains the case that over the longer term there was a major shift in the understanding of extra-Parliamentary activity, together with a series of changes to the lexicon of politics. While we need to be cautious, there is some support for this view from the sheer levels of the use of certain terms in the popular press. In Table 1.1, I have used the British Library Newspaper Archive to chart the frequency of use of certain terms relating to politics in the popular press and this material largely confirms this pattern, registering major changes most in the period 1810–1850.[36]

In the first two decades of the nineteenth century there was more than to be expected (when compared to the number of newspapers) use of agitation, sedition, meeting, protest, popular and reform. In the period 1820–1840, there was a dramatic increase in the use of the terms agitation, reform, popular, meeting, platform, protest and demonstration (and, although there is not space to demonstrate this, the same happens with 'out of doors', reform, revolution, political and radical). Essentially, however, the more substantial spike for a range of terms is around the 1830s and 1840s. What is absolutely clear is that in both raw and relative terms the amount of newspaper 'talk' about these matters dramatically increased.[37] Figure 1.1 indicates that, against a baseline set by numbers of newspapers, all these terms show a substantial increase in use.

---

[35] Thomas Holcroft, *Memoirs of the Late Thomas Holcroft, Written by Himself; and Continued to the Time of His Death from His Diary, Notes, and Other Papers* (London: Longman, Brown, Green, and Longmans, 1852), p. 226.

[36] It is difficult to edit out multiple copies from the British Library Newspaper Archive and there is clearly a great deal of reprinting of material from London papers in local papers, but neither issue should skew figures seriously. While an ngram gives an account of the frequency of use, relative to the corpus of texts for that year, search facilities in the British Library corpus give us raw numbers of papers for each year, which means we then need to independently generate an account of frequency. The other thing to say is that the constant updating of the resources on the newspaper archive (albeit usually by very small amounts) keeps changing the exact numbers but, if we treat this as a snapshot and are tolerant of minor inexactitudes, the picture it gives overall seems reasonably faithful.

[37] The probability values for frequency of the terms against the total number of newspapers are all significant at $p < .001$. With thanks to Henry Bradshaw for running the numbers. Post-1840, the incidence of agitation and sedition drop.

Table 1.1 *Political terminology (reformist), 1770–1870*

Year range	Agitation	Reform	Loyal	Popular	Meeting	Platform	Protest	Political	Movement	Radical	Total newspapers
1770–1779	1,680	382	3,666	1,986	16,435	153	119	6,462	729	1,038	11,994
1780–1789	2,409	5,237	4,730	3,062	26,777	532	151	10,230	858	3,002	15,853
1790–1799	2,513	4,448	7,136	4,667	27,831	695	175	12,579	3,303	2,552	16,597
1800–1809	3,989	4,138	14,323	9,438	43,724	1,826	2,391	26,306	6,284	7,351	35,030
1810–1819	8,443	22,251	20,633	21,403	103,957	3,533	8,563	56,464	15,381	14,164	47,122
1820–1829	26,323	32,316	40,912	59,370	246,056	9,953	20,249	127,519	18,850	23,929	71,154
1830–1839	100,197	357,695	101,721	207,774	685,918	27,266	66,962	417,309	75,631	163,329	124,391
1840–1849	179,417	206,271	161,793	285,888	1,166,933	78,229	115,350	520,531	233,842	126,649	156,869
1850–1859	146,842	380,221	183,453	471,531	1,676,130	158,317	159,067	736,119	432,239	139,835	213,784
1860–1869	222,963	634,295	368,539	782,639	2,955,200	316,123	274,600	1,044,513	767,508	233,815	341,381

PERCENTAGE CHANGE IN INCIDENCE OF
NEWSPAPER TERMS AGAINST TOTAL
NEWSPAPERS

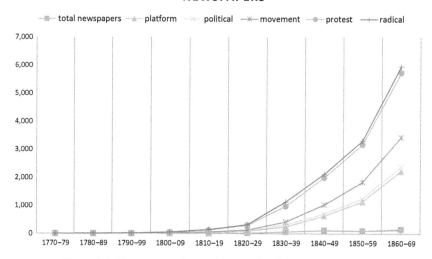

Figure 1.1 Percentage change in use of political terms, 1770–1870

Moreover, the incidence of political terms more generally has a similar pattern. If we analyse the incidence of more common political terms – crown, parliament, legislation, government, we get a similar increase in numbers, with the sharpest change between 1820 and 1840. And if we look at negative radical terms – such as despotism and tyranny, these also increase in use in the 1830s. One other element worth noting is that the 1790s is a decade in which there is a slight dip in the use of a number of terms – reform, out of doors, radical, demonstration, Parliament, crown and legislation (see Table 1.2). But it is difficult to avoid the impression that there is less political talk in this most political of decades, albeit that might well be a function of effective repression.

That this was clearly not just a change in the use of a few terms or only in terms associated with reforming activity suggests that there was a deeper shift in the lexicons employed in thinking about the political order and its foundations and a dramatic expansion in the sheer amount of talk, and these developments also suggests a link to changing practices.

Moreover, over a fifty- to sixty-year period at the beginning of the nineteenth century, people's conceptions of social and political order, of economic activity, of class conflict and of the sources of threats to liberty and a wide range of other aspects fundamentally changed. Not least, for

Table 1.2 *Political terminology (general), 1770–1870*

Year range	Despotic	Tyrannical	Political	Movement	Parliament	Crown	Government	Legislation	Total newspapers
1770–1779	18	648	6,462	729	25,788	15,224	20,808	56	11,994
1780–1789	28	582	10,230	858	41,298	20,963	32,393	86	15,853
1790–1799	37	876	12,579	3,303	31,789	17,069	42,397	57	16,597
1800–1809	641	1,177	26,306	6,284	54,237	35,650	84,686	568	35,030
1810–1819	2,939	2,526	56,464	15,381	99,147	73,345	129,057	2,819	47,122
1820–1829	6,651	4,518	127,519	18,850	212,824	127,927	247,609	11,225	71,154
1830–1839	24,951	21,247	417,309	75,631	603,110	325,431	713,872	59,691	124,391
1840–1849	23,669	23,435	520,531	233,842	818,826	467,320	1,121,058	130,103	156,869
1850–1859	49,145	24,355	736,119	432,239	1,054,368	614,384	1,767,047	156,905	213,784
1860–1869	40,898	29,016	1,044,513	767,508	1,500,602	948,753	2,711,625	258,298	341,381

many people there was a developing sense that they were on the threshold of a modern world (that they linked to a progressive conception of history) and that the old order was resisting these developments and failing to take their interests into account. But a crucial part of that process was that people came to experiment with and to engage in forms of activity that they began to think of as political, in a way they had not before – both because they had not participated in these particular ways and because they had not generally conceived of themselves as active contributors to what they understood as an élite (often corrupt) political world.

It is important to be precise here: people had always reacted to infringements of what they saw as their liberties, they would riot against injustice or when convinced that what they valued was being endangered and they would tell Lords to mind their own business – as in Eaton's parable:

> A certain peer celebrated for the suavity of his manners, purity of morals, and meekness of spirit, had been accustomed in his afternoon walk, to hold frequent conversation with a neighbourhood farmer, respecting his breed of cattle, the nature of the crops, mode of farming, &c until at last, emboldened by this familiarity, the farmer ventured to ask his Lordship's opinion respecting the War, and its duration – G**d***y***b***, says the noble Peer, how dare you speak to me about Politics – G**d****y***b***d, replied the honest Rustic, how dare you talk to me about farming.[38]

But most ordinary people (and that goes quite a long way up the social scale) thought of politics as something that was not really a part of their sphere – even if it was something that they might follow or discuss. Indeed, even among radicals, the common conception was that the private activity of men and women discussing and deliberating among themselves was not intrinsically political or politically consequential. This provides us with a basis for re-emphasising a point implicit in Cobban's original characterisation of the period as perhaps 'the last real *discussion* of the fundamentals of politics in this country'.

1.3   Private and Public

This absence of a dramatic change in the use of broadly political terms in the 1790s was clearly influenced by the successful repression unleashed by the government from the spring of 1792. Nonetheless, there is evidence that this was a repression waged against something that was not

---

[38] Eaton, *Politics for the People*, p. 96.

itself understood (at least initially) by many of its participants as political activity and this had some paradoxical outcomes. In response to increasing government interest in their activities and discussions, some clearly sought to dissociate themselves from the activity, but others reacted more stubbornly and often imaginatively to the challenge. My thinking here has been very much influenced by the work of John Barrell, in particular his paper on 'Coffee House Politicians', in which he makes a series of central points about the complexities of the private and the public.[39] My concerns here are slightly at a tangent in that they are concerned with what kinds of things people thought politics involved, and how its relationship to the private and the public was conceived. Nonetheless, I believe we share a sense that a key turning point for many people was 1792–1793, when many people responded to the Royal Proclamations and the development of the Reevite Association for the Preservation of Liberty and Property Against Republicans and Levellers (APLP) by trying to draw a line between their activities as private men and women and what they thought of as engaging in politics. For example, the young copyright lawyer, Sharon Turner (who later became the country's foremost Anglo-Saxon historian), noted that:

Under these circumstances (of intrigue and repression following the establishment of Reeves's Association) I continued in my resolution to avoid all political societies & meetings – to be connected with no political agitations & to *confine my own political* feelings and / ideas as they arose of whatever kind to my own meditations and *to my private* conversations with the friends I esteem.[40]

Turner clearly saw a distinction between politics and inquiry. He was curious about the London Corresponding Society (LCS) and he wanted to find out more about them but without joining or taking a part in any of their measures, so he asked Thomas Hardy to come to measure him up for a pair of shoes. When Hardy came, he quizzed him about the society and recorded what Hardy candidly replied and he followed up the conversation when Hardy brought him his shoes. He noted that Hardy's objective in presenting a petition to Parliament for reform was to 'cause much talk both in doors and out of doors & that was their object in it & wd be of benefit to them'. And he assessed Hardy as 'a modest man of plain, strong understanding'. Moreover, Turner's curiosity led him to attend a dinner of the SCI chaired by Horne Tooke only days before Tooke was arrested on charges of treason in 1794. But he clearly did not regard any of this activity on his part as political; nor did he link it to

---

[39] Barrell, 'Coffee House Politicians', chapter 2 in his *The Spirit of Despotism*, pp. 75–102.
[40] Sharon Turner, British Library Add ms 81089, fols 314–315, emphasis added.

'political agitations' – that is a phrase he seems to associate with the agitation of ordinary people by government, linked to government or against government.

It is this sense that ensured that Turner was far less complimentary about the APLP (despite his own innate conservatism) and its invitation to all and sundry to communicate with them in support of their desire to suppress seditious publications –

they added what alarmed all who, without thinking of any conspiracy or confederacy, were conversing with the usual freedom of Englishmen on the exciting events of the day. I will not say that such a Society was useless or ineffective but it was of a dangerous and obnoxious character and was convertible into an instrument of tyranny and of much private malignity and mischief. The indictment and verdict and sentence against John Frost for what he said at the Percy Coffee house – *merely words* – nothing done – confirmed these suspicions and spread much alarm.

Turner was a friend of the line-engraver William Watts and in 1794–1795 he fell in love with Watts' daughter Mary. Turner was concerned for Watts because he was very outspoken in his criticism of government and his support for France. But Watts' outspokenness also threatened to jeopardise Turner's matrimonial hopes because another young man, a 'Mr S.', who became a regular visitor to the family, was also a rival for Mary Watt's hand. That was a major concern because Mr S. seemed able to travel effortlessly between France and England and raised suspicions that he was a spy. That meant there was a danger that he might pressurise or blackmail Watts into agreeing to the match. Turner saw in Watts a man of strong private opinions but with no practical intent or activity, who seemed suddenly vulnerable in the new inquisitorial circumstances of the 1790s.

No one was more credulous of these aggravating reports than Mr. W – tho no one could be more innocent or more incapable of Treasonable projects or seditious movements than he was. He would not have stirred a yard from his fireside to give them the least favor or assistance. But he loved to sit in his chair and criticise whatever was going forward. He was a Diogenes in his talk – but nothing like him in his manners. He had a keen sense of what was wrong and expressed vivaciously what he felt and saw it wherever it existed. But this was confined to no party, government profession or Country. He exposed what he thought erroneous in the measures of the French Convention as earnestly as in those of our own Parliament and Ministry. He was a skirmishing Utopian waging war with defects and evils whenever he perceived them, but he kept clear from all Societies and public meetings or places of general resort and only indulged his acute fluency and well-meaning fault finding, seldom without some good grounds among his particular friends in his own hospitable parlour.

But under the influence of these rumoured inquisitorial proceedings, and from that impression of our own importance which we all partake of, Mr. W – thought he was a marked man.[41]

And under these polarising forces, Turner could see that the status quo was rendered increasingly unstable – less because of the thinking of the reformers than because of how the government saw their deliberations and activities and because of how they then reacted to government pressures.

> It was a day of battle & alarm. Each party had so much right in their theories & reasonings & so much wrong in their practises – that my mind vibrated from one to the other – affected by the fervor of the fervent on each side, until it became unable to judge soundly what ought to be – or what wd be the result ... Yet I could not repress a very anxious curiosity & warm interest in the events that were daily occurring – for the happiness of myself & everyone seemed to be involved in the uncertain issue – The future was never more impenetrable to human sagacity than it was in 1793 – and 1794 – Stern and wary prudence was for that time the most necessary quality – My mind partook of this character.[42]

We might doubt that last statement –it is clear that Turner's sense was that there was a private arena for reflection on matters of politics but that this was increasingly broken in on – in part by the Royal Proclamations against sedition, in part because of the arrest and trial of a number of people (including John Frost whom Barrell discuses), but perhaps mostly by inciting others 'without' politics to take up its inquisitorial spirit. What was being put at risk was precisely: 'conversing with the usual freedom of Englishmen on the exciting events of the day'. The right of Englishmen to free private deliberation was under threat. Moreover, he saw the activities of the societies as pushing each other to countenance in reaction more active measures, leading to increasing suspicion and to agitation that threatened the stability of the order. His reference to 'political agitation' must, I think, be taken as agitation deriving from or affecting the political sphere – although the use of agitation is very common, *political agitation* is a phrase whose use is mainly from the end of the first quarter of the nineteenth century, suggesting that it is not conceived as a distinct form of agitation so much as a sphere affected by agitation.[43]

Turner holds to a distinction between 'conversing with the usual freedom of Englishmen on the exciting events of the day' on the one

---

[41] Ibid., fol 413, 415.   [42] Ibid., fols 314–315.

[43] Turner himself uses agitation frequently to refer to his emotional state – but uses the phrase political agitation three times, twice to emphasise his refusal to be involved with it in Britain and once to register his inamorata's endorsement of his avoidance of such activities.

hand and a wider sense of a public activity on the other. For many, perhaps especially the literary radicals of London in their 'private conversations with friends I esteem', there was also a sense that what they were doing in such activities was not directly tied to what they saw as the core meanings of 'politics'. Indeed, there was a sense that politics and politicking was part of the problem, not a component of any appropriate response. But that line was one which was increasingly under strain, as can be seen from Turner's comments and from those of Thomas Muir in his trial for sedition.

> Mr Waddell has stated to you what passed after the meeting was over, in private company in the unguarded hour, when the mind dreads no danger, and when vigilance is asleep. Can anything prove more strongly than the deposition of this man, the innocency of my conduct? The conversation related to politics, and to new publications; and surely /materials of that kind are infinitely more noble in their nature, than those that deform convivial society, and disgrace the man. He remembers me speaking of Mr Flower's book on the French Constitution ... It is true, I recommended Mr Flower there, because I recommend his principles everywhere, – I will do so still; will do so in your presence, in the presence of the Court, and to this great audience. You, who wish for a Reform in Parliament, read and weigh well the lessons, which this good man has given and inculcated. Let personal reformation precede public; let, the torch of knowledge lighten the path of liberty; but above all, let sound morality, and genuine Christianity be the goals from which you commence your political career. A people ignorant – never can enjoy freedom; a people immoral – are unworthy of the blessing ... Among my papers, there is not one which can be construed into guilt. They chiefly consist of pamphlets unconnected with the politics of the day.[44]

Men like Turner and Muir distinguished between public political activity and reflections of a political nature or the consumption of 'a dish of politics'. As a result, they did not see politics as necessarily public in character as against private – as if there was a simple binary division between public/politics vs private/non-political. Rather there was an important distinction between speculation about politics and the public activity of politics, with the former being conceived of as a largely private activity pursued by men in their private capacity that reflected on politics but was not in itself a form of political action and that was a matter for deliberation and reflection between friends and acquaintance. In Kant and Habermas's terms this sounds 'public', but in the participants' minds (who lacked that terminology) it was a matter of private conversation between men linked by acquaintance and friendship.

---

[44] *An Account of the Trial of Thomas Muir, Esq., Younger of Huntershill, for Sedition*, Robertson ed. (Edinburgh: J. Robertson, 1793), pp. 94–95, 124.

That gives us the following matrix:

	Political	vs	Non-political topics
Public activity	A. Parliament, Government, The Court		B. commerce, fashion, etc.
vs			
Private activity	C. foreign news, intellectual speculation about government and parliamentary activity, debating societies		D. domestic/ household matters

If that is right, we can see that one thing that happened in the 1790s was that the government began to associate private political speculation and discussion with sedition – or, as Barrell shows, it made things, formerly regarded as private, matters of public concern and open to political prosecution. In effect, it attempted to characterise activity in **cell C** as activity in **cell A**, and thus as in direct conflict with the current division of political labour and as potentially seditious. The claim of a right/duty to deliberate about practical politics, if it was treated by government as a form of political activity, would inevitably also be seen as simultaneously challenging the authority of the government.

The pressures of the government and the loyalists forced reform organisations such as the SCI and the LCS to pose much more sharply the question of whether they were associations of private men with interests in discussion and the circulation of literature – or whether they sought an active political role. And, following the creation of Reeves's Association, it became clear to many that the former was no longer an option – that they had to take a public stance. That in turn exacerbated the tensions with men such as Godwin who were concerned about associations disturbing public tranquillity by taking up the political challenge. Moreover, because they were acting outside the parliamentary structures that they were seeking to influence, it encouraged the interpretation that their conduct was seditious: for the government, sedition was anything that they saw as leading to a disturbance of the peace, which might involve merely the bringing into contempt, hatred or ridicule either institutions or prominent persons (indeed, the truth of a statement was seen as irrelevant to its tendency – so that true statements that brought or risked bringing institutions into contempt were as seditious as those that were false).[45] On this reading, the radicals' activities were seen as encouraging a predictable breach of the peace, with malicious

---

[45] See William H. Wickwar, *The Struggle or the Freedom of the Press 1819–1832* (London: George Allen & Unwin Ltd., 1928), pp. 18–28.

intent being formally interpreted merely as a 'foreseeable tendency'. Hence Turner's anxieties about the security of Watts, whose talk had no active component but might nonetheless be taken as a challenge to political authority. It was then partly as a function of government and loyalist activity that older ways of distinguishing forms of discussion and activity were strained to meet changing circumstance and in doing so violated a widespread sense of the character and importance of the public–private distinction. But there was also another dimension.

In legitimating the reporting of 'seditious' talk and philosophical speculation, and in making the discussion of political ideas in private places both politically consequential and public, the government simultaneously empowered loyalists to claim their own activity as public *and political*; that is, as connected to the activities of government and parliament *and* (in contrast to radical activity) as legitimate. As Hannah More put it in 1808: '... the alarming state of public affairs fills all men's minds with one momentous object. As every man is a patriot, every patriot is a politician'.[46] And that move further encouraged the fragmentation (although I don't want to claim there were no other causes of fracture) of the divisions between public and private and political and non-political – opening up the distinctions to further interrogation and challenge both by those loyal to and by those who were critical of the status quo.

One immediate response to this incursion among some of the friends of reform was the redoubling of attempts to underline the private character of political discussion and speculation, and thus to strengthen the claim that private discussion and activity was not directly political (to insist that **C** was **C**). That, in turn, further re-enforced a way of thinking about private discussion that saw it as centrally concerned with moral improvement and the development of sound principles. These were seen as the necessary precursors to wider change in society or the reform of the political system; but the emphasis placed on them also encouraged a progressivist but quietist dimension of the reform movement, that one can see practiced especially in literary and cultural circles and for a time at least came into the ascendency in the reform societies and that saw emancipation largely in terms of self-development through deliberation, rather than necessarily preceded by institutional change. One way of thinking about that development is that most people began the decade thinking of politics as largely circumscribed within the purview of the elite and considered their own discussion as private, being political only

---

[46] Hannah More, *Coelebs in Search of a Wife*, edited by Patricia Demers (Toronto, Canada: Broadview, 2007), p. 280.

in their subject matter. As government became more concerned about the spread of opinion and its discussion of reform, its own reaction (as it censored, arrested and imprisoned people) forced many people to reflect on whether their activities could be defended as wholly private. But that process of reflection encouraged a reading of the government's actions as increasingly autocratic and encouraged people to reinterpret their own activity and to consider other steps they might take to challenge these incursions on private space. While some sought to insist that private discussion was rooted in and restricted to a private domestic world and its networks of acquaintance and sociability, others were led to consider a more public political dimension to their aspirations.

Was this insistence on the private character of their activity unreasonable? It is difficult to see it as such. Since they had never been invited to participate in politics it would be hard to regard what they had been doing for years as such participation. In addition, what many of these people were most interested in was discussion and deliberation. In their private conversations they sought a form of candid exchange of ideas in which people could disagree and through which they believed there could be some progress in knowledge and understanding. Government and politics had its own limited sphere, but the progress that the literary radicals believed in was one fundamentally orientated to intellectual improvement. Hence the desire to protect deliberation from politicisation and interference.

This move, I am arguing, proved to be an unstable solution. Extra-parliamentary speculation or activity about political matters was consistently and successfully typed as political *and* public in character by government and loyalist activity, even as those who engaged in it were trying to insist on its private character and its centrality to what it was to be an independent agent. But, in becoming typed as public, it also changed the way in which public political activity was understood. The language of the rights of free-born Englishmen moved from being largely an expression of self-congratulation, first to an increasingly defensive set of claims for liberties threatened by the state and then, in turn, began to take on a language of positive claims for ancillary rights (so as to ensure the preservation of liberties of thought and expression), to be distributed on the basis of equality (each has a right to contribute, not just persons of quality). In this way, the exercise of independent thought and agency, the prerequisites for any human progress, came increasingly to be seen not just as negative rights but as positive claims that had political consequences and were a legitimate component of public and political life. And this fed into a conceptually revised understanding of what politics should involve and to what it referred, and that generated a further change in understandings of what it was to be a full member of the society.

Clearly, these were not overnight transformations and there remained competing strands of understanding throughout the 1790s, but my suggestion is that this development was of wide significance and profoundly affected literary and cultural circles and the circles of the middling orders, even if it also reached down into the artisan and tradesman classes and subsequently spread more widely in the workers organisations in the 1820s and 1830s. In the process of this change many strands of thinking and activity contributed; but this shift typifies the change from the debates of the 1790s to the radicalism of the late 1810s and early 1820s and then those of the 1830s. This means that it is not the best way of characterising 1790s Britain to say that it was an era of popular politics, although it was an era in which the conversations, organisations and publications of ordinary people began to be attributed an immediate political salience. In response and over time, people came to claim the participation that government both attributed to some (as loyalists) and denied them (as reformers), as a set of rights that they sought to secure and exercise.

We can see some of the reactions to this changing world in the responses of people in the 1790s and early 1800s and also a little later. Moreover, continuing a line I have defended for some years about the importance of studying both loyalist and radical thinking together, I want to suggest that the government response and the rise of loyalism played a major part in this shifting lexicon.[47] As indeed did the popular mobilisation of 1803–1805. The secretary to the London Institution, William Upcott, found himself in danger of being called up when the government mobilised men in response to Napoleon's threat of invasion:

The internal situation of the country at this moment, add to my uneasiness. Nothing but a French Invasion is now their theme. I must own *that* does not alarm me, but the measure making use of to repel it. That the French should attempt a landing on this island is folly to suppose, but their end is answered even if they keep us in a continual dread of it, taking every means in our power to prevent its completion.

For this purpose extraordinary plans are adopted – doubling the force of the militia, increased my fears.[48]

Upcott was saved from the ballot for the Militia by the intervention of a benevolent friend who gave him the money to allow him to sign up to the

---

[47] Especially in 'Disconcerting Ideas: Explaining Popular Radicalism and Popular Loyalism in the 1790s', chapter 3 in my *Reforming Ideas in Britain*.

[48] William Upcott Diary, BL Add ms 32,558, fol 40v.

local Volunteer regiment and to produce the necessary uniform and equipment. It was clearly the lesser of two evils. But being bullied into signing loyalist addresses or being forced to enlist in the Volunteers so as to avoid a worse fate provided a series of incursions into people's private and domestic social worlds that forced them to rethink their understanding of the political world as something outside and beyond them. By bringing that political world into their private space, it also opened up that space for political aspirations that had previously been kept apart from it.

The wider thesis is that a great deal of the radicalism in the years immediately following the French Revolution was essentially intellectual in character and was not in itself intended as a direct and organised political challenge to the powers that be. People wanted to discuss events, they wanted to talk about politics, they sought to correspond with others and to engage with them on a range of subjects, from the more speculative to issues of the need for parliamentary reform. The French Revolution certainly encouraged this – not least because, after a century of almost constant war with France, people began to see the prospects for a lasting peace and for progress. But the reaction of government and a popular campaign against those proposing parliamentary reform, especially in London, with the use of Royal Proclamations and prosecutions for sedition, forced people to reflect on their intentions and activities and led many to seek to underline the private character of their proceedings. At the same time, the increasing reluctance of the government to recognise that line made many fearful that there was a concerted conspiracy against the liberties of the people being conducted in tandem with the war with France. Consequently, people's doubts about the legitimacy of and their hostility to the British political system grew as repression and the loyalist propaganda developed. In their opening responses to the French Revolution and in their arguments for parliamentary reform, few people had much sense of how they might effect a transition from what they saw as a rather self-serving and corrupt form of political administration to a more apolitical conception of good government. They were exercising their minds and conversations on political matters in their private capacities and they were obeying. But their government was increasingly unprepared to trust those distinctions.

In his *The Annals of Parish*, John Galt's Minister mentions the case of the man who opened a bookshop in 1790 and 'took in a daily London paper for the spinners and weavers, who paid him a penny a-week for the same; they being all greatly taken up with what, at the time, was going on in France'. The bookseller, he claims, turned a 'whawp' (curlew) in the nest and had to decamp, but the Minister reports that

I could not, however, think any ill of the man notwithstanding; for he had very correct notions of right and justice, in a political sense, and when he came into the parish, he was as orderly and well-behaved as any other body; and conduct is a test that I have always found as good for a man's principles, as professions.[49]

Galt hereby reproduces the distinctions of the 1790s with some accuracy – with the Minister seeing men becoming suspect on the basis of opinion, not conduct; recognising that a man's opinions might have led him astray in some respects but that it is on their basis, rather than on the basis of his actual conduct that he is forced to flee. Yet, in retrospect, he was able to evince a broad tolerance for a diversity of views subject to orderly conduct.

What emerged towards the end of the 1820s was a new set of claims about political rights linked less to universalism (although those idioms continued to be used) and more to the rights of particular groups and communities, often linked to the rights of labour. What is also striking is that these bodies saw the problem as centrally concerned with bringing the attention of those in Parliament to their needs and concerns, and they increasingly saw a reform of political representation in Parliament as essential to ensure that they were listened to – and they began to claim their own activity as a form of political agency. The strategy that was ill-formed in the 1790s, of demonstrating the views of the people in favour of reform through their attendance at mass meetings and through the delegates elected to a national convention (ill-formed because, while there was some precedent, there was real uncertainty on all sides as to what such action could mean – sufficient to legitimate Lord Chief Justice Eyre's verdict of constructive treason for seeing to 'over-awe' parliament[50]), became more clearly conceptualised as a form of popular representation, expression of grievance and petitioning, through the 1810s. And it was driven by the hope that such representation would influence Parliament (without denying to it its independence of action). The failure to secure relief led increasingly to the view that Parliamentary reform was even more essential to secure the good of the people and that means had to be found to ensure reform despite the resistance of so many in Parliament. That was a view that the more middling orders and intellectuals found hard to subscribe to – on the one hand dogged by fears of the chaos of popular insurrection and the lessons of the French Revolution (and the Gordon and Birmingham riots) and on the other by

---

[49] John Galt, *The Annals of the Parish* (Philadelphia: M. Carey & Sons, 1821), p. 186.

[50] Barrell, *Imagining the King's Death*, pp. 297–300; T. M. Parssinen, 'Association, Convention and Anti-Parliament in British Radical Politics, 1771–1848', *English Historical Review* 88 (1973), 504–533.

a desire to ensure that the voice of the educated retained a degree of influence, indeed ascendance, over the popular cause. They sought to retain the autonomy of their private communications; while the innovations on the popular front came from a few gentleman leaders, such as Major Cartwright, Thelwall, Henry Hunt and others, and more generally from those most affected by the post-war slump and its ensuing hardships. And the struggle for the freedom of the press and for the right of self-expression was precisely a struggle fought between reformers and an old order, which saw their demands as bringing institutions and people (such as the Prince Regent) into contempt and as detaching people from their affection for and loyalty to the political system. This was unquestionably (by their definitions) seditious activity and at the end of the war the government seemed wholly resolved to ensure that such activity would not be permitted to undermine the government and the institutions of the country. But seeing things in this way made 'political' things that people may not have previously seen as such and it increasingly set the lines for the struggle between popular forces on the one hand and the forces of order on the other.

There is no teleology here – as if we head inexorably towards a natural view of what politics involves, to a natural view of a line between public and private or to particular claims about our rights and responsibilities in relation to politics. There is never a wholly stable content to politics, because those in power are themselves engaging in contestation over the boundaries between those inside and outside politics and reflection on the relative tolerance to be afforded to opposition both within and without. In this period the term 'politics' became more freighted, extended to new areas of activity, decoupled from parliamentary activity and opened to a wider body of people. Those changes were not inevitable; they reflect a period of turbulence and conflict and the dynamics of that process gave a particular inflexion to the forms these changes took and to the way people understood their world. The evidence shows a distinctive constellation of commitments that the attempt to mobilise popular loyalism in particular helped bring into being, which is why there is so much discussion of the rise of loyalism by those who were its intended targets. People saw this was something new – that it broke in on their lives in a way that opened them up to direct interpolation by political power. What they didn't quite see was that it came to change what they themselves thought of as politics – but my suggestion is that this was essentially what happened.

One dimension of the change was the development of a form of mass mobilisation and the bearing of arms by ordinary citizens: not so much from the state down, as in the *levee en masse* of the French Revolution, but as a voluntary activity that the state was initially uncertain how to deal with and only in 1803–1805 fully took up and promoted.[51] Another dimension concerned libel and the freedom of the press and a gradual process of shifting away from the prosecution of words to the prosecution of actions[52] – a process in which attempts to keep tight control over the reforming press essentially collapsed in the first thirty years of the nineteenth century and thereafter contributed to a very widespread European view that Britain offered a degree of freedom of expression that was largely absent in the post-restoration states of Europe. Finally there was the development of forms of popular partisanship and demands for the interests of particular groups and classes to be taken forward – in which the more universalistic language of rights or the more defensive language of the rights of free-born Englishmen became expressed as sets of claims from particular classes or groups for a recognition of their rights, which in turn developed into an appeal on the basis of social class and contribution.

Some of these changes were the result of the government's response to the radicalism of the 1790s. In the face of demands for reform, the government initially issued Royal Proclamations, solicited loyal addresses and encouraged prosecutions for sedition and, in 1794, 1798, and 1803, also for Treason, while also suspending the Habeas Corpus Act (from March 1793). In 1795 it added the Treasonable Practices Act and Seditious Meetings Act (the 'Gagging Acts'), which sharply delimited the right to public assembly and to hold meetings. It also added the Insurrection Act in Ireland (1796), establishing curfews and providing the death penalty for secret oath taking. Further repression followed the mutinies at Spithead and the Nore and the insurrection in Ireland in 1798, leading to Irish Union, the Combination Acts, directed against workers' associations, the further repeated suspension of habeas corpus, and then the arrest and long-term internment of a number of leading members of the old radical societies. These measures were followed in the subsequent two decades by the Framebreaking Act (1811, directed against Luddism) and the Unlawful Oath Act (1811, directed against both radicals and Luddites). Then, following the rise of unrest in the wake of Waterloo and its consequent economic disruption, 1817–1820 saw suspensions of Habeas Corpus, an act making attacks on

---

[51] See Cookson, *The British Armed Nation* and Austin Gee, *The British Volunteer Movement, 1793–1815* (Oxford: Oxford University Press, 2003).

[52] See Wickwar, *The Struggle* and Michael Lobban, 'From Seditious Libel to Unlawful Assembly: Peterloo and the Changing Face of Political Crime c1770–1820', *Oxford Journal of Legal Studies* 10(3) (Autumn 1990), 307–352.

the King treason; further legislation against sedition; the Peterloo Massacre; the passing of the Six Acts, to stop disorder, outlaw military training, control public meetings and to strengthen powers against the free press; and culminated in the execution of Arthur Thistlewood and his associates in the Cato Street Conspiracy to blow up the cabinet.

At the beginning of his memoir, *Passages in the Life of a Radical*, Samuel Bamford noted the development of Hampden Reform clubs throughout the country from 1815 and the spread of William Cobbett's books and his direction of the people 'to the true cause of their suffer-ings – misgovernment; and to its proper corrective – parliamentary reform. Riots soon became scarce, and from that time they have never obtained their ancient vogue with the labourers of this country.'[53] Bam-ford certainly purveyed a roseate view of the developments. Nonetheless, it is clear that the government measures in the 1790s and early 1800s led to the framing of popular political activity in new ways and that this was co-eval with a widening sense that people's views had some right to be heard – leading to a developing process of jostling for the high ground over what counted as legitimate forms of political expression.

These changes were clearly influenced initially by events in and debates on France. Indeed, an emerging language of popular politics was also an issue for the French, although popular activity and debate developed an intensity and an acceleration in revolutionary Paris that both traumatised French attitudes to popular activity and convinced them that the real threat to liberty lay less with the traditional system of government and politics and more with the anarchic consequences of popular power. That produced in a very different French response after the Revolutions of 1830: there the order progressively restricted the franchise in the 1830s and 1840s, saw the problem as one of a subterra-nean process of equalisation of status that threatening to expand into demands for social and economic equality and it turned to explore what kind of political system could best protect liberty against these forces. In contrast, Britain slowly (and certainly reluctantly) moved towards a way of integrating political movements and popular activity into the existing system of representation and its institutionalisation in Parliament. Indeed, it is striking how far activists in other European states came, post-1830, to see Britain as exceptional and distinctly liberal in its traditions of responding to popular concerns. One component of this was a developing acknowledgement that popular opinion had some political legitimacy – the challenge for many European states was to

---

[53] Samuel Bamford, *Passages in the Life of a Radical: Autobiography* (1842), edited by Henry Duxley, v.ii (London: Internet Archive, 2014), p. 7.

identify an arena that they could afford to acknowledge as allowably political (rather than merely seditious or insurrectionary) and that could be accorded a certain degree of legitimacy by the formal political system. States took different routes on this – and, as a result, their 'political communities' and their histories took very different paths towards modern worlds that are in consequence importantly different on many dimensions.

These issues raise questions about whether scholars of the period have done enough to try to understand the shifting character of people's conceptualisation of their actions and thoughts and how far they have seized on a range of material as being intrinsically political in content and as thereby having a wider or deeper significance than merely as literary or aesthetic form. I don't think that what I have said blocks all such claims – but I think it should encourage us to worry more about how people conceptualised their behaviour and their institutional and civil context and the lexicons they use in doing so – above all, so as to avoid any retrospective application of modern (if similarly local) understanding of the nature of politics. In Chapter 2, I turn to examine in detail the impact of this shifting set of distinctions on the experience of debate and discussion in the 1790s.

2   Disagreement and Deliberation

2.1   Convergence

One element in the troubling of the concept of politics and its relationship to debate and discussion can be seen in the way in which people in the 1790s understood and negotiated questions of disagreement. Religion remained one major area of disagreement in Britain, although it was one that the eighteenth-century state reasonably successfully cordoned off from the political domain. The result was a public confession of rather latitudinarian Anglicanism, which kept open a broad church, around which Catholicism and various strains of Dissent were accorded toleration and kept largely off stage and out of political life by the Test and Corporations Acts. Anti-popery remained a potentially disruptive element at the popular level (and was effectively and destructively exploited in the Gordon riots of 1780) and Church and King could be mobilised to similar effect (as they were in the anti-Priestley riots of 1791 in Birmingham), but the political order was not being torn apart by religious conflict and the Anglican Church and the State remained ascendant. For the most part, people came to tolerate different religious views so long as they were not introduced into the political process but remained private or a part of non-political public debate. Certainly, these disagreements were not expected to generate controversies that spilled over into the political sphere – in large part because they submitted to an order that emphasised the privatisation of belief. Indeed, Hannah More expressly complained that even Anglicanism had become essentially a wholly personal and private matter, that rarely extended even to a 'dish of chat' about religion:

As in the momentous times in which we live, it is next to impossible to pass an evening in company, but the talk will so inevitably revert to politics, that, without any premeditated design, everyone present shall infallibly get to know to which side the other inclines; why, in the far higher concern of eternal things, should we so carefully shun every offered opportunity of bearing even a casual testimony to the part we espouse in religion? Why, while we make it a sort of point of conscience to leave no doubt on the mind of a stranger, whether we adopt the part of Pitt or Fox, should we chuse to leave it very problematical whether we belong to God or Baal? Why, in religion as well as in politics, should we not act like people who, having their all at stake, cannot forbear now and [/] then adverting for a moment to the object of their grand concern, and dropping, at least, an accidental intimation of the side to which they belong.[1]

For More, religion (so long as it was the right religion), was something that ought to feature much more in discussions and debates, rather than becoming wholly privatised, although that evangelical perspective also risked destabilising the existing consensus. In the traditions of Dissent, theological matters were often very intensely debated, and its members also contributed extensively to wider debates on philosophy, morality and theology. For many from this tradition, there was a reluctance to accept that the breadth of toleration and its nature were wholly settled questions. The exclusions from public office that applied to Dissenters were increasingly seen as indicative of a residual intolerance in the Anglican State that was deeply unjust. Some looked to America and saw in the Virginia Statute of 1786 a more tolerant order:

Whereas almighty God hath created the mind free; that all attempts to influence it by temporal punishments or burtherns, or by civil incapacitations, tend only to beget habits of hypocrisy and meanness, and are a departure from the plan of the Holy author of our religion, who being Lord of both body and mind, yet chose not to propagate it by coercions on either, as was in his Almighty power to do ...[2]

The statute prompted Richard Price to comment

Had the principles which have dictated it been always acted upon by civil governments, the demon of persecution would never have existed; sincere inquiries would never have been discouraged; truth and reason would have had fair play; and most of the evils which have disturbed the peace of the world, and obstructed human improvement, would have been prevented.[3]

The Virginia Statute was resolutely directed to theological matters, but there was an equivocation in much written by Rational Dissenters that

---

[1] Hannah More, *Strictures on the Modern System of Female Education with a View of the Principles and Conduct Prevalent among Women of Rank and Fortune*, vol. 2, 3rd ed. (London: T. Cadell, 1799), v.ii., pp. 50–51. In keeping with my opening chapter, I take this to be about people taking deliberative sides in relation to political events, not with practical action.

[2] Virginia Statute, 1786, cited in Merrill D. Peterson and Robert C. Vaughan, *The Virginia Statute for Religious Freedom: Its Evolution and Consequences in American History* (Cambridge: Cambridge University Press, 1988), p. xvii.

[3] Richard Price, July 26, 1786, Letter to Mr. Urban, *The Correspondence of Richard Price: Volume III February 1786–February 1791*, edited by Bernard Peach and D. O. Thomas (Cardiff: University of Wales Press, 1994), pp. 45–47.

suggested a broader reading. Consider, for example, Joseph Priestley's comment:

It is universally understood, that REASON and AUTHORITY are two things, and that they have generally been opposed to one another. The hand of power, therefore, on the side of any set of principles cannot but be a suspicious circumstance. And though the injunction of the magistrate may silence *voices*, it multiplies *whispers*; and those whispers are the things at which he has most reason to be alarmed.[4]

For many, a belief in the sovereignty of individual conscience in matters of religion had no *necessary* connection with ideas about the rights of individuals with respect to politics. Yet it was certainly mooted in this period (and clearly Priestley believed) that there was some such connection. On this view, the right of private judgement could naturally be generalised from the dimension of religion to that of politics, so that all opinion (and participation) ought to be tolerated that did not threaten the security of institutions that protected the liberties of all individuals. This meant that the boundary between politics and religion was not wholly secured and remained potentially open to question.

In Britain, in the late eighteenth century, the vast majority of religious sects accepted the existing division between the secular and the theological and accepted that different rules applied in each sphere. Protestant dissenters certainly chaffed against the restrictions of the Test and Corporations Acts, but in many ways they did so because they felt their loyalty to the state was not in question and believed that disabilities – which some still thought could be appropriately applied in some cases (such as Catholicism) – should no longer be applied to them. In the course of the debates on the Acts and their potential repeal between 1787 and 1790, many made claims about the sanctity of private judgement and the evils of enforced conformity, but that case was a conditional one – given that belief was important *and was not prejudicial to the security of the political order*, then it ought to be tolerated.[5]

One basis for that claim could be found in the view that faith and belief were a function of the direct personal relationship between the individual conscience and God. On this view, there could be no grounds for a secular power to intrude in that relationship – so long as it remained essentially private and not a threat to the authority of the state. Within

[4] Joseph Priestley, *An Essay on the First Principles of Government and on the Nature of Political, Civil, and Religious Liberty*, Peter Miller (ed.), *Political Writings* (Cambridge: Cambridge University Press, 1993), pp. 56–57.
[5] See G. M. Ditchfield, 'The Parliamentary Struggle on the Repeal of the Test and Corporation Acts, 1787–1790', *English Historical Review* 89 (1974), 551–577.

Rational Dissent, however, there were many who saw the primacy of the right to private judgement as rooted in a more direct appeal to truth (rather than in faith).[6] For those who did, fidelity to one's beliefs in one's relationship to God could be linked to a view of truth as a matter of rationally grounded belief. Making that link made possible the breaking down of the barriers between religious belief and belief and knowledge more widely.

This raised a number of potential challenges. If conscience was to be understood as a function of the agent's unmediated and inscrutable relationship to God, then differences in beliefs were to be expected. If, however, belief in God was seen as a matter of rational apprehension of an objective truth, then the failure of others to perceive this truth raised questions about how to understand failures on the part of others to perceive the truth and questions about how to react when others would not be persuaded. How should one explain the fact that people continued to disagree; and how should that disagreement be reacted to? This second issue became more acute when, instead of dividing the world up into spheres of belief to which different principles applied (religion and matters of faith, as against politics and matters of argument and interest), we begin to see the whole of life as a single sphere in which the same principles are applicable across all instances and issues. When William Godwin insisted that 'truth is in reality single and uniform, and it is irresistible' he was claiming that there is no natural line between religion and politics, between faith and knowledge.[7] And if truth is single and uniform, why did people disagree, how should we understand their disagreement and how might they be brought to agreement? This was a central issue for Godwin – given his willingness to see the *raison d'etre* of the secular world as a search for truth and (derivatively) virtue – but I also want to suggest that it might also have been a much more widely held position that would have been taken as threatening the status quo.

In this chapter I want to focus firstly on the expectations that radicals had of discussion, argument and the clash of mind on mind, how far they considered other forms of communication and persuasion, how they distinguished appropriately deliberative forms of disagreement and inappropriately non-deliberative attacks on their positions and how they thought the latter should be responded to. I then turn to examine the way

---

[6] On Rational Dissent see Knud Haakensson (ed.), *Enlightenment and Religion: Rational Dissent in Eighteenth Century Britain* (Cambridge: Cambridge University Press, 1996), especially John Seed's essay '"A Set of Men Powerful Enough in Many Things": Rational Dissent and Political Opposition in England, 1770–1790'.

[7] Godwin, *Enquiry*, III, vii, p. 102.

in which these understandings changed as reformers came under increasing pressure as the private/public divide was progressively violated. There were further pressures as some members of Godwin's networks turned against their former allies and denounced them and their political commitments. I explore the ways that those who retained faith in their commitments, despite this fragmenting radical community, responded to this development, and I analyse some of the different grounds that contributed to the haemorrhaging of Godwin's circles.

Mind has a perpetual tendency to rise ... it is the duty of individuals to publish truth without diffidence or reserve ... The more it is told, the more it is known in its true dimensions, and not in parts, the less it is possible that it should coalesce with or leave any room for the pernicious effects of error.[8]

In these radical literary circles we can recognise a very strong aspiration for a distinctive form of candid, deliberative and progressive form of discussion, centring on the clash of mind and mind (a commitment that owed a great deal to Dissenting views of the importance of private judgement and the pursuit of truth and that found affinities with many who had a background in Dissent, especially among the younger generation, and to those who had attended the Dissenting Academies in the 1770s and 1780s). In the 1790s its advocates needed to find ways of responding to what they saw as unreasonable government opposition to their claims for a full toleration and subsequently to what was seen as the irresponsible and insincere attempts of loyalist forces to smear those arguing for progress. As the decade proceeded, that issue was further exacerbated by defections from the radical cause and from friendships and groups of acquaintance. These prompted suspicions of opportunism, but also raised issues about the demanding nature of the radicals' aspirations and the tensions between their strong egalitarianism and the very inegalitarian society in which they lived. Over time, confidence among the intellectual radicals began to wane, in part moderating their expectations and at the same time fuelling doubts and encouraging a retreat from the openness they had demonstrated in the earlier part of the decade.

I begin by exploring the character of the relationships to which the literary radicals aspired. Clearly there were many commercial and professional relationships that look very much like the weak ties of a free-market economy. At the same time, I will suggest, if one scratches the surface of many of these, we can see that family connections and embeddedness in localities and in sets of relationships point towards a picture of London's culture and people's relationships that remains

---

[8] Godwin, *Enquiry*, VIII, viii, pp. 461–462.

marked by strong and traditional ties. In contrast, the disinterested benevolence that Godwin aspired to and his and his associates' hopes for a deliberative culture focused around the exercise of private judgement and the pursuit of truth and justice, looks like a particularly demanding form of disinterested friendship. These were not weak ties, nor were they the traditional strong ties of family and connections. Rather, they were much more like a very intensive form of the disinterested friendships that Allan Silver's discussion of Adam Ferguson's account of friendship points to – which we might think of as a new form of deliberative strong tie.

These disinterested strong ties came with certain preconditions – not the least of which was a presumption of the fundamental equality between participants. True deliberation had to exclude any claim to differential status or to authority. Nonetheless, Godwin and his friends were trying to practice such a discourse in a deeply inegalitarian society, which seems initially to have tolerated and supported them. As that setting reacted to the political pressures of events in the 1790s and as scrutiny and spying insinuated themselves in these intense private relations, the tensions between these discursive relations and people's more traditional stronger ties and their more particular interests become more obvious and unsettling. Absolute candour and free and open discussion might work in a relatively egalitarian society, even when placed under various forms of duress, but this was not an egalitarian society. It was strongly marked by class and status divisions and these had powerful effects on the extent to which relationships that aspired to being equal and disinterested could survive.

We can recognise these deeper inequalities even in relationships that on the surface look more familiar and equal. In the wider society of male friendship, élite men were often perfectly willing to include other men of lower status in their debates and society, often with little regard for their morals and reputations, being interested only in their talents or sociability (which is not a position that most women could take). Nonetheless, an underlying consciousness of distinction remained clear. John Taylor noted, with respect to Frank North:

Soon after he became Earl of Guilford I met him and he saluted me in his usual free, open, and good-humoured manner. 'Before I answer', said I, 'I must know whether I am speaking to Frank North or to Lord Guilford?' – 'Oh! Frank North for ever, among old friends', said he, and we renewed our intercourse, as far as the difference between our ranks admitted, for the remainder of his life.[9]

---

[9] John Taylor, *Records of My Life*, 2 vols. (London: Edward Bull, 1832) v.1., p. 128 – Taylor's clause is about ranks worth noting.

Taylor was touched to receive a commendatory letter from Mr George Hardinge (barrister), nephew of lord Camden, in reference to a few lines Taylor had written for an Inchbald play, 'though I had not the least acquaintance with him. I returned his civility, of course, and once afterwards passed him in the street, but did not think it proper to make myself known.'[10] Here too, the lesser man waits for the greater to condescend to identify him as an equal.

There were clearly rules about social deference and, while they could be waived, they were to be waived by the higher status individual. Male friendships, then, might well look like, and sometimes be, a case of 'disinterested relations', linked by a general sympathy and not dominated by calculation or seeking advantage. But they often took place across class and status divisions and they masked differences that, under pressure, could become salient and could undermine their independence from instrumental concerns, professional connections and familial relations. While Ferguson thought of this realm of disinterested sociability as relatively robust we can see that, in the often very demanding form in which Godwin and his associates pursued it, it might be vulnerable to political pressure, to disillusion and betrayal, to disagreements about the requirements for a secure and progressive society and to rumbling social and status differentials that could be triggered by displays of presumption.

2.2   Candid Deliberation

Even on the most rationalist of accounts of discussion, some disagreement was clearly to be expected. Conversation and deliberation involving the 'clash of mind and mind' were central to Godwin's account of human progress. People had to exercise their private judgement, but they also needed to engage in deliberation as a way of testing and further developing their understanding. Godwin was suspicious of any dependence on the ideas of others: we have to assess ideas on their merits rather than taking them on the authority of others. But he was not solipsistic: open exchange and debate were central to his sense of the march of truth. He was clearly not alone – many others influenced by the ideas of the enlightenment and stimulated by the opening events of the French Revolution, similarly saw 'mind' as progressive and understood progress in terms of the improvement of intellectual capacity and knowledge. They did not necessarily believe that truth was instantly communicable

[10] Ibid., v.1., 402.

but there was confidence that open discussion would produce a convergence of belief and, through that, the unfolding of progress. Among those
in circles of Rational Dissent, and more widely amongst those with a
certain amount of learning and with interests in science and literature,
there was a powerful sense that this progress was being made and would
spread from the intellectual élite to the masses through education and
from the domain of theology and religious belief to the broader political
and social world. The American and French revolutions (which were
read as the overturning of arbitrary government based on force and
fraud) did not cause this belief, but many people read these events as
further grounds for holding such beliefs. Indeed, the enthusiasm in many
circles in response to the opening stages of events in France might best be
understood as arising from their sense that this was confirmation for a
rather inchoate belief that they were living in an age of rapid and progressive change.[11]

The younger generation of Dissenters especially responded by seeing
progress in still more secular and social (not just theological or intellectual) terms while retaining their expectations of convergence. Godwin
and many of his friends in London's literary and extra-parliamentary
social circles took this tack. Godwin was not a hot head – he saw the
need to move slowly and not to precipitate or exacerbate conflict. He
understood that people needed time to take on board new ideas and to
adjust and adapt themselves to them. But he believed that things were
changing, he anticipated further and much more extensive changes and
he saw it as a duty to promote such change. Holcroft was equally
committed, as were many of the younger men they influenced and many
of their contemporaries. For these men, the opening of the 1790s seemed
to encourage expectations for the advancement of mind and for social
and political change that had been a part of their hopes through the
second half of the 1780s. Holcroft's *Anna St Ives* (published at the
beginning of 1792) represents that confidence no less than Godwin's
Enquiry, published almost exactly a year later. And, while Godwin's
discursive style tends to be taken as distinctive, it is clear that Holcroft
operated in a very similar manner. Sharon Turner had encountered
Holcroft at William Watts's home, but was some time later paid a visit
in his rooms in Lincoln's Inn:

---

[11] Significant as the leading Catholic power in Europe – hence Priestley's claim about
Louis's execution involving the striking off of the first of the horns of the beast of the
apocalypse. Clarke Garrett, *Respectable Folly* (Baltimore: Johns Hopkins University Press,
1975), p. 133.

His conversation has been that of an intelligent, but peculiar and paradoxical man. He made truth, which he pronounces Trewth, every thing. As I saw he was using the word in some sense different from its common meaning, I asked him to explain to me what he intended by it for I felt Pilate's question 'What is truth?' to be fully applicable at this moment.[12]

His answer was – 'By truth I mean, that which produces the greatest public good'. I suggested whether some other word might not better express his principle, but he thought not, and gave me reasons which I did not quite comprehend for its exact propriety. I saw it was a hobby horse that wd not be parted with and that he was not pleased that I did not perceive its happy applicability. It was obvious that he called truth what his great friend Godwin called Justice, each making his favorite word the cardinal point of his own theory.

But Turner also commented on the mode of Holcroft's discussion:

He lectured me precisely as if I were his pupil and was not very patient at my inquisitorial remarks. He speaks [371] very dogmatically and formally, yet with considerable force of language and energy. It was interesting, as an intellectual effusion, but fatiguing to listen to him. He expected your immediate apprehension and adoption of his ideas and does not like to be put to elucidate them or to hear objections to them.[13]

Turner was a naturally cautious man, who was not likely to subscribe to ideas he had not tested and weighed, and he clearly felt he was being pressured by Holcroft. Yet, his experience raises a wider set of questions about how discussion, persuasion and the transmission of ideas (and truth) were supposed to operate. 'Trewth' was central to the literary radicals: it was both what communication and deliberation sought to track and to expand, and it was an obligation on the part of the agent to speak and pursue the truth.

For Godwin, at least in the first edition of the *Enquiry*, candour was an obligation irrespective of the consequences. He shared that view widely with those raised in traditions of Rational Dissent: candour was a core duty – a way of communicating, both as a mode of expressing one's thoughts and beliefs, and as a mode of listening – one that had to give due weight to what others said. In his *Enquiry*, Godwin argued that the obligation to speaking the truth overrode other more prudential objectives, such as preserving one's life![14] Discussing a Jacobite, who encounters loyalist troops pursuing but not recognising him, he addresses the question of whether it is right to lie to save oneself:

---

[12] John 18:38, 'Pilate saith unto him (Jesus), What is truth?'
[13] BL Add ms 81089, fols 369–371.   [14] Godwin, *Enquiry*, IV, iii, s.ii, pp. 238–52.

We must not be guilty of insincerity ... He that, having laid down to himself a plan of sincerity, is guilty of a single deviation, infects the whole, contaminates the frankness and magnanimity of his temper (...) and is less virtuous than the foe against whom he defends himself; for it is more virtuous in my neighbour to confide in the apparent honesty, than in me to abuse his confidence.[15]

The kind of intensive deliberation that took place between Holcroft, Godwin and others was clearly difficult to replicate on a mass scale and the rather dry speculative arguments Godwin advanced in his *Enquiry* also had limitations. Scholars have increasingly recognised Godwin's own concern with the problem in the shifting ways in which he sought to support the progress of truth. Recent work by David O'Shaughnessy on Godwin's writing for the theatre and by Jon Mee and Vicki Myers on rhetoric and the *Enquirer* has broadened our appreciation of his attempts to convey his principles more forcefully and compellingly to a wider audience.[16] His disappointment at the speed at which Joseph Gerrald had consumed *Caleb Williams* while in his prison cell awaiting transportation only confirms this sense that he was ambitious to do things in all his work that would go beyond mere entertainment and the telling of stories:

And, when I had done all, what had I done? Written a book to amuse boys and girls in their vacant hours, a story to be hastily gobbled up by them, swallowed in a pusillanimous and unanimated mood, without chewing or digestion. [Gerrald] told me that he had received my book late one evening, and had read through the three volumes before he closed his eyes. Thus, what had cost me twelve month's labour, ceaseless heartaches and industry, now sinking into despair, and now raised and sustained in unusual energy, he went over in a few hours, shut the book, laid himself on his pillow, slept and was refreshed, and cried, Tomorrow to fresh woods and pastures new.[17]

It was an unusual moment of self-doubt for Godwin in the first half of the 1790s – but it speaks to the extent to which he was ambitious for his work to enlighten communication and to change the world in which he lived. His hopes with respect to the theatre are captured in a note among his papers:

---

[15] Ibid., IV.iv, s.ii, p. 135.
[16] David O'Shaughnessy, *William Godwin and the Theatre* (London: Pickering & Chatto, 2010); Mee, *Conversable Worlds*, pp. 156–167; and Victoria Myers, 'William Godwin and the *Ars Rhetorica*', *Studies in Romanticism* 41(3) (2002), 415–444. Also, thanks to Pamela Clemit's growing volumes of Godwin's letters, readers can see Godwin's own struggles with candour in his most intimate friendships: *The Letters of William Godwin: Volume I: 1778–1797*, edited by Pamela Clemit (Oxford: Oxford University Press, 2011) and *Volume II: 1798–1805* (Oxford: Oxford University Press, 2014) (hereafter *Letters of WG*).
[17] Don Locke, *A Fantasy of Reason*, pp. 70–71.

Why is the drama useful?

Because it is eminently subservient to the discovery & propagation of truth

Moral truths, if they have not been discovered, have in this method been elucidated & enforced

It does that, which sermons were intended to do: it forms the link between the literary class of mankind & the uninstructed, the bridge by which the latter may pass over into the domains of the former

In comparison with this object, of what consequence is it, whether it does or does not inculcate les petites moralités.[18]

These scholars have added considerably to our appreciation of Godwin's purposes and of the extent to which they informed the broad range of his work. More widely, as Jon Mee's *Conversable Worlds* shows, there were different modes of conversation, from the polite, to the robust, to the clash of mind on mind.[19] People had different understandings of the conventions and distinguished different degrees of acceptability in the manner of conversation. And there were different conventions for different circles and over time these conventions changed, as did the circles. Circles associated with Rational Dissent shared a particular view of how such argument should proceed: candid, not conversational; truth orientated, not for enjoyment and entertainment; committed and serious, not light or witty.[20] In many respects Godwin and his friends took that form to its extreme. Indeed, Sharon Turner's diary suggests scholars might have underestimated quite how demanding this sort of exchange could be. When Turner was discussing Holcroft with Watts's daughter, Mary (a friend of Sophie, Holcroft's daughter), she told him:

He (Holcroft) did not mean to be disagreeable but he often was so, though he was very civil to her she could not avoid being in some awe of him. She knew his daughters were. When he meant to be most gracious it seemed awkward and unnatural to him to be so. Even Godwin, his chief associate, sometimes was afraid of him. At times when she was visiting his daughters, she had seen the two friends sit for a quarter of an hour together with their arms folded looking first at the floor, then at each other without speaking a word as if afraid to begin their arguing battle. When it took place both were sturdy – for both had their peculiar opinions; but Godwin was so cool and wary as to have great advantage.[21]

---

[18] Abinger MS Dep c. 21, fol 57.
[19] Mee, *Conversable Worlds*, introduction and chapter 1.
[20] See D. O. Thomas, *The Honest Mind: The Thought and Work of Richard Price* (Oxford: Oxford University Press, 1977); Martin Fitzpatrick, 'Toleration and Truth', *Enlightenment and Dissent* 1 (1982), 3–31; and my 'Democratic Virtues: Between Candour and Preference Falsification', *Enlightenment and Dissent* 19 (2000), 23–44.
[21] Diary of Sharon Turner, BL Add ms 81089, fol 281.

This conversable world was one in which people argued. The argument was not a battle so much as a process involving the sincere expression of conviction which was meant to be deeply explorative. Moreover, it changed people's minds and their behaviour – as it was intended to. Most people would also have brought to it an implicit back-up account as a way of explaining why other people seemed snared by pre-conceptions and rigidities – in terms of corruption, self-interest or fraud and the gains that arose from power. That helped them to account for the delays and resistances. From this position it was easy to believe that Burke had been purloined by a pension, that the government was serving very particular interests and that it was becoming despotic because of the tendency of power to distort people's judgements, which would account both for its resistance to the voices of reasoned argument and its habitual recourse to force. In the case of Rational Dissent there is evidence that such explanations were widespread and that many people were consequently tempted to take a more retiring approach to the world, even as early as the very early 1790s in the light of the failure of attempts to repeal the Test and Corporations Acts. But not all were dismayed: Richard Price, writing to Priestley, pointed out that 'You endeavour very kindly to comfort me over Mr Burke's abuse but I have not been much impressed by it ... Such has been the fate of most persons who have aimed at mending the world and opposed the corruption of the world.'[22] Nonetheless, there was increasingly widespread loyalist activity directed against Dissenters and reformers more broadly that, over the last decade of the century, led to increasing withdrawal from public debate and a drawing in amongst a close group of friends, neighbours and co-religionists in many areas of the country. As we should expect, this was less acute in areas of dissenting strength – Cookson cites Norwich, Nottingham, Leeds and Liverpool, but also Exeter, Shrewsbury, Warwick, Derby and Sheffield.[23] And in a rather different way, because of its size and radical traditions, there was also London. In such places there was resistance to this 'quietism'; even so, those engaged needed some

---

[22] Richard Price, *The Correspondence of Richard Price: Volume III February 1786–February 1791*, edited by Bernard Peach and D. O. Thomas (Cardiff: University of Wales Press, 1994), p. 337.

[23] John Cookson, *The Friends of Peace* (Cambridge: Cambridge University Press, 1983). But the story in even these towns is a complex, varied and local one, as evidenced in Martin Fitzpatrick's 'The View from Mount Pleasant: Enlightenment in Late-eighteenth Century Liverpool', *Oxford University Studies in the Enlightenment* (formerly *SVEC*) 2008 (1) (2008), 119–144; and in the broader survey of anti-dissenting attacks in David L. Wykes, '"The Spirit of Persecutors Exemplified" The Priestley Riots and the Victims of the Church and King Mobs', *Unitarian Historical Society, Transactions* 20 (1) (1991), 17–39.

understanding of why a premeditated and carefully contrived 'persecution' was happening and how it ought to be met.[24]

I have suggested elsewhere and underlined in Chapter 1, that the political, literary and cultural world of Britain from 1792 saw an escalation and polarisation of political conflict.[25] What began as a literary and philosophical debate was no longer merely a discussion or conversation. Words were seen as weapons and the boundaries between the expression of ideas and their practical application became more blurred. Moreover, it became an increasingly bitter conflict, generating on the one side forms of popular mobilisation and protest and invoking on the other the full penalty of the law, government repression and the mobilisation of loyalism. In that context, with an increasingly Manichean division of reformers and loyalists, how were people to understand and explain their opponents' positions? Moreover, in such conditions people faced the supplementary question of at what point candour and the exploration of truth might become impossible? Could there be a point at which people might come to see the other as sufficiently malign, corrupt and autocratic to warrant giving up on candour? And at what point in the period did people begin to feel it was no longer possible to argue one's case or to do so with candour.[26] Possible dates for such a moment include the defeat of the attempts to repeal the Test and Corporations Acts in 1790; the destruction of Priestley's home and those of others in the Birmingham Riots in July 1791; the issuing of the Royal Proclamation against seditious writing in May 1792, the rise of Reeves's Associations for the Preservation of Liberty and Property Against Republicans and Levellers (from December 1792); the Treason Trials of 1794; the Gagging Acts of 1795; the suppression of the Irish Rebellion in 1798; or the repeated suspension of *habeas corpus* and then the incarceration of radicals in March and April 1799?[27]

The sense of solidarity among literary and philosophical reformers living in London gave some grounds for confidence. Nonetheless, these men and women did increasingly come to believe that the government was engaged in a conspiracy against their liberties, even if they also believed that time and numbers were on their side and that the people would awake to the imposture practiced by the government and the loyalists with its alarms about Jacobinism. They had no doubts that the

---

[24] Cookson, *The Friends of Peace*, p. 13: 'persecution, premeditated and carefully contrived'.

[25] See my *Reforming Ideas in Britain*, especially chapters 1–3 and 11.

[26] See my 'Candour, Courage and the Calculation of Consequences in Godwin's 1790's', in Eliza O'Brien, Helen Stark and Beatrice Turner (eds.), *Godwin and Fear* (forthcoming).

[27] Until the expiration of the suspension of the Habeas Corpus Act in 1801.

methods used by their opponents were deeply suspect. In February 1793, Godwin accused John Reeves (the founder of the Association for the Preservation of Liberty Against Republicans and Levellers) of dashing the means of propaganda from the hands of the reform associations only to pick them up and use them for his own purposes. He professed (and there is every reason to think he was being sincere) that the use of pamphlets, squibs, songs and handbills served only to disturb the population. In effect, he doubted their value as a means of spreading truth and enlightening the population and he reprimanded Reeves for taking the same tools and doing so to excite the vulgar 'to pull down the houses and destroy the property of the dissenters'. Moreover, he went on to deny that Reeves was a sincere friend of the constitution – 'Every sincere advocate for the Constitution will wish for no better than a fair and tranquil field of debate and an honourable surrender on both sides of all the means of inflammation ...'. But Reeves was not a sincere adherent since 'every disputant that breaks out into rage, scurrility, and violence, proves that he has no confidence in the strength of his arguments. If you believed what you pretend to believe, you would scorn to take advantages; you would not fear for the event in the contest.' But he predicted that within months Reeves' followers would discover his plot against the liberties of all. For Godwin, the people could be deceived, but not indefinitely, and those who imposed upon them would be discovered and disdained.[28]

The same understanding was at work in his letter of March 1793 to Sir Archibald Macdonald, save that, for Godwin, the standing of Attorney General made his attack on freedom of expression still more dangerous. He quoted Macdonald as saying that 'Intemperate speaking is pregnant with danger', and responded by accusing him of being still more of a danger to public tranquillity: 'it is your conduct that is pregnant with danger – danger to a cause you pretend to espouse, and not to the words of an intoxicated tallow chandler. There is no method that leads so surely and so suddenly to the dissolution of power, as an endeavour to stretch it beyond its ability.'[29]

We might think this was merely a tactical rhetorical strategy, but it was so extensively deployed by Godwin and by others and was so much in keeping with his principles and his profession of them that there are

---

[28] See 'To Mr Reeves, Chairman of the Society for Protecting Liberty and Property ...', signed Mucius in William Godwin, *Political and Philosophical Writings of William Godwin*, edited by Mark Philp (London: Pickering & Chatto, 1993), vol. 2, pp. 16–19.

[29] 'To Sir Archibald Macdonald, Attorney General', signed Mucius, in Godwin, *Political and Philosophical Writings*, vol. 2, pp. 20–23.

grounds for taking it at face value. Government, for Godwin, was founded on opinion.[30] Inflaming that opinion, or usurping authority in the name of jeopardy or security, risked disturbing the orderly progress of truth and understanding and that threatened the stability of the social and political order.[31] He was as critical of the reformers when they resorted to scurrility and rabble rousing as he was of the government when it did so, because he thought – indeed, in the light of the Gordon riots and the Priestley riots, he knew full well – that opinion could run wild when artfully stimulated, with dramatic, indeed terrible consequences. He also saw the vulgar as misled, in want of education and enlightenment and as being exploited by both sides, who incited their hostility for their own purposes.

In the early 1790s Godwin saw himself as holding the line between responsible deliberation and the agitation of the public mind that he associated with the government, loyalists and some reformers and their associations. He did so in his debates with members of the reform organisations; in his remonstrations in *Cursory Strictures* and his *Considerations* (which were written in terms that were equally critical of the government and of the activities of the reform societies and those of his friend John Thelwall); in *Political Justice* and its revisions; and in the *Enquirer* and his shift to a more conversational mode. He held that line throughout the 1790s. He was not put off by the Birmingham riots, nor by the course of French events, nor by the draconian sentences delivered by Braxfield against his friends for attending the Scottish Convention, nor by the challenges of the Treason Trials and then the two Acts. His disappointment in the war was rehearsed early[32] – as were his fears that this too was a matter of policy – 'the cause of the present war is despotism, the consequence is anarchy'. What could a person do in this situation? Godwin thought an individual might do much:

You may have an eminent share in the meritorious task of saving your country! It was with great difficulty that the people of England were drawn into the snare that was spread for them. A long apparatus was necessary of panics, and associations, and signatures solicited through every corner of the island, and crafty invectives in behalf of a murdered monarch whom no man was in earnest to save. At last it is but like a nocturnal intoxication which may vanish before morning.

---

[30] *Enquiry*, II, iv, p. 105; Hume's 'Of the First Principles of Government'.
[31] For tools to think about loyalist tactics see A. O. Hirschman, *Rhetoric of Reaction: Perversity, Futility, Jeopardy* (Cambridge, MA: Harvard University Press, 1991).
[32] In his 'Essay against the Reopening of the War with France' – a manuscript probably from early in 1793, printed in Godwin, *Political and Philosophical Writings*, vol. 2, pp. 31–61.

There is a sure and easy path. Let each man who reflects have an opinion upon the subject. Let him not have a half-faced opinion, but one that carries his heart and soul along with it. Let him exert his powers to clear away the darkness that clouds his neighbour's mind. Let him do this and in a little month perhaps we shall regain a station of tranquillity. In a little month we shall have driven far off the catastrophe which otherwise too surely threatens us, and which the heart of every man of humanity and discernment bleeds to contemplate.[33]

Godwin saw insincerity, collusion, corruption and subterfuge in the government, but he stuck to the principle of the free exchange of views, the measured tones of argument and the pursuit of truth. He did not try to persuade the designing Machiavels in government, but he wanted to show the people that they were being misled. In that sense he believed that candour and argument would change people, even when government forces blustered and confused them. That situation, however, did not persist. It came under increasing strain as people from within Godwin's circles turned against him.

2.3   Friendships

For Godwin, the way 'to clear away the darkness of his neighbour's mind' was through disinterested friendship that was rooted in mutual esteem and the practice of debate and discussion. Godwin had many such friendships, but they often proved less secure than he expected. Consider his relationship with Samuel Parr, with whom he had been on good terms for some years, visiting him on several occasions in Warwickshire and meeting with him in London during Parr's visits to town. In November 1794 Godwin kept him up to date with the progress of the Treason Trials, by which Parr was appalled:

Is it possible my friend that any baseness can be more foul, any injustice more pernicious, and treason more atrocious than the deliberate technical, systematic perversion of the law? ... I can make allowances for the projects of statesmen, the errors and prejudices of princes, and even the outrages of conquerors, but when I see the ministers of public justice thirsting with canine fury for the blood of a fellow creature, my soul is all on fire.[34]

Parr was a committed Whig, who clearly felt that the government was crossing the line of acceptable conduct. He certainly did not approve of the reformers' activities, but it was the government that concerned him most:

---

[33] Ibid., p. 58.   [34] MS Abinger c.2, fol 65v, 10 November 1794.

I very strongly disapproved of the Convention, I would oppose the doctrine of universal suffrage, I look with a watchful and perhaps with an unfriendly eye upon all political associations, I wish to see the people enlightened but not inflamed, I would resist with my pen, and perhaps with my sword, any attempts to subvert the constitution of this country, but I am filled with agony when the Laws intended for our protection are stretched and distorted for our destruction.[35]

There is some suggestion that Godwin and Parr's daughter Sarah Anne may have had a flirtatious attachment to him, possibly an 'understanding'.[36] Parr clearly thought of Godwin as a friend. His letters were often informal: he set up dinners for him in Warwickshire with people whom he thought would interest Godwin; in 1795 he wrote to Godwin to express his hope that he sought some 'wary counsellor' before publishing his *Considerations*, given the 'lengthened and the strengthened fangs of the law'; and in the same letter he reassured Godwin, who had told him 'with strong symptoms of anguish' that some of his friends seem to have deserted him. 'Are you sure then that these deserters even had a claim to the honourable appellation of friends?' Indeed, he declared 'Upon many questions of politics and morals and upon all subjects of religion, I differ from you as widely as any human being can do. Yet I shall ever do ample and open justice to the magnitude of your talents, nor shall I fall rashly in with the reproaches of those men, who arraign the rectitude of your intentions.'[37] And he wrote fulsomely in praise of *Considerations* in December 1795, if despairingly:

But of Politics no more. For my heart sinks within me when I see the strides which Mr Pitt is taking, not to strengthen the monarchy, according to his specious pretext, but to form an imperious and gigantic aristocracy according to the wishes and the prejudices of his new associates. My hope is that the King will discern the snare and will act with the people against their common betrayers.[38]

Having received news of Godwin's becoming a father (but not yet aware of Wollstonecraft's death), he teased him about the contradictions between the philosopher, 'who would set reason upon the throne where she is to hold all the passions, all the affections & all the powers of volition under the most absolute sway ... Even Mr Godwin finds by Experience that he is not unassailable to the feelings of a Father & a Husband.'[39] The following day, having heard the news about Wollstonecraft, he wrote again, expressing his sympathy for Godwin's 'most deplorable & irreparable loss'.[40]

[35] Ibid., fol 66v.   [36] See Chapter 4.   [37] MS Abinger c.2, fol 130r–v.
[38] Ibid., fol 134v.   [39] MS Abinger c.3, fol 81v.   [40] Ibid., fol 86r.

For all the appearance of deep friendship and mutual respect, however, the relationship did not survive the growing hostility to reformers. When Parr was in London briefly in June 1798 Godwin saw him twice (this being after the publication of Godwin's *Memoirs* of Wollstonecraft in January of that year) and the following year he sent him *St Leon* (1799) together with a note denying a story that he had heard that Parr was advancing, that he had abandoned his atheism[41] and converted to Christianity. In the conclusion to his letter he referred to James Mackintosh, whom Parr had been seeing in Norfolk. Godwin said he hoped that Parr had 'settled accounts with him (Mackintosh) as to your opinion of his political lectures' – suggesting this was something they had discussed. And he went on to describe Mackintosh as loading

indiscriminately the writers of the new philosophy with every epithet of contempt. Absurdity, frenzy, idiotism, deceit, ambition & every murderous propensity dance through the mazes of his glittering periods: nor has this mighty dispenser of honour & disgrace ever deigned to concede to any one of them the least particle of understanding, talent or taste. He has to the utmost of his power contributed to raise a cry against them, as hollow, treacherous, noxious & detestable, & to procure them either to be torn to pieces by the mob, or hanged up by the government.[42]

Parr did not reply. He was in London in April and Godwin called on him twice but Parr was 'not at home'. He had heard that Parr had preached his Spital Sermon at Christ Church Greyfriars, Newgate, but had not seen its contents, and assumed that Parr would have treated his subject very differently from Mackintosh's *Discourse on the Study of the Law of Nature and Nations*.[43] He was to be disappointed and he wrote to ask why Parr had turned on him and why he had done so in so public a forum. Parr wrote him a very lengthy reply working through Godwin's letter systematically and setting out his reasons for breaking with Godwin and for his friendly reception of Mackintosh's views and expression, with which he could find no fault.[44] He denied he had ever sought Godwin's acquaintance with any zeal; he said he was offended by the passages in the *Enquirer* in which Godwin speaks 'irreverently' about the founder of

---

[41] Godwin's faith collapsed soon after he began his career as a Dissenting Minister in 1779, although he vacillated for many years between deism and atheism, and his discussions with Coleridge in 1799–1800 probably brought him as close to a more orthodox position, if temporarily, than at any other point in his mature years.

[42] Godwin, *Letters of WG*, v. ii, p. 123.

[43] James Mackintosh, *Discourse on the Study of the Law of Nature and Nations* (London: np, 1799).

[44] MS Abinger, c.5, fol 113r–118r, dated 29 April 1800, transcribed in Godwin, *Letters of WG*, ii, pp. 191–194.

Christianity; he proclaimed that he had not in 1794 'been shocked in common with all wise and good men' by Godwin's *Memoirs*; and he lamented the effect that Godwin had had on two or three young men whose talents Parr esteemed and whose virtues he loved (including Joseph Gerrald). It was a deeply hurtful letter – so much so that Godwin wrote out a point by point refutation of Parr's claims.[45] And he lashed out in a draft accusing him of a consummate betrayal:

If I could ever be prevailed upon to present to the public the luxuriant, & but short-lived vegetation of your professions of regard as they now lie by me in my closet, contrasted with the expressions of this letter & the frivolous reasons by which they are attempted to be supported, your character would be placed in a light, in which it was never yet the lot of a human being to be exhibited.[46]

In his *Thoughts Occasioned ... by Parr,* Godwin drew attention to those who had welcomed and stuck by the French Revolution through its bloodiest days only to turn against France and the possibilities of human progress in 1797. In contrast, Godwin had remained consistent – less radical than many in relation to 'the practical principles of the French Revolution' and often censured for his luke-warmness, but nonetheless consistent. The rise of Napoleon – whom Godwin described as 'an auspicious and beneficent genius' – had preserved the great principles of the revolution and 'every thing promises that the future government of France will be popular, and that her people will be free'.[47] What had turned the English friends of liberty from the true path was something wholly distinct from events in France: it was the failure of the more general cause of reform at home. As that was silenced, so had their own enthusiasm been dimmed. And it was only 'now that these persons come forth to sound the alarm; now they tread upon the head of the monster whom they regard as expiring; now they hold it necessary to show themselves intemperate and incessant in their hostilities against the spirit of innovation.'[48]

In these comments, Godwin was effectively trying to resist the tide – to insist that his position was both reasonable and unchanged. And he was turning on those whom he saw as swimming with the tide of public opinion – where doing so indicated a defect in character, candour and commitment. For Godwin, the philosopher should not waver in his

---

[45] Godwin, *Letters of WG*, ii, pp. 188–191.   [46] Ibid., ii, p. 135.

[47] 'Thoughts Occasioned by the Perusal of Dr Parr's Spital Sermon, Preached At Christ Church, April 15, 1800: Being A Reply to the Attacks of Dr. Parr, Mr. Mackintosh, the Author of an Essay On Population, and Others', in Godwin, *Political and Philosophical Writings*, vol. 2, p. 169.

[48] Ibid., p. 169.

commitment to truth and to his principles, even when (as he did in later editions of *Political Justice*) he revised his thinking in the light of further argument and deliberation. That was not a case of bowing to public pressure and the vagaries of opinion; it was a process of reasoned debate and judgement. But, while he might have experienced that in the first half of the decade, by the end it is clear that disagreement in intellectual matters between friends had been displaced by a collapse of the discursive sincerity, with its candour in pursuing the truth, and replaced by tirades of polemic and denunciation from men he had formerly regarded as friends. The position he took throughout his reply to Parr was that of a vilified innocent, who was above the storm and above reproach, but was being sacrificed to a set of cowardly motives by men who should know better. That meant that he had to have a way of explaining the shift in attitudes of those who now regarded him the enemy and as irresponsible radicalism incarnate. Before turning to his concern with Parr and Mackintosh, Godwin sketched a view of the character of opinion that owed a lot to Burke and Hume. He did not insist that the former friends of France had changed merely from 'worldly wisdom and personal interest':

It is not in the nature of man to like to stand alone in his sentiments or his creed. We ought not to be too surprised when we see our neighbours watching the seasons and floating with the tide. Nor is this fickleness by which they are influenced, altogether an affair of design. It is seldom that we are persuaded to adopt opinions, or repersuaded to abandon them, by the mere force of arguments. The change is generally produced silently, and unperceived except in its ultimate result, by him who suffers it. Our creed is, ninety-nine times in a hundred, the pure growth of our temper and social feelings. The human intellect is a sort of barometer, directed in its variations by the atmosphere which surrounds it.[49]

Moreover, it was not so much the change that Godwin complained of – more that 'instead of modestly confessing their frailty and the transformation of their sentiments, they rail at me because I have not equally changed.'[50] Holcroft, on the other hand, refused to believe that people with whom he had engaged in such deep and enlightening discussions with could simply reverse their views. In January 1799 he noted:

I learn ____e____ intends to read lectures on law, in which political government is to be introduced, and the established systems of this country highly praised. Expressed the pain I felt, that a man of such superior powers should act so false a part, and so contrary to his convictions, of which I must, in all human probability, be able to form a tolerably accurate opinion from the many conversations I have had with him. His judgment was (and, doubtless, still is, for his faculties are in

---

[49] Ibid., pp. 169–170.   [50] Ibid., p. 170.

their full vigour) so clear, his perceptions so penetrating and his opinions so decided, that I can conceive no possibility of their being so totally changed.[51]

Both Godwin and Holcroft saw the change as involving a falling off from honesty and openness, a dereliction from candour and the abandonment of the collective development of mind and the pursuit of truth. As such, it also testified to the growing fragility of the deliberative, disinterested community that they saw themselves as members of in the first half of the decade and which they saw as crucial to the further development of mind.

Godwin's sense of the mind as an often passive register of changes around it was not a sudden or major departure for him.[52] His *Enquiry* represented progress in terms of a general process of enlightenment in which all must move pretty much together, although some are inevitably in the vanguard. In *Caleb Williams*, Godwin first fully explored the extent to which opinion could be something that resisted being brought under the command of reason. Prejudice and presupposition repeatedly undo Williams and he and Falkland are unable to reason together because of the societal prejudices (and inequalities) that they have in various ways inherited. For Godwin this was a growing recognition of the difficulties of winning the argument by appealing to reason alone. His gradualism, his suspicion of political activity and associations and his own contained and careful deliberative manner all pointed to his acknowledgement of the challenges that people face in commanding their faculties so that reason and rationality would direct their beliefs, rather than opinion, rumour, interest, emotion and prejudice. We might treat that as increasing conservatism on Godwin's part, or increasing realism. Either way it suggests a more nuanced account of disagreement, and a less optimistic account of its overcoming. Nonetheless, he could still feel betrayed and duped by people when they turned against him, and it is clear that he thought that they were acting shamefully.

Godwin accused Mackintosh of reneging on his commitments and friendships. Mackintosh, a little later in life, rather conceded the point:

If I committed any fault which approaches to immorality, I think it was to Mr Godwin. I condemn myself for contributing to any clamour against philosophical speculations; and I allow that, both from his talents and character, he was entitled to be treated with respect. Better men than I am, have still more wronged their antagonists in controversy ... But I do not seek shelter from their example.

---

[51] Holcroft, Memoirs, pp. 248–249. His reference is clearly to James Mackintosh's Lectures.

[52] As I have argued in 'Godwin, Thelwall and the Means of Progress', in my *Reforming Ideas in Britain*.

I acknowledge my fault; and if I had not been withheld by blind usage, from listening to the voice of my own reason, I should long ago have made the acknowledgement to Mr. G., from whom I have no wish it should now be concealed.[53]

And in compensation Mackintosh brought Godwin back into his circle after 1813, when Godwin's fortunes were dramatically diminished.

Parr was another matter.[54] Godwin admitted that there was no apostasy there, since it had always been clear that he did not share Godwin's views, but Parr had 'joined his high-engendered battles' to those who 'flocked to the slaughter of those standing in defence of liberty'.[55] Godwin and Parr had debated with each other on many occasions.[56] What was different about the Spital Sermon was that it was an attack from the pulpit and by innuendo; one that turned their private exchanges into a public denunciation and was coupled with Parr's repudiation of their friendship. 'I will accuse him, as king Lear reproaches the angry skies, that, if he were not of my political kindred, and "owed me no subscription, yet I call him servile" auxiliary that he has "joined his high-engendered battles" to theirs.' Above all, it was Parr's non-deliberative, public rebuke and the penetration of loyalism into his private relationships and the candid and conversational world of the early 1790s that so disturbed and distressed Godwin.[57]

A similar experience was associated with Basil Montagu, one of Godwin's young acolytes, who gave up his legal career briefly after reading Godwin's *Enquiry* and became extremely close to Godwin, travelling with him in the Midlands (and visiting Parr) in June 1797. The relationship cooled around 1799/1800, with Montagu forming stronger links with Wordsworth and Coleridge and their circle. Nonetheless, there

[53] James Mackintosh, *Memoirs of the Life of the Rt Hon. Sir James Mackintosh*, 2 vols. (London: Edward Moxton, 1835), i, p. 134 (extract of a Letter to Mr Sharp written 9 December 1804).

[54] Farington says that Mackintosh's changes of commitment were simply a result of self-interest and records a story of Mackintosh and Parr at dinner with Sir William Milner, mentioning Quigley (O'Coigly), a United Irishman and associate of Arthur O'Connor and others, who were tried for treason in June 1798. O'Coigly was the only one found guilty and hanged. Mackintosh said that O'Coigly seemed to be a character of the worst kind, to which Parr replied: 'No, Jemmy, not of the worst kind; He was an *Irishman*, might have been a *Scotchman*; – he was a *Priest*, and might have been a *Lawyer*, He was true to His cause, and might have been an *Apostate*, Jemmy.' Joseph Farington, *The Diary of Joseph Farington*, edited by, Kenneth Garlick, Angus Macintyre, Kathryn Cave and Evelyn Newby, 16 vols. (New Haven, CT: Yale University Press, 1978–1998), VIII, p. 3008.

[55] Godwin, *Political and Philosophical Writings*, vol. 2., pp. 177–178; *King Lear*, III.ii., lines. 18, 21–23.

[56] On 7 and 8 July 1795, and probably also on 5 July 'Arraigns P. J.', see *Godwin Diary*.

[57] See Barrell, *The Spirit of Despotism*.

was a resurgence in their friendship at the end of 1809 and they continued to meet occasionally until the end of Godwin's life. In May 1799, Godwin wrote to Montagu saying that he had heard from Fanny Holcroft that Montagu planned to take holy orders and was engaged in writing an answer to *Political Justice*. Godwin was reluctant to believe the story, but uneasy that it might have been true – 'I suppose it to be an idle & groundless fiction from beginning to end, but I have sometimes detested myself for excessive & preposterous confidence, and I do not like to be duped.'[58] This was followed by a brief surge in visiting, with Montagu staying over on one occasion, all between 12–24 June 1799. Their next contact was a long letter from Godwin, referring to a reply to his previous letter, in which Montagu had indicated he was writing a pamphlet, but which Godwin rather dismissed on the grounds that 'You have talked to me of too great a number of essays & pamphlets, for any one of them to make an impression.' And he insisted that Montagu had done nothing to clarify the situation when they had seen each other repeatedly in June, but had subsequently published his piece (similarly to Parr, using the public domain to challenge a friend's views).[59] Godwin's letter was furious: he clearly felt that Montagu had dissimulated, falsified his position and was now attacking him with little restraint. Montagu had also told him that Godwin needed to compare what he (Montagu) had done with what he had resisted – 'If what you have resisted be the attacks, sarcastic & serious, of your friends & relations, it is just in point of construction to infer that what you have done is finally to yield to those attacks.'[60]

The difficulties in sustaining one's commitments to reflection and to standing apart from the flux and pressures of the times are also evident in other sources. As we have seen, Sharon Turner's friendship with William Watts and his developing admiration and affection for Watt's daughter Mary was beset by anxieties about the political climate. Watts himself became alarmed and, when Turner went away on holiday in the summer of 1794 and Mr S. (a feared spy) took the opportunity to propose to Mary, her distress and anxiety, coupled with Watts' alarm (and Turner's failure to declare himself before he left town), led Watts to push her to accept and it was only with difficulty that Turner extricated her. Throughout the courtship, Turner insisted that he did not want any

---

[58] Godwin, *Letters of WG*, v. 1, p. 82 (the letter is dated June, but Clemit points to the date as May on the basis of the diary).

[59] No longer extant or identifiable, but Godwin's letter indicates that Tobin ridiculed it, which led Montagu to withdraw it before publication. Godwin, *Letters of WG*, ii, p. 85.

[60] Godwin, *Letters of WG*, ii, pp. 84–6, quotation p. 85.

involvement in politics: he was a regular guest at Watts', he met Hardy to talk to him about the LCS and wangled a seat at the SCI dinner in May 1794 only days before Tooke's arrest, he attended the Treason Trials and he met and talked with Holcroft and others about philosophy and matters of the day. None of this counted for Turner as 'political activity' – he was a private individual, engaged with friends, finding out as much as he could about people's ideas, but not himself political. But if he sought to draw that line, he was increasingly conscious that the government, the loyalist associations and those paid to inform were redrawing those lines and equally conscious that the atmosphere was such that emotion and irrationality had intensified and often precluded clarity of communication and consistency of conduct.

Turner married Mary Watts in January 1795, shortly after her eighteenth birthday. Her father had equipped her with a good education and Turner thought her a lively and intelligent young woman with a sound fund of good sense. His diary/memoir is silent about their first eighteen months of marriage (which included the birth of the first of their thirteen children), but when he resumed his narrative of their life they were both clearly relieved to be out of the world of such anxieties. Turner's activities had turned to expanding his law practice, debating with his scientific friends, and to his examination of the authority of the Christian tradition, for which he dedicated time to learning Hebrew. He read his wife works of religious controversy and they discussed the arguments. He had been brought up within the Anglican tradition, she had been brought up wholly outside the church. Nonetheless, he recorded her saying to him:

'Do go on to examine this subject. I have not myself time nor sufficient ability, but I see you are taking every trouble to find out the truth and are seeking it fairly, When you have finished, let me know the judgment you pronounce decisively upon it and as I can confide in your impartiality be assured I will make your opinion mine'. As the dear creature has been educated with every prejudice against Christianity and is indeed a very acute reasoner against it, I was charmed to find that she kept her mind as candid and so open to conviction. I told her that I should use every care to form my decision on the rules of sound reasoning and that I only wished her acquiescence in proportion as she found my arguments and conclusions to be just.[61]

This rather disheartening statement signals the couple's withdrawal from an active participation in argument and deliberation for them both. She trusts him; he is focused on matters of religion and has turned his back on political discussion and reflection – with a rather palpable sense of relief!

[61] Add ms 60647B, fol 24.

One of the surprising things for many about Godwin's position in his reply to Parr was his identification of the *late* 1790s as the turning point in the reaction against reformers – well after the French extremism of 1792–1794 and the height of government repression in England in 1794–1795. That dating was symptomatic, not so much of the further revival and extension of anti-Jacobinism and loyalism (although that may have been a component), but of Godwin's sense that there was a dramatic collapse of confidence among those who had continued to side with the cause of reform after the summer of 1792. It was in the late 1790s (rather than after Birmingham, the September massacres or the execution of Louis XVI and Marie Antoinette) that middle class and professional men and women, many of whom were associated with Rational Dissent or sympathetic to its positions, tended to turn inward and at which groups began to fragment under pressure. Godwin's sense of that fragmentation was clearly very personal, but it probably did capture a wider experience, perhaps especially in London in the late 1790s. The breaking up of allegiances may also have been exacerbated by the furore created by Paine's *Age of Reason* and by the linking of infidelity to reform (both by zealots and by their denouncers). Godwin's *Memoirs* of Wollstonecraft also alienated several of his acquaintances and provided a ready target for intrusive attack on the private and domestic lives of radicals and there is no doubt that the reaction against the *Memoirs* shook Godwin. Moreover, issues of religion became the subject of further doubts on Godwin's part at precisely this time. In the late 1790s Godwin's atheism was seriously and systematically challenged in discussions with Coleridge and others – as if his doubts about doubts reflected a more general unease and uncertainty in the period. It was also in this period that Godwin's material fortunes began to sink. By the early 1800s he was composing a list of 'Amis perdus' – somewhat prematurely since some (like Mackintosh) did reconnect with him. But the list is significant: it includes George Dyson, Basil Montagu, James Stoddart (whose sister married William Hazlitt), Samuel Parr, John Pinkerton, Elizabeth Inchbald, James Mackintosh, Maria Gisbourne/Reveley, John Arnot, Henry Dibbin, Hannah Godwin, Amelia Opie, William Bosville, Francis Burdett, and Thomas Kearsley. And he coupled this with a list of Whigs who were keeping their distance.

The list is significant because it represents Godwin's own anxieties about a deliberative social world that seemed to be slipping away from him; and because it captures a fragmentation of the tight circles of conversational and personal friendship and acquaintance that existed in the 1790s. Moreover, it represents a shift in perspective from one, in 1795–1797, in which he was prepared to make the kinds of compromises that would have to be made to serve in parliament and when he actively contemplated that possibility, to a situation a year or two later when that looked like a major piece of hubris – because of Fox's withdrawal from Parliament as a result of Pitt's 'Terror', but more so because of Godwin's loss of standing in that more élite Whig world.[62] In fact, the list displays many sides of Godwin's anxieties – some of these friends were people he offended because of his marriage to Wollstonecraft (Inchbald) or by his behaviour after (Reveley/Gisbourne) or by his rather high-minded attitude to love affairs amongst his disciples and his sister's apprentices and his own housekeeper (Dyson, Dibbin, Fell and Hannah Godwin). Others, such as Parr, Montagu, Stoddart, Mackintosh, Bosville, Burdett and Kearsley, seem to be connections he lost between 1797 and 1806 largely, but not wholly over his philosophical views, including those on marriage.

2.4   Doing Justice

We should pause here to consider a further element relating to money in some of these relationships. Some forms of disagreement arose very directly from apostacy and developing political disagreements, but another reason for people distancing themselves from Godwin was his requests for loans or gifts that later became legendary in his circles – Don Locke entitled one of the chapters in his biography 'The monster with the maw'.[63] Disinterested friendship, as reflected on by Ferguson and Silver, presumes that interests are catered for in other components of people's lives, creating possibilities for precisely 'dis-interested' friendship. Certainly, Godwin was committed to disinterestedness, but he gave a considerably broader scope to the concept.

I hold my person as a trust in behalf of mankind. I am bound to employ my talents, my understanding, my strength and my time for the production of the greatest quantity of general good, so great is the extent of my duty.[64]

By the end of the *Enquiry* he is clear that this extends to property. The duty does not completely discount my interests, but it weighs these as part of the whole – 'If the extraordinary case should occur in which I can promote the general good by my death, more than by my life, justice requires that I should be content to die.'[65] In contrast to Silver/

[62] See my *Godwin's Political Justice* (London: Duckworth, 1986), pp. 198–199. See also his diary for entries for Debrett's, which stop in July 1797 and never resume.
[63] Locke, *A Fantasy of Reason*, chapter 19.   [64] Godwin, *Enquiry*, II, ii, p. 56.
[65] Ibid., 56.

Ferguson's view of the liberation of friendship from interest, because these are satisfied elsewhere, Godwin's picture is one in which those disinterested relationships are to regulate every aspect of people's lives. That is an exceptionally demanding perspective that ruptures the cordoning off of disinterested friendship from interests and permits the introduction of claims on others that go beyond their mutual respect and shared sets of intellectual concerns and affections, to the point of making claims in the arena of personal and economic interests.

The practical implications of this creed were not evident early in Godwin's career. From his autobiographical fragments it seems that earlier in the 1780s there may have been a good deal of reciprocity and mutual help among his cohort of very close friends (especially Marshall and Fawcett), in which the better-off provided succor to the more disadvantaged (where this might be understood largely as a strong tie rooted in shared circumstances and history).[66] In the early 1790s, Godwin was comparatively flush thanks to his work on the *New Annual Register* and subsequently because of the support Robinson provided him while he wrote his *Enquiry*. He had no family responsibilities and no household to keep and, with a much smaller social circle, he could maintain a flow of balanced reciprocity – that he could represent in the more glamourous colours of justice and disinterestedness. By the 1800s his situation was dramatically changed – his needs were considerable and it would have been harder for his growing list of creditors to have much sense that they might anticipate repayment let alone reciprocity. Some friends, like Wedgwood, insisted that what they were doing was giving gifts – but given that most of his acquaintances had relatively restricted resources and had less intense relationships with him, gift-giving was rare and could not be relied on. Crucially, one-sided supplication, the expectation of unreciprocated benevolence and his consistent defaulting on debts began systematically to undermine his standing and thereby his equality, with consequences for the intimacy of his acquaintance and the possibilities of candour and confidence. As his financial troubles multiplied the tensions between his ideals and the realities of the relational world of the 1790s and 1800s began to bite.

Godwin's requests for help should be understood in part in the light of his own willingness to be generous to those in need when he was able. In relation to a number of his young acolytes and his friends he provided a range of support and saw doing so as demanded by the duty of justice. As he emphasised in his *Enquiry*, we should be able to weigh people's needs

---

[66] William Godwin, *Collected Novels and Memoirs of William Godwin*, edited by M. Philp (London: Pickering & Chatto, 1992), v. 1, pp. 44–46.

and their merits and our abilities to help meet those needs and in doing so we are merely giving practical expression to our judgement that such support is necessary to conform to justice. Moreover, Godwin was often able to find people willing to give or lend him money (and this was often to support others). But his sense of the demands of disinterested benevolence by the 1790s was not a matter of close reciprocity that had operated in these earlier circles linked to his education and first vocation. Rather, he rejected the claims of reciprocity and preached a disinterested consequentialism that he sought to spread more widely across his now much greater range of contacts. And he did so on the grounds that they seemed committed to a similar emphasis on deliberation, reflection and judgement in weighing the claims of others. That extension, however, presumed much when it went beyond mutual esteem to make claims on the distribution of goods and money. Pure disinterested benevolence was liable to come into direct conflict with people's practical interests and concerns. That meant that Godwin was appealing to an ideal of equality that was in sharp tension with the dramatic inequalities and property relations that marked the world in which he moved. As his financial problems increased, as his circles contracted, and as people turned inwards and against him, so too did the tensions between principle and the practice increase. What he wanted to present as claims of justice, would likely have been received as importuning in his own interests.

Matters were further complicated by the fact that, in Godwin's philosophy, specific obligations had rather little weight – they should certainly not over-ride our duty to act on the imperative dictates of reason.[67] Indeed, Godwin seems to have thought that, like promises, they have no special standing when an agent is deciding how best to act. But for most of Godwin's contemporaries, financial debts were specific obligations that did have a special weight (even if you often kept people waiting for payment).

On both these counts – mixing the language of disinterestedness with the sphere of financial and economic interests and giving little weight to financial obligations – Godwin's conduct created tensions with those to whom he appealed on principles of disinterested benevolence. The possibilities for misunderstanding and resentment were considerable. For example, Godwin borrowed £100 from Ralph Fell, a younger and hardly wealthy man, who married an apprentice of Godwin's sister Hannah (much to Godwin's disgust). Moreover, he cited Fell as someone to whom he owed money when writing a letter to Thomas Wedgwood on

---

[67] Godwin, *Enquiry*, III, iii, 'Of Promises'.

14 April 1804, which pointed to his pecuniary embarrassments. In response, in a letter on 15 April Wedgwood promised to send a cheque for the sum owed. There is no reason to doubt that he did so. But it seems that a more imperative case arose and the money never made its way back to its intended recipient. Godwin wrote to Fell on 25 August 1805, to tell him there was simply no possibility of him repaying the money that he acknowledged that he borrowed.[68] This was pressing a philosophical point rather hard against the practical necessities that the disappointed creditor then had to face.

Godwin may well have supported others, but he seems increasingly rarely actually to have done so without getting the money from still others. And he was himself increasingly in need, with the result that his borrowing and 'begging' began to compromise his claims to equality as a fellow autonomous, deliberative agent. His construction of his deliberative world as a fundamentally egalitarian one was being subverted in relation to many in his wider circles by the inequalities that his need for money underlined and reproduced (as he failed to repay). This is partly why it is so difficult (because it is embarrassing) to read Godwin's letters about money – seeing him trying to appeal to the language of disinterestedness while being clearly 'interested' – thereby subverting his own commitment to fully candid relationships, since these became mired in these more 'interested' and sordid realities, which he tend to present as having rather little to do with him![69]

As Don Locke recognises, one of the targets for Godwin's borrowing was Sir Francis Burdett. Godwin's relationship with the baronet suffered a sharp decline after 1799.[70] In that year he had dined frequently with him (usually as Tooke's) and during his travels in December of that year he had stayed over and then ridden back to London with him. Thereafter, they met largely at Tooke's and Godwin was increasingly writing to Burdett. It seems highly probable that his friendship with Burdett's declined not so much because of a change in views (since there is little evidence of that) but because Godwin pushed a reading of their relationship, and their equality, that alienated Burdett. When Godwin wrote to Burdett (although only one letter is extant, tentatively

---

[68] Godwin, *Letters of WG*, ii, pp. 305–306; 358: letters 372 and 420.
[69] Several of Godwin's friendships were threatened by his asymmetry with respect to financial relationships, coupled with his assumption of egalitarianism in his discursive relationships even in the later 1790s and 1800s – for example with Joseph Ritson (in January 1801), MS Abinger c.6, fols 127r–128v; c.7, fols 18r–18v and fols 20r–20v and c.15, fol 71r. And damage quickly spread and became endemic.
[70] Locke, *A Fantasy of Reason*, p. 229.

dated 17 May 1800) he was almost certainly asking for money – and Burdett refused.[71]

When Godwin listed Burdett among his 'amis perdus', his 'loss' was less a matter of the frequency with which they met and more a sense of the declining degree of intimacy accorded to him, brought on by his pressing of his financial needs. That might have been somewhat repaired in 1806, when both men called again on each other, as well as occasionally meeting at Tooke's, but it also looks as if Godwin blundered again by sending Burdett a second series of letters about money, thereby curtailing the prospects of further friendship.[72]

In many other cases, Godwin found disagreement underlying the estrangement with his former friends, such as: John Stoddart[73], whom Godwin encountered in 1796 and immediately announced to him that he had 'found a treasure'; John Pinkerton, a curious man and an unlikely companion for Godwin, with a history of literary forgery, the use of pseudonyms and with a number of illegitimate children and abandoned women to his debit, whom he saw regularly in 1798 and 1799 and who eventually told Godwin that 'in scarcely one principle of religion, morals, politics or literature is there a shadow of agreement between us', which, as Godwin noted lightly 'would strip our acquaintance of many charms';[74] or William Bosville, a relatively wealthy man and a keen supporter of reform, who assisted both Horne Tooke and William Cobbett (when the latter was in prison between 1810–1812) and whom Godwin saw largely at Debrett's, which he stopped visiting in the summer of 1797 and to which he never returned after Wollstonecraft's death, even though he had once considered a parliamentary career (and even though Holcroft continued to visit).[75] In such cases the loss of friends arose from their rejection of his views and of his view of the kind

[71] Godwin, *Letters of WG*, ii., pp. 139–141, dated [?17 May 1800], although, because of the deletion of Burdett in the diary entry on 17 May, 4 June 1800 might be more in keeping with the diary evidence – there were also letters in 1802 and 1804 that lie in the scope of this volume of the letters but do not seem to have survived.

[72] MS Abinger c.9, fols 97r–98v (21 April 1806); c.9, fols 102r–103v (2 May 1806); c.10, fols 7r–8v (see also Godwin's note c.18, fols 73r–v, 18 October 1806 abut his inability to repay and c.10, fols 11r–12v – a note from Burdett's brother in response on 31 October 1806, and Godwin's reply c.18, fol 78r, written on the same day). See also an undated, but probably earlier letter written by Godwin (in which he says he has been an author for eighteen years – suggesting 1801), asking for a loan, c.20, fols 79r–80v).

[73] Farington meets Montagu and Stoddart together in November 1796 – describing Montagu as a 'natural son' of the late Lord Sandwich, who had 'imbibed in a violent degree the speculative principles of the new Philosophers ... Stothard [sic – the editors index the entry to Stoddart] appears to be a pupil of the same doctrines, but expressed himself more prudently', III, pp. 700–701.

[74] *Godwin's Letters*, v. ii., pp. 101–102.   [75] See Holcroft, *Memoirs*, pp. 190–256.

of egalitarian deliberative relationship he believed he shared with them. There may also have been an element of this in his sense of his growing distance from the Whigs. Godwin himself clearly saw his position as increasingly isolated. But what seems to have hurt him most were former friends turning on him, and doing so publicly, as with Mackintosh, Parr and Montagu. Turning their private friendship and understanding into a series of public and political attacks on his ideas, and thereby subverting his own sense of their deliberative commitments to each other and of the community of equals these presupposed.

There was relatively little decline in the overall numbers of people Godwin listed in his diary in the late 1790s and 1800s. Nonetheless Godwin clearly felt that he was marginalised and excluded. It is also likely that his sense of increasing isolation was more widely shared – especially amongst dissenting friends and acquaintance. After Wollstonecraft's death, he had come to rely on Johnson more, but that circle was also diminished, with the *Analytical Review* closing in the summer of 1799 and both Joseph Johnson and Gilbert Wakefield spending time in prison. Thomas Brand Hollis' circle was also being eroded and its dissenting members were increasingly distant from Godwin.

This was not the end for Godwin, but my sense is that by the early-1800s (c 1800–1805) he felt that it might be and his confidence in the progress of truth was shaken. In his reply to Parr, he wrote:

Long habit has so trained me to bow to the manifestations of truth wherever I recognize them, that, if arguments were presented to me sufficient to establish the uncomfortable doctrine of my antagonists, I would weigh, I would revolve them, and I hope I should not fail to submit to their authority. But if my own doctrine is an error, and if I am fated to die in it, I cannot afflict myself greatly with the apprehension of a mistake, which cheers my solitude, which I carry with me into crowds, and which adds somewhat to the pleasure and peace of every day of my existence.[76]

This was almost a shift from truth to consolation – with an abandonment of the obligation to test one's beliefs rigorously. In fact, I think it is better (if perhaps rather charitably) understood as Godwin recognising that such self-examination demanded a conversational, discursive dimension and that, with the collapse of that discursive community, this had become increasingly difficult. Indeed, it is then scarcely surprising that Godwin's conversational world should dramatically contract, especially after the completion of the *Thoughts* on Parr in May/June 1801 – as is

---

[76] William Godwin, 'Thoughts Occasioned by the Perusal of Dr. Parr's Spital Sermon', in Godwin, *Political and Philosophical Writings*, pp. 190–191.

clear from the almost complete disappearance of topics of any substance noted in his diary between 1801 and 1808.

2.5   Modifying Deliberation

Godwin's personal experience was certainly distinctive, but it had much in common with the experience of others in the decade, particularly in the broader community of Rational Dissent and in London's literary and cultural circles. In each case this was a wider legacy of the polarising political conflicts of the decade. Godwin's representation of his experience was of a community that remained relatively close and united into the late 1790s, despite riots and controversies, deaths and emigrations. It was a community that retained a commitment to reform and that became primarily directed to the campaign for peace, but that collapsed at the end of the 1790s. It is less clear where we should draw the boundaries of that community, the degree of its overlap with Dissent and its connections to the wider literary and mercantile communities of the period. Godwin's aspiration at the beginning of the decade was of a face-to-face world linked by candour, conversation, and deliberation – and, in practicing what he hoped to find, he helped in part to construct such a community. That world was central to his sense of who he was and what he stood for and it was central also to the self-conception of many of his closest friends and acquaintances and to their sense of the standards of belief and argument that they had a responsibility to adhere to. They faced a hostile world from early in the 1790s and that took its toll (with emigrations and imprisonments). But it did so without really threatening their self-conception, largely because they developed strategies for explaining why people failed to recognise the truth and because they took a longer view that was more positive.[77] But Godwin's sense of the fracturing of his own conversational communities identified a much more problematic development, one that destroyed the social and intellectual world with which his own beliefs were deeply entwined. The result was increasing doubt and a switch to a stronger sense of individual faith and justification. Moreover, it was a wider experience of a dissolving

---

[77] This is not to ignore the various 'demêlés' Godwin had – brought about by the demanding character of his expectations – and, according to some of his interlocutors, by his ill-humour. Marshall had a major disagreement with him in April 1795 about Marshall's proposal to publish a set of letters, given freely to him by an acquaintance, which he hoped would make him a bit of money to save him from the bailiffs. Godwin's objections to the plan were, for Marshall, little more than a display of petulance. The spat meant that they did not see each other for nearly two months! But, crucially, they were able to resolve their differences. MS Abinger c.2, fols 91–92.

set of associations and networks that were no longer joining people together and sustaining their social circles, their collective narrative and their confidence. Godwin may have been especially vulnerable, given his movement from circles linked to what was an extraordinarily close community of dissent in the 1780s and early 1790s, into the wider literary, political and cultural world of intellectual radicalism after 1793. But he was not alone in that movement and it seems likely that many others from a variety of backgrounds were touched by the same process.[78]

Godwin's doubts about his own conduct emerged in this period and his confidence in his opinions and judgements was clearly shaken. Indeed, Holcroft's diary reports an interesting conversation in relation to their commentary and criticisms of each other's work – a practice that they had carried on for many years without apparent difficulty. Holcroft began his account by detailing what he had said to Godwin:

H: The first part of your criticism which I have read has, I own, both pained and surprised me. When you brought your tragedy (*Antonio*) to me, you gave a minute detail of the rules I was to observe in criticising your work, that you may properly benefit by my remarks, which rules you have yourself not in the least attended to. One of the first of them was not to find fault in such an absolute and wholesale style as might at once kill your ardour, and make you, if not disgusted with your work, yet so doubtful as at once to damp all further progress. Yet, having read mine, you come with a sledgehammer of criticism, describe it as absolutely contemptible, tell me it must be damned, or if it should escape, that it cannot survive five nights that the characters and plot are but transcripts of myself, and that everybody will say it is the garrulity of an old man ...

Holcroft, while admitting that an author's judgement on his own recently completed work was extremely fallible, nonetheless took the view that his play (*The Lawyer*) 'contains some of the strongest writing I ever produced'. And he recorded Godwin as replying:

I thought it my duty to speak my thought plainly ... My language was unqualified, but there is this distinction between my critique and yours, of which I complained. I have used no triumphing banter, which you did.

---

[78] Seed, '"A Set of Men Powerful Enough in Many Things', pp. 140–168, emphasises the withdrawal from radicalism and public controversy among Dissenters; Fitzpatrick's *The View from Mount Pleasant* tells a more complex story that shows some stalwart commitment to enlightenment and to radicalism in the Liverpool movement. My sense is that this more complex story is right, but that this makes the narrative increasingly local and in many cases it is likely that people sought solace in activities that were increasingly private. In Godwin's London circles that may also have been the case, contributing to his sense of a shift in culture in which his own position is marginalised.

H: Not in that part of my remarks which was general; nor ever, but when I supposed it would make you more clearly perceive the defect which I wished you to amend, than any other method I could take.

G: There is another difference between us. Though I certainly give myself credit for intellectual powers yet ... I am so cowed and cast down by rude and unqualified assault that for a time I am unable to recover. You, on the contrary, I consider as a man of iron.

H: It is true, I have been so hardened in sufferance, by the difficulties I have had to overcome, that when such attacks are made upon me I think I may say, however egotistical it may sound, I can ... shake them from me Yet if you imagine that sensibility is destroyed in me, the mistake is strange and unaccountable, considering how well you know me. On the present occasion, I lay wakeful and ruminating full three hours on the injustice and wrong nature of your remarks. At length I recollected the folly of such uneasiness, created chiefly by the pain it gave me to think you could act so improperly, and then I recounted to myself your great virtues, and how very trifling such blemishes are, when placed in comparison with them.[79]

Holcroft says to Godwin that he thinks it right that he should inform him of the perturbation he had suffered, even if he was able to overcome it. 'We then walked and conversed on other subjects till dinner-time.'

While, to us, this may be merely an amusing anecdote about the bruising character of candour, it clearly meant more to both men than that. Their belief in absolute candour and the importance of speaking the truth irrespective of its costs had been laid aside. Both men felt more vulnerable and fragile and for both the practical need for approval (and for their work to be successful) had become more urgent. And their trust in each other had become less all-embracing and more conditional. Indeed, Holcroft's appeal was for his friend to recognise his sensibility and to moderate the communication of truth – and Godwin's response seemed to ask the same. In his *Memoirs*, Holcroft's editor quotes a story that Holcroft had told him deriving from the time he spent in Paris, in 1801–1802, when his wife was buying fish in a market but was undecided as to what to get. The stall holder said to her: 'Prenez cela, car votre mari est un brave homme'. Louisa replied: 'Oui, cela se peut bien; mais comment savez-vous qu'il est un brave homme?' 'C'est égal', answered the girl, 'cela fait plaisir à entendre'.[80] Holcroft was stoical about French morals; 'The difference between words and things is certainly less marked in France than in England: how far this is an advantage or a

---

[79] Holcroft, *Memoirs*, pp. 246–247.

[80] ['Take this because your husband is a good man'. Louisa replied: 'Yes, that may well be; but how do you know he's a good man?' 'It doesn't matter' answered the girl, 'it is pleasant to hear'.]

disadvantage, I do not, for my own part, pretend to decide'.[81] The compliment was effectively an untruth – and part of the 'manners' which he and others had so staunchly challenged in the 1790s (following the lead of Rousseau). By 1803 such forms seemed less dangerous; and truth similarly seemed less urgent and potentially too costly.

Holcroft went abroad, only returning in 1802. Following the publication of Godwin's *Fleetwood* (1805) the two men irretrievably fell out because Holcroft took one of Godwin's characters in the novel to be based on him and to be attributing to him some responsibility for the unhappy suicide of his son – something that Holcroft had experienced with Godwin when they sought to prevent Holcroft's son running away to go abroad in 1791.[82] They were reconciled only as Holcroft lay dying in 1809.

These cumulative losses of people who had played major parts in his life from the early 1790s changed Godwin's conversational world. It was not extinguished, but dramatically transformed. His trust in his friends was undermined and his confidence in his own abilities took a battering. Moreover, his sense of the importance of being able to communicate across partisan lines seems to have evaporated. He no longer preached to the unconverted, because he was no longer confident that they could be swayed by force of argument, or that his argument was, in the end, the most convincing. The shift from philosophy to consolation, indicated in the passage I cited from Parr, may not be a universal experience for Rational Dissent or the friends of reform, but few remained unchanged by their experience in the 1790s as they emerged into the first decade of the nineteenth century.

In the 1790s we see several things happening. The increased pressure for religious and political reform, just at the point at which relations with France were deteriorating fast, produced an increasing differentiation and polarisation of opinion. In the case of someone like Parr, this was not an immediate process, but developed over time, something that would have depended very much on the circles in which people moved and their sense of loyalty to partisan positions held back in the 1780s. Nonetheless, over the decade, people felt forced to commit more firmly either to support or seek to challenge the government, and the costs of doing the latter rose. As they rose, people were also forced to recognise that their conduct could no longer escape scrutiny and that they were potentially answerable in public for what they said in private

---

[81] Holcroft, *Memoirs*, p. 261.
[82] William Godwin, *Fleetwood, or the New Man of Feeling*, 3 vols. (London: Richard Phillips, 1805).

conversations and discussions. That development had a corrosive effect on the confidence and candour of many who had been more outspoken earlier in the decade. At the same time, at least in London, there existed a set of literary and cultural circles in which there was a long-standing practice of speculation and intellectual experimentation.

If we merely look at what people wrote and argued and what they were prepared to say in public or to intimate friends we are in danger of missing the dimension of how they conducted their lives. How they acted in public and private and how they negotiated that boundary, how they deliberated and how they framed those debates, who they saw and in what circumstances and how far their public pronouncements and their personal conduct lined up are all crucial elements in coming to grasp quite how these deliberative practices and their associated culture evolved over the period of the Revolutionary and Napoleonic Wars. People's experience and conduct also changed and those changes then influenced their expressed convictions and commitments. To grasp this, however, it is necessary to look more carefully at the way in which people's social worlds worked. To do this, I begin by analysing how the social lives of women from the middling orders in London operated in this period; I then examine the apparently more radical circles of women writers committed to challenging the status quo in the 1790s, before turning to consider the challenges that the egalitarian hopes of many of these people navigated in the fundamentally inegalitarian nature of gender relations.

3   Plurality
Women's Circles in London

Godwin aspired to a form of open, candid deliberation, conducted amongst equals, but such relationships were exceptional and many other dimensions of people's relationships demanded their attention. Moreover, whereas such deliberation implied something like a shared public sphere we need to recognise the plurality of London society. My sense is that this is insufficiently acknowledged in the historiography. In particular, there is a tendency to take a masculine model of disinterested friendship together with a wider set of weak ties in an open public sphere and to apply it to women's circles, perhaps especially circles of radical women.[1] This exaggerates the character of men's sociability; but it equally certainly mischaracterises that of their wives and daughters and of most single women. One of the things that points to the multiplicity of circles and to their relatively discrete character is the sheer size of London in the period. For those making their lives there it was important to have connections and contacts that were partly instrumental, partly confirming and protecting of social identity, partly acting as a means to encounter prospective spouses, for oneself, one's relations or one's children (especially daughters), and partly emotional and affective. To develop those relationships required a substantial delimiting of the million

---

[1] I deal with 'radical women' in Chapter 4. The involvement of women in élite political circles is well discussed by Elaine Chalus, *Elite Women English Political Life 1754–1790* (Oxford: Oxford Historical Monograph, 2005), Amanda Foreman, *Georgiana, Duchess of Devonshire* (London: HarperCollins, 1998), and Judith S. Lewis, *Sacred to Female Patriotism: Gender, Class, and Politics in Late Georgian Britain* (London: Routledge, 2003). The study of more middle class female experience was the subject of Leonora Davidoff and Catherine Hall's *Family Fortunes: Men and Women of the English Middle Class 1780–1850*, revised ed. (London: Routledge, 2002) – on which see Kathryn Gleadle's 'Revisiting *Family Fortunes*, Reflections on the Twentieth Anniversary of the Publication of *Men and Women of the English Middle Class, 1780–1850*', *Women's History Review* 16(5) (2007), 773–782, together with her survey at the beginning of *British Women in the Nineteenth Century* (London: Palgrave, 2001). One component I wish to emphasise here is the importance of geography: London had an effect on the dynamics of interaction for many women in the more middling and professional classes and it is examples of these women whom I focus on in this chapter.

London souls. People had to find their 'little platoon', as Burke referred to it.[2] And these little platoons did not make for a unified culture. The Dunbar number of a natural limit to the number of people we can know suggests that they were quite little[3] – especially if one considers that for many their meaningful relationships would include their own servants, the servants of others, shopkeepers, merchants, family and so on – that is, people closely connected to the domestic environment. I want to put more flesh on this argument by looking at two examples of such circles. Both are cases from outside the aristocracy and concern people who came from professional backgrounds, although they both moved in circles that brought them into some contact with that more élite culture. I have chosen them because of their essentially professional/middling class status, their links to the world of musical entertainment and to artistic and architectural circles and because they are firmly based in London in the period with which we are concerned. These were not radical women. Nonetheless, understanding how their circles worked can help provide us with a background for examining those who identified themselves with the cause of reform and the critique of society.

3.1   Marianne Ayrton

Marianne Arnold/Ayrton was the daughter of the composer Samuel Arnold and was the wife of the impresario William Ayrton. She used her diary to record the people she met – although it is likely that her record is more complete for the early part of the diary. Consequently, I have focussed on her record of events from January 1802 to September 1809, when her diary breaks off for a long period – after which, for some periods, we have only her husband's later transcription of her notes (which, in the copy he made for the earlier period, omitted some 50 per cent of the content!).[4]

At the start of the diary, in January 1802, Marianne Arnold was thirty, single and living with her parents, although there was an engagement/understanding with William Ayrton. In the next seven years she married Ayrton, buried her father, had five children (losing one in infancy) and she was shortly to lose her eldest daughter at five years of age. In the diary

---

[2] Burke, *Reflections*, p. 96.

[3] As discussed in the Introduction, see Dunbar 'Neocortex size', who posits an upper limit of c 150 people.

[4] BL Add ms 60372, 60373 and BL Add ms 52351: Marianne Ayrton's diary for this period (1802–1809) consists of two parallel notebooks – one in her hand, which is messy but has about twice the number of entries as the other – which is William Ayrton's 'transcription'.

she recorded contact with approximately 185 people.[5] These included a number of doctors, some domestic servants and many relatives. If we look at the groups of those who appear five times or more in the record there are thirty-one such individuals, but they are quite tightly grouped.

There was Marianne's mother (née Mary Ann Napier); her father, Dr Samuel Arnold, the composer, (b. 1740 but who died early in 1802 at the start of her diary); her brother Samuel, and his wife Matilda Catherine née Pye (one of the few individuals to be referred to by her christian name). Also, her (initially) future husband William Ayrton (they married on 17 May 1803), his brother Scrope, his sister Elizabeth Paris (1762–1847), whose family account for a further eleven contacts; and his father (Edward Ayrton, 1734–1808). These eight individuals provide c. 135 entries over the period. In addition, her godmother, Mrs Mallet, was also a visitor in ten cases and it seems likely that James Warde Tobin who married Jane Mallet (the daughter of Marianne's godmother) in 1807 was one of the Tobins recorded. The Pyes (connected through her brother Samuel Arnold's marriage) also account for a further group of contacts. And there is either a brother of William Ayrton or a cousin referred to as Bart (although it is possibly a nickname for William), who accounts for thirteen contacts and who is clearly a very close family link, given that he carries Marianne up the stairs after the birth of her second child. Collectively these various family members account for twelve of the thirty-one frequent contacts.

Four people who were seen frequently were connected to the medical treatment of the family: the surgeon Anthony Carlisle (1768–1840), Dr Nelson (who managed Marianne's pregnancies and deliveries), Dr Pullinar (who seems to have been called in for the children especially) and Thomas Bradley (1751?–1831) of the Westminster hospital was also a focal point for contact, probably in relation to Dr Arnold's treatment for an injury that he received four years before his death. While Nelson and Pullinar seem to be entirely professional contacts, Carlisle and his family came to dinner and he invited the Ayrtons to his home, as did Bradley and his wife and children who, as a group, account for four individuals mentioned at least five times and account for a further 125 encounters (accounting for a further seven of the thirty-one frequent contacts).

The Burneys also account for two of those with five or more contacts, mainly Captain (probably James) Burney and Sally (probably Sarah nee Payne) Burney. There may have been some prior contact between the Burney and the Arnold families, but Marianne expressly groups them

---

[5] Approximately, because her handwriting is very small and not easy to read and discriminating between Mr, Mrs and Miss is not always easy.

under 'Later friends', rather than friends from her childhood, so they may have come with her marriage. Their friendship might well have been enhanced by the fact that the two households were living in the same street a few years after Marianne's marriage. Dr Edward Miller, from Doncaster, was a musical contact linked to her father (who trained one of Miller's illegitimate sons as an organist), who stayed with them for a week in July 1805, thereby becoming a frequent contact.

Only ten of the thirty-one most frequent contacts are not easily accounted for by family, medicine and the Burney family and these are: The Granvilles; Mr and Mrs Hamilton; Mrs Jones; Mr Leeds; Sir F Nicolay/Nicolai[6] and his family and Thomas Ward (and Mrs Ward). The Granvilles, Hamiltons and Nicolais are mentioned in her list of later friends and she sees a great deal more of the Nicolais and to a lesser extent the Hamiltons than of the Granvilles, Jones, Leeds and the Wards, who were each seen only about five times each. At the start of one notebook she lists the friends of her childhood and adolescence, but she sees very few of these (many of whom were clearly considerably older and were friends of her parents) after her marriage, suggesting that these other connections were ones that her marriage brought to (or imposed on) her.

What this suggests is that the bulk of Marianne Ayrton's life, both before and immediately after her marriage, despite living near the centre of London, was dominated by contacts with family and family friends and that she had a rather circumscribed social life. Of course, she quickly became practically busy, with young children, but this did not mean that people did not call or that she remained at home. But when she did receive, or go out, she did so with people drawn from a very small group. She was not physically isolated, living in Sloane Street and then in James Street, where she was a neighbour of Captain Burney and later of Charles and Mary Lamb (whose evenings her husband frequented, although she seems only rarely to have visited them). She appears to meet the Dunbar number over the period, but it is clear that a very high proportion of her contacts were with a very small core of that group, some twenty-four individuals at most.

3.2   Eliza Soane

Was this an exceptional case? If we compare Ayrton's experience with that of Elizabeth Soane, wife of Sir John Soane, the architect, we can see

---

[6] Possibly the connection is through music. Nicolay/Nicolai may be the same as identified as being a page to the King, and as an enthusiast for music, in Laetitia Matilda Hawkins, *Memoirs, Anecdotes, Facts, and Opinions*, 2 vols. (London: Longman, Hurst, Rees, Orme, Brown, and Green, 1824), p. 44.

some similarities, even though Eliza was older and not bound by the responsibilities of a young family. As far as we know Mrs Soane kept her diary only from 1804–1811.[7] She had married Soane in 1784, when she was twenty-four, and began the diary twenty years later when her surviving two sons, John and George, were eighteen and fifteen, respectively. As a young woman she had lived with her uncle George Wyatt, who was the City Surveyor of Paving with whom Soane had worked, and it was at her uncle's that she first met Soane and where he subsequently courted her.

Between January 1804 and June 1811 she noted seeing c. 230 different people. She saw fifty of these at least five times (not including her husband and her two sons) (twenty-three of those more than ten times and twelve of them more than twenty times). Indeed, those she sees five times or more account for some 870 contacts; of these, those she sees ten times or more (23) account for some 670 contacts; and those she sees twenty times or more (12) account for 516 of those contacts: this signals a degree of concentration in which a few people were seen very often.[8] She had an active life, she was not tied to the house as much as Marianne Ayrton was and she hosted many dinners, both at Lincoln's Inn Fields and at Pitzhanger Manor, their house in Ealing. She went on holiday to Margate from the end of August each year until the beginning of October and, although she kept no record of those whom she met there or spent her time with, there are obvious continuities – Mrs Wheatley went with her in 1804, the Beecheys in the following year and so on.[9] There were regular visits to Soane's brother William and other family members and Soane's friends in Chertsey.

Her most frequent (more than ten) contacts include several people connected to Soane and to art circles: Sir William Beechey (1753–1839), portrait painter, and his second wife Anne (1764–1833), a miniature painter; Sir Francis Bourgeois (1756–1811), landscape painter; the sculptor and designer, John Flaxman (1755–1826) and Mrs Flaxman (née Anne Denham, 1760–1820); Edward Foxhall, a fellow student of Soane's who specialised in decoration, his wife, and their daughter, Fanny, who sometimes stayed with Mrs Soane; Thomas Leverton (1743–1824), architect and surveyor and his second wife (née Rebecca

[7] With some short breaks – it is possible that this and other material has simply not survived.
[8] The average number of contacts for the whole group of those seen more than five times is 17.7; for those seen five-to-ten times the average is 7; for those seen ten-to-twenty times the average is 14; and for those seen above twenty times the average is 43.
[9] There is some reference to people she saw in her letters from the coast, but not in the detail that we have for the diary.

Craven) whom he married in 1803; Lucy Loutherbourg, the wife of
Philip Loutherbourg (1740–1812), the landscape painter and designer;
Mrs Malton, the widow of Thomas Malton, the younger (1751–1804),
the architectural draughtman – whose admission to the Royal Academy
Soane had helped block, and whose son Charles had a rather unsuccess-
ful apprenticeship with Soane; the painter Joseph Mallord William
Turner; Mrs Wheatley (née Clara Maria Leigh, 1769–1838), widow of
the painter Francis Wheatley (1747–1801) and a miniaturist in her own
right, who subsequently married the actor and miniature painter Alexander Pope; Mr 'Marcey' (probably Giuseppe Filippo Liberati Marchi
(1735–1808), painter and engraver); Mr and Mrs John Patteson, a
supporter of Soane from his first trip overseas, when they had travelled
together; James Spiller, an architect; George Wyatt – Mrs Soane's uncle
whom Soane had first met while working on the aftermath of the Gordon
Riots and through whom he met Elizabeth; Mrs Taylor, probably the
wife of John Taylor (1757–1832), author of *Records of my Life*; Ann Selina
(Nancy) Storace (1765–1817), the singer, whom Soane had first met in
Florence where he heard her sing aged 14 and whom he and Elizabeth
Soane had befriended after she left her husband in 1784, with Soane
undertaking some work on her house. Nancy Storace often appeared
with the singer John Braham, with whom she lived for nearly twenty
years, producing a son in 1802). Lord and especially Lady Bridport (née
Maria Sophia Bray, 1746–1831 and Alexander Hood Viscount Bridport,
1726–1814) appear a good deal; they were former clients of Soane, but
the relationship between Mrs Soane and Lady Bridgeport clearly became
a close one. Mrs Cook is probably one half of Mr and Mrs William
Cooke (1730–1810) of Walthamstow, a client of Soane's for works in
1783 and 1784 whom he visited socially, on at least one occasion taking
his future wife – (it is also possible that Mrs Cook was the widow of
William Cooke, a model-maker, who died in 1791 and who may have
been a relative of Foxhall, who tried to get elected to the post of Housekeeper to the Royal Academy).[10] In addition, although they remain
largely unreferred to in the Diary, it seems likely that Mrs Soane would
have had fairly frequent communication with the various pupils and
assistants who worked at the Lincoln Inn Fields house (from 7–7 in the
summer, and 8–8 in the Winter!)[11]

---

[10] Farington, *Diary*, vol. IX, p. 3204, 20 January 1808; vol. IX, p. 3209, 27 January 1808.
For Soane's domestic life see Susan Palmer, *At Home with the Soanes*: Upstairs,
Downstairs in 19th Century London (London: Pimpernel Press, 1997).

[11] Dorothy Stroud, *Sir John Soane, Architect*, 2nd ed. (London: Giles de la Mare, 1996),
pp. 65–66. These hours changed in 1810 to 9.00 a.m. to 8.00 p.m. – see Margaret
Richardson 'Learning in the Soane Office', in *The Education of the Architect*, Proceedings

Those less directly connected with Soane's interests and work are: Mrs Exley (probably a neighbour of the Soanes in Lincoln Inn's Fields)[12]; Mr and Mrs Kinderley (a lawyer and his wife, to whom the Soane's second son George was articled for a period after leaving Cambridge); Ann Levick (daughter of Mrs Soane's Aunt), Mrs Elizabeth Levick; Miss Woodmeston (a cousin of Mrs Soane); and two unidentified people, Mrs Treves (possibly the wife of Treves, an associate of the Prince of Wales, influential on the building of Brighton pavilion)[13] and Vaux (probably a surgeon, who attended Soane's badly infected finger).

Most of these connections are not simply 'meetings'. The contacts, especially with her female friends, were important to Mrs Soane and she gives us hints of that in the details recorded in the diary (in a way that Ayrton does not, although it is possible that similar dynamics were at work in her relationships). She performed services for them and gave and received gifts – buying lemons and other supplies for Lady Bridport, making 'doyleys' for Mrs Lytleton and Mrs Kindersley, giving a necklace to Lady Beechey, and a locket to Mrs Wheatley, her bonnet (that she had made at Mrs Kinderley's) to Mrs Such. She took people to the theatre, for drives in the park and, of course, she fed them and was fed by them. And she received gifts, shared shopping expeditions and was entertained and treated by others. There is an ongoing 'economy' in the diary, as she took money to the bank, paid servants, bought material and clothes, etc. – but there was also an economy of gift-giving, servicing and reciprocating – where the reciprocation was not necessarily in the same currency. For example, Mrs Malton was clearly not wealthy, having lost her husband and raising seven children on her own, but, while the diary is largely without tone, it seems that she played an important role for Mrs Soane in giving her company when Soane was away. These elements are features of a social and emotional economy of mutual support and exchange which helped tie people's social worlds together, giving them depth and meaning, even as they also made their relationships more complex and less transactional in character and consequently strengthened the normative grip of each other's evaluations and tightened their group more closely.

Eliza Soane was not an especially secluded woman. She had her friendships, but these also brought her to a range of public venues and she was active in the wider commercial society, in ways that make the

---

of the 22nd Annual Symposium of the Society of Architectural Historians of Great Britain (London, 1993).

[12] See the will of Ann Exley NA Prob-11-1573-269.

[13] See Farington, *Diary*, vol. V, p. 1920, 17 October 1802 and p. 1921, 21 October 1802.

binary of public and private difficult to sustain. She shopped on her own and with others and on her own part and for others; she frequented the theatre, exhibitions and concerts (paying usually in the order of six shillings for a theatre ticket, per person, but sometimes a pound for concerts, especially benefits); she went to see pictures in Somerset House, the Turner and Shakespeare Galleries and elsewhere; and she bought pictures at auction without any obvious consultation with her husband (and the John Soane Museum suggests she had a good eye and that she was not afraid to spend money on art, paying on one occasion nine guineas); she went to Vauxhall Gardens and to operas with her friends and her sons – and to church in much the same company; she went to Astley's Circus and to concerts at 'Mr Heavysides'[14]; she visited the Pantheon to see 'Lunardy's balloon'[15]; she called regularly on her husband at the Bank of England; and when he was away (most usually) she visited friends to enjoy a dance with them. Marianne Ayrton was more constrained, but she also attended concerts, oratorios, church services and other public events – indeed we can see a certain amount of overlap in their interests, although not to the point of them being in the same place at the same time – as far as we can tell.

In neither Ayrton nor Soane's case should we think of these as tightly restricted circles. But we might usefully reflect on how their circles were formed and what gave them a degree of coherence. We also need to consider what the norms and conventions of these circles required of their members. As I have argued, the size of London in the late Georgian period made it a half anonymous city that posed a set of challenges to be negotiated. It was not possible to know it all, or for one to presume that one would meet one's acquaintance, just by entering the city. There was, then, some anonymity, but also some accompanying isolation; but, unlike the modern city, it was not so large that a person could easily be wholly anonymous. Those who lived there had to make the city work for them and they did so in part by finding both social and geographical 'lay-lines', by which to connect themselves to people and activities in the city that they wanted or needed to engage with. One's 'given' acquaintance (through family, spouse and profession) provided them with a baseline and set of contacts by which they could navigate the wider city. In the cases of these two women, we can see both family and their husbands' professional connections and interests playing a very large part in the construction of

---

[14] Probably John Heaviside (1748–1828), surgeon and museum proprietor, who may well have held small concerts in his museum or home.

[15] Vincenzo Lunardi (1754–1806), balloonist, who held exhibitions of his balloon at the Pantheon, Oxford Street.

their circles and their social lives. Soane's circles revolved resolutely around the art and architecture world and Elizabeth Soane was inducted into it before her marriage (because of her uncle's position). Marianne Ayrton had some similar connections in the world of music, because of her father's friendships and contacts and those of Ayrton, although her attendance at events seems rarely to have been part of a large group.

Circles in these worlds were also multiple. If we look at references in Vic Gatrell's careful analysis of the artists in the Covent Garden area, *The First Bohemians* (2013) and compare those he lists as significant in the area to those in Mrs Soane's circles there is actually relatively little overlap – despite the short walk from Lincoln Inn Fields to Covent Garden.[16] Soane, Beechey, Wheatley and Marchi are only passingly mentioned, de Loutherbourg, Flaxman and Turner especially receive more attention, but Sir Francis Bourgeois, Pope the actor and miniaturist, Patteson, Storace, Braham, the architectural scholar John Britton and Mrs Wheatley are not mentioned at all. The bulk of Gatrell's book analyses a slightly earlier period, but it is not restricted to it and it certainly includes these later years. The differences give us a sense that the heart of Covent Garden offered contacts with one constellation, while other constellations existed in close proximity around it – or, at least, it did so for the partners of those active in these spheres. Clearly, the Royal Academy served to bring certain groups of artists together and those who ran it were able to control both membership and financial support for artists' widows and families in difficulty. And that power almost certainly helped pull people into its orbit and influence. But it did not subsume other groups and centres, for example around the engraving trade, around print shops and so on. It also seems likely that there were similar circles around church music, oratorios, concert halls and musical theatres; or differentiated theatrical establishments around patent and unlicensed theatres; or those that revolved around the book, newspapers and periodical trades. Nor should we assume these areas of activity were wholly united – Soane does not bring all RAs back to his house – Joseph Farington (the artist networker *par excellence*), for example, did not appear in the period of Mrs Soane's diary, although he did dine with Soane in the previous decade.[17]

The pool of people created by an area of activity was far from unified and may have divided in different ways – although it is also likely that the wider circle provided something like a reference group for its members, even if they baulked at association with all of them and might themselves

---

[16] Vic Gatrell, *The First Bohemians: Life and Art in London's Golden Age* (London: Allen Lane, 2013).

[17] Farington, *Diary*, vol. III, p. 703, 27 November 1796.

be overlooked by others. Moreover, members of these circles were also interested in connections to other worlds and groups. Some people (almost always men) were more consistently peripatetic than others – Farington seems to have an insatiable thirst for information concerning multiple worlds (as we will see). Yet, interestingly, he has practically no connection with Ayrton's circles, makes no reference to the singer Nancy Storace and a great deal of his diary involves reporting on what his other contacts say about others (or what they say others say about people in a wider public domain). Moreover, people could share participation in a public domain without having a relationship: Mrs Ayrton and Mrs Soane clearly enjoyed the theatre and concerts, but they were part of an audience – they saw the performance, but did not know the actors and may well have been largely ignorant of most of their fellow spectators. Elizabeth Soane's connections with Nancy Storace and the tenor John Braham derived partly from her husband's personal history and professional contact and they do not seem to have led to a wider acquaintance with the world of vocal music and opera (although there were other connections through design and scene painting with de Loutherburg). In general, there seems to be more evidence of a city of multiple domains than of a single homogenous world.

3.3   Norms of Conduct

In these circles people were attentive to the norms and conventions concerning conduct that governed them. As I suggested in the Introduction, these norms were policed – indeed we might distinguish collective forms of policing and the policing that husbands or other family members might engage in. There was a certain latitude, but perhaps especially that afforded by men to other men and by some men to some women. John Taylor, the memoir writer and an intimate of the Soanes, captured something of the 'surveillance' function that many men played with respect to their wives. In discussing the painter John Opie and his first wife (Mary Bunn), who had absconded from Opie with a Major Edwards, whom she subsequently married, Turner apologised for her on the grounds of Opie's being so engaged in making his career. Her 'fall' was the result of 'Unavoidable neglect plus the persevering attention of a gallant'. He went on to say 'I am well acquainted with her, and introduced my former wife to her, which assuredly I would not have done if I had observed any incorrectness of conduct or manners.'[18] The remark exhibits both a latitude we might not expect and demonstrates Taylor's

---

[18] Taylor, *Records of my Life*, v.i., p. 303.

normative control of his wife's companions. That said, Taylor was an associate of Farington, but was clearly not privy to Farington's information (from Robert Smirke) that the first Mrs Opie had already had two illegitimate children when Opie married her – with Opie equally not being aware of this and with the children being raised elsewhere. When her son was arrested for stealing a watch and incarcerated in Newgate, he discovered his mother's address and wrote to her asking for assistance. According to Farington, she refused and told him he would destroy her life if his existence were known of. Farington presumed that, since it was a first offence, he would escape execution, despite being sentenced to death, and would be transported instead (but, like so much in Farington, he does not follow this up for us!).[19]

Clearly Farington did not make it his business to spread information or Taylor would have had a different attitude. Rather, he seems to have hoarded it. Indeed, his diary gives us a cumulatively rather unattractive picture of Opie, together with a powerful sense of how men tended to stand together in their circles in support of their members. While Opie's divorce was being finalised he met a young woman, Miss Elizabeth Mary Booth, who came as a pupil (perhaps following Opie's commission to paint her father Benjamin Booth, c 1790) and had very good financial prospects (£4,000 pa) and he engaged her affections. He asked Farington to plead his cause with the father (a lawyer), whom he thought likely to be obdurate. Farington initially demurred, suggesting it might be better to wait until the divorce was completed! Once that was achieved, Opie repeatedly came back to Farington and succeeded in engaging him to act for him with Booth who was, as predicted, unhappy about his daughter being united to a painter of apparently uncertain means. The struggle to secure Miss Booth went on some time, until, it seems, her friend Mrs Hily Addington helped her see how potentially imprudent the match might be.[20] Within a matter of months Opie had turned his attention to Amelia Alderson, although he had also clearly at least reflected on the possibility of marrying Mary Wollstonecraft and considered a Miss Jane Beetham.[21] Amelia's father, Dr Alderson, was also

---

[19] Farington, *Diary*, vol. VIII, p. 3113, 27 August 1807.

[20] Ibid., vol. III, pp. 704–706, 708, 711, 713–714, 717, 720, 722, 724, 726, 732, 735, 737, 742, 743, 744–763, 29 November 1796, although Addington's judgement appears on 11 January 1797 and there is still discussion of Booth's father and son's more moderate opinions on 5 February 1797. See also Shelley King, 'Portrait of a Marriage: John and Amelia Opie and the Sister Arts', *Studies in Eighteenth Century Culture* 40 (2011), 27–33.

[21] Farington, *Diary*, vol. III, pp. 705–706. The ODNB entry on Opie makes much of Jane Beetham, who is described as a pupil of Opie's, but does mention Farington's part relating to Miss Booth.

clearly concerned about aspects of the match and, while Amelia seemed to be happy with her choice, Opie kept her on short quarters and when he died suddenly in 1807 she was amazed to find (as were his friends) that he had over £12,000 squirreled away. In all of this, there was no sense that others in Opie's circle had any responsibilities to these various women – indeed, Farington's sense of his responsibilities seems to have been to assist Opie in doing what he wanted. When he resisted, it was because he thought that Opie's timing was poor.

Such forms of masculine ascendancy seem to us extreme, but they were hardly unusual. The fencing master Henry Angelo (who taught Soane's sons and drank tea with Mrs Soane) recalls how Sheridan, who married the singer Miss Elizabeth Ann Linley (1754–1792), could not 'endure to hear his sweet bride, "warble her native wood-notes wild;" though, to do justice to her memory, art had amply improved her strains ...'. Angelo spent a Christmas with both families – at Richard Brinsley's house in Orchard Street: 'We kept it up to a late hour; and music making part of the after-supper entertainment, Madame Linley asked her daughter to sing a certain little favorite air: but a single glance from her juvenile lord and master, kept her mute.'[22]

Sheridan may well have been influenced by the fact that the world of the theatre and performance (potentially also the arts more widely), by giving such public prominence to certain women, simultaneously raised questions about their respectability. This might have been linked to their availability to the gaze and fantasising of a large male public.[23] Men might discount the significance of such rumours, perhaps because such doubts also allowed them to imagine the availability of such women. But other women often did not do so. John Taylor, for example, commented in relation to the novelist Mrs Inchbald, a widow living on her own (whom Charles Lamb described as the 'only endurable clever woman he had ever known'[24]): 'Though scandal was formerly not uncommon among the theatrical community, I never heard the least impeachment

---

[22] Angelo, 85–87. In contrast, see Canning's *Journal* in relation to Jenny Linley (Elizabeth's sister), pp. 86–87, where she sings for them. George Canning, *The Letter Journal of George Canning 1793–1795*, edited by Peter Jupp (London: Royal Historical Society, 1991).

[23] This would be so even when they did not appear as themselves; that is, actresses portrayed certain women and often became associated with certain roles (as with Mary 'Perdita' Robinson), but (especially male) audiences seem often to have found it challenging to distinguish the person and the part. See Charles Pigott, *The Female Jockey Club* (London: np, 1794), pp. 75–84.

[24] Betsy Aikin-Sneath, *Georgian Chronicle: Mrs Barbauld and Her Family* (London: Methuen, 1958), pp. 149–150.

on her character, nor do I believe she ever gave occasion for the slightest insinuations.'[25] In contrast, her twentieth century editors suggest that she probably had a long-standing affair with Sir Charles Bunbury (1740–1821).[26] Taylor seems double faulted (given his assessment of the first Mrs Opie), although it may be that he had no real interest in being certain about a person's propriety, what mattered was the appearance of things and how that would be read by others.[27] What is clear is that Inchbald invested a great deal in preserving her reputation and she took an essentially intolerant line towards women she believed would taint her by association (as with Wollstonecraft when her status as Mrs Imlay was revealed to be counterfeit). It is also striking that, despite her proximity to and potential professional sympathies with Mary Robinson (whose liaisons with the Prince of Wales and others had been notorious), they do not seem to meet (on the basis of extant correspondence and both Inchbald's and Godwin's diaries – in the latter, proximity is deducible by the number of entries in which the two women were part of a clearly walkable circuit of calls that Godwin made).

Female concerns about propriety and about associating with those whose reputation was somewhat tarnished was often very severe. Perhaps especially when the individual concerned felt threatened – Mrs Soane became troubled by a young and rather foolish vicar's daughter named Nora Brickenden who seemed to be setting her cap at her husband in the summer of 1813. Eliza Soane wrote to her husband to make clear her concern saying, 'I boast of being a plain *matter of fact woman* of my own sex, yet those who act systematically wrong I should ever wish to shun.'[28] The letters to Soane relating to the 'affair' from Richard Holland, the man who had introduced Soane to Miss Brickenden, are difficult to make clear sense of. Holland wrote on 26 June 1811:

My girls [Holland was single but surrounded himself with young people, including a niece, Mary Holland, who seems to have been John Soane's goddaughter] were delighted with your good humour and kind attention to them, which it will not be easy to erase from their memories, nor should I wish it. *Your* [god]*Daughter* is all warmth and affection, and I am sure feels a real

---

[25] Taylor, *Records of my Life*, v.1, p. 399.

[26] Elizabeth Inchbold. *The Diaries of Elizabeth Inchbald*, edited by Ben P. Robertson, 3 vols. (London: Pickering & Chatto, 2007), v.2, p. 378.

[27] See Soile Ylivuori's 'Rethinking Female Chastity and Gentlewoman's Honour in Eighteenth Century England', *Historical Journal* 59(1) (2016), 71–97, for a more nuanced conception of reputation than the common tendency to think (with Richardson's *Pamela*) that 'virtue' and 'virginity' outside marriage were the sole standard of honour for women. The situation is clearly much more complex.

[28] Gillian Darley, *John Soane: An Accidental Romantic* (New Haven: Yale University Press, 1999), p. 221.

friendship for you. *Your Friend* [Brickenden] desires her *dutiful respects to 'My Lordship'*, so I am to word it: *Little Pickle* says you will find her a *Great Pickle –*, if you have to contend with her in London, which she says she threatened.[29]

Almost two years later he wrote again to say that he was surprised and hurt to hear that Soane had been 'gallanting about another lady' in Mrs Soane's absence, advising him to be cautious, lest he alienate Mrs Soane's affections. He continued:

I only wish for the sake of Your character, and particularly for Your easy reconcilement with Mrs Soane, when she comes to know of such extraordinary attentions, that it had been my Mary's friend, Miss Nora Brickenden. You might *then* justly escape censure because I can assure You that *She* is a lady of strict virtue and honor, and such as I should be bold to recommend to Mrs Soane, should she return before she the said Nora leaves London, but it cannot be her.

He went on to say that Soane 'may be tired' (most plausibly, of being teased) and might think Holland

somewhat deranged. To be grave then, I did hear of Miss Brickenden's intention of going to London, and thought to have troubled you, if she did, ... to have asked you to introduce her to Mrs Soane ... Hearing she was gone I depended on your gallantry, should you hear of her arrival, which I more than suspect you have ... Oh these women! And forgetting you are a married man, and a man so full of engagements *already*. I fear you gave them too much encouragement at Coombe Royal, but this you need not tell Mrs Soane, only assure her that Miss B is a friend and favourite of ours, and one whom I can recommend to her notice ...[30]

Holland was certainly being arch – and his subsequent letter three weeks later opens 'I am now writing serious and in confidence' and goes on to express his gratitude for the attentions shown by Soane and Mrs Soane to 'my friend *Nora* ... but I shall be very much concerned if you suffer those attentions, through regard to me, to annoy, or be in any way inconvenient either to Mrs S, or yourself'.[31]

There was almost certainly material in these letters expressly designed to put Mrs Soane's mind at rest and there is certainly some anxiety about Holland being blamed by Mrs Soane, but what is more striking is Holland's refusal to see any possibility of impropriety, and his equal refusal to upbraid Soane with any seriousness on his conduct. Male solidarities, it seems, were ones that were far less judgmental than were female solidarities. And women could see this – and could tell when they

---

[29] Arthur T. Bolton, *The Portrait of Sir John Soane RA: 1753–1837* (London: Butler and Tanner Ltd., 1927), p. 169. It is not clear how significant it is that Mrs Soane's diary jumps from March 1811 to June of the same year (when there is only one entry); and then resumes on 2 November, although the entries thereafter are sparse.
[30] Bolton, *Portrait*, p. 175.   [31] Ibid., p. 176.

were being set up: Mrs Soane clearly grasped that her husband had
written to Holland asking him to write a letter that could act as some
kind of cover! On 1 August 1813, Mrs Soane wrote to her husband:

I am sorry you had the trouble of getting an explanation from Mr Holland, as
I really think there is much more fuss made about Miss B than she deserves; for in
my opinion, any woman turned thirty, that affects to be romantic, and professes
platonic love, tis only a cloak for intrigue – she should recollect, in London, as well
as the country, there are all ways gossips that are ready to propagate what they *see*
and what they *guess* and I must say, tis rather surprising your friend Mr Holland,
who certainly knows the world, should have considered a romantic lady, a fit
companion for his niece.[32]

Indeed, Mrs Soane saw herself as having to defend herself against some
of her own friends who seemed in league with her husband. She had
broken with Mrs Wheatley in June 1805 over a disagreement, but it looks
as if her husband subsequently used Mrs Wheatley (who was invariably
broke) for various tasks, paying her a sum of seven pounds and four
shillings on 28 May 1807 (shortly before Mrs Wheatley's marriage to
Alexander Pope the actor and miniaturist on 25 June 1807), reintroducing
her into Mrs Soane's society in 23 November 1813; and then paying Mrs
Wheatley a further £8.8.0 on 1 July 1813 – possibly to undertake a
miniature of Miss Brickenden). Mrs Soane was not amused.

Excluding or cutting others certainly did not have to serve directly
personal interests. Fanny Burney, for example, reacted strongly to a story
from her father in relation to Mme de Stael and M. de Norbonne, who
were staying near them with Arthur Young: 'I do firmly believe it is a
gross calumny ... In short, her whole coterie live together as brethren ...
I would, nevertheless, give the world to avoid being a guest under their
roof, now I have heard even the shadow of a rumour; and I will, if it be
possible without hurting or offending them'.[33]

Similarly, Anne Aikin described her family's attitude to Mary Shelley:

The ladies of my family, though great admirers of Mrs Godwin's writings, were
too correct in their conduct to visit her, and the same objection was felt to Mrs
Shelley. When many years after this time, my aunt Lucy was at a large party at
Mrs Daniel Gaskell's, a lady who liked to collect every kind of lion in her rooms,
she brought up Mrs Shelley to introduce her to my aunt ... my aunt, however,
resolutely turned her back on the fair widow, much to Mrs Gaskell's dismay, and
to the surprise of my brother, a very young man who had escorted his aunt to the
party, and was himself enchanted with Mrs Shelley's beauty and manners.[34]

---

[32] SM Archive 4/B/8/6/7 (Fair copy 4/B/8/6/8).
[33] Frances Burney, *Diary and Letters of Madame D'Arblay*, edited by Muriel Masefield
(London: G. Routledge & Sons Ltd., 1931), p. 237.
[34] Aikin-Sneath, *Georgian Chronicle*, p. 189. The occasion was probably in the early 1830s.

This field of social interaction was additionally complicated by men who insisted that their wives receive the appropriate respect from the wives of others. Samuel Rogers noted that Charles James Fox had cut Sir James Mackintosh in the Louvre during the Peace of Amiens because Mackintosh's wife had not visited Fox's wife (formerly Mrs Armistead) after he had formally announced their marriage in 1802 (it had taken place in 1795).[35] And whether one could insist on one's wife being accorded acknowledgement depended a lot on relative status. In this culture where the élite called the tune on the admission of others to their society, the assumption for the most part was that men accepted other men as individuals – the courtesy was not extended to those connected with them: 'Indeed, society is so consti-tuted in England, that it is useless for celebrated artists to think of bringing their families into the highest circles, where themselves are admitted only on account of their genius. Their wives and daughters must be content to remain at home.'[36] Even in parliamentary circles, among comparative equals, mutual regard among members was not extended automatically. Anne Lister reports a discussion with Sir John Astley, MP for Wiltshire, and his wife Lady Astley, who said 'the gents of the House of Commons knew each other quite well, but that did not at all apply to their wives'.[37]

As we have seen in the Introduction, acquaintance, and a wide acquaintance, would have been useful in broader terms (as weak ties) and for many would have been mainly linked to professional concerns, even though they were often conducted largely as matters of sociability, ostensibly freed from express calculation. But it is not clear that this was true for women or as true (and I will go on to raise questions about how far it was in fact true for men). Many women's sociability remained bounded by familial connections and by the professional activities of their husbands. For them, these relations are 'given' and have a much less open and voluntarist character than those of men – in the sense that men's relationships were potentially multiple and choice-based, whereas women had them more commonly thrust upon them by family, marriage and domestic responsibilities. And women's relationships were, conse-quently, more 'interested' – more essential to their holding their place in society and the respect of those around them and more freighted with

---

[35] Samuel Rogers, *Recollections of the Table Talk of Samuel Rogers*, to which is added Porsoniana, edited by W. Sharp (London: Moxton, 1856), p. 85.

[36] Ibid., p. 209.

[37] Anne Lister, *The Secret Diaries of Miss Anne Lister*, edited by Helena Whitbread (London: Virago, 2010), p. 284.

anxieties about appropriateness and propriety.[38] One consequence of the difference is that women had to invest heavily in their narrower circles and their particular relationships and found it hard to escape these (and were often censorious of those who sought to or who compromised them). Men, in contrast, could be interested in others just because they found them of interest and they could tolerate a great deal – although they might not introduce all their friends to their families.[39]

These complexities may have been one reason that the very terms troubled Amelia Alderson, leading her to reflect on what exactly she was to make of the people with whom she socialised in London and to say: 'I wish you would invent some word warmer than acquaintance & less warm than friend – as the latter word owing to the poverty of language is frequently applied where it does not belong.' She went on to say that she flattered herself to think that Wollstonecraft shared her attachment to people to whom she was connected by early impressions – and whom she had 'long loved and have a claim on her affections to which perhaps their talents in the eye of reason give them no claim'.[40] It is significant that this is a question she asked of London and in that group, as if forced to reflect on the substantial ties of friendship rooted in the past and in 'necessary relations' to those who could claim the title 'friend' in a way that her London connections could not. Yet, the sense of communion with these less connected companions seemed to her to be more than mere acquaintance. As we shall see, while this is what Alderson felt about her radical London companions, the touchstone for her expectations remained these older, essentially unchosen relations. It was in part these older relations – unconnected to talent and virtue – that Godwin encouraged her to root out of her breast on the first meeting (and his earlier comment may well have triggered the issue for Alderson in discussion with Wollstonecraft). And while we may take Godwin as wholly intellectually (or ideologically) driven and exceptional, he might also be seen as conforming more fully to the male model of a public

---

[38] See Silver, 'Friendship in Commercial Society'. Silver does not discuss women's friendships, but his account of male relationships in the eighteenth century in relation to early modern society is suggestive of the contrast.

[39] See for example, the relationship between William Godwin and John King, discussed by Pamela Clemit, where Godwin attends dinners at Kings but then refuses to act as a character witness at a court hearing on King's affairs – 'I can dine at a man's table, without being prepared to be the partisan of his measures & proceedings'. Clemit, *Letters of WG*, v.1, p. 150. Pamela Clemit and Jenny McAuley, 'Sociability in Godwin's Diary: The Case of John King', *Bodleian Library Record* 24(1) (April 2011), 51–56.

[40] MS. Abinger c.41, fol 4r. Amelia Alderson to Mary Wollstonecraft/Imlay. See also the discussion of types of relationship by Robert Paine, 'In Search of Friendship: An Exploratory Analysis of Middle-class Culture', *Man* 4(4) (December 1969), 515–519.

world of associating with other men for their qualities, independent of older ties. Certainly, he constantly reached out to others – as in his attempts to 'woo' Flaxman (as had earlier wooed John Stoddart) to come and dine, writing to him in 17 October 1802,[41] and then repeating the invitation in June 1803, saying that although he had not come on the previous occasion he was asking again – 'Because, judging by what I have seen of your works, & heard of your character & conversation I should be glad to know more of you.'[42] Such attempts at interpolation on the basis of (apparent) equality and respect for abilities were often ignored by Godwin's more élite associates – and may well have been seen by some as transgressive of social norms, but it seems to have been more acceptable amongst those in literary and cultural circles who may have accounted themselves as, broadly, his equals. In contrast, even more suppliant importuning was risky for women – and tended to be undertaken as an epistolary level only. They were not expected to reach out – and doing so could easily put them at risk from those they approached, especially when they reached out to men.

Maintaining appearances and reputation was partly about projecting a status for oneself so as to guide the conduct of others toward oneself. Women were especially vulnerable to male intrusion and insult. There was no code of honour for women to identify, manage and revenge an insult – except by proxy through one's husband or a member of one's family if the insult derived from a man.[43] And it is clear that many men acted in ways that women found inappropriate, intrusive or in various ways compromising of their self-presentation and self-conception and they were especially vulnerable the less they could rely on familial or spousal male protection and/or the more their associates behaved in ways that exposed them to such forms of inappropriate contact. Anne Lister's Yorkshire diary shows her repeatedly concerned about the coarseness of those with whom she associated, despairing of finding a circle in which she would be comfortable and appropriate and being alienated from her father by his 'vulgarity'. She clearly felt the danger that association with him would leave her open to more pointed and intrusive remarks and

---

[41] Clemit, *Letters of WG*, vol. ii, p. 290.

[42] Godwin to Flaxman (16 July 1804. BL Add ms 39781, fol 44).

[43] A point made by Mary Robinson in *A Letter to the Women of England* (London, 1799) and *The Natural Daughter* (1799), edited by Sharon M. Selzer (Toronto, Canada: Broadview Press, 2003), p. 5: 'If a man receive an insult, he is justified in seeking retribution. He may chastise, challenge, and even destroy his adversary. Such a proceeding in MAN is termed honourable ... But were a WOMAN to attempt such an expedient, however strong her sense of injury, however invincible her fortitude, or important the preservation of her character, she would be deemed a murderess.'

behaviour from others. She also despaired at the behaviour of her Aunt (to whom she was generally more tolerant) when travelling in North Wales:

We do not cut a figure in travelling equal to our expenses. My aunt is shabbily dressed & does not quite understand the thorough manners of a gentlewoman. For instance, taking the man's arm so readily to Snowden. Indescribable! George, too, is a clown of a servant, too simple in the manners of the world.[44]

When she visited London, on the way to France, with her father and sister, she reflected: 'Surely this is the last journey I shall ever take with my father and Marian both together. But seeing this street (Park Crescent) made me think. Well, perhaps I am repaid, for nobody knows me.'[45] But the sense of being compromised by the company she kept was persistent. 'Heaven grant this to be my last journey with my father. I am shocked to death at his vulgarity of speech and manner … I am perpetually in dread of meeting anyone I know.'[46] In Yorkshire too there was a constant risk of insult: the diary records her outrage at receiving letters from men suggesting marriage or making lewder propositions and she clearly faced a degree of harassment in her locality. That she was single and committed to remaining so (and was a committed lesbian, which was not broadcast, although she was conscious that her attire was often rather masculine) seems to have made her more of a target. But her diaries are an important case of sustained reflection on the challenges of carving out a circle and set of standards that could afford her an intellectual and cultural society that she could feel was appropriate to her social status and intellectual abilities. Moreover, her setting down of her experience and distress at being approached by men who failed to accord her appropriate respect betrays a mix of concerns about personal and social vulnerability and her own personal and social ambition.

The threat of masculine (or less commonly female) violation of one's standing – to be treated disrespectfully in public or as someone of a group whose status one did not identify with – was just one element in a wider problem about exposure to various forms of intrusion that one's status would not always pre-empt.[47] The diaries kept by women and letters between them were rarely wholly candid about such matters. Revealing oneself and one's humiliations in letters would risk only further exposure, since letters were often passed around. Nor were diaries sacrosanct – Anne Lister wrote sections dealing with these matters and with her affairs

---

[44] Lister, *Diaries*, p. 216.   [45] Ibid., p. 238.   [46] Ibid., pp. 238–239.
[47] For some of the complexities of women's position see Soile Ylivuori, *Women and Politeness in Eighteenth-Century England* (London: Routledge, 2018), chapter 4.

in code. Nonetheless, it is difficult not to believe that a great many other women experienced some such conduct (not least because it was a staple of the female novel throughout this period). To project one's status successfully was to be able to command an appropriate degree of respect and recognition in the conduct of others toward you. In 1798, Elizabeth Smith and her mother and aunt set off at 11.30 p.m. to climb Snowden so as to see the sun rise from the summit. Her mother and aunt stopped at about 1,000 feet but sent her on accompanied only by a guide (who spoke only Welsh) whom they had picked up at the base. This is not entirely Austenian lady-like behaviour, but it underlines the importance of getting things right and commanding the appropriate respect so as to ensure one's security – and also, perhaps, the differences between observable behaviour in towns and the more secluded activities of the country.

Status could not always guarantee respect: Lady Bessborough reported to Granvillle Leveson Gower that a sequence of letters had been sent to her daughter, Lady Caroline (Lamb, née Ponsonby), which were filled with 'every gross disgusting indecency that the most deprav'd imagination could suggest – worse, indeed, than any thing I ever heard, saw, read, or could imagine amongst the lowest Class of the most abandon'd wretches.'[48] Social status clearly could not protect women against such intrusions (and there may well have been an unspoken anxiety that Lady Bessborough's own conduct (with Leveson Gower) had exposed her daughter in some way, and concerns also that the material came from a member of their own set). Women further down the social scale faced a triple problem of dealing with rapaciousness from above, from within their status circles and the difficulty in signalling their status to command the distance they sought from those they regarded as owing them some deference. And it seems likely that the greater degree of anonymity available, as in the city, and the greater the chance of meeting strangers, the more such boundaries might be in danger of being crossed. In Catherine Hutton's exuberant novel, *The Welsh Mountaineer* (1817), our heroine is arrested as a thief in London because she was riding on her own in the city early in the morning – and so lacked the accompanying servants and status markers that would have shielded her from such assumptions.[49]

When visiting London, people had to balance the pleasures of the city against its dangers. They did so, largely, by staying with or moving

[48] Bessborough to Leveson (v. 2, p. 3).
[49] On Hutton, see Mary Ann Constantine's '"The Bounds of Female Reach": Catherine Hutton's Fiction and Her Tours in Wales', *Romantic Textualities: Literature and Print Culture, 1780–1840* 22 (Spring 2017), 92–105.

around with family and close friends. When Abigail Gawthern, a widow with considerable property living in Nottingham with her two children, Anna and Frank, visited London in 1802, when Anna was 18 and Frank 16, they kept company to a large extent with people they had travelled with or knew from home. A great deal was done together. While she underwent a small operation and was recuperating Gawthern allowed the two young people to attend the Lord Mayor's Ball on 19 April 1802 with their friends (they did not return home until after 4 o'clock) and her friends accompanied them to the opera, a dancing school, a concert and various entertainments. Nonetheless, Gawthern drew the line at one of their company's suggestion that he take them to a masquerade – 'I refused his offer, not thinking it quite prudent, neither do I approve of that entertainment.'[50] In the four months they were away from home they did a great deal of visiting and seeing entertainments (including 'the invisible girl', a sham fight on 'Wimbleton Common', Vauxhall Pleasure Gardens, the British Museum, trips to the theatre, to watch a balloon flight, and visits to Windsor, Eton, Richmond, Hampton Court, Greenwich, and so on) but this was conducted as a group. It was clearly important for people of means and some connections to monitor carefully the activities of their young people in the city, challenging as that must have been, especially in relation to their connections with the opposite sex. Anna had already had one proposal in Nottingham (from a man twice her age) and when she was back there in October she had another. It is clear that her mother was concerned to manage her transition to marriage extremely carefully, and that meant ensuring that she had the right social skills, a degree of cosmopolitan experience and an

---

[50] Abigail Gawthern, *The Diary of Abigail Gawthern*, edited by Adrian Henstock, *Thoroton Society Record Series XXXIII* for 1978 and 1979, (Nottingham, 1980), 24 May 1802, p. 93. Note, even Canning found this an 'exceptional' sort of entertainment when he first attended one in April 1795: 'I had never in my life be at a masquerade, publick or private, and was therefore all delight and admiration. Tish at her first Ball at Bath was nothing to me in point of friskiness. From Mrs Crewe's, where I stayed till the company began to thin, Wallace seduced me to the Public Masquerade at the Haymarket, which I found at least as dull and disgusting as the other had been pleasant and lively. I stayed however some time to see the humours of it – but when at about ½ past 4 o'clock the gentlemen began to get quarrelsome and the ladies drunk and sick, I whipped my domino into my pocket and waked home to the Temple to my bed.' Canning, *Letter Journal*, p. 238. It may be that the character of the masquerade changed in the last decades of the eighteenth century, becoming more 'risqué': Fanny Burney notes attending a masquerade – and being cornered by a woman dressed as a nun, in 1770, when she was seventeen, but without any special comment about the propriety of such entertainment. Dror Wahrman points to the dramatic decline in their frequency in the last eighteenth century in *The Making of the Modern Self*, pp. 157–165, and he is following Terry Castle's *Masquerade and Civilization: The Carnivalesque in English Culture and Fiction* (Stanford, CA: Stanford University Press, 1986).

appropriate range of accomplishments, but without having exposed her reputation to risk or her sensibilities to insult.

Something of the control of male/female relations through norms of propriety slightly lower down the social scale can be seen in the diary of William Upcott, who worked in a bookseller's, but also developed an interest in ancestry and autographs and eventually became secretary to the London Institution. As a young man in London in 1803–1807 (he was twenty-four in 1803) he was used to moving about freely with a number of young women, some visiting the town, others living or working in some capacity (often as servants or in the houses of relatives) in the capital. Upcott was averse to marriage and to entanglements. He does not seem to have been predatory (except when collecting auto-graphs and manuscripts later in life). His young female friends in London seem to have trusted him and he seems to have been fond of them. When the prospect of money and marriage enters into his thinking he turned a calculating, but still reluctant eye – saying of one girl:

Miss C...g, the daughter of the landlady at whose house I took a night's lodging – Since her father's death it is well known she is to be in possession of 1500 £ which has caused a variety of suitors to spring up which otherwise would have ... fallen into utter neglect. Lovers of all ages from 20 to 55 have now paid their addresses to her. But the one the most eager and least accepted is this said N – Not a day passes but he forces himself into her company, and produces some ill applied compliments.

He went on:

I moreover did, what I said is now of little importance – and if I offered her my arm it was what others neglected was to do – suffice it to say – If inclination had not been wanting – I could soon have upset all the addresses of her various pretended inamoratas – But she is a person not suited to my taste. – A good figure, tolerably handsome, wanting education. Of her disposition I can say but little – but that little in praise of her. In her conversation I found out her acquirements were few, but those of a necessary kind. – Her fortune in some instances is desirable – but her person not wholly so – Her family is far from respectable, (at least their calling not so) and their company to be, by no means coveted. These circumstances considered – I was no wise inclined to make pretensions.[51]

In another instance, he met a girl in the country who subsequently came to London for surgical treatment for a lump in her breast, and he showed her around the town:

we visited all the parts from the extremity of the eastern to the end of the western. We saw plays & farces, Drury lane, Covent Garden, Astleys – the circus etc. were

---

[51] British Library, Add ms 32,558 32v–32r, Diary of William Upcott.

all visited in their turn. I showed her all the attention I was capable of – and from being so continually in her company perhaps grew partial toward her. Her personal appearance certainly forwarded the partiality – aided by her interesting tho' unfortunate situation.[52]

When she was operated on, he registered his anxiety and distress for her in eloquent terms. Upcott subsequently felt she behaved badly to him, although this was later accounted for, but his recurrent concerns about marriage clearly affected this relationship: 'I am almost persuaded I shall not resolve to alter my condition – I cannot brook the idea of being compelled to endure the miseries of a married life. – I have seen so few proofs of substantial happiness arising from it in my family. – that common prudence forbids my taking measures to bring it to bear.'[53]

When Upcott took a perambulation with a companion around the Midlands, they sought out another friend, only to find that he had set off on a walk with his wife and two young women. They overtook the group only for Upcott to be deeply offended by their reception:

... truly we were amply repaid for our trouble in finding them! For two such Asses as the strangers seemed to be, I never was in company with before. – not an atom of freedom – not the smallest particle of affability – not a shadow of politeness or good breeding was to be found in either – no, they surpassed every one that I know in Ill behaviour! And heaven preserve me from such tribe for the future! To show them civility was literally throwing pearls before swine. The idea of offering them my arm struck them with astonishment. 'Twas a crime almost second to treason to make the attempt – and even the squeamish Anne Moore shrank from such an offence – and seemed as much terrified with it, as if it had been the paw of a lion.[54]

Upcott's complaints continued – he was clearly immensely annoyed! They returned to tea and then took a walk to return the two women to their homes, but, while there was some more rational conversation over tea, and although 'we treated them all with the greatest civility, ... it was no use; the moment they got into the open air – they became as intractable as ever'. What Upcott seemingly failed to recognise was that, as outsiders, he could not expect these young countrywomen with some pretensions to status to be unconcerned about how their behaviour would look to those who lived with them through the year. Taking the arm of a young man in the city might be a protection and an excitement – taking it in the countryside might be the occasion for gossip and rumour. When staying near Shrewsbury or visiting a young 'lass' he had been introduced to in London and who had moved to Kingston on Thames,

[52] Upcott Diary, BL Add ms 32558, fol 58r.   [53] BL Add ms 32558, fol 60r.
[54] BL Add ms 32558, fol 115r.

there seems to have been no similar restriction, so he found it hard to comprehend. But it may simply be that a slight shift in social standing (and perhaps a difference in social aspiration) created this apparently incomprehensible conduct (or that the former cases saw him as eligible and as a potential husband). For the young women in the Midlands, Upcott and his friend could well have been seen as a threat to their reputations and future prospects in the local community.

London was certainly not free of such concerns in relation to the free movement of young women. Sharon Turner's courtship of William Watts' daughter Mary, then only sixteen, revolved around walking in London. On one occasion, Watts sent his daughter and two of her young friends to Turner's rooms in Lincoln's Inn, from Titchfield Street, a mile or so away, to deliver a book to him.[55] Turner took the opportunity to show them Lincoln's Inn gardens and to walk through a series of Parks with them, before conducting them home. Watts, nonetheless, was hesitant about allowing a further walk with Turner (despite Mary being accompanied by her friends). Without these walks it is unlikely that the evening salons that Turner attended at Watts' house would have sufficed to develop their relationship, but Watts was clearly concerned about how far being conducted around town, even in a group, was appropriate for a young lady.

It is by no means easy to pick out the conventions and expectations relating to movement and association in the city, partly because there was considerable variability in terms of how cautious, trusting, daring or modest the participants were and partly because different practices were followed in different social circles and in relation to different social statuses. Amelia Alderson seems to have moved freely about the city, accompanied sometimes by old friends, albeit these were men with some connection to her family. In 1794 she attended the Treason Trials, apparently on her own. She was then 25 and had been running her father's household since her mother's death in 1785. And she was a spirited and independent minded young woman. But, evidently, she did not behave in London in ways that she thought would incur unacceptable reputational cost or risk. This might have been because her core reputational perspective and reference group was her native Norwich. But it was also linked to her involvement with radical and dissenting circles which were willing, at least in some respects, to challenge the conventions of society. Having said that, her family and friends

---

[55] The hard to get hold of, J. M. Lequinio, *Les préjugés détruits* (Paris: De L'Imprimerie Nationale, Et se trouve Chez Desenne, Debray, Libraires, au Jardin de la Révolution, ci-devant le Palais Royal, 1792).

were unable to act to protect her interests in relation to Opie's miserliness – a Norwich marriage might have been more manageable.

We have noted that men might have concerns about those with whom their wives associated. Clearly, wives also had concerns about their husbands, although they had much less ability to set the terms of the marital relationship than did men. Mrs Soane clearly has moments of jealousy arising from her husband's attention to other women (which might have been wholly innocent). But she herself would have been concerned to ensure that no reputational doubt could be attached to her conduct. She therefore had to consider carefully how far those she associated with might cause her collateral damage. Her anxieties about her son George and his treatment of his father, and then his own unsanctioned marriage, were partly reputational ones.[56] This policing of one's own actions and that of one's family and associates was clearly an issue for many of the women in the period, who sought both to have an area of freedom, while trying to ensure that it remained uncompromised in the eyes of others who would matter to one's social position.

Marianne Ayrton *expressed* no such anxieties, but largely because she seems to have lived largely within her family circles – and perhaps also because of an enduring sense of vulnerability to her husband. Having had a long-standing engagement to her, William Ayrton seems to have made difficulties over the match at the last minute such that, at one point, she was thrown into despair. He quickly withdrew his concerns about the arrangements and married happily. He was rather cloyingly sentimental about his wife and took great care to preserve her diary (while taking it upon himself to transcribe it and quietly edit out what he must have thought of as a large amount of inconsequential matter!). Clearly, on his construction, he was a doting husband. But there is no doubt that Marianne felt she had come close to losing him, and that was at the age of 30 after having had a long association with him, making a subsequent relationship less probable. We see very little of her participation later in her life when she lived in close proximity to the Lambs and the Burneys and when her husband was a frequenter of the Lambs' evening discussions. Indeed, she may well have had concerns and resentments at her husband's freedoms, but the only expression of these that remains is a brief note in her diary indicating that we are unlikely to find any further evidence: 'I hope I have destroyed any, and every mem. that I have been tempted to make under the feelings of anger or distress of mind. If you

---

[56] She died before George had fathered a child to his wife's sister – daughters of James Boaden, Inchbald's biographer.

meet with any pray destroy them, or it my Darl, for I can recollect nothing now but unremitting tenderness and kindness.'[57]

We should also recognise that there were a number of women who were manifestly invisible and lacked the protection of such circles. These were the unacknowledged common law partners and the mothers of the children of men who refused to marry them. Turner's narrative of his courtship of Mary Watts made no mention of her mother. Farington noted dining with Watts and 'Mrs Watts spinster', indicating that the couple were not married.[58] On one occasion Turner records Watts as making reference to 'the entreaties of a lady in this house'. This might have referred to his partner who might have been his two children's mother, but otherwise there is complete silence on the issue.[59] William Watts was hardly alone. Horne Tooke looked after a son, Sidney Montague, and two daughters Mary and Charlotte Hart, without marrying their mothers – and famously asserted that he would never marry a pretty woman because 'she would be studious to be admired by others and to please anybody more than her husband'.[60] Thomas Rowlandson left his whole estate to 'Betsey Winter Spinster', his companion for twenty years and about whom we (and probably his contemporaries) know (and knew) nothing.[61] The miser John Elwes had two sons, by his housekeeper, at least one of whom had a number of children out of wedlock;[62] Charles Dibdin also had two illegitimate sons whom he did not treat well – whether from one or two women (whom it seems likely he also did not treat well) is unclear;[63] and Godwin was friends briefly with John Pinkerton, who had a number of children, some by a common law wife, others by wives, at least one of whom he divorced.[64] In the provinces someone of the standing of Erasmus Darwin could intersperse his

---

[57] 31 December 1824.

[58] Farington, *Diary*, vol. II, p. 314, 10 March 1795, and p. 315, 16 March 1795; there is a further entry to Mr and Mrs Watts in vol. III, p. 839, 15 May 1797, which gives a seating plan for dinner.

[59] Sharon Turner, BL Add ms 81089, p. 399: It was '… chiefly to the entreaties of a lady in this house that I have permitted his (Mr S's) visits'.

[60] Michael T. Davis, 'John Horne Tooke', *Oxford Dictionary of National Biography* (2009), https://ezproxy-prd.bodleian.ox.ac.uk:2095/10.1093/ref:odnb/27545, citing Rogers, *Table Talk*, pp. 154–155.

[61] Gatrell, *City of Laughter*, p. 326.

[62] See Chapter 7 and my 'Unconventional Norms', in Kevin Gilmartin, *Sociable Places* (Cambridge: Cambridge University Press, 2017).

[63] See Holcroft's *Memoirs*, and Jon A. Gillaspie, 'Charles Dibdin', *Oxford Dictionary of National Biography* (2014), https://ezproxy-prd.bodleian.ox.ac.uk:2095/10.1093/ref:odnb/7585.

[64] Sarah Couper, 'John Pinkerton', *Oxford Dictionary of National Biography* (2008), https://ezproxy-prd.bodleian.ox.ac.uk:2095/10.1093/ref:odnb/22301.

two marriages with an affair with Mary Parker, by whom he had two daughters. He absorbed them into his household, before sending their mother off to marry someone else, as he himself then did.[65] Farington also mentions Sir John St Aubyn, who had several children by different women, but was never married.[66] It is not difficult to multiply the cases. The status of many of these women was null. Many were kept out of the public gaze by their men and few had any public visibility. The fellow diners of 'Mrs Watts, Spinster' on the one occasion noted by Farington, were Farington, Mr Gore and Mr and Mrs Hughes (the two women 'Watts' and Mrs Hughes seem to have been sisters). Tolerant (or libertine) men could admit such women as the partners of their companions and might require their wives to join their company in intimate gatherings. Sisters might also be willing (and allowed) to acquiesce. But there is little sense that these unmarried companions could appear prominently. Nancy Storace is somewhat of an exception, but it is difficult to tell how far she was more acceptable because of her art or because of the fact that she was married (dead though that relationship was). Her living for many years with Braham (and having a son by him) does not seem to have hindered her acceptance in Soane's circles, but she had celebrity and money and, therefore, some power, and also a history of connection.[67] The rules do not seem wholly hard and fast – but there do seem to be conventions that effectively excluded many of these women from the company of those who had some concern with respectability (perhaps unless, as Sally Engel Merry suggests with respect to gossip and sanctions, they could pull rank or in other respects had manifestly superior resources).[68]

Such complexities in people's social relationships might best be understood as part of a larger picture of a society constructed of little societies, which served to delimit people's openness to the massiveness of the city and the potential to lose oneself, and thereby allowed one to navigate it and to make it habitable, to forge relations, to find a path and pursue and develop sets of interests and to find entertainment, partners and security. But one's place in these smaller societies came with obligations and with certain costs – that were a condition for admission to groups that offered protection, access, and support. In late Georgian London it seems likely that men's circles were usually larger and more accommodating to

---

[65] Maureen McNeil, 'Erasmus Darwin', *Oxford Dictionary of National Biography* (2013), https://ezproxy-prd.bodleian.ox.ac.uk:2095/10.1093/ref:odnb/7177.

[66] Farington, *Diary*, vol. VIII, p. 3015, 10 April 1807.

[67] See the Introduction and Merry, 'Rethinking Gossip and Scandal', p. 283, on the insulating character of money.

[68] Merry, 'Rethinking Gossip and Scandal', pp. 286–287.

difference and deviance, but then men were rarely as exposed as women were. And, to reduce and control their exposure, women invested a great deal of effort in their circles and in cultivating friendships and associations that might prove useful for them personally and for their children.

In reflecting on these circles, the Dunbar number of 150 is suggestive. In fact, it does not seem wildly inaccurate, but it needs complementing with the important if often fluctuating difference between core and periphery. In our two central cases it looks like a core of around twenty-to-thirty close relationships might well be normal for most women in this period. Moreover, it also seems that there was considerable interaction within the members of the cores of these circles – so that if you are one of my core relationships, then others in my circle may well also be core relationships for you. Indeed, it makes sense to see these circles as gaining a degree of fixity from family, profession or particular sets of activities – for example, Marianne Ayrton's two families (Arnold and Ayrton), her husband and father's musical connections, her domestic situation and her immediate locale. And for Mrs Soane, again her family, her husband's (and uncle's) circles and professional contacts and the spin-off from these in terms of her capacity for patronage and her domestic connections around the household, her entertainments, etc. In both cases, these identities and activities help provide a degree of consistency of social position from which to look out and assess oneself, one's associates and one's influence. A 'set' that was continually in flux would not be a set and could not provide a sense of rootedness and foundation; but in most cases there was a relative fixity holding these circles together. And it was that relative fixity that both required and allowed a degree of policing and, amongst women, this was done in part by gossip – and the attempt to gain information about others and to ensure that there was none that others had against oneself. That is, they were often not powerfully strong ties, but they were ties that people often sought to strengthen insofar as they could.

This assumes that there is repeated interaction within a set, even if the content of that set changes over time. My sense is that really core people total more like thirty. If that is so, then we should expect London to have had many non-interlocking or only marginally interlocking circles; and we should expect those to have had a certain pattern – often around activities and reinforced by certain kinds of institution, such as for the arts, the Royal Academy, publishing around St Paul's Churchyard, newspaper production, literary circles, the theatre, music, around party or Westminster or government business. Within these multiple circles there was scrutiny of those in the circle – they knew one another and they may have judged one another, but the way they did so would have had considerable variability. It is clear that the damaged reputations of some could create collateral damage to those who associated with them – especially (perhaps almost wholly) for women. But it also seems that there were subtle gradations, indulgences and forgivenesses – this was rarely a matter of categorical judgement but was something that was heavily context and status dependent, that linked to certain role responsibilities (for example, mothers in relation to their children) and power differentials. Hence the importance of the informal testing and projection of standards through conversation and the relaying of information. This makes it important not to overgeneralise. These complexities required a considerable alertness for many, especially those who were at some disadvantage in relation to the particular social circle, but who needed it personally, professionally or socially, more than it needed him or her or who was an outsider in certain ways, or was trying to make their name and make progress in their profession for which certain connections mattered greatly. But this also meant that, for many circles, there were a great many people who were not of much interest, who sat below the threshold of awareness or of whom awareness might be extremely superficial. Where they bump into these circles they might generate contempt or condescension or perhaps conditionality – until they have been 'talked through', gossiped about or otherwise subjected to some sort of accreditation. And some of these people might then get to move in these other circles with the right kind of passport.

Most men do not seem to have shared much of the details of their business or much of their information and their wider social knowledge with their wives or families. In many respects it seems that they were more open with each other. This might be less so when their relations were 'interested' and they had to be prudent in sharing information or exposing their own activities, but it is clear that men forged relationships with other men on the grounds of shared ideas, estimations of character and convictions of shared tastes and values. In that process, they strengthened what were often initially weak ties of acquaintance into stronger, disinterested, quasi-fraternal relationships. In contrast, for many women their relations with other women were rooted in family, marriage and interests, albeit with some of those relations potentially offering a sense of intellectual affinity, mutual regard and affection. In general, however, most relationships bore the hallmarks of mutual recognition within a limited range of gendered roles, practices and possibilities and it was from such bases that these more 'disinterested' friendships might take off. Nonetheless, when the invasive intervention of loyalism and the powers of government broke into these masculine spheres of private discussion and friendship, it seems clear that men were significantly more exposed than women, whose friendships were less closely allied to their intellectual commitments and senses of affinity. Just as we should not see these distinctions as wholly either/or, so we should not think that women's society was all of one type. Nonetheless, what I believe we see in the 1790s was a largely masculine intellectual culture that was ambitious for greater equality and deliberative exchange, forming sets of relationships that had a markedly different character from those based on family and interest (by which women's relationships remained much more systematically marked), being violated and consequently broken up by the intrusions of loyalist suspicion and government spies. What I have done in this chapter is to lay some of the groundwork for giving an account of the social underpinnings of the intellectual phenomena I discussed in the opening chapters. What I want to turn to in Chapter 4 is a more detailed examination of how far women in broadly reform circles might be seen as socially linked in different ways than those whom we have discussed thus far, and how far, when they were, it left them still more vulnerable than their male counterparts to the storm of reaction.

4 Radical Literary Women

4.1 Women's Circles

I have been arguing that there was a more plural and disjointed character to a great deal of London's cultural and social life in the 1790s and 1800s than we often recognise. People had their social locations, defined in large part by family and status and by their own or their husband's trade or profession. They knew something about some people outside these orbits, but often did not know them or much about them. While a good deal of effort went into managing one's social relationships, the pools from which one might draw were to a considerable extent given.[1]

We can see this with respect to Marianne Ayrton and her pre-marital list of friends, when compared to those she sees on a regular basis after her marriage. Essentially, while her family remained a focal point, those earlier friendships (which were predominantly made up of older people who were friends of her parents) had very little influence over her circles post-marriage, which derived largely from Ayrton's connections. Similarly, Eliza Soane clearly brought some friends and relatives to her marriage, but most of the central members of her circles came from links with her husband's professional interests.

In the case of the dramatist, novelist and sometime actress Elizabeth Inchbald, while we are missing a substantial part of her diaries, it is clear from those that do exist that her connections were largely a mix of theatrical and familial connections. The bruising exchange between her and Godwin in the wake of Mary Wollstonecraft's death makes clear that she did not see herself as having anything like a 'circle' – certainly, she did

---

[1] That does not mean they women in such positions were 'non-political' – much would depend on family and connections. But it adds a component to the analysis of more middle class women's participation that is not always attended to. Work on middle class circles of women, especially in relation to Dissent, can be found in the early chapters of Kathryn Gleadle's *Borderline Citizens: Women, Gender, and Political Culture in Britain, 1815–1867* (Oxford: British Academy/Oxford University Press, 2009); see also Barbara Taylor, *Mary Wollstonecraft and the Feminist Imagination* (Cambridge: Cambridge University Press, 2003), especially the opening sections of chapter 6.

not see herself as orchestrating one. Referring to the refusal of Inchbald's close friends the Twisses to accept Wollstonecraft after her marriage to Godwin on the grounds that she had presented herself as married to Imlay, he depicted them as 'sacrificing to what they were silly enough to think a proper etiquette'. In contrast, he portrayed Inchbald as 'a person so out of all comparison their superior' who should have 'placed her pride in acting upon better principles ... They could not (they pretended) receive her onto their precious circles. You kept no circles to debase & enslave you'.[2]

Yet, in the immediate wake of the French Revolution, and with a rising tide of pressure for Parliamentary reform, many scholars believe that there was something like a confluence of a number of serious literary women in London who looked for progressive social change and who challenged the limits of the education of women and their subordinate place in society.[3] Certainly, it was a period of intense literary production for women – we might list, for example: Fanny Burney, Catherine Macaulay, Anna Barbauld, Joanna Baillie, Helen Maria Williams, Mary Wollstonecraft, Elizabeth Inchbald, Mary Robinson, Mary Hays, Maria Edgeworth, Elizabeth Hamilton, Elizabeth Fenwick, Amelia Alderson, Mrs Radcliffe, Charlotte Smith, Harriet and Sophia Lee, Hannah More, Sarah Trimmer and so on. Moreover, it is clear that there was active participation of women in the debating life of London, with all-women debating societies before 1788 and continued involvement in certain societies thereafter.[4] It is also clear that a range of women participated in publishing and print-making and contributed to the literary world, either on their own account or in support of their husbands (such as Thelwall's wife Susan) or other members of their family.[5]

[2] *Letters of WG*, i., p. 241. See also Roger Manvell, *Elizabeth Inchbald: A Biographical Study* (Lantham, MD: University Press of America, 1987), pp. 98–108. Manvell suggests that Godwin proposed to Inchbald in 1793, based on an entry in the diary (although this claim actually rests on Ford K. Brown and Charles Kegan Paul's biographical work on Godwin rather than on the diary itself). The reference is probably 16 September 1793, 'Call in Inchbald, talk of marriage'. This more likely describes a topic rather than a proposal!

[3] A suitably cautious claim for this is made by Arianne Chernock, *Men and the Making of Modern British Feminism*, (Stanford, CA: Stanford University Press, 2010), p. 3.

[4] Donna Andrew, *London Debating Societies, 1776–1799* (London: London Record Society, 1994), pp. xi–xii.

[5] See Mee, *Print, Publicity and Popular Radicalism*, pp. 53–60. For the early nineteenth century see Christina Parolin, 'The "She-Champion of Impiety": Female Radicalism and Political Crime in Early Nineteenth Century England', in *Radical Space: Venues of Popular Politics in London 1790–1845* (Canberra: ANU Press, 2010), pp. 83–103; and Iain McCalman, 'Feminism and Free Love in an Early Nineteenth Century Radical Movement', *Labour History* 38 (1980), 1–25. For engraving circles see David Alexander, *Caroline Watson & Female Printmaking in Late Georgian England* (Cambridge: The Fitzwilliam Museum, 2014).

Sharing an activity does not make a social circle. Moreover, the writing of novels and pamphlets is not in itself an especially *social* activity and, while plays probably may have involved some playwrights in various aspects of production in the theatre, this usually involved people who were not themselves writers. Men with literary ambitions had opportunities to meet with their fellow toilers through their 'apprenticeships' in the reviews, periodicals and newspapers, but these opportunities were rarely extended as frequently or as inclusively to women.[6] And aspects of the wider elements of this male culture of deliberative sociability, in the form of meetings in coffee houses, taverns, booksellers, clubs and societies, were only exceptionally open to women. Joseph Johnson's support for Mary Wollstonecraft was certainly unusual. Mary Hays relied on a certain amount of advice from Wollstonecraft, but never secured the same kind of inclusion that Wollstonecraft did. The sense that we get from studies of the art world is that it was, at heart, a highly masculine culture, which condescended to a number of women artists (Angelica Kaufman, Clara Wheatley, Mrs Flaxman, etc.,); but these women did not get to operate in the same way as men, either on the wider public stage or in the more professional art world. They were tolerated, sometimes encouraged, but not fully integrated, especially in areas associated with the professional world which were highly masculine – such as dinners, drinking and managing institutions linked to the arts. And this was a world which, unlike medicine, Westminster politics, government offices, law, science and engineering, etc., actually did admit and recognise, up to a point, the contribution of women as participants in the field. In many respects, within the arts, it is the fine arts, literature and, perhaps above all, the theatre and concert performance, that women could attain some potential public status and role, but in each case never quite to the degree or with the same social consequences that were afforded to men.

Nonetheless, we might think that the shared literary concerns and political interests and affiliations of several of these literary women would have encouraged them to associate with each other and to seek such connections as they could make. Moreover, in what many of these women wrote, they pointed to forms of female solidarity and aspired to membership of a more rational and egalitarian form of social order that would, in itself, require a different mode of operation.

---

[6] While it is important to recognise that women had a public voice, as Anne Mellor does in *Mothers of the Nation: Women's Political Writing in England 1780–1830* (Bloomington, IN: Indiana University Press, 2000), it is equally important to recognise that this is a constrained inclusion.

Nonetheless, the evidence supports a sense of an emerging collective identity and of a female group of deliberative friendships only to a very limited extent, and then in relation to just one sub-group of these writers in London. This is the group with evidence of iterated interaction around Mary Robinson, Mary Hays, Mary Wollstonecraft, Amelia Alderson and Eliza Fenwick. This analysis rests principally on Godwin's diary, complemented by Inchbald's diary and by the surviving correspondence of these women (which is inevitably incomplete). Nonetheless, these materials allow us to construct something of a picture of these literary women's interaction in London.

Many connections were by no means intensive. I have not included Helen Maria Williams in this discussion because she left for France early and did not return.[7] Wollstonecraft met her in France – and reported to her sister 'I shall visit her frequently, because I *rather* like her, and I meet French company at her house. Her manners are affected, yet the *simple* goodness of her heart continually breaks through the varnish, so that one would be more inclined, at least I should, to love than admire her.'[8] There is nothing substantive in Mary Hays's letters in relation to Helen Maria Williams, but Hays' correspondents do talk about Williams in the 1810s. In a letter in December 1813, Penelope Pennington refers to Hays' superior abilities, but says that she herself has been accustomed 'to the intimate Association of some of the first Literary, and Talented Characters of the Age' and enumerates 'as my *more* particular Friends, the celebrated Mrs Piozzi, – Miss Seward, – Hannah More, – Helen Maria Williams, the late ingenious Dr More, Mrs Siddons's &c &c'.[9]

That is a somewhat surprising list. More, Seward and Thrale/Piozzi and one suspects others on it would not have thanked Pennington for the link to Williams.[10] In the 1790s Thrale had noted with regret Williams' fall:

---

[7] Although there are some rather puzzling references that seem to be to Williams being in Britain on 8 March and 7 April 1795 in Godwin's diary, for which there is no further evidence.

[8] Mary Wollstonecraft, *The Collected Letters of Mary Wollstonecraft*, edited by Janet Todd (New York: Columbia University Press, 2003), Letter 118, 24 December 1792, p. 215; see also p. 225; 229 where she refers to Mrs Stone (John Hurford Stone's wife, displaced by Helen Maria Williams – although Wollstonecraft does not comment on that); 248, which relates that Williams had encouraged her to burn her manuscript on the French Revolution; and there is a reference in a note to Godwin, from July 1797 (p. 430), who seems to have been wanting to send a letter to HMW.

[9] Mary Hays, *The Correspondence (1779–1843) of Mary Hays, British Novelist*, edited by Marilyn L. Brooks (Lampeter, Wales: Mellen Edwin Press, 2004), p. 508.

[10] As noted in Chapter 3 and discussed further in this and the next two chapters, the contemporary clustering of women by others often linked people whom we see as diametrically opposed in principles, but who contemporaries saw rather differently and as similar in certain respects.

Helen Maria Williams is on the Point of Sacrificing her Reputation to her Spirit of Politics. She went from England with Mr Stone a married Man who left his Wife here, but *She* would go to *France*: a foolish Thing some People thought, but I said there had been always an old Classical Connection between *Helen* and *Paris*.[11]

Thrale made no reference to Wollstonecraft, but her connection with Williams was longstanding. Then, in the early Autumn of 1794, she noted:

I have heard from Helen Williams again, tis just two years since She wrote last, & beg'd an Ansr but I was fretting about Cecilia Thrale's Health & thought little of any other Concern but that. I had however discretion enough not to correspond with a /895 profess'd Jacobine resident at Paris, tho' She requested a Letter very sweetly indeed, & with much appearance of true Regard for *me*: my refusal to answer such a Request from such a Writer put me in mind of the brutal housekeeper in Clarissa … This was exactly the reason why I did not write to her then, but now She is escaped from Paris poor Soul! I think I may congratulate her on having had Power & Will to leave the Wretches: but I fear *Reputation* has been left behind somehow – I *fear* so; tho' perhaps no real harm has been done. One could not write *then*, because there was no way of conveying a Letter but through some French Man … but now one may send a Letter by the Post, I think I will send a Letter. Helen Williams is a very fine Genius.[12]

Her suggestion that 'Reputation has been left behind' is coupled interestingly with the thought that 'perhaps no real harm has been done'. Then in February 1795 she noted: 'Helen Maria Williams has totally lost her Character – as a *Woman*, she lives with Mr *Stone* who has a Wife alive – Mr Chappelow says comically that She is *petrified*: we once as he observed thought her *nemini secunda*.'[13] She then relates a story of John Philip Kemble attempting to rape a Miss De Camp in the Green Room at the theatre,[14] and his being given the cold-shoulder by audiences as the story spread, which she found somewhat heartening – she concluded that:

no Sin but *one* seems punished by the World's Disapprobation …; and there is *some* Idea, – a *faint* one, – about the Point of Honour amongst Women too; Helen William's Friends are all ashamed of *her*. When Stone's *real* Wife followed her Husband to Basle in Switzerland, wither He had fled with his newer Connexion, fair Helen, – leaving the first poor Soul behind; in hope She would be Guillotined

[11] Hester Thrale, *Thraliana: The Diary of Mrs Hester Lynch Thrale (later Mrs Piozzi) 1776–1809*, edited by Katharine C. Balderston (Oxford: Oxford University Press, 2014), vol. II, 1784–1809, p. 848 (October–December 1792).

[12] Thrale, *Thraliana*, vol. ii, pp. 894–895.

[13] 'second to none', ibid., p. 910 (February 1795).

[14] See the depiction in BMS8730, The Rape of Proserpine, A Dramatic Tail (Aitken), 15 February 1795.

by the Terrorists: *his* Conscience smote him, and he would at least have behaved *civilly*, but the second Lady stormed and cried, and obliged him to drive Mrs Stone from his Door, at which she intreated for Bread – Oh Tempora! Oh Mores!

Yet in a footnote, she added: 'I have a Notion however that Helen will lick herself clean after all.' And that did indeed seem to be the case. She remained a favourite with radicals – Mary Robinson praised her and Lady [Emma] Hamilton in the same breath, saying that they exemplified the fact that 'an English woman, like a prophet, is never valued in her own country. In Britain they are neglected, and scarcely known; on the continent, they have been nearly IDOLIZED.'[15] Williams welcomed John and Amelia Opie and Anne Plumptre when they visited Paris in 1802–1803 and introduced them to several eminent friends of freedom, including the Polish patriot Count Tadeas Kosciusko.[16] When Henry Crabbe Robinson had been in company with her in Paris in February 1815 he reported that, although 'I was not prejudiced in her favour ... she rose in my esteem. She has no un-English feelings, And retains her original love of liberty.'[17] Nothing was said of her domestic arrangements – as Thrale predicted, she seems in part 'to have licked herself clean' – or, at least, clean enough for visitors to Paris.

I have also not included Elizabeth Inchbald as a figure in this circle, since she seems a clear case of someone who did not altogether relish the idea of a coterie of literary women – the evidence we have suggests that Godwin introduced her to Mary Wollstonecraft and that they met three times at the theatre, but not otherwise. Certainly, there was no great affection between them. In contrast, Inchbald and Alderson did have some history. In Brightwell's *Memorials* of Alderson, there is a letter from Alderson to her friend Mrs Taylor in which she reported that on the 26 August 1794, during her visit to London, she and Mr J. Boddington (a family friend) had called on Godwin, who said he had talked of her to Inchbald, who had recollected her and expressed a wish to see her. They later paid her a visit, finding her '... as pretty as ever, and much more easy and unreserved in her manner, than when I last saw her'.[18] They later developed quite a close relationship, but the evidence we have suggests that this was not until after Alderson's marriage to Opie, and was probably more in the 1800s than the 1790s (the diary for 1807 shows the first sign of intimacy, although we lack many of the earlier diaries). In this later

---

[15] Robinson, *A Letter to the Women of England*, p. 65.
[16] Celia Lucy Brightwell, *Memorials of the Life of Amelia Opie, Selected and Arranged from Her Letters, Diaries, and Other Manuscripts*, 2nd ed. (Norwich: Fletcher and Alexander 1854), pp. 98–114.
[17] Hays, *The Correspondence*, correspondence 577.   [18] Brightwell, *Memorials*, p. 43.

period Inchbald called on (by then) Mrs Opie, on several occasions during and after the final critical phase of John Opie's illness (suggesting that they must have seen something of each other in the preceding years). These connections are also evident in James Boaden's *Memoirs of Inchbald* concerning the meeting with Mme de Stael in 1813; and from Inchbald's later diaries of 1814 and 1820). In the 1790s, two of the three recorded contacts between Alderson and Inchbald (in Godwin's diary) took place at the theatre and one of these is unclear as to whether Godwin's contact with them in the same venue involved them being with Godwin at the same point in time (such are the vagaries of Godwin's use of 'adv' to indicate having seen someone, but where doing so could be at any point in the visits he paid that day). Also, Wollstonecraft refers apologetically in a letter to Amelia Alderson for having spoken rather sharply of a certain lady (Inchbald) in Alderson's presence and Janet Todd suggests that she did so because Inchbald was already a friend of Alderson's and had acted as her chaperone in her first visit to London.[19] Evidence for this is hard to find and implies a visit to London some time prior to her stay with Boddington and her first London encounter with Godwin. Moreover, if we are to believe Inchbald's own strictures, voiced with respect to Wollstonecraft ('I did *not* know her – I never wished to know her – as I avoid every female acquaintance who has no husband, I avoided her') it makes it unlikely that she would have played quite that role (although see the further discussion of Inchbald later in this chapter).[20]

According to Godwin's diary, Inchbald also met Maria Reveley and Harriet Lee, but again largely at the theatre, and neither appears in her own diary for 1793. There is no evidence of any contact between Inchbald and Mary Robinson, the Fenwicks or Hays.[21] Alderson was not central to any London circle as a visitor, although she is an interesting outsider who forged a set of relationships across a number of divisions that those living in the city were more likely to respect. Other visitors to or temporary residents of the city include Charlotte Smith, Anna Letitia Barbauld, Anne Cristall and Anne and Belle Plumptre (whom Alderson knew from Norwich, and the fact that Belle had accompanied Alderson

---

[19] Wollstonecraft, *Collected Letters*, no 321, 11.4.1797, pp. 408–409.
[20] Godwin, *Letters of WG*, i., p. 238; see also Guest, *Unbounded Attachment*, p. 83, and Inchbald's letter to John Taylor reflecting on her 'nervous apprehension' of new acquaintances, 'Especially if they are of my own sex' (MS Eng. Misc. e 143, fols 25v–26, 32r–v).
[21] Although, in the last case, there is an entry in her diary for 1820 that she 'Heard that Miss Hays's boarding house is broke up and she is imprisoned for debt'. This does not seem to be Mary Hays, and even if it was, it scarcely counts as 'acquaintance'. Inchbald, *Diaries*, p. 241.

on a visit to Godwin's 'cousin', Mrs Southren,[22] suggests that Godwin
also probably knew the Plumptre sisters from before this).[23] Although it
is difficult to be certain it seems probable that Godwin introduced
Wollstonecraft to the Plumptres, having met them in Norwich at least a
year earlier; that Barbauld was also someone with whom he had had
previous contact[24]; and that Anne Cristall might be someone
Wollstonecraft knew already (since Godwin met her at tea at Wollstonecraft's, her poetry was published by Joseph Johnson, and there is correspondence between Wollstonecraft and Anne's brother Joshua in 1790).[25]

Charlotte Smith met Godwin at John King's in May 1797, having just
come back into circulation in London. He then took Wollstonecraft to
meet her and that seems to have been their first meeting (certainly, he did
not refer to a previously existing acquaintance with Wollstonecraft in his
letter to Smith after his wife's death in October 1797). Evidence of
connections between Charlotte Smith and Mary Hays comes from col-
laborations between them in the 1800s, together with a letter to Hays
from Smith (responding to one of hers) in July 1800. In that letter Smith
refers to having made the acquaintance of Elizabeth Fenwick – 'Of
several new acquaintance, I know none for whom I am more interested
than Mrs Fenwick.'[26] There seems to be no evidence of any links
between Charlotte Smith and Amelia Alderson or Maria Reveley. In
contrast, Smith sent Inchbald a complimentary volume of *Elegiac Sonnets*
in May 1797 and referred to a discussion with her about the income they
had made from their novels (in slightly bitter comparison to Burney and
Radcliffe) in June 1797.[27] Mary Robinson is invoked only in a letter
about the portrait of Smith for *Elegiac Sonnets*, v. 2., when Smith referred
to 'Mrs Mary Robinson & other Mistresses whom I have no passion to be
confounded with.'[28]

The core of something like a London literary group of women seems to
have emerged briefly early in the second half of the 1790s and to have

---

[22] Alderson to Godwin, 28 August 1795, MS. Abinger c. 2, fol. 108r.
[23] Godwin's '1796 List' identified the years in which he first met people whom he regarded
as significant: Barbauld (1781); Williams (1787); Inchbald (1792); Radcliffe (1794);
Siddons (1795). In a second list, Wollstonecraft (1791), Reveley (1793), Mrs Robinson
(1796), Mrs Smith (1797) and Harriet and Sophia Lee (1798) make the cut, but then so
too do the Kingsman sisters in 1798 and 1799. Hays, Alderson and the Plumptres
do not.
[24] Godwin's '1796 List' suggests he had contact with Barbauld from 1781, although
whether Mr &/or Mrs is unclear.
[25] Hays, *The Correspondence*, no. 98.
[26] Charlotte Smith, *Collected Letters of Charlotte Smith*, edited by Judith Phillips Stanton
(Bloomington, IN: Indiana University Press, 2003), p. 350.
[27] Ibid., pp. 279–280.   [28] Ibid., 25 April 1797, p. 268.

involved Mary Hays, Mary Wollstonecraft, Mary Robinson and Eliza-beth Fenwick.[29] There was also some contact between some of this group and Amelia Alderson, Charlotte Smith and the Plumptre sisters, although this does not seem to have been especially intense in this period. These relationships were all relatively new in 1795–1796, except in the case of Hays and Wollstonecraft who had corresponded and possibly met in the autumn of 1792, before Wollstonecraft's departure for France in December 1792. Their correspondence resumed when Wollstonecraft returned in 1795 and, if they had not met in person before, they were brought together at dinner at Johnson's in the autumn of 1795, shortly before Hays invited Godwin to meet Wollstonecraft in January 1796. It seems likely that Hays met Mary Robinson through Mary Wollstonecraft in January 1797, either at dinner with Godwin at Robinson's on Sunday 22 January 1797[30] or shortly before at tea with Wollstonecraft.[31] Woll-stonecraft and Godwin coincided at Mary Robinson's on 1 June 1796, Godwin having met her regularly since February of that year, which suggests he may have made the introduction.[32]

It is unclear when Mary Hays met Elizabeth Fenwick.[33] Given Fen-wick's involvement in the Godwin household after Mary Wollstonecraft's death, the falling out at this time between Godwin and Hays and the absence of any recorded contact prior to October 1798, it is possible that they did not know each other long before. Fenwick seems to have been introduced to Mary Robinson and spent some time staying at Robinson's cottage in the Summer of 1800 (although Robinson privately confessed

---

[29] It is striking that Godwin's diary suggests that Helen Maria Williams's circle from the late 1780s to May 1791 involved very few women, and none regularly – although it may be that he systematically under-recorded those present in this early phase of his diary keeping.

[30] Hays, *The Correspondence*, p. 305.

[31] Wollstonecraft, *Collected Letters*, no. 296, p. 392.

[32] The most interesting coincidence, however, might be the publication in 1798–1799 of Robinson's *A Letter to the Women of England*, Mary Hays' *Appeal to the Men of Great Britain on Behalf of Women* (1798), edited by Eleanor Ty, 2nd ed. (Toronto, Canada: Broadview Press, 1998), and Mary Anne Radcliffe's, *The Female Advocate, or an Attempt to Recover the Rights of Women from Male Usurpation* (London: Vernor and Hood, 1799). Each of the three expressly cite Wollstonecraft and, while there is no evidence that Mary Ann Radcliffe knew her or the others, the publication of three such tracts suggests a wider movement of positive action. It was also the year of More's *Strictures on the Modern System of Female Education* and these follow the Rev. Richard Polwhele's *The Unsex'd Females: A Poem*, addressed to the author of *The Pursuits of Literature* (London: Cadell and Davis, 1798), for discussion of which see later in this chapter.

[33] And neither Lissa Paul, *Eliza Fenwick: Early Modern Feminist* (Neward, DW: University of Delaware Press, 2019), nor Wedd's edition of Fenwick's correspondence to Mary Hays is really illuminating on that question – such is the serendipity of surviving resources. Annie F. Wedd (ed.), *The Fate of the Fenwicks; Letters to Mary Hays (1798–1828)* (London: Methuen, 1927).

to being in despair at the noise that Fenwick's children made and at the over-attentiveness of Eliza to her young son, Orlando).[34] There is no doubt that Hays and Fenwick became very close and Hays did much to support and help her friend, but it seems likely that this element in their relationship developed around 1798. It also seems likely that Godwin introduced Hays to Alderson on 5 June 1796,[35] but there is no recorded contact between Alderson and Mary Robinson (and while Alderson in December 1795 relates to Godwin something Mary Robinson said in a letter to one of Alderson's acquaintances,[36] this does not indicate any other form of contact). There is also little to suggest much interaction between Alderson and Fenwick, apart from three meetings over a seven-year period (the first and last being at the theatre) and in October 1798 Fenwick was asking Hays to talk to Alderson about the prospect for starting a school in Norwich, suggesting any 'tie' would be very weak.[37] It is also around this time that the Plumptre sisters wrote to Hays asking her to come to tea with them and Alderson before Alderson left town in March 1798 and, then again, without Alderson, in November 1798.[38]

We should also acknowledge that in most cases these women were authors before they came into contact with each other and prior to the more intense period of their interaction around 1796–1799. Wollstonecraft was publishing from 1787; Hays from 1791; Alderson from 1790; Robinson was publishing poetry from the 1770s and her first novel *Vancenza* appeared in 1792. The exception is Elizabeth Fenwick, whose first novel, *Secresy*, was published in 1795. (The outliers are similar: Smith was well established as a novelist and poet by the end of the 1780s; Inchbald's plays were popular from the end of the 1780s and her first major novel, *A Simple Story*, was published in 1791).[39] This is not to say that their work was entirely independent from each other – Inchbald's *Nature and Art* (1796); Wollstonecraft's *Letters Written in Sweden, Norway and Denmark* (1796) and *The Wrongs of Woman, or Maria* (pub posthumously and incomplete in 1798); Hays' *Memoirs of Emma Courtney* (1796), all convey a somewhat shared agenda, while (I shall suggest) Alderson's *Adeline Mowbray* (1805) represents something of a retrospective reflection on the interaction of some of these

---

[34] See Sharon Setzer 'Original Letters of the Celebrated Mrs Mary Robinson', *Philological Quarterly* 88(3) (June 2009), 305–336, Letter 5, 20 August 1800.

[35] See Hays letter to Godwin in *The Correspondence*, 6 June 1796, p. 459 and *The Diary of William Godwin*, 5 June 1796.

[36] Bodleian MS. Abinger c. 3, fol. 2r.   [37] Hays, *The Correspondence*, p. 319.

[38] Ibid., p. 317.

[39] Elizabeth Inchbald, *A Simple Story* (1791), edited by J. M. S. Tomkins (Oxford: Oxford University Press, 1998).

writers a few years later.[40] But, while there is a good deal of productivity, there was not a great deal of interaction.

One reason that this interaction was limited in its frequency (if not its intensity) was that the norms and conventions of wider female society were in operation within the circles in which these women participated. Mary Hays comments in a letter to Godwin dated November 1795, in the course of a discussion of *My Fair Penitent*, in which the heroine has a lover who is not her intended husband,

> ... what humane & benevolent man, uninfluenced by selfish considerations, would wish to subject the woman whom he thought deserving of the highest species of friendship (for this ought marriage to be) to the world's scorn? Supposing that she might have sufficient magnanimity (though the circumstances which attend female education render this improbable) to trample on that scorn – still, she must suffer, & sharp wou'd be the conflict, the arduous struggle: besides which, she is not only shunn'd, as if infected by some contagious disorder, by, even some of the best & worthiest part of society (such has been the controul of prejudice) but, if she possess not an independent fortune, she loses, with the worlds respect, in many cases, the very means of procuring a subsistence ... These reflections recurred to me with additional force from a conversation that recently took place in a company when I was present. The connexion of Mrs Woolstonecraft (sic) with Mr Imlay (which, it is said, has not received a legal sanction) was the subject of discussion. Some ladies present, most amiable and sensible, & worthy, women, expressed their concern on a variety of accounts, & especially lamented that it would no longer be proper for them to visit Mrs W.[41]

Hays, of course, went to her friend's defence, insisting it would not interfere with her own visits. But the women pointed to her lack of experience of society and its tendency to see a single woman associating with someone of this character as someone who would be tempted to make the same mistake.[42] This was about six weeks before Hays brought Godwin and Wollstonecraft together for tea, for their first meeting since the latter's departure for France in 1792.

There was also clear conflict between Wollstonecraft and Inchbald over precisely this issue – and when Godwin upbraided Inchbald for her coldness, she answered frankly if not wholly precisely: 'I did *not* know her – I never wished to know her – as I avoid every female acquaintance

---

[40] Elizabeth Inchbald, *Nature and Art*, vol. 2 (London: G. G. and J. Robinson, 1797); Mary Wollstonecraft, *Letters Written in Sweden, Norway, and Denmark* (1796), edited by Tonne Brekke and Jon Mee (Oxford: Oxford University Press, 2009); Mary Wollstonecraft, *Mary and the Wrongs of Woman* (1798), edited by Gary Kelly (Oxford: Oxford University Press, 2007); Hays' *Memoirs of Emma Courtney* (1796); Amelia Opie, *Adeline Mowbray* (1805), edited by Anne McWhir (Ontario, Canada: Broadview Press, 2010).

[41] Hays, *The Correspondence*, p. 408.   [42] Ibid., pp. 408–409, 20 November 1795.

who has no husband, I avoided her – against my desire you made us acquainted – with what justice I shunned her, your present note evinces, for she judged me harshly; *she first* thought I used her ill, or *you* would not.'[43] Never satisfied, Godwin wrote back, dismissing the Twisses who cut Wollstonecraft on their imagined grounds of 'proper etiquette', and telling Inchbald, as we have seen, 'I think you chose a mean & pitiful conduct, when you might have chosen a conduct that would have done you immortal honour. You had not their excuse. They could not (they pretended) receive her into their precious circles. You kept no circles to debase & enslave you.'[44]

Godwin clearly had a point: Inchbald had little in the way of a 'circle'; her contacts were mainly family friends and connections to the theatre. But he also underestimated how her relative isolation would have made her more dependent on the support of the friends and wider acquaintance that she did have. What he failed to do was to bring her into membership of his circles (indeed, the evidence suggests that she resolutely resisted such inclusion). He assumed she would identify with him because of her talents and her apparent support for progressive ideas – she was clearly unwilling to put at risk what she already had and knew that she could rely on to do that.

Mary Hays, while she defended Wollstonecraft, also had reservations about the conduct of those she met. For example, she expressed herself reluctant to engage with those who took a brighter view of the world than she did:

I thank you for introducing Miss Alderson to me – her spirits appear unbroken – she does not look at if sorrow ever/touch'd her heart. I am not sure her manners entirely pleased me – I mean to say that I have some unfashionable & obsolete notions & prejudices – I love the retiring delicacy that sometimes shrinks from observation. – Assured, fearless & self-satisfied, Miss A must have long since forgotten to blush or to hesitate –.[45]

Alderson, then, was not quite as a young woman should be for Hays. Yet Alderson herself had much respect for *Emma Courtney* – 'I am delighted with Miss Hays's novel! I would give a great deal to have written it.'[46] And in a letter to Godwin of 27 December 1795 she told 'General Godwin' that he had 'a very skilful aide de camp in Captain Mary Hays – I felt two or three almost irresistible impulses while reading Emma Courtney to take up my pen and send her my blessing directly, but did not, for I thought it would seem conceited (as if I thought my praise of

[43] Godwin, *Letters of WG*, i., p. 238.   [44] Ibid., p. 241.
[45] Hays, *The Correspondence*, pp. 459–460.
[46] Wollstonecraft, *Collected Letters*, p. 393; n.828 MS. Abinger c. 41, 18 December 1796.

consequence to her) – so I breathed "blessings not loud but deep"'.[47] Moreover, in November 1796 she was asking Godwin to pass her good wishes on to 'Miss Hayes' – while expostulating 'Fye upon her' for fleeing from the field in response to criticism from Towers.[48] Moreover, Alderson had a degree of awareness as to the dangers she was courting in associating with this group of women, whose reputations were somewhat under siege. And we get a sense that they knew and appreciated this – Mary Wollstonecraft, for example, addressed her 'My dear Girl', a term of endearment not used to others.[49] Godwin introduced Alderson to Wollstonecraft (as Mrs Imlay) on 9 June 1796, taking her to tea at Hays's where Wollstonecraft was present – Hays's reaction was, as we have seen, lukewarm; Wollstonecraft, in contrast, spent the evening with her on 4 August 1796 with some pleasure – 'Elle est trés jolie – n'est pas?'[50]

Two further women are significant in this nexus, one a partial presence, the other an absence. The partial presence is Maria Reveley, who had had an indulgent continental upbringing by her father (who had abandoned her mother and kidnapped their daughter) and whose education was described in the following terms by Mary Shelley: 'Having no proper chaperone, she was left to run wild as she might, and at a very early age had gone through the romance of life.'[51] She married Willey Reveley, whom she met in Italy when she was eighteen, and they struggled financially when her father disowned them. Godwin and Maria had a close friendship that developed an independence from his acquaintance with Willey Reveley, and that prompted his proposal to her in the summer of 1799 after her husband's sudden death. All of which receives the fuller attention it deserves in Chapter 7. But her significance here is that she is one of the few women outside of literary circles who (as far as we can tell) came into regular contact with the core group of Wollstonecraft, Hays, Fenwick and Robinson that I have been discussing.

Godwin could have done us a better service if he had been more scrupulous in his diary in distinguishing when Reveley referred to Maria and when to Willey, and in being more precise as to when 'meet' entries after a visit means that he met people at that visit or met them after – but

---

[47] MS. Abinger c. 3. fol 2r .   [48] MS. Abinger c. 3. fol. 41r.
[49] Wollstonecraft, *Collected Letters*, p. 408, 11 April 1797.
[50] Alderson referred to Wollstonecraft as Mrs Imlay in a letter dated 17 August 1796 (MS binger c.3., for 33–34). Wollstonecraft's assessment of Alderson is in *Collected Letters*, no 225, p. 345, 4 August 1796.
[51] Kegan Paul, *William Godwin*, 1.82. See also Edward Pope's paper on William Godwin, The Reveleys and the Jenningses of 8 February 2012 on his website exploring the Godwin circles.

it looks as if Maria Reveley met and knew, at least slightly, all the women in this group – including Inchbald (possibly) and Alderson – with the exception of Mary Robinson (in part because her residence was rather out of town), although Reveley certainly seems to have met Robinson's daughter (at a theatre outing). Contact with Hays seems to have been slight; contact with Fenwick in the aftermath of Wollstonecraft's death and in the beginning of 1798 was more intensive; and contact with Wollstonecraft, although certainly not fully recorded in Godwin's diary, seems to have blossomed into a more substantial friendship – to the point that Wollstonecraft was able to share some gentle mockery of Godwin in a conspiratorial note to Reveley. The note implies that they both knew of his tendency to write in French in relation to affairs of the heart and it suggests they had both experienced Godwin's susceptibility to enthusiastic female admirers of his work. Godwin had missed a previous dinner, when he was away from London visiting Parr and Thomas Wedgwood in Etruria, and Wollstonecraft wrote to Reveley to say that the same group was to be re-united just after his return: 'Pray come or he will be *in despair* (that ought to have been said in French) at not being able to keep his engagement with you). Your coming to this party is not to prevent you from paying me a visit *hap-hazard*, alone, when I will shew you one of Mr Godwin's epistles, I mean one addressed to him, from another Fair in intellectual distress – But this *entre nous*.'[52] There were also notes about visits involving their respective children (Fanny Imlay and Reveley's son Henry). Similarly, the links with Eliza Fenwick became strong: Fenwick was with the Reveleys when Willey Reveley was taken ill in the summer of 1799 and she stayed to provide support for Maria following his death. In the case of both women, there is clear evidence of a friendship and set of connections that goes beyond the record in Godwin's diary.

The second person, notable by her absence, is the novelist Ann Radcliffe. Her husband was a professed sympathiser with democratic principles, and they were certainly in London in March–May 1794 and in May and August 1795, since they met Godwin on a number of occasions, but there is no record of them mixing more widely – indeed, barely any trace of them even in Farington.[53] There is no correspondence

---

[52] Wollstonecraft, *Collected Letters*, no. 334, pp. 424–425, 26 June 1797.

[53] Farington, *Diary*. Radcliffe's literary output in this decade is prodigious: Ann Radcliffe, *A Sicilian Romance* (1790), edited by Alison Milbank (Oxford: Oxford University Press, 1993); *The Romance of the Forest* (1791), edited by Chloe Chard (Oxford: Oxford University Press, 1999); *Mysteries of Udolpho* (1794), edited by Bonamy Dobrée and Terry Castle (Oxford: Oxford University Press, 2008); *The Italian* (1797), edited by Nick Groom (Oxford: Oxford University Press, 2017). Yet these texts are largely devoid of political sentiments – and remain widely embraced by respectable literary culture.

(even with Godwin: we know he wrote to her, but no letters survive). Like Fanny Burney, but without her political views, Radcliffe was not part of this particular slice of literary London and seems to have had no interest in exploring it further – although the control exercised by her husband over her legacy after she died suggests that he may also have had fairly firm views of the importance of maintaining propriety.

What I have tried to do thus far is to take a careful look at the evidence we have for interaction between the women writers whom we associate with support for France and for reform in Britain in the 1790s. The results are not very encouraging. Many of these women seem to be rather isolated; they move in their own circles; a few interact with each other with any intensity only briefly (around 1796–1798) and then in different groups from around the 1800s. Part of this rather fragmented picture may well be to do with professional jealousy and competition (see, for example Charlotte Smith's letter to Thomas Cadell, in which she mentions speaking to Inchbald, and in which she complains about the price received for her work in comparison to her competitors).[54] Some is a matter of domestic circumstances: Smith, Fenwick, Robinson and Wollstonecraft had responsibilities for children while desperately trying to make a living; and those who were (or had been) married (Robinson, Inchbald, Smith and Fenwick) rarely found being so a source of solace. It is also clear that Inchbald and Smith, at least, were conscious of a need to avoid reputational damage if they were to sustain an audience for their work and if they were to maintain the coterie of friends and acquaintance in which they were supported and valued. They were also very clear about their vulnerability to a hostile press, who reached for the easy trope of incontinent sexual conduct as a way of tarnishing their reputations.[55] The major drop in subscriptions from 817 to 283 for Charlotte Smith's *Elegiac Sonnets* between the 1784 edition and the 1797 edition is indicative of some of the damage done to her reputation by her political leanings. In contrast, Mary Robinson had little to lose in terms of reputation or with respect to women's acceptance and she relied on a group of predominantly male admirers from her past – although the predatory behaviour of her lover Colonel Tarleton towards her daughter speaks eloquently to her consequent vulnerability. As for Wollstonecraft, she was clearly not prepared to produce a second child out of wedlock if she could avoid it and had no choice but to brace herself for the reaction to the collapse of her standing as Mrs Imlay as the lesser of two evils.

[54] Smith, *Collected Letters*, pp. 279–280.
[55] see Kenneth Johnston, *Unusual Suspects* (Oxford: Oxford University Press, 2013), pt 2, pp. 113–116.

In wider circles Hays was simply mocked and vilified – despite her having what were, on her own account, rather old-fashioned notions of propriety and decorum ('I am not sufficiently French in manners ...').[56] In many respects, then, this was an increasingly hostile environment for women who strayed from the norms of propriety and/or who sought to speak out in relation to politics in the wider public culture (where that transgression was often reacted to with insinuations implying manifold others). They faced political reaction and ridicule, aspersions were frequently cast on their personal lives and conduct and they faced reaction from within their own circles insofar as their conduct was perceived to be unorthodox.

One irony here is the extent to which the linking theme across a great deal of their work was the critique of contemporary manners and social conventions. And their interest in Godwin was often in the idea that private judgement and involvement in deliberative discussion should guide conduct and that societal prejudices and norms should be criticised and set aside in favour of the fuller and freer expression of – indeed the living out of – their ideas, principles and commitments.[57] In particular, as women, they were conscious of the greater constraints that operated on their sex and they were also articulate about the extent to which women themselves were often responsible for the exclusion and isolation of other women. But it is also true that they did not need the stimulation of the febrile political atmosphere of London in 1794–1799 to be conscious of this since they would have had myriad earlier experiences of the oppressively restricting order of society that women encountered. The developing hostilities in the political press towards those who questioned the social and political order nonetheless forced them and their associates to make decisions about sides and about how far they wanted to appear to their public in ways that might bring considerable costs. The French Revolution may well have encouraged their explicit articulation of these views, but they were hardly responding to a new experience. Insofar as they had a sense that there might be a more enlightened age dawning, it must also be said that, in practical terms, they critiqued boundaries more often than they transgressed them (save when in France – as with Wollstonecraft and Helen Maria Williams – which was also a wider trope – mistresses and unfaithful wives of the élite tended to use the continent for their amours and to give birth to their illegitimate offspring). We do not, for example, find much evidence in the correspondence of

---

[56] Hays, *The Correspondence*, p. 444.

[57] Or, as Mary Hays emphasises in *The Victim of Prejudice* (London, 1799), edited by Eleanor Ty (Toronto, Canada: Broadview Press, 1998), what they saw as central was 'independence'!

these women of a willingness to reach out to the silent female cohabitants that littered London, even if in their novels they were prepared to defend those who fell victim to masculine desire.[58] If we reflect on our earlier discussions of the disinterested friendships among men and the place of gossip in monitoring and shaping the behaviour of women in their circles and familial settings, we can see some of these women as gesturing to the former and as trying to establish a different kind of relationship based upon intellectual interests and affinities, but these possibilities seem to be dramatically more curtailed for women than for men and more consistently subjected to the discipline of being talked over by others.

These women were certainly not entirely conventional. Wollstonecraft and Robinson were far from being so; Hays put some practical commitment behind being taken seriously by men of her acquaintance; and it is difficult to know quite how unconventional Maria Reveley had ventured to be. Above all, they were tolerant of each other and their choices and could see the grounds for their unconventionality. Indeed, even those who look most committed to the protection of reputation and conformity to traditional norms were not uniformly so. In Inchbald's diary for 1793, she records dining with her old actor friends Mary Lane Whitfield and her husband John on a regular basis, usually at the Whitfields. Boaden reported that 'Mrs Whitfield seems to have occupied the first place (of her female friends) most decidedly this year (1787): they could hardly pass a day apart, and they lived near each other.'[59] Then on 8 July Inchbald recorded 'Heard Miss Whitfield was gone off with a gentleman'; on 10 July 'Heard what had befallen Miss Whitfield'; and on 14 July 'dined at Mr Babbs, Miss Whitfield there'; on 16 August 'Mrs Whitfield and Miss Whitfield dined here'; and on 7 September 'Witnessed Miss Whitfield's articles'. This succession of events is pretty cryptic but nonetheless suggestive. The Whitfields were two of Inchbald's oldest friends from her theatrical past – who had eloped together to France in 1771 in the same year Inchbald went to London and first met her husband. She was alive to their interests and would have been anxious for their daughter and concerned that the issue be resolved satisfactorily – as it seems to have been, through something like

---

[58] As in Wollstonecraft's *Wrongs of Woman* (1798), Hays' *The Victim of Prejudice* (1799), Inchbald's *Nature and Art* (1796), Mary Robinson's picaresque novels on speed, *The Natural Daughter* (1799), edited by Sharon M. Selzer (Toronto, Canada: Broadview Press, 2003) and *Walsingham, or the Pupil of Nature* (1797), edited by Julie A. Shaffer (Toronto, Canada: Broadview Press, 2003), and Alderson's *The Father and Daughter* (1801), written as Amelia Opie.

[59] James Boaden, *Memoirs of Mrs Inchbald, Including Her Familiar Correspondence …*, 2 vols. (London: R Bentley, 1833), v. 1, p. 251.

a cover-up and her signing-up to an apprenticeship. She did not have a problem with seeing the girl, probably because she was effectively 'family', perhaps also because the event was one which might be disguised and forgotten, and almost certainly only because the girl must have proved repentant and tractable. But it is clear that Inchbald would have responded differently to someone who sought to vindicate their conduct, unless the elopement issued in marriage. Miss Whitfield was not a reputational threat to Inchbald, but she perceived an association with Wollstonecraft to pose precisely that problem.[60]

Perhaps more surprising was the presence of Mary Wells (1762–1829) in Inchbald's diary, even though she was living with and had three children by Edward Topham,[61] who subsequently abandoned her, taking the three girls.[62] Again, Wells and Inchbald went back a long way. But Inchbald also knew that she was taking some reputational risk. Boaden says that, in 1787:

Her next favourite was Mrs Wells, who stood her ground notwithstanding the discreditable mode of her living with Topham. They (Inchbald and Wells) sometimes proposed a separation; and it often, we confess, surprised us to hear of the connexion: it could proceed from no impure sympathy, or even indifference to worldly maxims, on the part of Mrs Inchbald. She was above all suspicion herself, and her friend greatly below it.[63]

---

[60] BL, diaries, 1793 RP 2266, 1782 RP 4730.

[61] See Charles Pigott, *The Jockey Club* (London, 1792), pt II, pp. 91–93; pt III (1793), pp. 93–96. Both comment on Topham's relationship to Wells.

[62] Inchbald's diary for 1783 records a developing familiarity between the two women (Wells came to London in 1781), which was still well established in the 1788 diary (and on 23 June 1788 Wells called on Inchbald with her child (by Topham)). The only references in 1793 are 10 May 1793 – 'Yesterday heard Mrs Wells in a mad house' – and 10 September 1793 – 'Mrs Wells call'd _refused to see her'. In 1807, 10 July, 'Spoke with Mrs Wells in the streets'; and in 1808, 23 March, 'Mrs Wells called _ I would not send her money. She asked for a subscription. Mrs Wells called below'. Topham also has a number of entries in the diary (in 1788 only), but several of the entries indicate that he stays 'some time'. There is no record of her seeing Wells and Topham together and on the one occasion she calls on Topham she mentions drinking tea with Charles Este. (Farington has no entries on Wells, and Topham is mentioned only in relation to his employment of Heriot on the *World*; his criticism of Turner in 1804; and his attendance at a boat race in 1807). Farington also barely mentions Inchbald, although he noted in 1798–1799 that she had recently spent much time with Lady Abercorn, who eloped with a Captain Copley (Lord Abercorn's brother in law by his first wife), with Farington implying that Inchbald had been coaching her in a theatrical part (concerning the manner of leaving her children – although the *Ipswich Journal* of 17 November 1798 (page 3 – doubtless drawing on one of the London papers) described the Marchioness as 'wholly incapable of disingenuous artifice'). There's no evidence that Inchbald knew the Marchioness and neither Abercorn or Copley appear in her diaries (although we do not have them for those years), so it may all be entirely unsubstantiated, possibly malicious, gossip!

[63] Boaden, *Memoirs of Mrs Inchbald*, p. 251.

If there is a consistency here it seems to be that Inchbald was loyal to those in her past who had befriended and helped her in her theatrical career; that she herself sought to protect her own reputation; and that she was averse to relationships that involved new risks. She was also not a risk taker in venturing abroad: when she wrote to John Taylor about his writing a preface for a play she had written she wanted him to be clear about what she felt was of value in it:

Urge but with due modesty the Simplicity and also the Unity of the story. Then plead as my excuse for not giving greater variety of character in my habits of retirement, my sex, which forbids me the resorts of busy men – She (ie: Inchbald) cannot walk the Royal or Stock Exchange, feast at a Tavern Dinner, peep into a Coffee house &c. All her pretentions are sometimes to find a Window to the heart. Where as she takes a stolen glance she/beholds passions seen in embrio small as an atom – others full grown; and so varied, mingled, Riotous and contentious as near to burst the tender habitation. They are passions then, she undertakes to paint not manners.[64]

Moreover, it might also be that the changing political atmosphere of the 1790s, the ready recourse by loyalist writers to slurs of sexual incontinence and French ideas (see, for example, Hannah More's and John Bowles' claims that women were being corrupted by an imitation of French manners) had added greatly to the risks associated with becoming a public character linked to those known to be sympathetic to reform.[65] Nonetheless, Inchbald did not take the attitude to Mme de Stael that Fanny Burney took.[66]

We might characterise Inchbald as socially and professionally 'risk averse' and Hays perhaps as a risk-taker, at least in what she wrote, and also, to some degree, in the way she tried to live, given her friendships with William Frend and subsequently with Charles Lloyd. Inchbald was contained; Hays seems anything but. And yet, if we look at the sources we have for how Hays in fact behaved, there was little with which people might take exception. The vast majority of her contact with Godwin was conducted at her lodgings or at another person's home. She has tea at Godwin's twice, he has tea with her over twenty times; he calls on her nearly fifty times, she calls on him on fourteen occasions (which might

[64] Bod Lib. MS Eng Misc e 143 Letter book of James Northcote, fol 28r–v.
[65] More, *Strictures on the Modern System of Female Education*, p. 100. John Bowles, *Remarks on Modern Female Manners, as Distinguished by Indifference to Character and Indecency of Dress* (London: F. and C. Rivington, 1802).
[66] Burney, *Diary and Letters*, p. 237. Compare Boaden, *Memoirs of Mrs Inchbald*, v. 2, pp. 190–191. But Burney seems to be extremely risk-averse – which might be a function of her sense of the insecurity of her position, perhaps because she had connections to the court but was of relatively low status.

well mean merely that she dropped off a letter). We know from her correspondence that she had a landlady and a servant who may have operated in the character of chaperones,[67] and she reported that she was not accustomed to receiving visitors before mid-day or when dressing. She also said that she would be pleased if she and Godwin could meet one day with Mr Holcroft 'when there is not too much company. Mr H need not trouble himself to procure ladies to meet me, his daughter is sufficient, I am more used to, and therefore more at ease in, the company of men.'[68] All of which suggests that she was as concerned about the proprieties of how they met as much as other women were concerned about their reputations and social acceptance. And when Hays was pilloried it seems to have been largely (initially) by men – until the publication of *Emma Courtney*. Although Elizabeth Hamilton, who took Hays' review of her *Translation of a Hindoo Rajah* badly, took her vengeance in the character of Bridgetina Botheram in her *Memoirs of Modern Philosophers* (1800).

While Hays' letters were extended expressions of her feelings and beliefs and would have been imprudent written to many men, Godwin respected her privacy – and he was somewhat engaged (if in a very self-disciplined way) with the problem she posed to him – namely the achievement of a more philosophical perspective on the pressures, inequalities and resulting contradictions and turmoil of women's social and thus emotional worlds. She treated him as an authority, but also as an equal; she was deeply critical of his rationalism and yet looked to it as a way of disciplining her emotional life and reconciling her to her lot. She believed that he sympathised with her predicament and her sorrows. Indeed, following the meeting she arranged with Mary Wollstonecraft in January 1796, Hays pointed to Wollstonecraft's new recognition of Godwin's sensibility and goodness of heart, which, 'tho' a dear friend, the other evening, affected to rally you upon it, she has told me, that it has raised you greatly in her esteem'.[69] At the same time, she seems to have presumed too much of Godwin in expecting him to respond to her needs and we can see their relationship coming under increasing strain before Wollstonecraft's death. Godwin may have thought he could reason her out of her condition, but it became clear that she believed that that was inappropriate and that she was looking for sympathy and

---

[67] Hays, *The Correspondence*, p. 444.

[68] Ibid., p. 443. Inchbald wrote to John Taylor 'though I prefer the society of men to that of my own sex, and would dine with any one or even two gentlemen in company – Yet for even the return of youth and beauty I would not encounter above two men at one dinner, and they must both be old acquaintances.' Bod Lib. MS Eng. Misc. e.143. fol 55r–v.

[69] Hays, *The Correspondence*, p. 422.

support, more than guidance. His response, as in one of his letters, seems to be that, just because doing so would be useful is 'no sufficient reason. I must not only do things useful, but out of the various utilities select the best'.[70]

Were men similarly scrutinised and influenced? They seem to have been much less so. They had wider circles of acquaintance, were less likely to be examined or condemned for irregular personal conduct (unless – as we have seen in Chapter 2 – they thrust it in the public domain in the way Godwin did in his *Memoirs*), and they had stronger professional connections and contacts that they could rely on (or thought they could rely on) into the future. William Beloe, for example, commented

Generally speaking, in London at least, there is great liberality among literary men, a ready disposition to interchange communications, which may be mutually useful, to accommodate one another with the loan of books, to point out sources of information, indeed to carry on, by sort of common treaty among one another, a pleasant, friendly and profitable commerce.[71]

This speaks to the distinction drawn earlier between strong and weak ties. Men had many more weak ties by which they were also connected to a wider world and they worked some of their weaker ties and encounters up to become deeper, disinterested, intellectual relationships. They were both more in the moment and seemed more protected from it by their connections.

Nonetheless, it is worth reflecting further on what men might have been looking for in their relations with others. There is much to be said for the view that they were not primarily interested in acquaintance as a way of serving their interests, but were looking for friendships founded on sympathy, mutual understandings and disinterested commitment. Certainly Godwin, Holcroft and a number of their close associates were often barely reliant on family connections and, in the first seven or eight years of the 1790s, seem primarily concerned to establish close intellectual and deliberative relationships. They saw themselves as pushing back the darkness of political, religious and social institutions, through the exercise of reason and judgement in discussion. That ambition does not seem to have been as widely evident among women, although it was an ambition that at least some manifested in the form of contributions to public, printed debate. But with respect to personal deliberative

---

[70] Ibid., p. 462.
[71] William Beloe, *The Sexagenarian: Or the Recollections of a Literary Life*, 2 vols. (London: F. and C. Rivington, 1817), i, p. 196.

relations, this was for the most part a question of a type of relationship conceived of by men as something that they sought with other men. Moreover, as we have seen, several women (such as Hays, Robinson and Williams) shared rather negative expectations of other women while themselves wanting a seat at a largely masculine table of discussion. At least among these writers there was not a strong sense of a desire for a deeper form of female solidarity that excluded men. But this raised a further set of issues: How far was it possible for more egalitarian relationships to function between men and these women? How clearly could the boundaries of intellectual relationships be established without risk of being seen as evidence of unorthodox social or sexual relationships? And how far was this a case of conforming to an extremely masculine discourse at which they would inevitably be at a disadvantage? We can see from Kathryn Gleadle's work on British youth at the time of the French Revolution[72] that there was an intense sense of a cultural shift (at least in some places, such as Norwich) that was registered even (perhaps especially) by the young and that led them to expect (and sometimes to demand) more egalitarian treatment from their elders and associates. And it is clear that this was also true for at least some of the women who interacted with Godwin's circles in the 1790s – such as Sarah Anne Parr, Amelia Alderson, Nan Pinkerton and others. We can begin to grasp some of the complexities of these relationships by considering Godwin's relationship to several of these women in particular.

There is, however, a supplementary question, in the light of the discussion of this chapter and Chapter 3, about how far these women – whom I have argued were for the main only very loosely connected – were responded to by loyalists and those committed to moral reform. Was theirs an individual or collective public profile, to what extent was it one that was anathematised and how was that done?

4.2   Identifying the 'Unsex'd'

In William Beloe's, *The Sexagenarian: Or the Recollections of a Literary Life* (1817), Alderson was lumped together with Wollstonecraft, Hays, Helen Maria Williams and Ann Plumptre (and to a much lesser extent Elizabeth Inchbald) for a collective telling off, with some personal jibes thrown in for good measure. Alderson was described as follows: '... the flattering attentions she received from her childhood, so far spoiled her,

---

[72] Kathryn Gleadle, 'The Juvenile Enlightenment: British Children and Youth during the French Revolution', *Past and Present* 233 (November 2016), 143–184.

that whatever she does, or says, or writes, is somewhat tinged with vanity and self-conceit, and that perhaps no more perfect picture was ever exhibited in society, of a *Precieuse*.'[73] And the collective picture was sharply dismissive:

Oh for the good old times! When females were satisfied with feminine employments, with cultivating their minds so far as to enable them to instruct their children in useful learning only, and to regulate their families with judicious economy; to learn those graces and that demeanour, which obtained and secured love and esteem, nor suffered the Laban images of foreign vanities to contaminate their tents. Daughters of England, be not beguiled; be assured that the study of politics is not essential to female accomplishments, that the possession of this Machiavellian knowledge will neither make you better mothers, wives, or friends; that to obtain it, a long life, severe study, and the most laborious investigation are indispensably necessary.[74]

Beloe's view was retrospective, as were the memoirs referring to Inchbald written by James Boaden and John Taylor. As such, it does not seem to have been quite as obvious to men and women at the time that this was a group that was at the heart of a new morality. One basis for thinking that they were seen as a group comes from Richard Polwhele's *The Unsex'd Females* (1798), which combined a wide and varied group for satiric condemnation – Wollstonecraft, Hays, Barbauld, Ann Jebb, Mary Robinson, Helen Maria Williams, Charlotte Smith, Miss Aikin, Angelica Kaufmann, Emma Crewe, and Ann Yearsely – implying a strong sense that there was a group of women writers and painters who were to 'Gallic freaks or Gallic faith resign'd'.[75] That text drew most heavily on three sources: George Dyer's *Poems* (1792); the fourth part of T. J. Mathias's *Pursuits of Literature* (1797) and Godwin's *Memoirs of the Author*.[76] Dyer's Ode VII 'On Liberty' refers directly to Wollstonecraft's second *Vindication* and claims that 'the most sensible females, when they turn their attention to political subjects, are more uniformly on the side of liberty than the other sex', explaining this by their need to resist the tyranny of

---

[73] Beloe, *The Sexagenarian*, p. 415.   [74] Ibid., p. 364.

[75] Polwhele, *The Unsex'd Females*. See William Stafford's detailed analysis in *English Feminists and their Opponents in the 1790s: Unsex'd and Proper Females* (Manchester: Manchester University Press, 2002), chapter 1; Eleanor Ty, *Unsex'd Revolutionaries: Five Women Novelists of the 1790s* (Toronto, Canada: University of Toronto Press, 1993); and Katherine Binhammer, 'The Sex Panic of the 1790s', *Journal of the History of Sexuality* 6(3) (January 1996), 409–434, although it is not clear that the decade is especially unique.

[76] George Dyer, *Poems* (London: J. Johnson, 1792); Thomas Mathias, *The Pursuits of Literature: A Satirical Poem in Dialogue. With Notes. Part the Fourth and Last* (London: T. Becket, 1797); William Godwin, *Memoirs of the Author of A Vindication of the Rights of Woman* (London: J. Johnson and G. G. and J. Robinson, 1798).

custom. He went on to mention Ann Jebb, Helen Maria Williams, Mrs Laetitia Barbauld, Mrs Charlotte Smith and Miss Hays ('an admirer and imitator of Mrs Charlotte Smith'). T. J. Mathias provides the epigraph and title for Polwhele's poem – 'Our unsex'd female writers now instruct, or confuse, us and themselves, in the labyrinth of politics, or turn us wild with Gallic frenzy',[77] and he had earlier referenced 'Mrs Charlotte Smith, Mrs Inchbald, Mrs Mary Robinson, Mrs &c. &c., though all of them are very ingenious ladies, yet they are most frequently *whining* or *frisking* in novels, til our girls' heads turn wild with impossible adventures, and now and then are tainted with democracy – not so the mighty magician of the MYSTERIES OF UDOLPHO.'[78] The most extensive satirical comment in Polwhele's poem was reserved for Wollstonecraft, and she, and Godwin's *Memoirs*, provide the rising crescendo to the work, but it is striking how little precedes this in terms of identifying a coterie of women.[79]

Indeed, although there were barbs in various places against individual women writers in the early and mid-1790s, when *The Decline and Fall, Death, Dissection, and Funeral Procession of his most contemptible lowness the London Corresponding Society, &c.* (1796)[80] was published it contained a satiric reference to 'Six virtuous female citizens, All clad in white, walking two and two' and singing 'the following patriotic lines in praise of modesty:

> Brightest gem upon the earth,
> *Mother Windsor* gave thee birth;
> Sister of chaste Dian's train,
> Like our *Armstead*, without stain.
> O! though *Luna* of King's Place,
> Joy of *Copenhagen* Race;
> *Jones's* bronze and *Thelwall's* eye
> Heave, O! heave, a heavy sigh;
> For the London Corresponding Society is for ever gone,
> And all the *Modesty* of REBELLION *is undone.*'

[77] Mathias, *Pursuits of Literature*, p. 238.

[78] *Pursuits of Literature*, First Dialogue (London, 1794), p. 58.

[79] It also, as Stafford points out, drew on George Dyer's *Poems*, in which Dyer identified the most sensible women, who are on the side of liberty, as Macaulay, Wollstonecraft, Barbauld, Jebb, Williams, Smith and Hays. See the discussion of Mathias and Polwhele in Amy Garnai, *Revolutionary Imaginings in the 1790s: Charlotte Smith, Mary Robinson, Elizabeth Inchbald* (Basingstoke, Hampshire: Palgrave/Macmillan, 2009), pp. 5–6, 71, 81–82.

[80] Anon, *The Decline and Fall, Death, Dissection, and Funeral Procession of his Most Contemptible Lowness the London Corresponding Society, &c.* (London: George Cawthorn, 1796), pp. 22–23.

The six virtuous females are

Citizen Armstead,	Citizen Benwell,
Citizen Windsor,	Citizen Malton,
Citizen Maynard,	Citizen *Lady Brown*.

This was satire that relied on a knowing and élite audience. It mentioned some of the reformers late from the Treason Trials (including Tooke, Thelwall, Holcroft, and Joyce) and also Citizen Lee, but when pillorying women it produced none of those we now associate with radicalism in the capital. Instead, we have Fox's mistress Mrs Armistead (by then his wife, but undeclared); a reference to Nancy Parsons, then Lady Maynard, who had a long career as mistress to members of the élite and as a prostitute, before marrying Lord Maynard with whom she then conducted an open marriage[81]; Mrs Benwell who was probably an actress (and was attacked for her size in the Morning Herald on 1 March 1793 and linked with Nancy Parson at Brighton in August (29) 1798 by the *Oracle and Public Advertiser*'s gossip columns; and Mrs Windsor (whom Vic Gattrell describes as a 'bawd'[82]). The reference to Malton may have been to the wife of the architect and engraver – although that remains puzzling.[83] And Mrs Brown may have been a reference to the estranged natural daughter of Lord Thurlow (by Polly Humphries – who ran Nando's Coffee House), who married a man with what her father regarded as no education or conversation. For all Thurlow's support for Pitt, he was in his later years (around this time) also very close to John Horne Tooke. This looks like an attack on Fox and his friends (who are represented as including the treason trial defendants) and on the fashionable 'ton' – but this choice suggests that the links between the reform organisations and their agenda and women's literary circles were not obvious to contemporaries, perhaps until Godwin's *Memoirs* gave satirists a richer vein to exploit, which they did in part by widening the scope of the attack to other authors (and artists) and from whiggish politics and élite blue-stockings to a wider swathe of contributors to the literary world.

Nonetheless, it is worth being cautious in assuming that 1798 marked some form of conclusive turning point. Hays, Robinson, Smith and Inchbald continued to produce work and, as we have seen, there are indications that the degree of intimacy between Hays, Fenwick and Robinson increased at the end of the decade. And there was something

---

[81] See ODNB, and Pigott's *The Jockey Club*, Pt 1, pp. 9–11 and *Female Jockey Club*, pp. 124–125.

[82] Gattrell, *City of Laughter*, pp. 406, 408, 688.

[83] The Mrs Malton we have encountered in Chapter 3, who was a close associate of Eliza Soane.

of a resurgence in 1798–1800, with a number of (now much less well known) novels coming from this group and a cluster of pamphlets on women's rights by Hays, Robinson and Mary Ann Radcliffe.

The other thing to consider is that the attacks on these women were not, for the most part, distressingly invasive (whereas Godwin must have felt that the reviews of his *Memoirs* of Wollstonecraft were). Indeed, if we look at the caricatures of the period, we can find very few references to this group – and references are often merely allusive. Many historians tend to treat the graphic satires of the period as a commentary on the times that would have been legible to a wide audience, leaving no indiscretion unmasked, but it is striking how narrow its representations were.

Although Polwhele's *Unsex'd Females* was a product of Anti-Jacobin circles which employed Gillray, there was almost no visual representation of the majority of these women.[84] The one exception was Mary 'Perdita' Robinson, who was represented in some forty-two caricatures produced between 1780 and 1812. But the vast majority of these come from between 1782–1784 and concern her relationships with the Prince of Wales and Fox, and most of the later prints include her in relation to either or both these men. The one print to cite her writing was Gillray's monumental *New Morality; – or – the Promis'd Instalment of the High Priest of the Theophilanthropes, with the Homage of Leviathan and his Suite* (July 1798), which depicts a cornucopia spewing forth radical texts, one of which bears the title of her novel *Walsingham, or the Pupil of Nature* (1797). That print swept up a wide range of reference to radical – or merely unconventional – thought: and it encompassed Charlotte Smith, Helen Maria Williams and Mary Wollstonecraft. But none of them were personally caricatured – rather we can identify them only because of reference to their books. Moreover, Gillray included only four of the women on Polwhele's list. There was an earlier print where Barbauld and Williams appear together along with Macaulay – '*Don Dismallo Running the Gauntlet* '(1790), but that was the only occasion on which a group of radical women were personified. And most radical men were not treated so differently – Godwin appears as a braying ass reading *Political Justice* in 'New Morality', but his subsequent appearances are entirely in the form of references to his books: as in BMS 9286 (1798) [*Frontispiece from an Unidentified Pamphlet*]; BMS 9371 (1799) *The Night Mare*; BMS 9522

---

[84] Using the indexes and cataloguing in Dorothy George's compendious Catalogue of Prints in the British Museum. The collection is not complete, but it is very extensive and I have found no exceptions in the 2,000 or so British prints that are held in the Bibliotheque National de France or in those held in the John Johnson and Curzon collections in the Bodleian.

(1800) *The Apple and the Horse Turds*; and BMS 11941 (1812) *The Genius of the Times*.

This relative paucity of representation should give us pause. It seems probable that satirical prints and caricatures were largely designed for an élite rather than a wide popular audience, that they relied heavily on representing people in ways that would be legible to people in the know, and they were deeply entangled in the world of contemporary parliamentary and court politics. The sweeping up of the odd literary radical in a print was a way of casting slurs on the *literati*, but there was no real point in representing them – not least because they were not widely known and would not be recognisable. Theatrical women like Robinson (who was constantly in the centre of society in the 1780s) would be recognised by élite males, who doubtless enjoyed the representation of her apparent availability. In contrast, Inchbald's only appearance in caricature is a walk-on part in BMC 9086 (1797) *A theatrical candidate*, in which Sheridan objects to his stutter and the candidate replies 'So did Mrs Inchbald'. The other radical women were not known in this way – and the representation of Williams, Barbauld and Macaulay/Graham in *Don Dismallo* relies on a near explicit identification in the print (Miss H M W__s; Mrs B———d; Mrs M__y G____m) and on their reputation as respondents to Burke's *Reflections* rather than by their being 'recognisable'.

For the buyers, renters and viewers of prints, reference to these women's work could be carried merely by allusion to their writing and, despite the invitation to salacious representation that Godwin offered in his *Memoirs*, there was no real interest in taking that up. How then to understand Polwhele's little barb? We probably need to think of it as having a different type of circulation – a jeu-d'esprit in literary terms (or a set of nasty patronising male jibes) directed to a classically informed and élite audience intended to ridicule its targets and entertain its readers. Not so different from prints, perhaps, save that the literary form allowed greater licence and more express identification and thereby recognition.[85]

The lack of much interest in representing the literary radicals can also be seen in relation to male radicals. Seen from the perspective of the satires and prints, the struggle was largely a parliamentary one, and it relied on a familiar cast of characters, often with references (such as to their flings with Mrs Robinson) dating back many years. And it is worth

---

[85] The different circles of circulation are also indicated by the fact that seditious writings were prosecuted throughout the decade, whereas, as M. Dorothy George says in the Introduction to vol. VII of the *Catalogue of Political and Personal Satires Preserved in the Department of Prints and Drawings in the British Museum* (London: The British Museum, 1942), vol. vii, p. xvi: 'Purely political proceedings involving graphic satire seems to be limited to the case of Peltier, prosecuted at the instance of Napoleon.'

noting how gradual the assimilation of new characters was. Entering politics in 1793–1794, George Canning makes two early appearances, where his identity relies on a report he is carrying of the (wholly unrelated) trial of Betty Canning and in a third he is represented as a schoolboy. His first real personification is in December 1797 in Cruikshank's *The Victorious Procession to St Pauls. Or Billy's Grand Triumphal Entry*, some four years into his parliamentary career.

Similarly, the representation of male radicals was strongly skewed to the parliamentary and historical. Horne Tooke has a long history of appearance that was exploited; but Hardy was referred to rather than represented until *A. Alan. Gardiner.* (BMC 8814) in June 1796; and while Thelwall features more widely, it is difficult to detect a settled representation and most versions included references to his lectures to identify him. There were three or four portrayals of a wider array of radicals by Robert Newton: *A Peep into the State Side of Newgate*, *Soulagement en prison* and *Promenade on the State Side of Newgate* were commissioned as group portraits by Holland, but they are not caricatures.[86] When popular radicals were caricatured it was usually in forms that did not rely on recognising them as individuals, but as types: see, for example, *London Corresponding Society alarm'd*. The prints suggest that the audience does not know them and does not need to know them – the type is enough.

Indeed, if there is a moral panic in this period in relation to female conduct, it seems as much directed against the élite and what they wear rather than against the literary radicals. The caricaturing of women's fashions seems to have had a resurgence after 1796, with critiques of a 'Directory style', that favoured loose clothing and the exposure of décolletage, and occasionally more, coupled with suggestions of a growing laxity in public morals, also derived from the French and supported by the modern system of infidelity and modern philosophy – that

holds up gratitude to contempt and which despises the sacred impulses of paternal love and filial piety … a Philosophy which inculcates to every individual that his own casual and capricious notions of right and wrong are to supersede those ancient rules, which are taught by divine wisdom, or established on the basis of human experience, and which have hitherto been regarded with reverence, and considered as the tests and bulwarks of morality …[87]

---

[86] See Iain McCalman, 'Newgate in Revolution: Radical Enthusiasm and Romantic Counterculture', *Eighteenth-Century Life* 22 (February 1998), 95–110; Mee, *Print Publicity and Political Radicalism*, chapter 4; and David Alexander, *Richard Newton and English Caricature in the 1790s* (Manchester: Manchester University Press, 1998), pp. 36–38.

[87] John Bowles, *Reflections on the Political and Moral State of Society at the Close of the Eighteenth Century*, 2nd ed. (London: Rivington, 1801), p. 127. It is at this point that Bowles praises Mackintosh's lectures on the Law of Nature and Nations.

The arch loyalist John Bowles saw concerns with luxury and matters of dress as indicative of corruption. 'Cultivated manners are calculated chiefly to make an impression on cultivated minds; but dress is more exclusively an object of sense, and it is, therefore, most fitted to operate on the mass of Society.'[88] And, in his later *Remarks on Modern Female Manners* (1802), which was partly drawn from the earlier publication, he launched an unrestrained attack on contemporary female fashion. For Bowles, 'Female modesty is the last barrier of civilised society. When *that* is removed, what remains to stem to torrent of licentiousness and profligacy.'[89] He accused the new fashions of supporting 'indecent modes of dress, which are more and more prevalent among women of all classes ... evidently invented for the purpose of exciting sensuality, and of inflaming passions that stand in the greatest need of restraint'.[90] Moreover, Bowles saw this as a practice developed amongst the élite and spreading through their influence throughout society, especially to 'those ranks, where it can be but little counteracted by education or reflection, [and] must inevitably prove an inexhaustible source of prostitution and debauchery ...'[91] Much the same line was taken by Nicholas Wraxall in reflecting on the change in customs, etiquette and form in the 1790s, and who identified a sea-change in attitudes around 1793–1794:

... though gradually undermined and insensibly perishing of an atrophy, dress never totally fell till the era of Jacobinism and of equality in 1793 and 1794. It was then that pantaloons, cropped hair, and shoestrings, as well as the total abolition of buckles and ruffles, together with the disuse of hair-powder, characterised the men; while the ladies, having cut off those tresses which had done so much execution, and one lock of which purloined gave rise to the finest model of mock-heroic poetry which our own or any other language can boast, exhibited heads rounded '*à la victim et à la guillotin*', as if ready for the stroke of the axe. A drapery more suited to the climate of Greece or of Italy than to the temperature of an island situate in the fifty-first degree of latitude, classic, elegant, luxurious, and picturesque, but ill calculated to protect against damp, colds, and fogs, superseded the ancient female attire of Great Britain, finally levelling or obliterating almost all the external distinction of costume between the highest and lowest of the sex in this country.[92]

It is always difficult to know quite how to interpret caricature, especially the social satires which combine making fun of their subjects, especially women, with a degree of artistic licence and prurience. But there was a

---

[88] Ibid., p. 147. [89] John Bowles, *Remarks on Modern Female Manners*, p. 16.
[90] Ibid., p. 11. [91] Ibid., pp. 11–12.
[92] Nicholas Wraxall, *The Historical and Posthumous Memoirs of Sir Nicholas William Wraxall 1772–1784*, edited by Henry B. Wheatley, 5 vols. (London: Bickers & Son, 1884), vol. 1 (of 5), p. 99.

spate of satires levelled against women baring their breasts and sallying forth into the public sphere to advertise their revolt against what Bowles regarded as merely natural standards of decency.[93] What is clear is that women's dress, which was always a somewhat contested terrain throughout the eighteenth century, was attributed clear ideological associations, in particular in relation to the Directory and subsequently the Consulate and Empire, and that loyalists sought to portray its adoption in Britain as the sure and certain road to French manners and the subversion of all that was decent. And, while that was not a reading that women themselves had much chance to rebut (although they might ignore it), it must inevitably have heightened their awareness of their self-presentation in public, and further fuelled concerns about how far their appearance could be read in ways that would harm their social standing and reputations (and this was, certainly, a double edged sword – to stand condemned for failing to accord with the fashions or for failing to warrant the

---

[93] See for example, James Gillray's *And Catch the Living Manners as They Rise* (H. Humphrey, 1794, BMS 8567); *Ladies Dress as it Soon Will Be* (H. Humphrey, 1796, BMS 8896); *The Fashionable Mama* (H. Humphrey, 1796, BMS 8897); *Lady Godina's Rout, or, Peeping Tom Spying Out Pope Joan* (H. Humphrey, 1796, BMS 8899), and then a series around 1810. Richard Newton adds to the representation in *Shepherds I Have Lost My Waist* (W. Holland, 1794, BMS 8569), *Peep into Brest with a Naval Review* (R. Newton, 1796) (see Alexander, *Richard Newton and English Caricature*); Issac Cruickshank's more comprehensive set includes *Too Much and Too Little* (S. W. Fores, 1796, BMS 8904) and *The Graces of 1794* (S. W. Fores, 1794, BMS 8571), *Symptoms of Lewdness or a Peep into the BOXES* (S. W. Fores, 1794, BMS 8521), *Dividing the Spoil* (S. W. Fores, 1796, BMS 8880); and *The Rage, or Shepherds I Have Lost My Waist* (S. W. Fores, 1796, BMS 8570) (see Gattrell, *City of Laughter*, pp. 361–375). Rowlandson adds *Buck's Beauty and Rowlandson's Connoisseur* (1799) (in Kate Heard (ed.), *High Spirits: The Comic Art of Thomas Rowlandson* (London: Royal Collection, 2013), pp. 152–153. The fashion was also denounced on the dual grounds of immodesty and Gallic influence by Polwhele in *The Unsex'd Females*: 'Scare by a gossamer film carest,/Sport, in full view, the meretricious breast; ...'! Opie's portraits of Wollstonecraft (1796), and Alderson (c 1800) follow the high waisted, muslin gown fashions, as did the engraving of Lawrence's portrait of Inchbald, so this is not entirely a fashion that the literary radicals repudiated, although none of them came even close to the exposure of décolletage that the prints portrayed. Interestingly, the bare breasted motif was used in depicting Mary Robinson back in 1783 in *Florizel and Perdita* (B. Pownall, 1783, BMS 6266). (There was an earlier spate of prints in 1793 depicting the fashion for false pregnancies and for bulking out various parts of the female anatomy – see Rowlandson's *Cestina Warehouse or Belly Piece Shop* [np, 1793, BMS 8387]; Cruickshank's *The Frailties of Fashion* [S. W. Fores, 1793, BMS 8388]; Gillray's *A Vestal of -93, Trying on the Cestus of Venus* [H. Humphrey, 1793, BMS 8389]; James Aitken's *Female Whimsicalities* [William Dent, 1793, BMS 8390]; *The Pad Warehouse* [Bon Ton Magazine, 1793 – see Wahrman, *The Making of the Modern Self*, p. 67]). Of course suggestive nudity would sell prints, but there is also a sense that there was something to caricature here – both in relation to fashion and in relation to dance in the theatre (see *Modern Grace, or The Operatic Finale* [5 May 1796] and the series of prints concerning Mlle Parisot – see Gattrell, *City of Laughter*, pp. 371–374).

respect of others because of one's dress and demeanour). The provincial papers in this period followed their London cousins in reporting in detail the clothes and fashions of London, with often ferocious precision and with a degree of pointedness: for example, the *Ipswich Journal* for 30 January 1796 reported on the elegance of Lady Charlotte Campbell's dress and on the inadvisability of certain women following her example, saying

she was the first, who disregarding the *artificial shape* given by *stays*, Introduced *short waists*. The elegant person of her ladyship appears to most advantage when nature is unrestrained, and therefore her short waist is uncommonly graceful; but the little *Dutch-Built Dames*, who have foolishly adopted the same fashion, look as if they were *peeping out of a puncheon* which had been covered by a petticoat.[94]

The 'short waist' crisis is clear in caricatures from 1794 and became an iterated theme in satires of the fashion world for the next several years. Nonetheless, the most straightforward way of interpreting such satires is to see them aimed at the aristocratic circles around Parliament, with the intent of lampooning those members of the élite connected to fashionable society.

What is a little surprising about Bowles's intervention is that it was hardly in the first flurry of representation, but that may well have been because his concern was primarily prompted by the gradual spread of this fashion and its associated principles down through the social world and by his own sense that those well beyond court circles were being drawn to a flimsiness of costume that was both overly stimulating and sensuous, thereby encouraging immorality – and inadequate as a covering for the climate, thereby encouraging mortality! But this was something that literary radicals also saw as food for critique – Mrs Inchbald made use of the trope in *Nature and Art* where the death of Lady Clementina was reported: "'Yes", answered the stranger; "she caught cold by wearing a new-fashioned dress that did not half cover her, wasted all away, and died the miserablest object you ever heard of"'.[95]

The audiences addressed by prints, satirical poetry and so on were not identical. Moreover, the transparency of reference was often quite restricted and often relied upon an audience in the know. Insofar as the literary radicals were targeted, the audience's 'knowingness' about this group of women writers, as in other cases, relied rather heavily on seeing as intimately connected people who were not in fact so close, sharing little more than the fact that they wrote and claimed some public attention with some sympathy for reform (although attacks did not get the

---

[94] *Ipswich Journal*, 30 January 1796, No. 3299.
[95] Inchbald, *Nature and Art*, XLIV, see also chapter VII.

measure of Mrs Radcliffe, or really of Inchbald, and they often lumped together those favouring a reformation of manners and those looking for a reformation of the position of women and of politics more widely). In retrospect, people developed a stronger sense of a coterie of women literary radicals. In the fray, in 1797 and 1798, different loyalist contributors lashed out in different ways, often relying on traditional associations and old news (as with Helen Maria Williams and Mrs Barbauld). What is surprising is that there seems no comparable visual trope of the artisan democrat to characterise these women writers – and when women were attacked in prints they remained largely aristocratic or related to fashion and fashionable society. As with the artisans, there is no need to know them beyond their works – unlike the beautiful, fallen women of the theatre who are portrayed, they lack allure and interest. Nonetheless, there does seem to be a case for seeing Godwin's *Memoirs* as especially ill-timed, and as encouraging the loyalist press to scoop together a wide range of women whom they disliked on one count or other so as to tar them with Gallic sympathies, infidelity and immorality.

5 Gender and Deliberative Equality

The women I discuss in this and the next two chapters were all connected to Godwin's life and several had unconventional relationships with him, albeit in very different ways. Seeing how they interacted with him can help us appreciate some of the complexities of the emotional, social and intellectual culture in which Godwin (and others) moved in the 1790s and its troubled relationship to a wider set of societal norms and expectations. The first I want to discuss is Sarah Anne Parr, the daughter of Samuel Parr, the literary cleric and headmaster in Warwickshire, who (as we have seen) subjected Godwin to a gruelling three-day critique of his *Enquiry* in July 1795 and in 1801 denounced him from the pulpit. Godwin almost certainly met Anne (as she signed herself) when he visited Warwickshire in 1794 and 1795, although he did not record her in the diary. In 1796 she visited London and stayed with James Mackintosh and his wife from at least 1 March to the end of April, by which time she had been joined by her younger sister, Catherine. During this period in London she wrote Godwin three letters that are certainly not characteristic of his wider correspondence.

On 21 March 1796 Godwin noted: 'Call on Montagu n, & mrs Mackintosh'. Although he did not mention Anne Parr, two days later she wrote to him as follows:

One miracle deserves another, and since you have to my infinite surprise been civil enough to call upon me, I am resolved to amaze you in return by writing a note to thank you for this extraordinary effort of politeness – I am sorry I was not at home, but perhaps if we had met we should have been less civil to each other, for I have even an increased antipathy to truth and precision because I daily find fresh reason to believe them mere cloaks for rudeness and affectation.

Is this not a shocking declaration, and do you not wonder at my stupidity in confounding the principles with the practice – Well, you may be shocked and surprised at your leisure, but I am obstinately resolved not to yield one solitary prejudice to your eloquence ... I leave town on Saturday morning, owing to an absurd prejudice I have of obeying my Father's orders – I am, with every possible prejudice against you, and for falsehood, Anne.[1]

Godwin clearly sought to follow this up the same day: 'sup chez mrs Mackintosh, w. S P; explanation'.

The vagaries of Godwin's system of annotation do not make wholly clear when they next met (or, indeed, whether she did in fact leave town on the 25th, but Godwin called on 'SP' on 1 April and dined on the 5th,10th and 13th April with Mackintosh and 'SP' or 'Ps'; on the 20th he 'sups at Mac's, w. S & C P' (Sarah Anne's sister Catherine), and on the 22nd he had '3 Parrs, 4 Mackintoshs, Inchbald, Imlay, Dealtry & Ht to dine'; he saw them again on the 26th and then was at the theatre with the Miss Parrs (Imlay refers here to Wollstonecraft).[2]

On 21 April, Anne wrote a letter from Nando's Coffee House at 2 o'clock in the morning, addressed to the 'most ungrateful of mankind' in which she upbraided Godwin again in the following terms:

Oh thou ungrateful, unfeeling, cruel, insulting, barbarous man, or to sum up thy iniquities in one word, thou Philosopher – art thou not ashamed, that is to say as much as one of thy sect can be ashamed, of conduct so atrocious. I am so angry that I would marry thee in downright spite, if I did not hold sacred the oath I swore six years ago never to marry – a wise man.[3]

The last (undated) letter is difficult to place but comes from the same period. She apologised for not alerting him sufficiently early to the fact that they could not come to dinner, since her father was engaged, but she invited him to come to Covent Garden to see Falstaff and a pantomime –

you may come by way of bear to my box if you feel yourself bearishly inclined – Put on your holiday coat, brighten your spectacles, brush your hat, stick it on one side, take a cane in your hand, and sally forth armed at all points if you are in good humour – if you are cross, stay at home and write a satire on the perfidy and forgetfulness of us women, quoting as an example the conduct of – Anne Parr.[4]

It is difficult to know exactly what to make of these notes – I doubt that they signify any serious interest on the part of Anne in Godwin as a marital prospect, but they are not entirely prudent letters and we might wonder what her parents might have said had they known they were

---

[1] Bodleian Library MS. Abinger c.3, fol 25r–v, 23 March 1796. The entry suggests that Godwin quietly censored his own intentions after the fact – describing himself as calling on Mrs Mackintosh – not on Sarah Anne Parr (who nonetheless recognises the visit as one to her).

[2] Another piece of Godwin's covert censorship – referring to Wollstonecraft in the form others would have referred to her.

[3] Bodleian Library MS. Abinger c.2, fol 88v, 21 April 1796.

[4] Bodleian Library MS. Abinger c.15, fol 59v, Undated.

being written. It might also be thought that they are symptomatic of a level of imprudence that could have helped her parents to predict her elopement with the insipid Mr Wynn in the following June. We also have no sense of to what extent they might have disturbed Godwin's repose. But Anne Parr is not the only young woman who seems to have this kind of teasing correspondence with Godwin around this time.

The other disturber of his repose was Amelia Alderson, about whom it is difficult to be wholly objective. Indeed, I want to suggest that this was a problem Godwin himself increasingly had. He was, as we should be, troubled by exactly how to read the tone of the letters and exchanges between them in the 1790s. And, in reading them, I want to make the case that they are evidence that something was happening to Godwin's emotional life that had substantial philosophical and practical implications for him and is indicative of a more general discomfiting by the destabilising effects of multiple layers of communication. This has wider consequences for Godwin's 1790s philosophical project (if that shorthand can be used) and for the role of the didactic in the sphere of intellectual exchange more widely. In exploring the impact of the changes, I want to make the case that this should change the way we think about social and sexual communication and the radicalism of the decade.

One traditional view of the decade is that the popular movement for democracy takes a major step forward. This position seems untenable, in part because the term is rather little used in the period and the reform movement for the most part is about improved parliamentary representation in a mixed system of government.[5] Moreover, where the term democracy was used, it was for the most part opposed to aristocracy, and the core component of this opposition was the issue of equality, albeit this referred to status and legal equality. People did not demand economic equality – indeed, when challenged by loyalists, most expressly disavowed it as a claim. But they wanted to be treated as equals in a system that was very hierarchical. Godwin was a more open defender of democracy than most of his peers but, again, his deeper concern was to protect the full and free and equal exercise of private judgement and public discussion and his rationalism and his belief in persuasion and the power of truth to move people rested firmly on an ideal of equal moral capacity. He was sufficiently confident to believe that he and his friends were more in the vanguard of intellectual developments than others; but

---

[5] See Joanna Innes and Mark Philp (eds.), *Reimagining Democracy in the Age of Revolutions* (Oxford: Oxford University Press, 2013) and *Reimagining Democracy in the Mediterranean* (Oxford: Oxford University Press, 2018).

he was also sufficiently shrewd to see that this did not give them a right to direct others. Rather, one had to try to move people through argument and discussion.

One problem that this gave rise to, and that Godwin returned to over and over again, was that equality had the effect of undermining didactic, intellectual relationships. Where intellectual relationships were no longer didactic, they became less bounded or their boundaries become more contestable, since the parties involved could press and challenge boundaries in different ways – and that opened them up to very different constructions, reactions and outcomes. Godwin wrote his *Enquiry* in full philosophical mode, laying out the argument for the reader in a calm, reasoned manner – very much above the fray! But, because of the success of the work, he was brought into contact with many people, especially younger people, who sought to engage with him and his ideas and who then raised a new set of issues for him about how to communicate and persuade.

On 29 June 1794, on a visit to Norfolk, Godwin dined with a mixed company with whom he discussed 'the punishment of kings' and which included Amelia Alderson (who would then have been twenty-four years old). In August of that year she visited London and she called on Godwin on 20 August. Godwin was not at home, but she called again with her host in London, John Boddington, on 26 August. They next met again at the end of September when they encountered each other visiting Gerrald in Newgate. But he also wrote to her on 8 September 1794.[6]

Alderson's epistolary report on their meeting in August to her friend Susannah Taylor does not read very favourably: Godwin appeared 'bien poudre' and 'in a pair of new, sharp-toed, red morocco slippers, not to mention his green coat and crimson under-waistcoat'. He interrogated her on where she was staying, making clear that he thought that staying 'out of town' with family and friends was somehow missing all the action. She defensively told him that she was bound by family affections – and he pulled out his trump card and asked whether she ought to admit of any other dominion than that of reason.

'But are you sure that my affections in this case are not the result of reason?' He shrugged disbelief and after debating some time, told me I was more of the woman than when he saw me last. Rarely did we agree, and little did he gain on me by his mode of attack; but he seemed alarmed lest he should have offended me, and apologised several times, with much feeling for the harshness of his expressions. In short, he convinced me that his theory had not yet gotten entire ascendancy over his practice.[7]

[6] Godwin, *Letters of WG*, v. I, p. 100, no. 53.   [7] Brightwell, *Memorials*, p. 42.

In Godwin's letter of 8 September he said to her:

I cannot forget your remark when I last saw you, that in your present visit you was governed by your affections ... to be governed by our affections in the company we keep, or the conduct we pursue, most usually means to discard our understanding ... But, if you excel in the degree you are capable of doing, you must not shut your eyes, but adopt a penetrating scrutiny into the persons you see & the principles you adopt ... These sentiments I have just written, however uncouthly expressed, prove not only the interest I feel in your well doing, but the uncommon esteem I have conceived for your merits.[8]

We don't know when Alderson wrote her description to Susanna Taylor – but there seems every likelihood that she did so before she received Godwin's letter. It is clear from later correspondence that Alderson had considerable respect for Godwin's judgement and valued what he said to her and that they shared a number of views on contemporary politics. Nonetheless, in the course of their friendship, Godwin ended up saying a number of things to Alderson which indicate a less than purely philosophical form of address – 'more of the woman', a 'coquette', a 'flirt', having no heart and, indeed, on one occasion he called her 'a bitch' and, on another, a 'reprobate and villain'.[9] The last came in a brief note he sent her after reading her comedy (which she probably left with him when she met him at tea at Holcroft's in 29 March 1796). He read it on 30 March and sent her the note on 1 April. Both the tone and the content are instructive:

Amelia, Are you in a hurry? No. Well then, I will criticise at my leisure. I could not refrain however from a first rapid reading the morning after I saw you. I can no longer withhold from you the general information that your comedy has, in my opinion, no inconsiderable merit, & that it agreeably surprised me.[10]

He explains it surprised him because he'd only read her tragedy, because comedy and tragedy are autumnal fruits of the human understanding, and 'Thirdly, because, reprobate and villain as you are, you will not be persuaded to cultivate the art of arts, The Art *par eminence*, the art of conversation: how therefore is it possible to suppose you have any thing in you?'[11]

---

[8] Godwin, *Letters of WG*, v.i, pp. 100–101. He comments on the contrast between the society at Southgate, where she was staying, and the society of the metropolis where 'the best communications of mind' would be available. And he is bluntly rude about her host, Mr Morgan – 'you are wretchedly deceived if you take Mr Morgan for a great genius'. George Cadogan Morgan had been a fellow student of Godwin's at Hoxton.

[9] Bodleian Library MS. Abinger c.3, fol 40v.   [10] Godwin, *Letters of WG*, i, p. 165.

[11] Ibid., i, p. 92; v.i, p. 165.

She responded with thanks in a note also dated 1 April. He re-read the play on the 9th , following dinner with her at Batty's on the 7th, and they met briefly again on 10 April (although Alderson was not one of the core party (Hts, w. Merry, Barry, Mackintosh's & S P; adv. A A & Richters). She then wrote him a fuller letter on 11 April, although it seems unlikely that they would have had any chance to discuss his deeper response. In the 11 April letter she clearly wanted to write to him formally to thank him for his trouble and his 'just criticisms' and because she was 'fearful that were I not to do so, your extreme aptness to misunderstand and misrepresent me would lead you to imagine that my self-love was more wounded than gratified by your endorsement of R. Twiss's note' (which seems to have been positive). She went on to say that she wanted to converse with him – 'I have many questions to ask, & I believe yr patience & forbearance to be of respectable dimensions rather than otherwise, consequently equal to the stretch which I may put them to.' But she then launched into a very cryptic set of comments that may be referring him to a discussion she had witnessed at Holcroft's on the previous evening, in which she might have thought that candour was being exercised to other ends than the promotion of truth:

I am now fully convinced of the existence of a Devil – but the fiend abideth not in the hot dwelling commonly assigned to him – no, no – Society is his dwelling place, & his name on earth is Ill humour – various are His shapes. Sometimes he assumes the form of serious discussion, & close argument – at others the more lively shape of *agreeable railing* – verily, verily he delighteth not in contradiction, but at its approach, he summons up all his force & attacks even Philosophy herself – Is this not true O Philosopher?

Perhaps you will think this self-same fiend is grinning over my shoulder while I am writing – but if he be, I assure you he turns his head away.[12]

When Alderson wrote to Godwin after the death of Mary Wollstonecraft she included an odd final paragraph – after a genuinely sympathetic and moving letter:

I have been told that you say I have *no heart* the severest of all assertions perhaps. But I shall not plead not guilty to the charge, as we never, I believe, take pains to confute a calumny, unless we are conscious it has some truth for its foundation – at least *my* experience says this, as perhaps so does that of others – I know not whether this charge implies an incapacity in me to be a *friend*, as well as a *lover*, but be it as it may, my own mind authorizes me to assert, and use my right of subscribing myself with the sincerest respect & friendship, Most affect yours, Amelia Alderson.[13]

---

[12] Bodleian Library MS. Abinger c.3, fol 30r–v.
[13] Bodleian Library MS. Abinger c.3, fols 99r–100v.

Godwin managed to quarrel with several people in the immediate after-math of Wollstonecraft's death. And, while his reply to Alderson started gently enough, he wound himself up as he progressed and ended with a characteristically unrestrained finale, picking up the accusation that he had said she had no heart:

To the best of my recollection I never said any such thing. I said indeed, you were a flirt. But that is no secret; everybody knows that. I might say that a flirt, quod flirtation, has no heart, but I know several admirable women who put on and off the flirt ... as easily as they put on and take off their clothes. In this respect you resemble Mrs Inchbald ... I do not, in my own personal judgment, approve the practice. I think it a very dangerous one ... I do from my heart and soul abjure and detest coquetry. If by rivers of tears I could wash it out of your character, I would shed them. But it lies too deep for that ... Coquetry trifles with the peace of the unwary, in the catalogue of whom may sometimes be found the most eminent of mankind; & it soils and makes cheap the character of the woman that practices it ... I had rather hear a woman laugh at religion and blaspheme her God, than see her profane and desecrate the testimony of those liberal emotions, which are calculated to bind by the noblest ties the two great divisions of the species together.[14]

This is an odd letter to return to a letter of condolence – although that too was a little peculiar. Read carefully, however, it seems that Alderson's coda simply tried to express her real friendship and affection for Godwin. That intention did not 'take' – such that there was no further correspond-ence between them and no visit until shortly before her marriage to John Opie. And their relationship was certainly much cooler subsequently, although Godwin's antipathy toward Opie probably played some role in that.

Nonetheless, the exchange was of a piece with their relationship. God-win's reference to 'the woman in you' (that Alderson picked up and tried to bat back) might have been about a sentimental attachment to family (which would suit his criticism of her accommodation in her visit to London in August 1794). But it might equally have been a matter of a certain style of communication.

One interpretation of what he meant when he said Alderson had 'more of the woman' might be, then, that she was behaving in a more conform-ist, less inquiring, less intellectual, more frivolous way. Alderson I think read it as accusing her of being capricious (rather than sentimental) – when she wrote for the second time in a week in February 1796, after a long period of silence, she remarked 'But you well know that there is no accounting for the caprices of woman – & that I alas, have a great deal of

[14] Godwin, *Letters of WG*, i, p. 259.

the woman still hanging about me – you know too well.'[15] But that sense of caprice needs to be coupled with his other criticisms of her – above all, that she resisted 'The Art' – that is – conversation. We might think Godwin is somewhat exacting, since the discussion that Alderson describes having in Eaton's bookshop with Eaton, his wife and Charles Sinclair, clearly indicates that she has 'conversations'.[16] Does Godwin mean something more? Certainly, she takes 'more of the woman' to mean that he expected something more – and better.

It is unlikely that he was expecting more than her upbringing and education in a dissenting community would have led her to expect – direct, candid communication. What he experienced, however, was a more volatile, coquettish, flirty behaviour. There is something surprising in this – Alderson's first novel, the *Dangers of Coquetry* (1790), was, after all, a representation and condemnation of precisely the kind of behaviour of which Godwin might have been accusing her. Indeed, her heroine's good upright husband, Mortimer, who dies fighting a duel as a result of his wife's coquettishness (and whom she follows swiftly to the grave from deep remorse), is also someone who asks of his wife that she rise above this. (There's no evidence that Godwin had read the novel, although it appeared before he began listing his reading; he did read *Father and Daughter*; and he read *Adeline Mowbray* when it came out (and he cannot have been especially offended by the latter since, in the 1830s, he started off by calling, his penultimate fictional hero Mowbray, before renaming him Cloudesley).[17]

Alderson was clearly aware of the dangers. But her mode with Godwin was only variably deliberative. And she shared that with Sarah Ann Parr – whom Godwin describes as 'a seducer', even if he also told Wollstonecraft 'You do not know, but I do, that Sarah has an uncommon understanding, & an exquisite sensibility, which grows in her complexion and flashes in her eyes.'[18]

Not all of the women whom Godwin met engaged in this kind of behaviour or were responded to quite in the way Godwin responded to

[15] 12.2.96 Bodleian Library MS. Abinger c.3, fol 20r.

[16] See Harriet Guest's discussion in her *Unbounded Attachment*, chapter 4, pp. 133–134; and Alderson's description in Brightwell, *Memorials*, pp. 43–45.

[17] Amelia Opie, *Father and Daughter* (1801) with *Dangers of Coquetry* (1790), edited by Shelley King and John B. Pierce (Ontario: Canada, Broadview Press, 2003), and *Adeline Mowbray* (1805), edited by Anne McWhir (Ontario: Canada, Broadview Press, 2010); William Godwin, 'Se Cloudesley' (1830), in Mark Philp (ed.), *Collected Novels and Memoirs of William Godwin*, 8 vols. (London: Pickering & Chatto, 1992), vol. 7.

[18] Ralph Wardle (ed.), *Godwin and Mary: Letters of Mary Wollstonecraft and William Godwin* (Lawrence, KS: University of Kansas, 1967), pp. 103–104; Godwin, *Letters of WG*, i., p. 225.

Alderson. We don't find Hays doing this, and Ann/Nan Pinkerton essentially gets told off by Godwin for her hectoring of him and by Wollstonecraft for trying to seduce Godwin. Both those women tried to compete on Godwin's home ground. But one way of reading Alderson and Parr's behaviour is that they successfully resisted both Godwin's interpolation of them as intellects to be brought on under his guidance and his own self-construction as the disinterested inquirer after truth and merit. He was serious in seeing in them this kind of intellectual promise, they were serious in both accepting and subverting that construction; he saw himself as immune to their attractions, they succeeded in confusing him over that; they were committed to equality, but demanded that they be treated as more than dialogic lieutenants.

We need to take seriously – and treat as self-referential – Godwin's comment that 'Coquetry trifles with the peace of the unwary, in the catalogue of whom may sometimes be found the most eminent of mankind.' Godwin knew that he was not good at that kind of exchange; and he had developed powerful philosophical grounds for thinking that it was inappropriate among the most serious minded. Yet these women (and a few others, probably including Inchbald and Reveley – but not the unconfident Mary Hays, the more mature and intellectual Wollstonecraft, the more established Harriet Lee, or the more experienced Sarah Elwes or Mary Jane Clairmont) disconcerted Godwin. I suspect Inchbald did so to a lesser degree – partly because, although more of the woman, Godwin had less intimacy and was more clearly under her direction when they met (since they usually met at her home). But Alderson and Parr were a different prospect (and perhaps, later, Nan Pinkerton – although we have very little evidence for her). We might think that this was because that was just the way they were, but I want to suggest another reason.

Godwin had little experience with women. All we know of his relationships from the first forty years of his life is that his sister Hannah attempted to interest him in a young woman called Miss Jay in 1785, but without success. In the early 1790s, when his reputation was growing, and his social life expanding and when he began to meet a wider range of women, he had already largely constructed his philosophical *modus operandi* and persona and, while that was a conscious set of commitments, driven by his belief in the necessity of advancing truth to the fullest extent of his powers, it was also less consciously a defence against his own social awkwardness. Moreover, his relationships with Inchbald, Hays and Alderson were established on the basis of his acting in the role of advisor, with Inchbald and Alderson in relation to their writing, with Hays in relation to her pursuit of truth and a degree of stoic equanimity.[19] Moreover, his mode of communication with the younger women was didactic – he recognised their special qualities, appealed to their minds, not to 'groom' them so much as to secure to himself a role with them that established his authority and protected his peace of mind, while 'developing' their abilities. On 26 September 1798, just over a year after Wollstonecraft's death, Godwin met by chance a Miss Emily Kingsman with Charles Kemble. He wrote to her the same day:

William Godwin to Miss Kingsman, Aldenham, Nr Watford

26 September 1798

Dear Miss Kinsman(sic),

As I did not say to you the things that I ought when I saw you, I feel myself prompted to say them to you now on paper. You overstepped the dull rules of old fashioned etiquette and ceremony by the action that gave me the pleasure of conversing with you. I therefore make no apology in the liberty I take in addressing you. As the scene that passed between us was wholly unexpected and afforded me no time for reflection, I the less wonder that I did not do all that I could have wished: I behaved coldly, and more like a mere scholar, than you had a right to expect from an author whom you honoured with some show of your approbation … I ought to have said to myself when a spirited conduct on your part so extraordinarily introduced you to me this morning, accident has thrown this lovely girl in my way, I ought to use the moment she affords me, in encouraging her virtue, in blowing the flame of her spirit, & endeavouring to render, as far as my powers may extend, the excellencies she now possesses as lasting as her life. This you had a right to expect from me, and I did nothing of this. Your accosting me as you did persuades me on reflection that you have a mind / capable of rising much above the vulgar of your sex. But you must treasure this gift, it is a talent that you may not neglect with impunity. You have it in your choice, like Hercules in the fable, to rise to what men of virtue must ever pay homage to, or to be lost in the grinding pursuits and the contemptible narrowness of soul, to which your sex is generally condemned. Allow me, if possible, twenty years hence to recollect our interview with exultation, and to say that the 26th September 1798, was not lost in my life.[20]

This seems like a return to old form – in which, from his Olympian heights, Godwin solicited an implicitly passive and duty-bound response from a potential female protégé. It is pretty clear that her family – who opened the letter, since Godwin had addressed it to Miss Kingsman, having been unaware of the existence of her elder sister – found it worrying. (Her brother – whom Godwin had met at Wedgwood's some

---

[19] See Chernock, *Men and the Making of Modern British Feminism*, pp. 79–80.
[20] Bodleian Library MS. Abinger c.17, fol 66r–v, 26 September 1798; Godwin, *Letters of WG*, v. ii, pp. 56–58.

years before – responded in a tone that was certainly chilly). If it is not downright unsettling, it is clearly very condescending. My sense is that this was the type of treatment that Alderson initially received, and she resented this. Moreover, and here lies the complexity of reading these relationships, she did so while being attracted to Godwin as an intellect, as someone who could help her literary activity, as a fellow sympathiser with reform and perhaps partly as a potential friend. As a result, in place of the unequal and rather subservient relationship that Godwin's attitude pushed her toward, by flirtatiousness and something like coquetry, together with a certain forthrightness in her letters and a teasing and unpredictable quality to her behaviour, she – and Sarah Anne Parr – unsettled Godwin. Moreover, they did so intentionally because they were looking (perfectly reasonably) for something more equal than the role of a pupil. Indeed, even if there was also some attraction, that could not trump the instinctive resistance to taking everything on his terms.

Certainly, it was a challenge to argue things out with Godwin – but Alderson could see the attractions of his style. In one of her earliest surviving letters to Godwin she reported that, having returned to Norwich, she had been in the company of those who were likely to form her society for the coming months in the town: 'and what strikes me most in them is, their eagerness to deliver their opinions tho' they violate propriety, & good manners by breaking forcibly in on the argument of someone else', and she goes on:

To have a talent for silence, [is] in my opinion a most desirable thing & I know no one who has this talent in such perfection as yourself – By silence I mean the power of *listening, patiently, & attentively* – even to *bad arguments, badly delivered* – were this talent cultivated as it ought to be, I should not the other evening have had the pain of hearing one person rudely interrupting another; that other exalting his voice to make himself heard in spite of the interruptions, till confusion & noise were the order of the day, and I thought myself in the national convention, but alas! There was no president & the bell was not rung.[21]

Nonetheless, Alderson resisted Godwin's 'conversation', turning their interaction into something both more charged and evanescent – something Godwin could not quite get a hold of and could not avoid finding both disconcerting and enticing. His accusation that she won't perfect the Art – was a reproach for resisting what he was supremely good at. When she asked Thomas Hardy to convey her apologies for delaying in writing to Godwin, Hardy's response was 'I do not wonder at your delay, for you must mind your p's and q's when you write to Citizen Godwin'.[22]

---

[21] Bodleian Library MS. Abinger c.2, fols 108r–109v, 28 August 1795.
[22] Bodleian Library MS. Abinger c.3, fol 16r, 5 February 1796.

But what is striking about both Alderson and Parr was that they did not really mind their p's and q's – indeed, they played fast and loose with them! It is true that Alderson could be meek and pleading when she wanted him to do something – but she had a much wider armoury of tactics. And her resistance to Godwin's deliberative style is significant: indeed, when he reproached her for coquetry on the grounds that it trifled with the peace of the unwary, he was also indicating that the serious conversationalist and the philosopher is necessarily unwary: that candid communication is unwary. And he was clearly unsure what he should make of communication that operated at several registers – teasing, flirting, sometimes engaging and sometimes not?

In a similar fashion, it is difficult to be certain as to exactly what we should make of Alderson's *Adeline Mowbray* (1805). In both her novels after *Coquetry* (that is, in *Father and Daughter* (1800) and *Adeline*) she takes as her central characters fallen/socially excluded women. But Alderson's achievement in *Adeline* (and to a lesser extent in *Father and Daughter*), and what sets her apart from Inchbald's novels, which have a similar concern with the failing Miss Milner in *A Simple Story* and the fallen Agnes in *Nature and Art*, was her ability to sustain the heroism of her women – they are not just passive victims. We are supposed to think that Adeline has had a defective education, but it is less clear exactly what that education should have been (or where it would have come from). Should it have been an education about society's hypocrisy, its intolerance, its exploitation of women, its wearisome sexualisation of relations, and so on? The novel is far and away the most subtle of the anti-Jacobin novels, to the extent that that is hardly the right label (and that label suggests a motive that may well have been absent). It conveys in unflinching terms societal hypocrisy, predatory masculinity and docile feminine complicity (of a particularly nasty kind in the case of Adeline's mother).[23] Glenmurray is a sort of Godwin – but one to whom Alderson is kind, if a little teasing, but gently so. He knows the costs that Adeline bears and as his health declines is aware of the dangers she faces – and so wants to marry Adeline (or as he knows he is dying, to marry her to his friend, who proves a disappointment); but it is her concern for his intellectual integrity that renders that impossible – and that is partly because she loves him (as, it seems clear, one might well do) for his integrity and his ideas.

---

[23] See James Mackintosh's reading: 'Mrs Opie has pathetic scenes, but the object is not attained; for the distress is not made to arise from the unnuptial union itself, but from the opinions of the world against it; so that it may as well be taken as a satire on our prejudices in favour of marriage, as on the paradoxes of sophists against it'. James Mackintosh to George Philips, 1804, in Mackintosh, *Memoirs*, v. i, p. 255. With thanks to Anne Verjus for pointing me to this.

We can also see her as using the novel to reflect on Godwin's work and his relationship with Wollstonecraft and to try to mark out for herself the points of difference between herself and Adeline. Above all, one key contrast is that Adeline is devoted to the 'Art of Conversation', to philosophising, and to following through deliberation with action, treating intellectual life as the core of virtue and utility as the basis for decisions. Adeline may partly be modelled on Wollstonecraft; but she was also modelled on what Alderson had declined to be. In doing so, the novel combined both an attempted vindication of her judgement; with an intense regret that someone as good as Adeline could only be destroyed – together with some confusion as to whether, in acting as she did, Amelia was herself being entirely true to her own beliefs and aspirations.

The other striking thing about Alderson was her apparent adventurousness. As a young single woman, she managed to gain Inchbald's affection and retained it into later life. She attended the Treason Trials; she went to the 1796 Westminster hustings with Godwin; she moved across many of the little platoons in London with apparent ease. She was well served by her Norwich connections and by her ability to interest people in her – and she developed acquaintances in a range of circles. But it is important that she did not openly break rules. A careful examination of her acquaintance with Godwin suggests that she did not take big risks. There were others present when they met (something that was much more important for how her conduct would appear to others than because doing so would invite Godwin to act inappropriately). Although she called on him, it seems likely that she was always accompanied, unless it was simply a matter of dropping a manuscript off.[24] Of the various contacts in which Alderson called on Godwin before his marriage to Wollstonecraft (or dined there, or had breakfast, tea or supper) each looks as if she is accompanied by another person. She seems, then, to have been scrupulous about her conduct and how it would be perceived by others. Indeed, in a letter to Godwin on 12 February 1796 she ends by asking 'How is Horne Tooke? – I long for another day at his house – but Mum! When we meet I will tell you why I did not visit him & his amiable daughters a second time – I sacrificed my wishes to – nonsense.'[25]

This suggests that Alderson had a prudent eye open to avoid becoming the subject of gossip and inuendo, perhaps tinged with a slight concern about masculine gallantry. Nonetheless she stood out in her relationship with Mary Wollstonecraft. They were introduced by Godwin; the two

---

[24] Of the 'call on Godwin' calls, none looks as if it was undertaken on her own, unless for the purpose of leaving something for him.
[25] Bodleian Library MS. Abinger c.3, fol 21v.

women developed an independent friendship; and Alderson did not waver in her friendship either before or after the marriage. She clearly thought of the pair as 'extraordinary characters' and while she certainly had reservations about them ('what charming things would sublime theories be, if one could make one's practice keep up with them; but I am convinced it is impossible, and am resolved to make the best of every-day nature'),[26] she did not consider those reservations as a sufficient reason to refuse their company or their affection. In this respect, she resisted the conventional route of cutting such women, as sketched and partly condemned in *Adeline Mowbray*, and she did so despite her friendship with Inchbald and the Twisses (who did cut Wollstonecraft) and despite the fact that, for many young women, such a relationship would have been feared for the reputational damage it might cause. That she was prepared to take that risk says much about her independence and contempt for 'nonsense', and something about the kind of marriage she aspired to. Farington depicted her as moving in much higher social circles than her husband John, but there is not much evidence of that from the sources we have before her marriage (Opie had been raised from a very poor background largely by the patronage of John Wolcot (pseud. Peter Pindar) who had advised him to maintain his rough manners). Their reputation, she seems to have believed, would not affect hers (or was seen as a price worth paying) – in striking contrast to the way many of the young women in the novel behave – with the exception of Emma Douglas, who was probably an alternative Amelia Alderson figure who married the man (Mordaunt/Opie) who was once entranced by an immensely able, virtuous, but fallen woman (Adeline/Wollstonecraft); and whose past was itself somewhat chequered but who had turned to a woman he could admire in a similar way, but without having to forgive her for her past. In her marriage to Opie, Alderson seems to have been embracing a preference for the face of things and plain speaking while resisting both the excesses of Godwinian candour and his philosophical didacticism.

It would be good to believe that Amelia Alderson got away with it. When she came to London her reference group was centred on Norwich and those linked to it and she did not aspire to marry wealth or privilege. But there is no doubt that the world she moved in while in London was a man's world, even if it was simultaneously for her an immensely exciting one. Her slightly gleeful report of Inchbald's claim that the world thinks Holcroft is in love with her, she in love with Godwin, Godwin in love

---

[26] Brightwell, *Memorials*, pp. 61–62.

with Amelia and Amelia in love with Holcroft was also an acknowledgement of the silliness of much of that world and the fanciful speculations
that were attached in particular to young, single women in society. She
clearly found some aspects tiresome – not least from the older gallants: –
'I had rather Mr Tooke should praise me to my friends than to myself.
I exult in his approbation but when he tells me I am pretty I cannot help
thinking he is laughing at me, smiling at the credulity of women, and
their [susceptibility] to flattery, however gross.'[27] Her objection was both
that their behaviour was wearing and that she disliked herself for being
responsive to their flattery. Godwin, after the initial 'bien poudre'
encounter, seems to have treated her differently, by appealing to her
intelligence, but in a way that could be equally stultifying and disciplining. And the wider 'society' and the devil in it was something of which
she was sharply aware. Certainly, her succumbing to John Opie's proposal might best be read in the light of Inchbald's description of him: 'the
total absence of artificial manners was the most remarkable characteristic, and at the same time the adornment and deformity of Mr Opie'.[28]
Opie was a curious man – chasing a marriage with Elizabeth Booth before
his divorce was settled and subject to rumours as to his attention to Jane
Beetham before (possibly coincidentally with) wooing Alderson. It is
unlikely that anyone in the know would have told her about these
amours.[29] On the contrary, men seemed to close ranks, leaving women
vulnerable to considerable misinformation and illusions. Similarly, as we
have seen, although she was convinced that their marriage had caused
Opie financial difficulties, forcing him to focus on the market for portraits
rather than landscape and history painting, his bank balance on his death
told a very different story! Their marriage seems to have been affectionate
and, as Shelley King points out, had benefits on both sides, but it also
speaks to the weakness of women's hands even in relatively companionate marriages with some equality to them. So, she did not escape entirely
unscathed.

---

[27] Bodleian Library MS. Abinger c. 3, 40v–41r.
[28] Brightwell *Memorials*, p. 65. See also King, 'Portrait of a Marriage'.
[29] King, 'Portrait of a Marriage', p. 32.

6 Negotiating Equality

6.1 A Vindication for Wollstonecraft

Amelia Alderson's resistance to Godwin's mode of debate and his didacticism discomfited him – as, most likely, did the antics of Sara Anne Parr. Such experiences, and those with Hays, infuriating as he sometimes seems to have found those, and with other women in his circles, such as Maria Reveley, forced him to think further about the picture he sketched in his *Enquiry* of minds stripped of emotion and sentiment and driven wholly by reason. That picture and his self-construction in its image did not survive unchanged by the experiences of 1792–1797. These friendships and acquaintances threw Godwin, but they also forced him to recognise that if he wanted relationships with women he needed to consider other styles of communication than that of didacticism from on high.

The ultimate fruit of that insight was his relationship with Wollstonecraft. In that relationship she was able to persuade him that there were other modes of communication – and he became less wilfully didactic with her. But her path was made easier by these younger women. Godwin's intellectualism was an extremely dominating style of discourse – indeed, one in which his emphasis on the intellectual seemed largely to eliminate the possibility of any other type of relationship – everything being reduced to reason and duty! What Alderson, Parr and Reveley opened up for Godwin was a richer mode of communication, involving affection, sympathy and sensuality. Without that, Wollstonecraft would not have responded to him and he would have not been able to learn from her, as he did during the writing of *The Enquirer*.

I have suggested that it was somewhat paradoxical that Godwin (and many of his friends) should seem to socialise so much when he (and they) had such a deeply critical view of the social conventions and false forms of communication which, in Rousseau-esque fashion, were seen as dominating polite society. Of course it is likely that he saw at least some of his social circles as different from those of the wider society; but while that might be so for some of the groups he moved in, it is difficult to see all his contacts as 'exceptions'. Another possibility, however, is that these circles were no more than a means for Godwin – above all a means to meet and then to engage with a few people whom he identified as of exceptional talent and ability.

Godwin retained throughout his life a commitment to the clash of mind on mind. He was suspicious of societies and, while he attended the Philomaths, this was more an adjunct to the close intellectual relationships he had already formed.[1] In his social circles he discriminated between those with whom he thought there could be improving conversation and those with whom he merely had acquaintance. Joseph Gerrald was certainly in the former category. As a result, for much of the time that Gerrald was in prison in London awaiting transportation Godwin tended to call on him on his own. At times the prison was clearly a very sociable place and Gerrald's friends dined with him and visited him on a regular basis. But the majority of Godwin's visits are made alone and, as far as we can tell, with the expectation that others would not be there. Godwin certainly did occasionally call with others, but he did not make this a regular practice, and it looks likely that he did not do so because he wanted to see Gerrald on his own – so he was seeing him, not as part of a network of support or solidarity, but to engage in intense conversational exchange.

This suggests that there is a major tension in Godwin's diary – between the complex interactions of networks on the one hand, that provide a wonderful opportunity to map social circles in London between 1788 and 1836; and Godwin's own intentions with respect to these circles. He clearly valued his connections; and after 1793 he lived in constant interaction with people. And many of these people were linked to cultural and literary experimentation, political reform and challenging the conventional wisdom. In that sense they were networks that were part of a wider cultural movement that questioned the status quo (albeit in different ways and with a variety of motives). Moreover, these networks enabled Godwin (and his friends) to do a lot of things, to support people, to borrow money and raise loans and gifts for dependents, to set up a business, to educate his children, etc. As Granovetter shows, weak ties can provide resources that are central to people managing their lives in many complex ways. But in something of a paradox, Godwin was not really interested in the weak ties of the network itself. He was interested

---

[1] See David O'Shaughnessy, 'Caleb Williams and the Philomaths: Recalibrating Political Justice for the Nineteenth Century', *Nineteenth-Century Literature* 66(4) (March 2012), 423–448.

in the possibility that out of these multiple encounters something more substantive and intellectually challenging and fruitful might be possible on a one-to-one basis.[2] Godwin's networks were weak; but they were important to him because they afforded opportunities for the emergence of the occasional strong deliberative tie that could meet his expectations (perhaps, more accurately, hopes) for relationships that would be mutually improving, educative, fulfilling, and morally enlightening – and deeply personally and intellectually engaging.

There is a wider issue here about network theory and the difficulties of mapping networks in ways that capture their variable significance, while also recognising that for many people networks are often thin or weak. In a range of Godwin's relationships, while he used his networks, he also sought to establish intense bi-lateral relationships in which he could experience the clash of mind on mind. The networks in which he moved were a means for meeting others, but he moved away from them when he could into more intimate relationships and settings.

The second thing to say is that this move from acquaintance to deep conversational exchange was considerably easier with male friends than with female acquaintances. This might partly be because of the kind of person Godwin was – since his intense and judgemental reasoning would have been found disconcerting (if oddly flattering) by many younger women. As we have seen, to be addressed by Godwin was to be accorded a certain kind of equality – certainly to be treated in a way that other men might never have treated them – even if that also implied a certain kind of pupillage! Hence the slightly odd letters with Amelia Alderson, Sarah Ann Parr, but in different ways also those with Mary Hays, in each of which we can see something like a struggle not to be interpolated wholly on Godwin's terms! But there were also, as we have seen, other social conventions that made intense intellectual relationships more contentious when taking place between the sexes.

Godwin's *Memoirs of the Author of a Vindication of the Rights of Woman* make it clear that his early meetings with Wollstonecraft in 1791 and 1792 were not a success. And in 1796 he betrayed some anxiety in his letter to Hays, in response to her invitation to tea to reacquaint himself with Wollstonecraft ('of whom I know not that I ever said a word of harm, & who has frequently amused herself with depreciating me') on 5 January 1796.[3] But there were early signs that each had changed (such

---

[2] References to Godwin's rather dull conversation in the early nineteenth century, perhaps especially from Charles Lamb, may well be misleading as a guide to his conduct when he lost the group and was engaged with a single individual.

[3] Hays, *The Correspondence*, p. 421.

as Wollstonecraft recognising that Godwin was more responsive to feeling and sensibility).[4] What these other relationships (from 1793–1796) had brought Godwin to see was the need for a wider range of responses and a more open and inclusive deliberative style that made greater concessions to full equality.[5] Wollstonecraft helped persuade Godwin that there were other modes of communication and that they had a legitimacy he had formerly been unwilling to ascribe to them. He did not wholly learn that lesson and he collapsed back into his more customary mode after her death, but his aspirations did become broader, more responsive to different modes of communicating and in that sense potentially more egalitarian. And he took these concerns to heart in relation to his writing.[6]

One consistent element in Godwin's thinking in the 1790s was a concern with how to bridge the gap between the enlightened and those less so. There is a note (as we saw in Chapter 2) reflecting on the potential of drama as a medium; and his collection of essays, *The Enquirer*, was constructed in a very different, more ruminative form that his *Enquiry*.[7] Written between 20 January 1796 and 27 February 1797 it can be read as marking the developing influence of his relationship with Wollstonecraft on his thinking. As they became closer, they engaged with each other's work and there were discussions of material from *The Enquirer* across the late summer and autumn of 1796. Moreover, essays such as 'Of Reasoning and Contention'[8] addressed the challenges of ascribing a 'real and *bona fide* equality' to children and can be read both alongside the book's declared purpose to consider education and more broadly in relation to communication in any relationship of inequality. In the second *Vindication*, Wollstonecraft wrote:

---

[4] Ibid., p. 422.

[5] In my *Godwin's Political Justice*, I was too resistant to the idea that his relationship with Wollstonecraft changed Godwin, not really seeing that this was part of a longer process of learning to negotiate with female interlocutors. I would, however, stand by the view that to explain the changes in terms of Godwin's emotional attachment to Wollstonecraft simply leaves unexplained why he might have become open to such a relationship. For a careful reading of Wollstonecraft's position at the time of their meeting, see Barbara Taylor, *Mary Wollstonecraft and the Female Imagination* (Cambridge: Cambridge University Press, 2003).

[6] This and the next three paragraphs draw on my 'William Godwin', in Sandrine Bergès, Eileen Hunt Botting and Alan Coffee (eds.), *The Wollstonecraftian Mind* (London: Routledge, 2019), pp. 211–223.

[7] See Mee, *Conversable Worlds*, pp. 156–167.

[8] William Godwin, *The Enquirer: Reflections on Education, Manners, and Literature, in a Series of Essays* (London: G. G. and J. Robinson, 1797), I, XI.

To render mankind more virtuous, and happier of course, both sexes must act from the same principle; but how can that be expected when only one is allowed to see the reasonableness of it? To render also the social compact truly equitable ... women must be allowed to found their virtue on knowledge, which is scarcely possible unless they be educated by the same pursuits as men.[9]

The Enquirer reflects on the necessary conditions for equal communication, as against merely making a presumption in favour of equality – so much so that it provides a leitmotif of the volume as a whole. And as Godwin reflects on the obstacles that inequality creates for the passing on of knowledge, values and principles, he and Wollstonecraft seem simultaneously to be working out how their partnership and communication was to be manifested and made equal, given that they brought very different experiences and commitments to the relationship.

As their relationship developed, this issue became a central matter that they had to resolve. One major obstacle to its resolution was precisely the developing physical and emotional character of their relationship – indeed the very terms in which Godwin later acknowledged this aspect implied difference – 'Mary rested her head on the shoulder of her lover ...'.[10] Yet the challenge for both of them was *not* to establish their relationship as one of her dependency on him. This was a challenge, given her experience, their relative financial positions,[11] their different educational and philosophical backgrounds and, above all, given the deep structures of inequality that pervaded Georgian society in general, but was equally prevalent in the apparently more tolerant and open literary and cultural circles of the 1790s. Wollstonecraft, by accepting (probably initiating) a sexual relationship, was putting herself in a dramatically more precarious position than was Godwin – indeed, it was an even more precarious one that she had had with Imlay while in France. Given the deep inequality in their respective vulnerabilities, and given their differently motivated resistances to marriage, we might see them as responding to these challenges precisely by diversifying their interaction, multiplying the registers they used and moving away from the direct deliberative exchange that Godwin had insisted on in his friendships earlier in the decade. We might see this as Godwin learning the language of affection and care, but what he emphasised was the language of equality and friendship, coupled with a disdain for claims

[9] Wollstonecraft, *A Vindication*, pp. 259–260.
[10] William Godwin, 'Memoirs of the Author of a Vindication of the Rights of Woman' (1798), in Mark Philp (ed.), *Collected Novels and Memoirs of William Godwin* (London: Pickering & Chatto, 1992), vol. 1, p. 129.
[11] Godwin writes to Wedgwood to borrow money to settle Wollstonecraft's debts before their marriage. Godwin, *Letters of WG*, i, pp. 194–195.

to authority – although he did fall into exhortation when he felt at an impasse,[12] and it seems clear that his assumption of the role of 'philosopher' was sometimes an issue.[13] Wollstonecraft herself comments on the importance of his recognising her different registers – to 'distinguish between jest and earnest' – even though this was hardly his forte; and he admitted to not knowing 'when your satire means too much & when it means nothing'.[14]

She clearly recognised that to sustain their equality she had to resist a solely philosophical register and had to persuade him that 'There are other pleasures in the world, you perceive, beside those know[n] to your philosophy.'[15] The relationship certainly had its challenges: her vulnerability was evident at the end of December 1796, when she was pregnant, low spirited and when financial difficulties prompted her to fear Godwin's indifference and the necessity of relying on her own resources: 'I am, however, prepared for anything. I can abide by the consequences of my own conduct, and do not wish to envolve any one in my difficulties.'[16] And as others have pointed out, there are clearly moments where Wollstonecraft feared that Godwin would be transformed into Imlay.[17]

They survived these moments. Godwin genuinely cared for her, even if he was sometimes confused and unsure as to how he should act. But his earlier experiences (with Alderson and Parr) seem to have been somewhat educative (and thereby fortifying) and to have been sufficient to get him to recognise that neither the philosophical mode nor conventional societal norms were the way forward, leaving him to try to enjoin registers in which both of them could find some solidity and comfort. Of course, he often got things wrong. In April, after their marriage, when they went to the theatre together with a larger company, including Inchbald and Alderson, and when Inchbald was 'base, cruel, and insulting' to Wollstonecraft, precipitating a quarrel in the household, Godwin took the high (dominant, benevolent, lecturing) ground: 'The sole principle of conduct of which I am conscious in my behaviour to you, has been in every thing to study your happiness. I found a wounded heart, &, as that heart cast itself upon me, it was my ambition to heal it. Do not let me be wholly disappointed.'[18] But Wollstonecraft too recognised the difficulties

---

[12] Wardle, *Godwin and Mary*, pp. 17, 23.   [13] Ibid., p. 37.   [14] Ibid., pp. 49–50.
[15] Ibid., p. 57. Letter dated 23 December 1796. They had seen Hamlet together on 31 October 1796.
[16] Ibid., p. 60.
[17] See, for example, Lyndall Gordon, *Vindication: A Life of Mary Wollstonecraft* (London: Virago, 2006), pp. 350–351; and Janet Todd, *Mary Wollstonecraft: A Revolutionary Life* (New York: Columbia University Press, 2000), pp. 446–447.
[18] Wardle, *Godwin and Mary*, p. 75.

of consistently effecting equality between them. In May she wrote: 'I am sorry we entered on an altercation this morning, which has probably led us both to justify ourselves at the expense of the other. Perfect confidence, and sincerity of action is, I am persuaded, incompatible with the present state of reason.' And she went on to underline how difficult it was to be certain whether he always acted for the right motives or indeed for those he professed to be moved by. And against that nice philosophical distinction she asked instead for a little 'romantic tenderness'.[19] But Godwin did also sometimes get it right, as in his letter while touring in the Midlands, when he wrote that,

after all one's philosophy, it must be confessed that the knowledge, that there is someone that takes an interest in our happiness something like that which each man feels in his own, is extremely gratifying. We love, as it were, to multiply our consciousness & our existence, even at the hazard of what Montagu described so pathetically one night upon the New Road, of opening new avenues of pain and misery to attack us.[20]

The central challenge that Wollstonecraft posed to Godwin was for him to recognise her as an equal, in a society in which there was little or nothing to support that, in a literary culture that in parts tolerated that aspiration but found little success in achieving it and where their developing emotional and sexual relationship inevitably made it still harder to achieve and maintain. On the face of it, Godwin was not promising material: he was forty years old and wholly inexperienced in relation to the opposite sex; he was a product of a highly masculine and highly intellectual cultural environment and had a very cerebral approach to the world; and he was dismissive of many women writers. But their relationship altered him and opened him up to new experiences, at least for a time. It forced him to reflect again and again on the problem of enabling equality in an unequal society, without patronising and infantilising his interlocutors. Their relationship became a stab at achieving deliberative equality and mutual respect in a deeply inegalitarian and gendered society. Godwin's candour about Wollstonecraft in his *Memoirs* was clearly meant to celebrate in part the equality they achieved. But he dramatically underestimated how damaging that candour would be (just as he underestimated how challenging his interlocutors could find it earlier in the decade). Others among his contemporaries might have done similar things behind closed doors, but openly to celebrate her life and her (and their) conduct in the febrile political atmosphere of 1797–1798 was a grave mistake. A very few other women saw their

---

[19] Ibid., p. 77.   [20] Godwin, *Letters of WG*, i, p. 215.

attempt for the extraordinary thing that it tried to be – Alderson was one and, much later, Mary Shelley another, but the *Memoirs* effectively threw a juicy bone to a wider public looking for ways to discredit the ideas of reformers (and above all women reformers) and it was seized on with gusto.

In his last letter to Alderson, before unbraiding her for coquetry yet again, Godwin reported: 'I am in the same house; I have her two children about me. They have no mother, & I am afraid I am scarcely worth having as a father: I feel as if I were the most unfit person in the world for the business of education. She was the best qualified of any person I ever saw.'[21] Godwin was clearly at sea – like Rousseau, he could write books about education, but did not see himself as a fit person to undertake it with his own children. His domestic life became a challenge and he ended up relying a good deal on Elizabeth Fenwick and Maria Reveley (until her husband expressed concerns) and employing a friend of his sister Hannah, Louisa Jones, from the time of Wollstonecraft's death until mid-1800. But he clearly 'wanted' a wife – and in *that* wanting, difference and inequality were clearly built in.

6.2 Godwin's Wooing

In March 1798 Godwin went to Bath, where he met the novelist and playwright Harriet Lee and over the next five months laid epistolary (and occasionally personal) siege to her. Reading these letters it is difficult not to be embarrassed for Godwin and to feel that whatever credit he may have earned in his relationship with Wollstonecraft and by his willingness to vary his style was being catastrophically spent. It is also difficult not to sympathise with Miss Lee, who must have been perplexed as to what she could have done to deserve such a testimony of Godwin's determination not to take 'no' for an answer. And yet, the letters are also revealing for what they do not mention, above all: Godwin's *Memoirs*, the different mores of London literary culture and the narrower confines, forms and distinctions of Bath and Bristol, the speed with which Godwin was seeking to replace his dead wife and the fact that she was a similar age to him and had clearly found it possible thus far to have resisted Godwin's fellow men and had found it possible to have coped, as he put it, 'without ever having lived: for that only deserves the name of life, where we feel existence at it were at every pore, where we melt with tenderness & affections unspeakable, where we glow with a generosity & disinterestedness with

---

[21] MS Abinger c.22, fol 68r; Godwin, *Letters of WG*, i, pp. 258–259.

which a life of celibacy must be forever acquainted. All else in sublunary existence, is comparative death.'[22] After an increasingly dogged set of arguments, Godwin, attempted to retire with grace in the final section of his last extant letter to Lee in August 1798, although he had already stooped to trying to enlist Lee's sister Sophia to his cause.[23] Miss Lee, however, seems to have handled the matter with discretion. It was the plight of many women to be subjected to such proposals, to resist them and then to be required to show absolute discretion about the foolish importuning to which they had been subjected. (Lee might well have had some earlier experience of this, having been attended by Thomas Laurence earlier in the decade, and might have become an old hand at doing what was necessary and what, if one was firm and patient, would ultimately prove sufficient).[24] Certainly, there seemed to be no wider suspicion of Godwin's flailing pursuit. When Lee returned to visit London in January 1799, Godwin saw her in the company of both Charlotte Smith and Elizabeth Inchbald, neither of whom seemed to have been aware of his 'courtship'. Godwin's diary records that he wrote to her again on 1 June 1799, but one hopes it was only to congratulate her on her *Canterbury Tales*, which he had been reading – and, doubtless, to correct a few errors.

Godwin's attempt to argue Lee into caring for him (he does not mention his children!) strikes us the more forcibly because we do not see this side of him in his relationship with Wollstonecraft. Of course, with Wollstonecraft their initial courtship was not epistolary for the most part and we can only speculate as to how it progressed.[25] He had to conduct his courtship of Lee largely by letter; in contrast, London had afforded him and Wollstonecraft possibilities both for association and a degree of anonymity. They called on each other with relative freedom and felt able to spend time together in a way that remained undetected for the most part by their contemporaries (although they were not entirely free from interference – 'I was glad you were not with me last night, for the foolish woman of the house laid a trap to plague me. I have, however, I believe put an end to this nonsense, so enough of that subject').[26] Their love affair grew out of a developing intellectual relationship and their shared concerns with

---

[22] Godwin, *Letters of WG*, ii, p. 28: see also his 'celibacy contracts and palsies the mind', p. 44.
[23] Ibid., ii, p. 53.   [24] See Farington, *Diary*, III. 866; IV. 1148.
[25] See, for example, William St Clair, *The Godwins and the Shelleys* (London: Faber and Faber, 1989), appendix 1.
[26] Ralph M. Wardle (ed.), *Godwin & Mary: Letters of William Godwin and Mary Wollstonecraft* (London: Constable and Co. Ltd., 1967), no. 97, p. 65.

literary matters. And their unconventional gradual cohabitation speaks to the extent that it was possible for an independent woman in London to achieve a degree of seclusion from the prying eyes of others. The ground on which he wooed Lee was very different and was far less friendly to Godwin, who seems to have been more comfortable falling into relationships than actively initiating them. Lee worked within the more traditional forms of visiting and polite conversation; he was clearly impatient with such forms. He sought to set philosophical terms to his courtship; she demurred. His earlier experience with young women was such that, although he might be disconcerted, he believed they might be flattered intellectually by his willingness to engage with them. The more mature and careful Harriet Lee showed little sign of recognising the honour he believed he was doing her. Because he was nonplussed by finding himself having to make efforts to be in her company and having to accept the conventions of that society and because he was impatient to resolve his situation, he blundered over and over again, leading her to set her boundaries more firmly. To some extent, he was undone by his assumption of the relative freedom of London literary circles; to some extent, he had a classically male blindness to how disconcerting such an approach must have been.

We have also seen that, shortly after the collapse of his wooing of Lee, he wrote a rather startling letter to Emily Kingsman, in which he raked up a variety of metaphors for the possibilities of mentoring her development (as a man of 42 to a young woman barely of age) as if he had learned little from his experiences with Parr and Alderson. To be fair to Godwin, what looks tantamount to grooming to us would almost certainly not have struck him in the same way (but then insight is not an inevitable masculine virtue). There is little beyond this letter to suggest that he was positively predatory; and much to suggest that his attitude to her was similar to his attitude to many young men with whom he developed close intellectual relationships – Basil Montagu, Thomas Turner, John Arnot, Thomas Cooper, Patrick Patrickson, Percy Shelley and others. Indeed, his reaction to meeting John Stoddart (aged 23 to Godwin's 39) on 14 January 1796 was not dissimilar – 'I want to know whether in exhibiting so many excellencies you have put a deception on me; or whether, as I like to believe, I have found a treasure.'[27]

These were not merely acquaintances or weak ties. They involved the search for a very different kind of relationship, based on sympathy and an appreciation of the other's merits and qualities and resting on the

---

[27] MS Abinger c.22, fol 8; Godwin, *Letters of WG*, i, pp. 147–148.

construction of a deliberative domain free from the pursuit of interest and dedicated to the advancement of knowledge and virtue. It was not the strong tie of family, occupation, locality and history, but one that stood apart from those particular determinants and sought a grounding wholly in the qualities of those involved. It was, in short, a bid for disinterested friendship. It is difficult to be sure of how widely such an attitude existed, but it was a central part of the self-representation of literary men in the 1790s as they pursued their agenda of intellectual progress.

Moreover, the concern to identify people of ability in the social circles in which Godwin and his friends moved was one which did not discriminate by gender. While that might be something we might commend, it is nonetheless difficult to ignore his failure to appreciate that his female acquaintances faced major difficulties in admitting such an approach. Godwin was rather stuck. His candour about his and Wollstonecraft's unconventionality could not but render both young women and women of any standing and reputation prudent about being associated with him (even if it might have increased his fascination for some). Among sympathetic men, and because he was male, he expected his infractions to be ignored or more positively to be respected for the commitments they represented; but, for women, association with him had to be handled carefully and openly. There was no one from his own circles whom he saw as able to fill the place of Wollstonecraft and, while his contacts brought him into a wider set of relationships, the norms of those circles were not as tolerant or as informal as he needed to allow a friendship to develop from which something else might then evolve (and it must be said, there is an air of desperation to his approaches that must have been additionally alarming).

That said, we should also recognise that Godwin's intellectual purposes also constrained him in his choice of partner and we should take seriously his praise for Lee's gifts as fitting her for the role he projected for her. The importance of a meeting of minds as the grounds for the conciliation of other parts was a central *desiderata* for Godwin, as emerged very clearly in his relationship with one of his young disciples the following year.

There were many boundary problems for Godwin in relation to those whom he welcomed so wholly into his society. He wanted to challenge the norms of domestic sociability for philosophical purposes – but such challenges might alarm his female acquaintance and it is also true that the practices of some of his male friends did not always meet his expectations. Consider the case of the writer Ralph Fell, whom Godwin met in 1797 and saw very frequently until 1804, when the relationship foundered because Godwin was unable to repay a debt.[28] Fell was friendly with Godwin's sister Hannah, but his involvement with Godwin's domestic circle became troubled at the end of 1799. Hannah Godwin was a single woman and a Mantua maker in London. She visited Godwin regularly, calling occasionally in the company of girls apprenticed to her business. In August 1798 she introduced her apprentice, Sarah Carey/Karre to Godwin, and Godwin met the two women with Ralph Fell in August and again in November 1799. In November 1799, Fell wrote to Godwin referring to his getting married (to Carey). Godwin was clearly angry about the relationship, suspecting that his sister was using his philosophical 'connections' as a means of securing husbands for her apprentices. His wrath is clear from the note he sent Hannah:

I am extremely mortified at your conduct in what has lately passed between Miss Carey and Mr Fell. You must have known, if you were capable of any accurate judgment, that it was the case of a young man of superlative talents and promise throwing himself away, from the most puerile, or rather the grossest motives, upon a creature comparatively worthy only of a dunghil. You ought, if you had any propriety, immediately to have consulted me on this subject. But I bear you no resentment. As I have said, I am only mortified, but not surprised by your conduct.[29]

His draft to Fell was equally unrestrained: 'But my judgment is clear: I will never see Miss Carey, as Miss Carey, so long as this business is in hand: if she should ever become Mrs Fell, I will treat your washerwoman with respect under that character, and will allow myself no retrospect to what is irremediable.'[30] Fell married Sarah Carey/Karre on 5 July 1800 at St Dionis Backchurch with James Marshall and Hannah Godwin as witnesses.[31]

Fell's marriage to Carey was followed by the marriage of another young friend and acolyte, Henry Dibbin, to Louisa Jones (Godwin's housekeeper) in May 1801 (at which Hannah Godwin was again a witness).[32] The two events led to a serious cooling in Godwin's

---

[28] Fell wrote *A Tour through the Batavian Republic during the Latter Part of the Year 1800: Containing an Account of the Revolution and Recent Events in That Country* (London: R. Phillips, 1801); and *Memoirs of the Public Life of the Late Right Honourable Charles James Fox* (London: J. F. Hughes, 1808). See above pp. 84–85.

[29] Bodleian Library MS. Abinger c.17, fol 9r–v. See HG's spirited replies, MS Abinger c.5, fols 14–17, and Godwin's subsequent responses, Bodleian Library MS Abinger c.22, fols 127–130.

[30] It seems likely he sent a toned-down version that does not survive – see Godwin, *Letters of WG*, ii, pp. 111–112.

[31] The certificate suggests that Godwin's references to Miss Carey involved a consistent misspelling of Sarah Karre.

[32] See http://edpopehistory.co.uk/entries/jones-louisa/1795-11-30-000000 (accessed 6 January 2019). See also National Archives TS 11473/1582 where Dyson writes to his

relationship with his sister. Their relationship may have been additionally complicated by Hannah's intimacy with Godwin's amanuensis James Marshall. In the 1790s she seems to have been very close to Marshall, and the evidence suggests that she fell out with Godwin in 1800 partly over her promotion of the Carey/Fell relationship. Prior to this, her friendship with Marshall was such that Godwin's mother expressed concern about it in a letter to Godwin:

> your poor sister is I fear a bad accernomist her heart too generous for her comings in ..., many people think her carrector injured by Marshal a married man, who I suppose dines with her on Sundays, is it not so, do you commend her, tell me freely, or advise her against it yourself, she will hear you sooner than any body else ...[33]

To our knowledge Godwin did not advise against it – perhaps assuming that Marshall was philosophically above reproach. Yet it is clear that there were a number of secrets being kept from Godwin even in his most intimate visiting circles: Godwin believed that Louisa Jones had decamped with George Dyson (when in fact he was only a witness to the wedding) and he reported as much to his young acolyte, the traveller John Arnot, who was himself in love with Jones.[34] It is unclear when Godwin found out the complete truth, but his reaction to Jones's marriage was uncompromising: she was barred from the house and forbidden to see the children again.

This makes clear just how treacherous the social terrain could become when people sought to dispense with traditions and conventions. On the one hand, Godwin found it difficult to read people's (especially women's) behaviour; on the other, protégés, acquaintances, friends and family were clearly failing, in Godwin's view, to act according to his high expectations. The exact form of those expectations with respect to personal relationships seems to have concerned the furthering of intellectual development and of capacities for contributing to the broader world; and they seemed to require affinities of mind between partners – promising a companionate, mutually educative, progressive and philosophical, not just a social or wholly sexual partnership. Or at least that was the case when he was (as he saw it) defending his friends against the attractions of Hannah Godwin's young apprentices. At the same time, they were acting in a curious social space – sharing some of Godwin's intellectual

---

father referring to Dibbin, who seems to have been an old school friend. My thanks to Edward Pope for pointing me to these materials.

[33] Bodleian Library MS Abinger c.3, fol 64v, 3 May 1797.

[34] This seems implied by Arnot's letter to Godwin, Bodlian Library MS Abinger c.6, fols 51–52, 10 October 1800.

ambitions alongside his sense that societal mores and customs were merely arbitrary constraints, while also being incompletely isolated from a wider social world that could impose costs on them for straying from more conventional paths. And Godwin found himself caught up in a range of conflicting imperatives and concerns, with the result that he was often disconcerted and occasionally outraged by the behaviour of others, when he thought they were betraying his principles. Indeed, friendships broke down because of his strictures (derived from strict philosophical principle). By 1805, he and Hannah had little contact – indeed, as we have seen, she was included in his list of 'amis perdus', which he drew up (probably) around 1805; a list that (as we saw earlier) named many of his former and younger friends – Dyson, Montagu, Stoddart, Arnot, Dibbin and Kearsley – and a number of other women – Inchbald, Reveley and Amelia Alderson.[35] Several of those on the list became alienated from Godwin in part because of the problems of policing the boundaries of these public and private spaces and connections. Dyson, Dibbin and Arnot were linked through Louisa Jones, Godwin's housekeeper; Godwin alienated Reveley by proposing to her so soon after the death of her husband in the summer of 1799 (despite their clear affection for each other)[36]; Inchbald froze Godwin out after his marriage to Wollstonecraft; and Amelia Alderson's earlier intimacy with Godwin cooled on her marriage to Opie. The list testifies to Godwin's misjudgements and mismanagement of the expectations of others and his over-statement of his own claims with respect to them. But it also speaks eloquently to the complex character of personal relations in the radical culture of sociability, conversation and candour in London at the end of the eighteenth century, to the difficulties in living in the light of one's private judgment in ways that were necessarily partly public, even when conducted in domestic space, and to the fragmentary character of radical social circles that could not protect them from the social mores of the wider groups of which they were members but against which they were in part reacting.

The dramatic misjudgement Godwin made in publishing his *Memoirs* of Mary Wollstonecraft suggests that he was largely unaware of the very limited public tolerance for his unconventional behaviour (or, more charitably, that he was too distraught to be cautious). At the same time, his behaviour with respect to Fell looks stultifyingly conventional and it is clear that there were other cases in which he found himself acting in ways that to the external observer look identical to the classic position of the

---

[35] See above chapter 2, p. 81. [36] *Godwin Diary*, 9 January 1795.

outraged patriarch of eighteenth century fiction.[37] There are then two contrasting sides – seemingly conventional opprobrium for some of his friends and their choices – and his own very unconventional relationships – not just with Wollstonecraft and subsequently with his second wife, Mary Jane Clairmont, but also, less intimate but not wholly intellectual, with a number of others including Elizabeth Inchbald, Maria Reveley, Amelia Alderson and perhaps also Sarah Anne Parr, Nan Pinkerton, Mary Robinson and Mary Hays. This list is rather impressionistic. Little exists to allow us firmly to determine Godwin's intentions, these women's expectations or the precise character of their relationships, but there is a clear sense in many cases that those who called on him and on whom he called were looking for a kind of intense intellectual relationship with him that was far from conventional and that this focus rendered the boundaries of their relationships with Godwin ill-defined and could generate difficulties and misunderstandings and possibilities for other dimensions of interaction to develop.

[37] His reaction in 1814 to his daughter Mary's love for Shelley and their subsequent elopement seems very conventional; but well before that, in 1804, he was involved in proceedings to rescue his niece Harriet who had run off with Thomas West, a married man, against whom he obtained a writ of habeas corpus, which produced an interview, but not a return. National Archive KB 1/32/2f.107. My thanks are again owed to Edward Pope for pointing me to this material.

7   A Private Affair

7.1   Calling and Numbers

As we have seen in relation to Wollstonecraft, it seems it was possible to shield one's developing relationships and intimacies from the awareness of one's close friends, at least for a period and up to a certain point. That does not mean that it was possible to do so without generating gossip, but that might well be restricted to women's circles – certainly there is little to suggest that there was a wholly porous membrane between male and female circles. At the same time, there were issues about how far women could afford to take such risks and over what period. The Godwin Diary Project is only one source on such matters, but it deals with a man who was in many respects unconventional, not least in his desire for intellectual relationships with women, albeit these had an inevitable element of instability because of the freighted character of gender relations in the society that could lead to reputational damage or to their tipping in more emotional and physical directions. The diary does, however, enable us to chart more systematically patterns of visits that Godwin paid to women and those he was paid by women, enabling us to deduce something about the norms that operated in his circles. I want to focus my remarks on the occasions on which Godwin saw women alone, either at his home or in theirs – something that he did to some degree, although much less commonly than was the case for his contacts with men.

I take the significance of them being 'alone' to be as follows. As I have argued, the reputation of women (in relation to men) was socially policed in this period, perhaps especially by other women. There were norms of conduct. Of course, people bent or sometimes broke them, but in doing so they risked their reputation, and that could lead to them being cut, ostracised from various circles, and could diminish their respectability and, for some, their consequent (marital) prospects. The costs to men were always substantially less – for many men, the point of having a past was, in part, to have something to put behind them! But for women these norms were extremely powerful and responsible men would have had some concern for the reputational risks run by their female friends. At the same time, these more intellectual circles shared a scepticism towards these mores and were often impatient of the restraints they placed on them. For example, in Godwin's letter to Maria Reveley when he courts her (much too) soon after the death of her husband, he begins: 'How my whole soul disclaims and tramples upon these cowardly ceremonies. Is woman always to be a slave?' And we have also seen Alderson's impatience with, but also her compliance with 'nonsense'.[1]

Most women sought to avoid providing food for gossip and speculation; many were also concerned not to be associated with women whose reputation might produce collateral damage; and many might be anxious, especially following Godwin's *Memoirs* of Wollstonecraft, not to be seen as being intimate with him. Radical women (that is, women who had liberal sympathies, supported reform and sought to challenge at least some of the polite conventions by which they were constrained) might or might not bend or break these rules; they might also be less judgemental about those they associated with; but in neither case could they expect to do so wholly without cost. Wollstonecraft was certainly concerned about such issues. When she returned to London from Paris she presented herself as Mrs Imlay and was taken by many to be exactly that. Indeed, Godwin, prior to the commencement of their affair and despite referring to her throughout his diary as Mrs Wollstonecraft, used the name Imlay in an unconscious reflex on the first occasion that he included her in a dinner party with his respectable friends (22–23 April 1796) – conferring a status on her he knew to be false but necessary to her.

As we have seen, Godwin was often unconventional – about whom he saw, how he saw them and in his attitude to conventional norms. He married after the fact, not before; he exhorted Wollstonecraft the day after the diary entry 'chez moi toute' – 'Humble! for heaven's sake, be proud, be arrogant!'[2]; in his many relationships with women he talked to them as a philosopher, irrespective of convention or offence; he was friendly with several women who were in various ways 'unrespectable' (such as Mary Robinson, formerly mistress to the Prince of Wales and subsequently to Col. Tarleton); and his *Memoirs* of Wollstonecraft made him both notorious and perhaps more interesting! This meant that the women he met had to consider how to respond to such an unconventional man. Above all, they would have been wary of being seen as being intimate with him – although someone like Mary Robinson who had little

---

[1] Bodleian Library MS. Abinger c.22, fols 117–118.
[2] Bodleian Library MS. Abinger c.40, fol 30.

to lose could use the same concerns teasingly to flirt with Godwin, as when she wrote to him, after he had visited her and stayed the night (when she was ill and rather isolated): 'I was extremely sorry, my dear Sir, when I found on opening my eyes this morning that you had kept your word, and departed without your breakfast' (one assumes it was not exactly 'on opening my eyes').[3]

Nonetheless, between 1791 and 1801 (in the December of which Godwin married Mary Jane Clairmont) there were many occasions on which Godwin recorded visits to or meals with women where no one else was recorded as present. Some can be eliminated because they clearly involved the domestic help Godwin needed with the two children. Some, but by no means all, were instances where Godwin and his visitor/host were not behaving strictly within the norms of propriety. For the historian the central issue is how these might be differentiated: not just by us but also by his contemporaries. How might others have seen these calls as something other than evidence of scandal? One principle that is likely to have operated in Godwin's circles is that people would have been concerned only where there was a *consistent* pattern of compromising behaviour. Also, married women might have had a degree of licence that single women did not – especially eligible single women. Older, well-established women may similarly have had this.

There were four main possibilities for Godwin seeing a woman on her own – the 'place' would be either his or her domestic space; and it might be a call or might involve a meal. Some categories are harder to establish than others. Godwin lists 'calls' to him in a way that does not make clear whether people are calling together or separately. For example, on 29 August 1800 he records 'Curran, Taggart, A Walker, H^t & Phebe G call'. Whether this is one or five calls (or something in between) is unclear, but they were probably five separate calls (Phebe G was Godwin's niece). The coding we used for the diary treats these as single calls, but we have emphasised that caution should be attached to that judgement and to this category.

We also do not know whether a 'call' or 'dine' where no one else is recorded really is a case of Godwin meeting the person alone. Godwin identifies housekeepers and servants in the diary only very exceptionally and on many occasions when it appears that Godwin was alone servants must have been in attendance. Of course, servants could be a mixed blessing: they could hold one's reputation in their hands and they could conspire for or against their mistress or master, so that people may often

---

[3] Bodleian Library MS. Abinger c.6, fol 41r.

have needed to maintain appearances in front of them as well.[4] More-over, what mattered reputationally was not whether two people were actually alone, but whether others assumed that they were.

If we set some of these concerns aside for a moment and look at the broader picture, we can recognise the following patterns. If we take the occasions on which Godwin recorded seeing women on their own and look at the busiest years, it is striking how far a single person accounts for around half of all such contacts. In 1793, 1794 and 1795 this was Elizabeth Inchbald; in 1796 and 1797 this was Wollstonecraft (these numbers hold up despite the fact that Godwin ceased to list Wollstone-craft in the diary after their marriage in March 1797); in 1798 this was Charlotte Smith; in 1799 and 1800 this was Sarah Elwes; and in 1801 this was Mrs Mary Jane Clairmont. In terms of total contacts across these years, there are 135 with Inchbald; 168 with Wollstonecraft; 28 with Smith; 116 with Elwes; and 56 with Clairmont. At this point, we might want more granularity.

Visits paid by Godwin to women when no other person was recorded as present were most frequently to Inchbald in 1793, 1794 and 1795; to Wollstonecraft in 1796 and 1797; to a cluster of women (Smith, Hays, Christie and Lee), each of whom was seen slightly fewer than ten times, in 1798 (after Wollstonecraft's death), to Elwes in 1799 and 1800; and in 1801 no one stood out.

Visits by women to Godwin when he was alone were far fewer. The only people who visited more than ten times in a year on their own were Wollstonecraft and Elwes. In 1797 and 1798, in the aftermath of Woll-stonecraft's death, Maria Reveley was also a frequent visitor. She came to help care for the children, but her visits caused her husband sufficient disquiet that she was forced to stop them. Reveley was a married woman; no single woman could have acted in this way without cost, except when enshrined in the capacity of a housekeeper or governess.[5]

Meals that Godwin had at women's homes on his own are in similar numbers to solo calls on Godwin. But even fewer people account for a very substantial proportion of such calls: Wollstonecraft, Smith, Elwes and Clairmont received Godwin more than ten times – and they account for a substantial proportion of such events.

Finally, meals taken alone with Godwin is the most exclusive group – only Elwes and Clairmont appear more than ten times. Moreover, of the

[4] See, for example, Opie's *Adeline Mowbray* (1805) for problems with servants.
[5] Roles that must have implicitly appealed to class and status differentials and a careful choreographing of conduct before others – especially given the possibilities of transgression – as with the case of Erasmus Darwin noted in Chapter 3, note 64.

forty such occasions between 1798 and 1801, Elwes accounts for twenty and Clairmont for fourteen.

It is clear that 1797 and 1798 were slightly odd years because from March 1797 Godwin continued to see Wollstonecraft, but no longer recorded their contact: also, from March he had a family home, changing the salience of several of the conventions; and from September 1797 he was desperate for help with his family in the aftermath of Wollstonecraft's death. 1798 clearly involves several people who were supporting Godwin's young family, such as Eliza Fenwick and Mrs Christie. Nonetheless, there is clearly a growing intimacy as we move through these categories. 'Calling' probably had components that were not fully registered in the diary, such as leaving a card, paying respects, etc., which might be highly conformist in character with respect to social manners. Also, while young women in particular might not have done much receiving of young men without supervision, it was not necessarily inappropriate to do so (as Fanny Burney's novels suggest), but it was something that would be 'read'. Women may also have been able to control the situation, through family proximity, servants or maids, to minimise their exposure. 'Mrs Perfection', as Wollstonecraft referred to Inchbald, clearly maintained control of Godwin's intimacy with her by restricting it to calls on her – of her 135 solo contacts with Godwin, all but 5 were calls he made to her, which suggests that she had a way of signalling to others that these were not occasions of unusual intimacy. Charlotte Smith also saw a lot of Godwin, especially in 1798, when she was in London a good deal, but she was married with ten children and, again, the vast majority of contacts took place at her home, with Godwin calling on her or, more usually, taking tea with her.

Those most at risk of accusations of impropriety were those who frequently called on or dined alone with Godwin or with whom he dined alone. There are three such people who stand out: Wollstonecraft, Elwes and Clairmont. We know a good deal about Wollstonecraft and I will say something about Mary Jane Clairmont in due course. Sarah Elwes has, thus far, been largely unnoticed and unidentified, but she offers us an especially interesting perspective on the problems that attached to encounters in private spaces.

7.2   Sarah Elwes

Sarah Elwes married John M. Elwes, the youngest of the two illegitimate sons of John Elwes senior, renowned as the meanest man in Britain on his death on 26 November 1789. In Dickens's *Our Mutual Friend*, Mr Boffin reads Edward Topham's *The Remarkable Life of John*

Elwes esq. to train himself up as a miser.[6] Sarah and John Elwes married on 23 December 1789. John may have been remarrying, he had a son by Margaret Olley Elwes in 1788 (but his will suggests that this son did not survive).[7] It was Sarah's second marriage, her first husband (from 1785) was Captain Thomas Haynes, who died on 26 December 1788.[8]

In October 1793 Sarah and John Elwes separated and in 1794 John Elwes brought an action in the Court of the King's Bench against a Mr George Samuel Harvey for criminal conversation with his wife dating from 1791. Harvey was approximately twenty-two years of age. Mrs Elwes was described as being between thirty and thirty-five years of age (John Elwes was forty-two). The case also cited another young man, Jasper Egerton, a lawyer who had acted as Mrs Elwes' representative and lawyer in the months leading up to the criminal conversation case. The case against Harvey was based on the testimony of various servants employed by John Elwes, who filed reports of lewd and intimate behaviour occurring in the back sitting room of the house (which was the main reception room) on various occasions. This included reports of Mrs Elwes's maid letting in Harvey (or Egerton) without the other servants' knowledge; of her taking the carriage with or having gone riding with one or other of the named gentlemen to Kensington Gardens,

and there quit her horses, and desired the same to be put up at some Inn or Public House in the Neighbourhood, and would remain in the said Gardens for several Hours together, and till after it was dark, and was almost constantly, at such Times, met either by Mr Harvey or Mr Egerton, and they used to retire into the most private and unfrequented Parts of the Garden, and remain there so long, that the Gate-Keepers have frequently taken Notice of it to the Servant waiting for her.[9]

Moreover, the claim was that

Mrs Elwes used very frequently to call upon Mr Egerton at his Chambers in Gray's Inn and on Mr Harvey at his Chambers in the Temple, and at other times,

---

6 Charles Dickens, *Our Mutual Friend*, 2 vols. (London: Chapman and Hall. 1865). The same Topham referred to earlier who lived with, and had three children by Mary Wells, Inchbald's friend, before abandoning her and taking the children with him. Dickens is referring to Edward Topham's *Life of the Late John Elwes*, which first appeared in London, published by Thompson, but was reprinted multiple times, often with slightly different titles. See above p. 140.

7 National Archive PROB 11/1591:129/110–112. Despite Scott's instruction at the Consistory Court that John Elwes should live chastely, he had at least one other child in 1804–1805, John Meggot Elwes, *Derby Mercury*, 1 May 1817.

8 Although it is difficult to be wholly certain, it seems likely that Sarah's maiden name was Allen and that she married Thomas Haynes in June 1785.

9 See Sarah Lloyd, 'Amour in the Shrubbery: Reading the Detail of English Adultery Trial Publications of the 1780s', *Eighteenth Century Studies* 39(4) (2006), 421–442.

in the Absence of her Husband, used to invite, sometimes the One, and sometimes the other of them home to her House, in Weymouth Street, and remained alone with them for a considerable Time.[10]

Reports of behaviour in the back sitting room came from the groom, who could see into that room from the loft of the stables (and from other servants whom the groom encouraged to join him in spying on his mistress). Another detailed servant's report describes his mortification at accompanying Mrs Elwes in public when she and her sister-in-law were in the carriage, drawing attention to themselves by boisterous behaviour.

... there was one gentleman in particular that spoke to her, who was Dr Hughs, who saluted her with a nod and a wink with his eye, and seemed to recollect himself that he knew my Mrs. Just as he come up with our carriage he then puts almost his whole body out of the chariot he was in, as perceiving it was my Mrs he then saluted her by saying 'ah how do yo do an old acquaintance' and stretched out his hand, but was obliged to go on as there were more carriages behind him in the procession, so he went on, there were many after that my Mrs laughed at, and threw herself backward in the carriage, there was two strange gentlemen come up to the carriage and examine the crest and on seeing it was darts, said damn it is the Elwes arms, so Elwes keeps a blowze or something to that's meaning, and by God said the other is his wife – they went away laughing together; many men stopped and looked at the carriage as said there is two whores, one said that he would sware to one, because of her lecherous eyes another who seemed to be a society man and said he would be damned if it was not a whore, and he want to drive her for one month; for nothing if she would let him stroke her once I don't know whether they heard them. I was so ashamed I was almost determined to tell my Mr; and I though myself resolved not to go ///her anymore, for all my acquaintances told me that I lived with a blowze.[11]

The court found for the plaintiff and awarded 100 guineas damages against Mr Harvey (taking into account his age and lack of resources). John Elwes followed up this case with a suit against his wife for an Ecclesiastical divorce or 'separation from Bed and Board and mutual cohabitation by reason of adultery', heard in the Consistory Court at Doctors' Commons, in which both Harvey and Egerton were named.[12] The Court found against her on 13 July 1796.[13] She immediately appealed against the judgement and the case was assigned to

---

[10] High Court of Delegates Judgment National Archive Del 7/1, p. 2.
[11] London Metropolitan Archive DL/6/662/179/3; DL/C/0562/177–179.
[12] Lambeth Palace Archives D675 and D 676, case number 3111; National Archive DEL 670 v. 2.
[13] *Morning Chronicle*, 14 July 1796, Law Intelligence.

Sir William Wynne, Bishop of London, in the Arches Court of Canterbury.[14]

Her appeal denied the items of the libel entered against her, pleading that the two visits of Mr Harvey were in fact made not to her, but to her sister-in-law Amelia/Emily Elwes, who used the house in Weymouth Street to entertain friends when her husband was absent, and that Harvey's visits were on matters of business. She claimed that she had consulted Egerton as a lawyer because of her husband's behaviour; that 'for a considerable time previous to the institution of the present suit, and from the beginning of 1791 [John Elwes] declared to several Persons he was tired of his wife, and was determined to get rid of her at all Events, and should be obliged to any Man to enable him to get rid of her'; and that John Elwes had used an intermediary, William Hayward, to offer to John Gray, a former servant of Elwes, a considerable sum of money if he could persuade Mrs Elwes to lie with him, or 'if he would at least put himself into, or under the Bed of his Mistress, in order that he might be detected in that Situation'. She also alleged that witnesses subpoenaed in the cause of Mr Harvey, and ready to rebut and falsify the claims of the chief witnesses used by Mr Elwes, had not been called in his defence in the original court hearing, to the injury of Mrs Elwes and expressly contrary to assurances to her by Mr Harvey, and that the costs and damages awarded to Mr Elwes by the court had not been paid by Mr Harvey or, if they had been paid, had been returned (suggesting they had conspired against her).

The Arches Court of Canterbury declared in favour of John Elwes on 6 November 1797. Notwithstanding, Sarah Elwes launched a further appeal, heard by the High Court of Delegates, which pronounced sentence on 26 June 1798, affirming the judgements of the lower courts.[15] There was no higher court of appeal. Either John Elwes feared he had insufficient evidence to go to the House of Lords and move from an Ecclesiastical divorce to a civil divorce or he had had enough of the institution of marriage. Sarah Elwes continued in her status as a wife, separated for matters of bed, board and accommodation, but still using the name and title of Mrs Sarah Elwes. In 1800 – while Godwin was on a trip to Ireland – in a case prosecuting Elizabeth Scoltock for stealing clothing from her, she testified 'I am the wife of John Elwes.'[16]

---

[14] Metropolitan Archive DL/C/562/177/2. National Archive DEL 1/670 v. 1; Lambeth Palace Archives G 155/18; G 155/79; G 153/89; E45/100; G155/79; MS Film 104, 105; Process books D 675, D 676.

[15] DEL 1/670 v. i, ii; The formal, printed declaration of High Court of Delegates verdict is at DEL 7/1. See also DEL 5/35; and DEL 6/52.

[16] *Old Bailey Online*, Case 489, 9 July 1800.

The interest in this case is that Sarah Elwes came to form a close friendship with Godwin after the conclusion of her round of court cases. She is additionally interesting because Godwin's early friendship with her runs parallel in the early months to his friendship with Ralph Fell and the tensions introduced into that friendship by Fell's relationship with Miss Carey/Karre. Sarah Elwes's history is also important because of how she was represented by others and because, when she began to see Godwin, a number of features of their behaviour, on the basis of the details in Godwin's diary, seem to replicate the conduct of which her husband had accused her. Godwin first recorded calling on her for tea on 3 May 1799 (which suggests that she may have written to him, since there is no evidence of any previous contact). He then called on her twice (6 and 9 May – on the later occasion she was not in) and had tea with her again on 11 May. On 18 May, the entry reads: 'Ride with mrs Elwes, Highgate, Hornsey & Hampstead: mrs Elwes calls.' He dined with her, apparently alone;[17] she called on him; they went to the theatre together early in June; four days later they walked together. On a handful of occasions, he met her with Jasper Egerton, but for the vast majority of their meetings they were alone. There was a break in their relationship briefly when Godwin turned to Maria Reveley after the sudden death of her husband in August 1799; but by October they were again seeing each other frequently. On 26 November Godwin's entry was: 'Post, w. S E; dine at Salt Hill; sleep' (Salt Hill is near Slough). The following day, Godwin called on Fox and Mrs Armistead (at St Anne's Hill, nr Chertsey), but he returned that night to Salt Hill to dine and sleep. No further mention is made of Sarah Elwes on this trip and there is no other similarly cryptic entry.[18] These last events are within days of Godwin's dramatic expostulations with Fell.

Godwin was clearly attracted to Sarah Elwes. Thomas Erskine (who acted for the prosecution in the criminal conversation case and again for her husband at the High Court of Delegates, alongside William Garrow) described her as an extremely beautiful woman, and Godwin clearly enjoyed her company.[19] Indeed, although his relationship with her collapsed after he began seeing Mary Jane Clairmont, he made several efforts to bring her back into his society and she became a family friend and regular visitor from 1812 until her death five years later (and she

---

[17] In the first hearing, under the eighth article of her evidence, Elwes was concerned to insist that she had not dined alone with Harvey on 18 August 1793 and that they 'never did dine alone together'. National Archive DEL 1/670, v. 1.

[18] Elwes may have been starting a longer journey: after this entry Godwin writes to her on 6 December, but she calls on him only on the 14th.

[19] *Morning Post and Fashionable World*. 18 July 1794.

bequeathed both of them items and some money in her will).[20] There is little to suggest Sarah Elwes pursued Godwin (and much to suggest that she stood back from the relationship at points when he turned to Maria Reveley and later to Mary Jane Clairmont). They were clearly at an impasse. She could not marry and, had she set up house with him or flagrantly cohabited, she would have lost her financial settlement.[21] Although Elwes had been concerned to limit his wife's claims on him, the settlement was significant. Correspondence in 1794 indicates that when she was dismissed from the house by her husband he agreed to allow her £40 per month for her maintenance and support (the naval pension she lost on her marriage to him was worth about £45 p.a.), which he then suspended in July 1794 when she applied for alimony, on the grounds that he had been paying the sum on the understanding that she would not do so.[22] The outcome of the disagreement in July 1794 is unclear, but on the commencement of the case in the Consistorial Court, Judge Scott allotted £550 annually to Mrs Elwes, for the duration of the suit.[23] Whether this changed subsequent to the finding of the High Court of Delegates is unclear. However, when Sarah Elwes died in 1817 her moveable property was valued at some £400 and she bequeathed £2,300 in 3 per cent consolidated annuities and £600 in the 5 per cent, which suggests the alimony was maintained.[24]

Godwin too was stuck. He wanted a wife, both for companionship and as a mother for Fanny and Mary. And he probably sought to avoid the further controversy (following the furore over the *Memoirs*) that cohabiting would produce. For her part, Sarah Elwes had much to lose financially and she probably did not want to gain responsibilities for two young children in a household of uncertain income.

Was Godwin a hypocrite in denouncing Fell's object of choice while he himself consorted with Elwes? My sense is that he certainly did not think himself to be. His relationship with Elwes does seem to have been in part about intellectual companionship – of the sort he had experienced with Wollstonecraft. It was in the wake of his relationship with Wollstonecraft

---

[20] Only one letter to her survives (identified by Pamela Clemit: 31 July 1810, MS Abinger c.21 fols 24–25) – although several were clearly written. This strongly suggests the subsequent elimination of papers by Mary Jane and/or Mary Shelley.

[21] Susan Staves, *Married Women's Separate Property in England, 1660–1833* (Cambridge, MA: Harvard University Press, 1990); Joanne Bailey, *Unquiet Lives: Marriage and Marriage Breakdown in England, 1660–1800* (Cambridge: Cambridge University Press, 2003); and Rebecca Probert, Julie Shaffer and Joanne Bailey, *A Noble Affair* (Kenilworth: Brandram, 2013).

[22] Metropolitan Archive DL/C/0562/178.

[23] Lambeth Palace, Process Books D 675, fol 38.

[24] National Archive Prob 11/1600 113r–4v.

that he wrote his idealised portrait of companionate love, both in his *Memoirs* and, subsequently, in his second major novel, *St Leon*, half of which was written during his friendship with Elwes.[25] If he was not being hypocritical it was because he saw himself and Sarah Elwes as having something like this sort of relationship. This may be why he was so attentive in his attempts to draw her back into his life later on – because he saw her as a woman of abilities and talents who had been exploited by and had fallen foul of the masculine world. Part of that later 'courting' may have been motivated by the difficulty such women had in gaining acceptance in any form of society; and, as in the 1790s, Godwin would not let a woman's reputation trump his own judgement of her worth. But other women behaved differently: it is striking that Godwin did not record meeting any single woman on any occasion on which he saw Elwes between 1799 and 1802 (and only two married women are recorded, both of whom Godwin met through Elwes and who were clearly part of her small circle). This may be a function of their purposes when they met – but it seems more plausible to conclude that Sarah's reputation was harmed by the criminal conversation and divorce cases and to be seen as connected to her would have been toxic for young, unmarried women.

Godwin's relationship with Sarah Elwes captures several aspects of his unconventional and conventional character and something of the difficulties of the norms and conventions governing sociability in domestic space. Each of the three central women in his life (Wollstonecraft, Elwes and Clairmont) had experienced the injustices of the patriarchal order in which they lived. All were abandoned by previous partners in ways that rendered them vulnerable to the respectable world (in Elwes case it is difficult to believe that her husband had not framed her to at least some extent). They were all attractive women.[26] And Godwin seems to have recognised them as victims and actively disdained the ordinary conventions that relegated them firmly to a very narrow private world. In keeping with his judgement of Mrs Fell, he responded to people's minds and their qualities, not to their reputations or superficial attractions. And, in the case of these women, he did partly re-establish them – bringing them into his circles (and joining theirs), challenging conventions and doing so with a degree of confidence and pride. But in each case, these women demonstrate how powerful the established

---

[25] William Godwin, 'St Leon: A Tale of the Sixteenth Century' (1798), in Mark Philp (ed.), *Collected Novels and Memoirs of William Godwin* (London: Pickering & Chatto, 1992), vol. iv.

[26] See Mary Jane's complaint in Bodleian Library MS. Abinger c.11, fol 50r.

norms were. Most of Godwin's female acquaintance (for all their attractions to radicalism and the new philosophy) did not do what these women did, they were much more careful about the proprieties, more conscious of their reputations, more aware (than Godwin) that they would pay costs for being seen as associating with him in particular ways (and places) or, indeed, for associating with his other women friends (as we have seen, sources suggest only low levels of interaction between these women and most of Godwin's other female friends). Godwin wanted to challenge convention, he wanted meetings of mind with mind, he wanted candour and engagement. He got these things from his male friends and especially from his male proteges but he also wanted something similar with the women he met – and therein lay the problem. Few were unconventional enough or were prepared to pay the price they would have to pay.

It is also true that those who appeared less conventional – such as Sarah Anne Parr, Maria Reveley, Nan Pinkerton, Amelia Alderson and Emily Kingsman – were able to discomfit him simply by appearing to be unconventional!

7.3   Maria Reveley

One central early relationship for Godwin seems to have been that with Maria Reveley – but she was married and there was an uncertainty on both parts about what their relationship was or might become. They seem to have been deeply attracted to each other and utterly unsure of how to deal with that – as suggested by the sequence of entries in the diary following an assignation at Greenwich with her (entered in the diary just as Greenwich): 'January 12, 1795 sup at Reveley's, courir dehors; January 19 sup at Reveley's l'eternal; January 24, tea Reveleys t.a.t., l'imposteur'.[27]

Willey Reveley died unexpectedly on 7 July 1799. Godwin called the following day, seeing the Fenwicks who were there supporting Maria. There is an undated letter to Maria Reveley (given as 17 July 1799 when he notes in his diary 'Write to M R'), which Godwin opens by challenging the conventions:

How my whole soul disdains & tramples upon these cowardly ceremonials! Is woman always to be a slave? Is she so wretched an animal, that every breath can

---

[27] See Edward Pope's discussion of this tangled relationship, which follows Farington's suggestion that she was having an affair with Jennings (although we should bear in mind that Farington was not always reliable, and was uncritical of his sources): http://edpopehistory.co.uk/content/william-godwin-reveleys-and-jenningses (accessed 6 January 2019).

destroy her, every temptation, or more properly every possibility of an offence, is to be supposed to subdue her? The ceremony is to be observed *for some time*. What miserable, heartless words! What is *some time* ...? – You know in what light such ceremonies have been viewed by all the liberal & wise, both of my sex and of yours.

Moreover, he makes clear what it is that he expects of her:

The conduct which propriety & a generous confidence in the rectitude of our sentiments dictated to us both, was too plain to be mistaken: to see each other freely & honestly as friends; to lay down no beggarly rules about married and unmarried men; & to say nothing *for some time* but what was the strict & accurate result of friendship.[28]

But Reveley, probably because of her own complex and mixed feelings, bought herself time by appealing to convention. In a letter in November, having been more wholly shut out, Godwin rehearsed their relationship in some detail, giving some idea of its complexity and the difficulty involved in sustaining it given the prevailing norms, concluding, in frustration, that 'If you are all at once become so thoroughly the slave of a miserable etiquette that you must not even risk seeing me alone, you may dine here with my sister; or order me to invite mrs Fenwick: where the heart is willing, such trifles are easily adjusted.'[29]

There are two odd events registered in the Diary at this time. On 16 August, just before his letter to Reveley, Godwin enters Meet 'M R & S Elwes' in his diary. This is a perplexing entry. The whole entry for the day is: 'Hume, p. 174. Meet M R & S Elwes: call on Fenwicks; sup, w. them, at Fell's'. The normal 'meet' entry is one in which he coincides with someone when he is engaged in some other activity or on a visit to someone else. Moreover, although the diary codes these entries as separate, unrelated activities, it is possible that Godwin did in fact meet the two women together. There is no other link in the diary between Elwes and Reveley, save on 9 November 1799, when Godwin enters 'Write to S E & M R^n' in the diary (a similarly odd entry given that the superscript 'n' usually indicates that the person has been called on and is not at home, but is not used for writing – although it could indicate that he did not send the letter). There are a range of reasons why Godwin might connect the two women in his mind; but he may also have encouraged Elwes to talk to Reveley about how their relationship stood. And Elwes was clearly stepping to one side: having been calling on and meeting with her on a very regular basis since May, following the

---

[28] Godwin, *Letters of WG*, ii, pp. 87–88.
[29] Ibid., ii, p. 110, [1 November 1799]; Bodleian Library MS. Abinger c.17, fol 93r–v.

19th August, Godwin's contact with Elwes was reduced to two letters that he sent her in September and this later one on 9 November, until she called on him again on 20 November 1799. It is difficult to know for certain (as mentioned, all the correspondence in relation to Elwes was carefully filleted from the collection at some point), but it does not seem entirely a coincidence that the entry for 26 November, 'Post, w. S E; dine at Salt Hill; sleep.', follows very quickly on from their reconnection. And the intensity of their calls remains undiminished until May 1801, when Mary Jane Clairmont appeared on the scene.

7.4   Mary Jane Clairmont

Mrs Clairmont was also a woman who engaged in some re-invention of her past. Although she passed under the name of Mrs Clairmont (which was the name of the father of her first child, Charles), she subsequently had another illegitimate child by Sir James Letheridge of Exeter, who paid her an allowance of 5 shillings per week for the child (Jane/Clare) until at least 1810. In the correspondence that survives from before she went to London, she signed herself either Mrs Vial (her maiden name) or Mrs St Julien.[30] Letheridge clearly wanted her to leave his district and to fend for herself – above all he was keen to stop her pestering him for support after his lordly munificence in agreeing to a settlement. At the same time, she managed to find friends and support and she was received by others as a distressed gentlewoman. These people helped her to leave debtors prison and to sort out her affairs, so that when she came to London she seems to have been largely free of debt and able to reconstruct herself on arrival in London as a respectable widow with two children. The story is told that she found herself living next door to Godwin and leant over her balcony and addressed him in the following terms: 'Is it possible that I behold the immortal Godwin'.[31] Lamb was appalled by Godwin's response: '... the professor is grown quite juvenile. He bows when he is spoke to, and smiles without occasion, and wriggles as fantastically as Malvolio ... You never saw such a philosophic coxcomb, nor anyone play Romeo so unnaturally.'[32]

---

[30] See www1.somerset.gov.uk/archives/, catalogue reference DD\DP 17/11, Papers of Dodson and Pulman, Solicitors of Taunton, Lethbridge estate papers (correspondence concerning Mary Jane Vial); and the transcriptions at https://sites.google.com/site/maryjanesdaughter/home (accessed 6 January 2019).

[31] Locke, *A Fantasy of Reason*, p. 205.

[32] Charles Lamb, *The Letters of Charles Lamb*, edited by E. V. Lucas, 3 vols. (London: J. M. Dent & sons & Methuen & Co., Ltd, 1935), v. 1, pp. 273–274.

This relationship was easier for Godwin to manage, since they shared the same building and meeting did not have to be a call or other activity visible to the public domain. He and Clairmont could meet and talk without witnesses and they could take things from there without being observed. Godwin had introduced Sarah Elwes to his amanuensis James Marshall and also to Ralph Fell, but the vast majority of their contact with each other involved just the two of them (at least until they drifted apart after the early summer of 1801). And Godwin essentially did the same with Mrs Clairmont, with Lamb being one of the relatively few to meet her prior to their marriage on 21 December 1801. Perhaps the most surprising thing about their marriage is that Clairmont was pregnant. Godwin may have had a principled stance against marriage, but he must by this point have been more than amply aware of the costs that women could face for their physiological vulnerability (although it seems that Elwes must in some way have 'managed' this). There was certainly nothing in his letters to Lee that suggested that he thought they might cohabit rather than marry (although he did encourage her to stay at his house when she visited London, which was both a protest against convention and a characteristic misjudgement). And one wonders how open Clairmont was with him about her past and financial situation and whether she felt she could risk a further illegitimate child because Godwin seems to have been so pliant with respect both to marriage and her interests (at least at the start of their relationship). But it may be that what we are seeing is evidence of a micro-culture that could be reasonably tolerant, because it was rather marginal to London's wider and more élite social circles. A culture that made no comment on the fact that Wollstonecraft's pregnancy clearly derived from well before their marriage, and that could be relatively forgiving if offences against the norms were not too blatant, and so long as the couple did not involve others or seek their public endorsement and acknowledgement prior to the marriage. A little bit Bohemian; but not very! (And the more Bohemian – the more isolated from wider social circles).

Godwin's second marriage clearly solved some of his problems with his household. He clearly did not see, or was not especially bothered by, his friends' hostility to Mrs Clairmont (Lamb – rather a hater of women – referred to her as 'a disgusting women', 'a damned disagreeable woman' and as 'that Bitch'),[33] and he managed to carry on pretty much as he had before. Indeed, part of Mrs Godwin's unhappiness might well have been that he used the marriage to manage his household, rather than focusing

---

[33] Locke, *A Fantasy of Reason*, pp. 205, 208.

on its potential for intellectual companionship. There clearly had been some intellectual spark between them: she was an able, productive woman, with literary skills, and Godwin used those to their advantage in the setting up and running of the bookshop. But it was neither a very companionate marriage nor a very equal one. In the very first letter to her from Godwin during their early courtship that survives, written while he was away from London, after complaining of the dullness of his companions, and describing the pleasures and follies of Blenheim, he concluded by saying:

My dear love, take care of yourself. Manage and economise your temper. It is at bottom most excellent; do not let it be soured & spoiled. It [is] capable of being recovered to its primeval goodness, & even raised to something better. Do not get rid of all of your faults. I love some of them. I love what is human, what gives softness, & an agreeable air of frailty & pliability to the whole.[34]

Written five months after they first met and just under three months before they married, Godwin had already set a tone of paternalist advice that was largely absent from his correspondence with Wollstonecraft. The intervening years seemed to have persuaded him that he would not find equality and that his other needs were more pressing.

7.5   Convention and Practice

What becomes clear is that, while Godwin was philosophically committed to being unbounded by convention, he often was. Moreover, that commitment made it harder for him to read these more challenging women's behaviour; he was unsure how far to treat them unconventionally and he found negotiating an alternative standard of appropriateness difficult; and even when committed to following through his unconventional conduct he could see that it was something that should be kept from his friends and acquaintances' inquiring surveillance. But an additional difficulty for Godwin in being unconventional for principled reasons was that he found it hard to judge how far those whose behaviour bent, played with or violated the conventions were acting from similarly appropriate motives. So Godwin's apparent inconsistencies and oddities were partly of a function of his desire for non-conformity and of the difficulty he found in responding to it.

Godwin's later despair in 1814 over the behaviour of his daughter Mary and step-daughter Jane/Claire Clairmont speaks eloquently to his appreciation of the power of social condemnation and exclusion over

---

[34] Godwin, *Letters of WG*, ii, pp. 242–243: 9 October 1801.

women and his concern that they not expose themselves in the way they then did with Shelley and Byron. He had, of course, not a leg to stand on – just the rawness of his experience of the reaction to the *Memoirs* and his rather conventional doubts about whether there was anything like a principle underlying their (and especially Shelley's) conduct. His inconsistency with his earlier writing and his principles was real enough, being generated by his concern about the costs of flouting convention; nonetheless, at some level he did try to hold to his intellectual commitments and he did so because he believed his conception of egalitarian relationships allowed people to realise goods, values and activity of mind that the conventions of their patriarchal society precluded.

I have tried to suggest some of the complexities of innovation in personal relationships and social circles in an age when inequalities and social conventions governing conduct were deeply rooted and powerful – perhaps less so in London's radical metropolitan culture than in country seats but, nonetheless, still an issue for members of Godwin's circles. He was concerned to jettison convention as an irrational constraint – but that was easier said than done, for others but also for him, especially with respect to women. The result was a complex interaction around calling and dining, above all around being known to spend time alone in domestic space with others. The diary shows that, despite his and his friends' radicalism, these norms were widely shared and complied with by most people and their transgression was clearly thought to be (and was) socially punished (as witness the silent mistresses of many men among Godwin's acquaintance). There were margins for experiment, but these could not be breeched unless you had nothing to lose or were prepared to take the chance that the anonymity of the city (or an excursion outside it) would provide protection.

I have also tried to show how small people's 'little platoons' might be – especially for women, and perhaps especially for literary women (especially where they also had domestic responsibilities). This narrowness of acquaintance increased their dependence on those with whom they associated, rendering the norms and expectations more powerful. A man, like Godwin, might partially rehabilitate a woman like Wollstonecraft – or Clairmont – but often incompletely, often within only a part of his acquaintance, and often with some cost to himself (and probably with a good deal of exclusion for her). But he could also pose a risk to the reputations of other women, who would have to consider carefully how their relationship with him and his consort might be seen by others.

The account I have given makes the case that, however gregarious radical culture in the 1790s might seem to have been, it was still very much masculine in character. Those wanting to challenge social conventions around gender relations found it hard to do so. Indeed, it seems likely that, despite their intellectual commitments, they found it hard to free themselves from those conventions – so that Godwin was unclear how to interpret unconventional behaviour on the part of those with whom he sought a different kind of intellectual relationship. And they, in their turn, were often interpolated in a way they sought to resist and had recourse to a variety of strategies to unsettle Godwin's determined pedagogy, which then puzzled him about what it was that they really wanted from him. This was especially so with younger women. But they served as an apprenticeship for him in dealing with a plurality of styles and registers of communication, which Wollstonecraft was then able to utilise in her own hesitant accommodation with 'the Philosopher'. Moreover, this experience was one which he then worked on intellectually, in his *Enquirer* and in *St Leon*, and he ruminated over the diverse ways in which it might be possible to bring his more philosophical concerns to fruition with individuals and audiences who were not of his background and training. At the same time, he was clearly overtaken at times by his own instinctive reaction to events: his physical awkwardness and inexperience at the beginning of his affair with Wollstonecraft were obvious to both and his emotional education at her hands then left him bereft and in an important sense 'stupid' after her death – unable to gain self-control, maudlin and self-indulgent, writing in a way that exposed them both to the kind of reaction they had sought to avoid in her lifetime and then lapsing into a pattern of activity that sought to solve his loss without recognising the importance of cultivating the kind of relationship that would be necessary to do that. The radical moment of the 1790s was in part a social and cultural one, a willingness to challenge the ordered hierarchies and conventions of the social world. But men who were willing to do that, for whatever range of reasons, did so with varying degrees of concern for the damage they might do to their female friends and partners, while still appearing to back the wider programme of such reform. In Godwin's case, as with *Adeline Mowbray*'s Glenmurray, the intellectual commitment was utterly serious, but unlike in Adeline's case, he was able to concede and to compromise, because both he and Wollstonecraft could see that her lot would otherwise be unbearable.

At the same time there are a deeper set of forces at work in this story, which concern the hubris of enlightenment reason in thinking it possible to escape from or wholly to tame the emotional and sensual character of human relations by the operation of the intellect. Godwin came up hard against the fact that relations between men and women (and between members of the same gender) were imperfectly rational, resistant to rules and conventions – indeed, in many cases, often reactive against such forms – and brazen in confrontation of the demands of rationality. It is unclear whether Godwin read Montaigne on friendship – he did note reading the essay on Sebond and other essays – but he would doubtless have read it according to his own bent. When Montaigne says: 'If you press me to tell why I loved him, I feel this cannot be expressed except by answering: Because it was he, because it was I',[35] he points to that primary emotional affinity as grounding their intellectual relationship. In contrast, the picture Godwin painted at the end of his *Enquiry* talks of assiduously cultivating 'the intercourse of that woman whose accomplishments shall strike me in the most powerful manner' with a willingness to 'consider the sensual intercourse as a very trivial object …'. It is not merely the case that Godwin overstated the power of reason over the senses; he also fundamentally resisted the idea that deep relations are as much a function of chance and coincidence as of reason and judgement and that it is out of such serendipitous elements that we develop our core commitments, our identities and our experience of happiness.

We might press further the question of how far some of these more middle class and professional men were able to realise their ambitions for rational exchange in their interactions with others, as against themselves also being more dependent on their 'little platoon' than they might acknowledge. Godwin certainly aspired to the clash of mind with mind, hoping to find among a wider acquaintance a group of like-minded people who would be the fit object of his friendship – where their fitness was a function of their ability and virtue. And, for a time, in the 1790s, he thought he had achieved exactly this; and he was able to feel this despite the fact that he must have been conscious of the huge inequalities and their associated power differentials encoded in the conventions of association in many of the circles in which he moved. For example, when it came to contacts with those who were socially his superiors Godwin was more often the supplicant than being more strictly an equal. His appendix on using servants to tell callers that the master or mistress of the house was 'not at home' speaks eloquently to both his condemnation and his experience of the practice.[36] He called on members of the aristocracy – they did not call on him. When they wanted to see him for some reason, they characteristically summoned him. Moreover, while the complexities of 'calling' are considerable, they were further complicated by the fact that Godwin probably had few facilities for receiving callers. But that simply underlines the extent to which material inequalities ran in

---

[35] Michel de Montaigne, *The Complete Works*, translated by D. Frame (London: Everyman, 2003), p. 169.
[36] Godwin, *Enquiry*, IV, iv, App II., pp. 145–148.

tandem with social inequalities. Moreover, these social conventions could be variable across space: having met someone at Debrett's bookshop and engaged in discussion did not mean that that person should be acknowledged if met in the street or in an exhibition or at a lecture: Holcroft records in his diary 'Met Sir F(rancis) B(urdett) in Bond Street, who reminded me of my promise; then H. who would not see me ('tis the fashion of these folks to those they think their inferiors) and afterwards C. Grey, M.P., who was less aristocratic, and gave me a nod.'[37] That Godwin, and some of his circle, wanted to break through such conventions does not mean that they could. What was open to them was to establish such ideal relations as, and when, and where they could. If we recognise this, we should also see that for most men, their circles might be in many respects rather similar to those of their wives, albeit expanded through relations based on their professional activities – but, nonetheless, delimited, focused, convention-governed – and Dunbar constrained.

This should alert us to the complex but often very conservative nature of London circles in the 1790s, which could be, in various respects, both unconventional and at the same time very rule and norm governed – with various concerns applying to men and women differently, and differently across various social gradations and status differentials (perhaps above all, married vs unmarried women), but also affected by the political ideas of the period and the partial rejection of forms of conventional compliance in favour of more reasoned and egalitarian forms of discourse and social exchange. Moreover, this was a world and a set of relationships and issues to which people were highly sensitive and attuned, so that people were very conscious of issues of conduct and behaviour; and it was an area in which behaviour was often not calculative and rational, but often deeply influenced by sentiment, emotion and affections over which they had rather imperfect control. Godwin's serial relationships all involved him falling into patterns of interaction in which he and his companions become entangled emotionally and then sexually. In no case does he seem to have set out with that as an objective and it is plausible to think that that is equally true for these women. Moreover, in many respects, he opened himself up to these sexual encounters in large part by assuming that he rose above the less rational aspects of human relations and by over-privileging the value and disinterestedness of the discursive (and probably the didactic) mode. It is possible there were elements of scheming in Mary Jane Clairmont's approach to Godwin – for whom an escape from her previous life and a return to respectability were clearly

---

[37] Holcroft, *Memoirs*, p. 249.

much to be desired. That case is much harder to make for Wollstonecraft or Elwes – although, unlike some of their acquaintance, they were not so hide-bound by convention that they felt constrained to avoid all risk of further relationships. In their cases – and possibly also that of Mary Jane (whose past must surely have counselled a degree of caution) – they were not looking for a relationship with Godwin, but they nonetheless developed one and then had to work out how to manage it. It may well have been that Wollstonecraft and Clairmont saw instances of people like Fox, bringing his long-term mistress and subsequent wife into a society from which she had previously been excluded, as an example of what marriage could do for them. But Wollstonecraft was also deeply critical of such conventions and the wider culture they rested on, and both women would also have been aware that the circles in which they moved might not be as tolerant or as receptive – and aware also that Godwin's power to command a wider respect for his partner would have been more limited.

The account I have been piecing together of the multiple and imperfectly intersecting circles and networks for the middling and professional orders of London in the period 1789–1815 is intended as a corrective to accounts which overemphasise the inclusiveness of London's literary and professional cultures. Instead it takes the view that, while there were spheres of public life and a developing public culture, these remain rooted in particular circles and relationships rather than becoming anything like a single public sphere. And these circles were deeply marked by personal friendships and loyalties, but also (especially for women) by concerns about propriety, reputation and conduct. In the febrile political atmosphere in the 1790s, women who stood out in any way – whether Mary Wollstonecraft or Hannah More[38] – increasingly became fair game to political attack and to scandal mongering (but often only among particular sections of the wider press). And that further exposed them to the scrutiny of their contemporaries and could raise questions about their suitability as companions or acquaintances. What is clear is that a great deal could happen beneath the radar, but women especially needed to be careful – about what they did, about how they saw whom they saw and about whom they associated with – and the more they appeared in the press, through publications, or in public entertainments and

---

[38] On Hannah More and the attacks on her, see Mellor, *Mothers of the Nation*, chapter 1; Anna Clark, *Scandal: The Sexual Politics of the British Constitution* (Princeton, NJ: Princeton University Press, 2004), chapter 6; Mitzi Myers seminal piece '"Reform or Ruin": A Revolution in Female Manners', *Studies in Eighteenth-Century Culture* 11 (1982), 199–216; and Claire Grogan's. 'Mary Wollstonecraft and Hannah More: Politics, Feminism and Modern Critics', *Lumen* 13 (1994), 99–108.

performances, the more careful they needed to be, especially if they lacked powerful male protection. They certainly contributed to dimensions of public discussion and debate, but their participation in the social worlds that undergirded this developing public culture was fraught with exclusions and dangers that they had to negotiate essentially through their 'little platoons'.

8   Music and Movement

To return to the subject of cooperation. It may be a curious speculation to attend to the progressive steps by which this feature of human society may be expected to decline. For example: shall we have concerts of music? The miserable state of mechanism of the majority of the performers is so conspicuous, as to be even at this day a topic of mortification and ridicule. Will it not be practicable hereafter for one man to perform the whole? Shall we have theatrical exhibitions? This seems to include an absurd and vicious cooperation. It may be doubted whether men will hereafter come forward in any mode gravely to repeat words and ideas not their own? It may be doubted whether any musical performer will habitually execute the compositions of others? ... All formal repetition of other men's ideas seems to be a scheme for imprisoning for so long a time the operations of our own mind.[1]

Godwin's sense of the encroachments of cooperation on the independence of individual judgement now seems bizarre, but it points to two features of his convictions that should be emphasised. On the one hand, he had an absolute commitment to the full and free exercise of private judgement. People should be moved by their own beliefs, rather than taking these on trust or on the authority of others. And in so far as they did less than this, thus far was their independence compromised and their behaviour rendered potentially vicious. While this commitment was partly generated by ideas about the development of reason and knowledge, it was also motivated by a series of concerns drawn in part from Rousseau about the way in which people come to base their expectations of themselves on the reactions and attitudes of others – where that literally took the person out of themselves and fixed their intellectual and moral compass externally to them. While there was a degree of disdain for the quality of performers in Godwin's comments, the clearly more troubling element was that they were to be brought into concert by something outside of themselves – whether a score, a conductor or a script.

---

[1] Godwin, *Enquiry*, VIII, vi., pp. 444–445.

Godwin canvassed a view that might most sympathetically be described as speculative. But his conclusions derived from more widely held beliefs and attitudes – about the importance of private judgement and the tyranny and corrupting influence of society. Holcroft, who was an accomplished amateur musician and played regularly with William Shield, who went on to become Master of the King's Music, nonetheless betrayed similar if less exaggerated concerns with respect to music in his novels. In *Anna St Ives* it is Coke Clifton (the vicious character whom Anna attempts to reform) who is transported by the glitter and glamour of public performances:

Last night we had a *Fête Champêtre*, which, it must be granted, was a most accurate picture of nature, and the manners of rustics! The simplicity of the shepherd life could not but be excellently represented, by the ribbands, jewels, gauze, tiffany, and fringe, with which we were bedaubed; and the ragouts, fricassees, spices, sauces, wines, and *liqueurs*, with which we were regaled! Not to mention being served upon plate, by an army of footmen! But then, it was in the open air; and that was prodigiously pastoral!

When we were sufficiently tired of eating and drinking, we all got up to dance; and the mild splendour of the moon was utterly eclipsed, by the glittering dazzle of some hundreds of lamps; red, green, yellow, and blue; the rainbow burlesqued; all mingled, in fantastic wreaths and forms, and suspended among the foliage; that the trees might be as fine as ourselves! The invention, disposition, and effect, however, were highly applauded. And, since the evil was small and the mirth great, what could a man do, but shake his ears, kick his heels, cut capers, laugh, sing, shout, squall, and be as mad as the best?[2]

Clifton is a rake and the slave of appearance. In contrast, Holcroft suggests that the highest emotional tone in performance is achieved when alone.[3] Moreover, while *Hugh Trevor* used a good deal of thinly veiled elements from Holcroft's own life experiences, including his learning the fiddle, the predominant tone in the discussion of music is to denigrate its social performance – with the culmination of this being in the description of an election and its marshalling of its resources for battle:

The day of beginning contest soon broke upon us, the word of command was given to muster, and all was in action. The friends of the opposing parties collected, each round their respective leaders: favours for the hat and bosom were lavishly distributed: the flags were flying: a band of music preceded each of the processions: and, when the parties approached the hustings, each band

---

[2] Thomas Holcroft, *Anna St Ives* (1791), edited by Peter Faulkner (Oxford: Oxford University Press, 1970), v.ii, Letter XXXVI, p. 116.

[3] Ibid., Letter XXXIV, p. 109: 'I have thought that she is most impassioned when alone, and perhaps all musicians are so'.

continued to play its own favourite air with increasing violence: as if war were to be declared by the most jarring discord, and harmony driven from the haunts of men.[4]

Despite his own clear enjoyment of playing and listening to music, Holcroft saw it as an arena in the social and political world in which the form was subordinated to the capriciousness of the dilettante and the tyranny of manners and was made instrumental to the demands of partisan conflict.

These concerns were not restricted to the two friends but were part of a wider suspicion of the practices of entertainment, glamour and perform-ance that literary and political radicals saw or imagined in the concert halls, theatres and salons of London. That suspicion was fuelled in part by their critique of manners, but also by their concerns about people being moved by forces outside of them and beyond their control. It is this latter set of concerns that I address in this chapter – the sense that musical performance, song and dance engage us and affect us in ways that are not fully under our control.

This dimension of music is rarely the subject of reflection by histor-ians. In much of the work on the politics of the 1790s and early 1800s, music and popular song, like caricature, tend to be used for illustration, not as subjects of study in their own right.[5] Of course, there are some pieces of shrewd analysis that track and analyse particular tunes or songs pointing to their deeper and more general significance, such as work on the tunes 'The Black Joke' and 'Derry Down'.[6] In this narrowing of focus, however, comes a tendency to essentialise their individual political

---

[4] Thomas Holcroft, *Hugh Trevor* (1795), edited by Seamus Deane (Oxford:Oxford University Press, 1978), Bk VI, chapter VII, p. 458.

[5] For recent exceptions, see: Susan Valladares, *Staging the Peninsular War: English Theatres 1807–1815* (Basingstoke: Ashgate, 2015); Oskar Cox Jensen, *Napoleon and British Song, 1797–1822* (Basingstoke: Palgrave Macmillan, 2015); Kate Horgan, *The Politics of Songs in Eighteenth Century Britain* (London: Pickering & Chatto, 2014); John Kirk, Andrew Noble and Michael Brown, *United Islands? The Languages of Resistance* (London: Pickering & Chatto, 2012); T. Baycroft and David Hopkin (eds.), *Folklore and Nationalism during the Long Nineteenth Century* (Leiden: Brill, 2012); Ian Newman, 'Civilizing Taste: "Sandman Joe", the Bawdy Ballad and Metropolitan Improvement', *Eighteenth-Century Studies* 48(4) (Summer 2015): 437–456; and Oskar Cox Jensen, David Kennerley and Ian Newman (eds.), *Charles Dibdin and Late Georgian Culture* (Oxford: Oxford University Press, 2018). For background see Nicholas Temperley, *Athlone History of Music in Britain in the Romantic Age 1800–1914* v. 5 (London: Athlone Press, 1981), esp. chapters 4 and 6.

[6] See Paul Dennant 'The Barbarous English Jig: The "Black Joke" in the Eighteenth and Nineteenth Centuries', *Folk Music Journal* 110(3) (2013), 298–318; and Gerald Porter's 'Melody as a Bearer of Radical Ideology', in Eva Guillorel, David Hopkin and William G. Pooley (eds.), *Rhythms of Revolt: European Traditions and Memories of Social Conflict in Oral Culture* (Abingdon: Routledge, 2018), pp. 240–264.

or social character and meaning and to treat them apart from the wider fabric of song, music and performance in which they appear.[7] Moreover, many political and social historians treat popular ballads as the most salient aural material but then focus on them predominantly as texts, whereas the legacy of cultural history might encourage us to locate them in a much wider musical spectrum in which such songs appear alongside tunes, hymns, military bands, Dibdin entertainments, Ranelagh Gardens performances, boys whistling in the streets and women selling and singing song sheets in the market. There are specialist literatures by musicologists that address some of these activities, but there are also more directly historical questions, such as are raised by David Hopkin in his work on France, about the ways in which this wider sonic world was an integral component of the cultural cloth of the period, being woven into people's practices and dispositions.[8]

My concern in this chapter is to take seriously the radicals' anxieties about being 'taken over' by music and performance and to consider a range of non-textual elements of music, dance and song for the ways in which these moved people, both emotionally and physically. I will argue that these features of sound and movement helped to weave people's daily lives into the political and military conflicts of the period and that this helps explain the resistance to these experiences on the part of many of the literary radicals. Much historical commentary is directed to what songs were saying about events and how they were saying it. In keeping with the broader line of argument of this book, I argue that we should also be interested in how 'things' happen to us at a less intellectual level and how these less fully conscious influences shape our commitments and conduct. My sense is that the radicals partly understood this, but that their strategy of refusal cut them off from a range of experiences that

---

[7] In Porter's discussion of 'Derry Down', for example, he claims that the tune is 'strongly associated with the emerging oppositional cultures of the late eighteenth century'. Porter, 'Melody as a Bearer of Radical Ideology', p. 245. This seems plausible in some periods, but not in others. For example, in sixteen of the twenty-two uses of the tune for political songs that I have identified between 1789 and 1815 the association is clearly with loyalism rather than radicalism. This should give us pause and suggests that such meanings are not intrinsic but are often a function of ongoing contestation.

[8] David Hopkin, *Voices of the People in Nineteenth-Century France* (Cambridge: Cambridge University Press, 2012); KCL's Project (https://musicinlondon.kcl.ac.uk/#) exemplifies the attempt to take these demands seriously. See also James M. Brophy, *Popular Culture and the Public Sphere in the Rhineland 1800–1850* (Cambridge: Cambridge University Press, 2007), chapter 2 – and especially the comment by Friedrich Hecker on p. 55: 'One learns a song for the first time, one sings it to thunderous jubilation and excitement of the moment, but in the still hours, in which one reflects and daydreams and during walks and hikes, the political song hums softly in the heart [...] the person becomes political.'

re-enforced their intellectualism but probably also weakened their appeal and influence.

8.1   A Fine Dance

In addressing areas in which we are moved in less than wholly rational ways, I want especially to consider the significance of dance in the period – as an experience that brought together music and movement and that often involved heightened emotion and pleasure for participants and their observers and was conducted in what was often a relatively close community of individuals. Eliza Soane had the misfortune to be married to a man who was not an enthusiast for dancing but, even with two sons approaching manhood, Eliza loved to dance. When Soane was away, she let the servants have a dance; and she often found opportunities for dancing ('1 April 1812, Wed Mr S out of town, had a little dance'[9]), as did her sons. There is no mention in her diary of her attending a ball, but when going to the houses of friends, a dance was something that she could occasionally find. The distinction is clearly not absolute, but 'ball' indicates a level of formality and organisation. What Eliza Soane enjoyed was the music and the movement; she seems not to have had much interest in the pomp! In the years of her diary from October 1804 to 1813,[10] she records having a dance – often seemingly impromptu, and rarely with Soane – on at least ten occasions. And these were clearly appreciated: 'Tuesday June 24 [1806] went to Ealing to meet company – had a dance, very pleasant.'[11] Moreover, she also notes when her sons go to a dance – as indeed do a great many of the diary keepers of the period, suggesting that, like the lessons that preceded their attendance, there was an investment (both practical and emotional) in their dancing.

The Nottingham widow (from December 1791) and mother of two, Abigail Gawthern, seems to have been similarly keen on dancing, having been taught as a child by a Mr Barker. She arranged lessons for her daughter Anna and son Frank, and she attended a range of events: 'concerts' (which seemingly often included dancing), balls, assemblies and less grand occasions in people's homes. Just over two years after the death of her husband and after a prolonged set of building works refashioning the family home, the completion of the renovation was celebrated with a 'ball':

[9] MrsSNB 8, f. r.21.
[10] Although we should recall that there is no record for the time spent at Brighton, which may have involved a good deal of dancing, although perhaps less when Soane was there.
[11] MrsSNB 6, f.v.3.

Jan 4 Our drawing room was opened with a ball, 15 couples; Mr Wylde and myself danced down the first dance; supped in the dining room; the company were all young people but Mrs Brough, Mrs Wylde, and Mr Neville.

Like Mrs Soane, she was concerned that her children could dance well and as her daughter Anna came of age there was a careful listing of those with whom Anna danced, the number of dances and the time they arrived home, often 3–4am. Indeed, at least two proposals to Anna seem to have emanated from prolonged encounters at balls. Provincial balls were not entirely genteel occasions: Gawthern noted that the ball following the country election of 1775 involved 'great mobbing and rioting'; and an election ball in December 1778 sounds similar: 'a great crowd broke into the assembly room' (although this did not seem to deter her participation: 'I had the honour of dancing a *minuet* with the member, the last I think I ever danced in that room, and country dances with Mr Clarke, Mr Medows's friend'). In April 1789, following the king's recovery, the Militia gave a ball (which she and her husband did not attend) which she reported as 'very riotous'.[12]

There's an interesting contrast here with James Oakes's Diaries from Bury St Edmunds, which did not comment on who danced with whom, but nonetheless recounted a wide range of public and private balls and dances, linked to the Assizes, elections, the local fairs and festivities such as Christmas, and so on. Oakes seems to have been especially interested in their success and he regarded their size as the key indication of this. On 19 October 1789 he is disappointed in the 'extremely thin' turnout for the '1st Assembly of the Great Week of the Fair ... not more than ½ Doz couple of dancers'; the 2nd Assembly, two days later, was more satisfactory 'Supposd to be between 2 & 300 Ladys and Gentn, 60 Couple of Dancers, very few minuets'. Two days later, at the 3rd Assembly, 'wch was most exceedingly full & brilliant. Suppsd to be nearly, if not altogether, 400 Ladys and Gentlemen, 80 couple [of] Dancers'. In 1790, the second Assembly could boast 'two Dancing Rows, say abt 80 couple [but] – only 4 minuets'. In 1791, having had a very successful assembly on 14 October with 80 couples (although 'Only 5 Minuets danced'), the first subscription ball a month later suffered 'the greatest want of Gentn Dancers ever remembered, began with 5 couple & at most could not make more than 11 couple'. In 1792 there were '80 couple of Country Dancers ... [but] Not one minuet dancd'. 1793 offered 'A most

---

[12] Gawthern, *The Diary of Abigail Gawthern*, pp. 30, 34, 49. This military engulfment of Nottingham seems to have continued through the 1790s, with the *Times* claiming in February 1793 that the town had more the air of a camp than a manufacturing town. See Gillian Russell, *The Theatres of War* (Oxford: Clarendon Press, 1995), p. 107.

brilliant Appearance, abt 90 Ladys & Gentlemen, 26 couple of Dancers'. The same success was recorded in 1794 (the second of which was 'Generally allowd to be as good a Ball as has been known for several years') and 1795, with fewer couples in 1796, and concerns about his daughter Charlotte's declining health removing them from the locality in 1797. In 1798 almost 60 couples were brought together in November to celebrate 'the late, glorious naval victories'.[13] Oakes' interest in minuets may be partly about the desire to watch the more formal, complex and elevated forms of dance. It is not at all clear that he himself was active in the dancing, but they provided a consistent point of comment in his diary – whether they be balls for adults or the regular ones held in the locality for children (also commented on in Gawthern). As such they were clearly a major event in the locality and often brought a considerable number of the business and local administrative community together.

These examples of the integral character of dancing to provincial communities can be re-enforced by the frequent references to such activities in other diaries and also by the fact that they feature widely in the novels of the period. For example, in *The Miser Married*, an unjustly neglected novel about manners, debt and the relations between London Society and provincial retreat, Catherine Hutton had a good deal of fun with the practices of the local dance in Monmouthshire society. The wife of the local clergyman organised an entertainment followed by a dance in a barn prepared for the occasion. Unfortunately, the strict rules of etiquette from London society remained in place:

... the laws of dancing are very severe upon us females. Like other laws, they were made, I suppose, by lordly man; and, therefore, made much in his favour. He enters the ball room; he looks round him, perhaps with a saucy air; he con/ templates a number of young women, who are placed in ranks before him, dressed in their gayest apparel, and their best looks; and he singles out the object of his choice. It is true that the poor victim has a veto. She can say, no; but then she forfeits the privilege of saying yes, as long as the ball shall last.[14]

The virtuous heroine, Charlotte, is trapped with the insufferable Mr Sharp, who seeks to monopolise her and has to be told that the convention is to change partners after every two dances, thereby permitting her true love to claim her intermittently. But despite the dangers, our less

[13] James Oakes, *The Oakes Diaries I: Business, Politics and the Family in Bury St Edmunds, 1778–1800*, edited by Jane Fiske, Suffolk Record Society, vol. XXXII (Woodbridge, Suffolk: Boydell, 1990), (1789), p. 261, (1790), p. 267, (1791), p. 274, (1792), p. 285, (1793), p. 296, (1794), p. 304, (1795), pp. 316–317, (1796), p. 338, (1798), p. 370.

[14] Catherine Hutton, *The Miser Married, a Novel in Three Volumes* (London: Longman, Hurst, Rees, Orme, and Brown, 1813), v. ii, pp. 132–133.

virtuous, more wordly heroine and predominant narrator is clear about the pleasures of the dance:

Dancing introduces a kind of familiarity that would be quite inadmissible in a drawing room. When a gentleman solicits the honour of your hand, it is not a figure of speech; your hand really belongs to him, for the time; and if he persists in taking it a little after the time, it would be very ill-natured to withdraw it – unless one did not like him. For my part I found something so admirably persuasive in the touch of a man I do like, even through two pairs of gloves, that I could not find it in my heart to cut short its eloquence.[15]

Dance was a crucial component of many of these diary writers lives, it was a staple for the late eighteenth and early nineteenth century romantic novel (and the occasion for numerous lessons on conduct, etiquette and morality) and it was something that people both enjoyed and invested in (in terms of time, education, clothing, energy and emotion). It has not, however, been much thought about in relation to the politics of the period or to the war. And yet, there do seem to be grounds for considering this angle.[16] In this chapter, I want to explore a range of dimensions relating to music and dance so as to go on to raise questions about how this dimension of social life was reacted to by the literary radicals of the 1790s.

Dances were, for most people, occasions of heightened experience. For most young people, at least, they were an exceptional entertainment and a source of excitement with opportunities to encounter people from one's wider social circles.[17] Dancing was also both a highly disciplined activity and an expressive one. Chivers' *The Modern Dancing Master* underlined this by beginning with a set of 'Observations on Deportment':

EITHER in *Walking* or *Dancing*, the *Head* should be properly situated, erect and free; the *Neck* and *Shoulders* will then appear in their true proportion and in their proper places, the Chest rather broad and full, and the *Back* straight; the whole forming an easy motion to the *Hips*, without which neither the *Knees* or *Feet* can have true command.[18]

---

[15] Ibid., v. ii, p. 170.

[16] I was first prompted to think about these dimensions by participation in Roger Parker's KCL Music in London 1800–1850 project (see note 3) and by a paper given at one of the meetings by Erica Buurman, which has subsequently been published as Erica Buurman and Oskar Cox Jensen, 'Dancing the "Waterloo Waltz"', in Kate Astbury and Mark Philp (eds.), *Napoleon's Hundred Days and the Politics of Legitimacy* (Basingstoke: Palgrave Macmillan, 2018), pp. 208–232.

[17] Almack's, for example, had a very restricted clientele with ferocious rules for admission. See E. Beresford Chancellor, *Memorials of St. James's Street and Chronicles of Almack's* (London: G. Richards Ltd., 1922), pp. 208–209. See also Captain Rees Howell Gronow, *The Reminiscences and Recollections of Captain Gronow* (London: np, 1900).

[18] G. M. S. Chivers, *The Modern Dancing Master* (London: published at the author's Salle de danse, 1822), p. 23.

In *The Juvenile Guide ... addressed to young ladies* (1807), the writer encouraged the activity in its appropriate form, recommending 'all the amusements which prudence allows. Of these I know none more calculated to enliven the mind, and give grace to the person, than dancing. When it is free from awkwardness and affectation, it is of all recreations the one most natural to young persons.'[19] A generation earlier, the *Polite Academy* had recognised that this was a partial freedom within restraint:

> Considering the efficacy of the exercise, and that fashion has abolished, or at least confined among the very few, the more robust methods of amusement, it can hardly be excused to neglect cultivating an art so innocent and agreeable as that of dancing; as it at once unites in itself the three great ends of bodily improvement, of diversion, and of healthy exercise.[20]

During the Napoleonic Wars and after the Bourbon restoration, the character of formal dancing began to change, from the popular country dances (originally *contra danses*) and minuets of the eighteenth century (with the minuets usually preceding the country dances), to include the cotillion (a more courtly version of the country dance) and its successor the quadrille (which was introduced by Lady Sarah Jersey at Almack's in London towards the end of the wars) and then the waltz (*c.*1812) and the polka (*c.*1840). In the process, the very much shared repertoires for dance and music in the eighteenth century became more class inflected as the nineteenth century developed. These changes also see a segue from the more formal and collective character of the minuets and country dances in the direction of a more intimate pairing of couples.[21] Most formal dances such as the minuet involved a good deal of intricate footwork but barely any physical contact between those partnered, with country dances largely restricting contact to the hands (as Hutton's comment suggests). Verbal interaction, especially in long country dance sets, was expected, although Chivers frowned on continuous conversation on the grounds that it would annoy others, but one did not grasp one's partner.[22] In the waltz, contact with one's partner became much more extensive: early public performances of the waltz were reported to contain hopping, stamping, and throwing one's partner in the air, although commentary in the period generally strongly censured such behaviour and the dance eventually took more constrained forms.

---

[19] Anon, *The Juvenile Guide, in a Series of Letters on Various Subjects, Addressed to Young Ladies* (London: Parsons & son, London Circulating Library, 1807), p. 18.

[20] Anon [H. Gregg], *The Polite Academy, or, School of Behaviour for Young Gentlemen and Ladies*, 3rd ed. (London: R. McDonald, Green Arbour Court, for Parsons & son, London Circulating Library 1771), p. 97.

[21] Temperley, *Athlone History of Music*, v. 5, pp. 113–114.

[22] Chivers, *Modern Dancing Master*, p. 27.

Even so, in 1814, Ellen Percy, the heroine of Mary Brunton's *Discipline*, when asked by the anti-hero Lord Frederick to dance a waltz at the ball at which she comes out, knows she should refuse, and it is a commentary on her imperfect character that while

so much native feeling yet remained in me that I shrunk from making such an exhibition, and at first positively refused; but, happening to observe that Lady Maria (his sister and her rival from school) was watching, with an eye of jealous displeasure, her brother's attentions to me, I could not resist the temptation of provoking her, by exhibiting these attentions to the whole assembly; and therefore consented to dance the waltz.[23]

There were still more questionable forms of dance. Nicholas Wraxall recalled spending an evening at William Hamilton's London home in 1801 where Lady Hamilton danced the tarantella, first with her husband, then with another guest, then with her Spanish maid, each of whom she is depicted as exhausting, casting off those spent and replacing them with the next:

... it would be difficult to convey any adequate idea of this dance; but the fandango and *seguidilla* of the /Spaniards present an image of it. Madame de Stael has likewise attempted to describe it, and has made 'Corinne' perform it at a ball in Rome with the Prince of Amalfi, a Neapolitan for her partner, but she has softened down its voluptuous features that render it too powerful over the imagination and the senses. Yet she admits the 'mélange de pudeur et de volupté' inherent in the exhibition, which conveyed an idea of the Bayadères or Indian dancing-girls ... We must recollect that the two performers are supposed to be a satyr and a nymph, or rather a fawn and a Bacchant. It was certainly not of a nature to be performed except before a select company, as the screams, attitudes, starts, and embraces with which it was intermingled gave it a peculiar character.[24]

A further new fashion at the end of the eighteenth century, that drew horrified condemnation from moral reformers, were balls for children. James Oakes mentions one in Bury St Edmunds, in October 1783, expressly referred to as 'the Children's Ball in the Evening' and another in January 'A Ball at Mr R. Adamson for our young Ones'.[25] George Canning went to 'a Child's Ball at Mrs Robinson's (Privy Garden)' in

[23] Mary Brunton, *Discipline: A Novel* (London: Longman, Hurst, Rees, Orme, and Brown, 1814), p. 36.

[24] Wraxall, *Historical and Posthumous Memoirs*, v. I, pp. 165–166. Wraxhall's comparison is with Mme de Stael's *Corinne, or Italy* (1807), edited by S. Raphael (Oxford: Oxford University Press, 1998), Bk VI, I, pp. 90–92, in which Corinne's performance conjures up the dancing girls of Herculaneum.

[25] Oakes, *Oakes Diaries*, pp. 230, 231; Canning, *Letter Journal*, p. 93; Gawthern, *Diary of Abigail Gawthern*, p. 61.

April 1794; Abigail Gawthern's children were at a ball given by Mr Ray in Nottingham in October 1794 that began at 6.00 and ended at 11.00.[26] Hannah More referred to them as Baby-Balls and was appalled by them:

This modern device is a sort of triple conspiracy against the innocence, the health, and the happiness of children; thus, by factitious amusements, to rob them of the relish for the simple joys, the unbought delights, which naturally belong to their blooming season, is like blotting out spring from the year ... They step at once from the nursery to the ball-room; and by a preposterous change of habits, are thinking of dressing themselves, at an age when they used to be dressing their dolls. Instead of bounding with the unrestrained freedom of little / woods-nymphs over hill and dale, their cheeks flushed with health, and their hearts overflowing with happiness, these *gay* little creatures are shut up all the morning, demurely practicing the *pas grave*, and transacting the serious business of acquiring a new step for the evening, with more cost of time and pains than it would have taken them to acquire twenty new ideas.[27]

In public balls and dances, dancing was a heightened experience, in part because it provided a distinctive social experience, an opportunity for fashionable display before one's peers, and a degree of competitiveness. It also involved risk. Getting things wrong, falling or otherwise making an exhibition of oneself were to be avoided at all cost. Captain Gronow details the humiliation of a rotund Lord Graves falling to the floor when trying to emulate the much admired *entrechat* (the crossing back and forth of the feet in the air) of his (French taught) partner, Lady Harriet Butler, during a quadrille at Almack's – a humiliation over which a duel was nearly fought.[28] To fall was to lose control; to dance was precisely to demonstrate it. Indeed, the physical and personal self-control of the dancer that Chivers sought to inspire (especially for women) extended well beyond the particular dance: 'Of so great importance is decorum in the female character, at all times, but especially in public assemblies, that an elegant writer has observed, "women ought to be very circumspect, for a mere appearance is sometimes more prejudicial to them than a real fault"'.[29]

Dancing involved a mobilisation of the body in a performance, accompanied by heightened sensation, anxiety, excitement and display. Its accomplishment would have been partly a matter of training and habituation to certain steps and motions, together with more consciously directed physical movements, alongside opportunities for conversation and exchange. This was a world in which posture and movement were

---

[26] Ray also clearly held balls for all ages – as in December 1795 and December 1798.
[27] More, *Strictures on the Modern System of Female Education*, v. i., p. 95.
[28] Gronow, *Reminiscences*, p. 298.   [29] Chivers, *Modern Dancing Master*, p. 25.

quite sharply policed – especially for eligible young women. That it was highly disciplined did not mean that it was not pleasurable; rather, well executed, it produced a heightened physical and sensory awareness that would have given an emotional charge to the subsequent memories and also linked them with past performances and social events. It was a chance to practice and display what one had learnt from one's dancing master or from the books of steps that circulated in polite society but, as is clear from Burney and Austen, the activity was always a complex mix of expression and control, exhibition and scrutiny, elation and anxiety.[30] Of course, the more formal events clearly raised the stakes to a much greater extent than the quiet, domestic occasions of practice or indulgence in the sheer pleasure of movement.

Dancing in more public contexts was also closely tied up with questions of masculinity, femininity and the performance of gender. In this period, the association of tunes with military themes and the prevalence of uniforms at the dances would have underlined masculine command and conflict, with some slippage between martial combat and engagement on the dance floor: with one's female partner, in rivalry in the 'lists and cards' and in the formalities of engagement to dance.[31] These associations would have become coupled with leading one's partner through the rhythms of the dance, inviting both a sense of partnership and subordination as a woman and of self-discipline and potentially mastery as a man – coupled for many with an acute sense of the fragility of that mastery.

This heightened emotional, physical and mental experience of self-discipline, bodily coordination and social and sensual regulation and excitement was unlikely to have been entirely fleeting. I want to argue that the referencing of other elements through tunes and titles and in the wider marshalling of people's appearance, dress and movement would have added further to its significance and to its effects. In this wider context, the names of tunes might also become embedded in people's memories, linking them to a particular collective reading of the past and its events. This points to a wider set of experiences in which such associations were forged relatively unconsciously.

---

[30] See, for example, Frances Burney's *Evelina* (1778), edited by Edward Bloom (Oxford: Oxford University Press, 2002) and her first experience of a dance (vol. 1, Letters XI XII); or the place of dancing in Jane Austen's *Pride and Prejudice* (1813), edited by R. W. Chapman (Oxford: Oxford University Press, 1923) or *Emma* (1815), edited by James Kinsley, new ed. (Oxford: Oxford University Press, 2003).

[31] See more widely the work of Matthew McCormack, including his *Embodying the Militia in Georgian England* (Oxford: Oxford University Press, 2015), pp. 134, 148.

8.2   Radical Questioning

As we have seen, at least some literary radicals in the 1790s were hostile to a range of forms of public entertainment.[32] Masked balls (which out-of-towners like Abigail Gawthern clearly saw as a step further than was advisable for young people)[33] went against candour and the open countenance of truth. In Inchbald's *A Simple Story*, Miss Milner's improper education is signalled by the enthusiasm with which she greets the opportunity to attend a masquerade at the home of 'the fashionable Mrs G' and by her lack of understanding of the horror of her Guardian and subsequent husband Lord Elmwood, who had previously been a Catholic priest, which is prompted by her desire to attend dressed as a nun. Moreover, there was a common stream of denunciation of the frivolities of 'Cards and dice, fiddling and dancing, and guzzling and guttling'.[34]

There was also a wider suspicion of dance among the literary radicals. Wollstonecraft linked it with the gallantry of the military and saw clearly the way in which young women were served up to society, with no real experience of sharing time and activity with members of the opposite sex of their own age. Being thus impressionable the ball merely served to cast them into the designing path of thoughtless and often predatory young men. At the same time, she attacked Dr Gregory for encouraging 'the innocent girl to give the lie to her feelings, and not dance with spirit, when the gaiety of heart would make her feet eloquent without making her gestures immodest'.[35] The same point, about the dazzling impact of the ball and its capacity to befuddle the young, is made in Eliza Fenwick's *Secrecy*: 'I have no power of description; my brain whirls from one

---

[32] Godwin, notoriously, looked forward to the end of concerts, which he associated with collective conformity rather than individual autonomy. Godwin, *Enquiry*, VIII, vi, p. 444.

[33] See above for her blocking the proposal of friends to take her daughter Anna to a masquerade when in London in May 1802. (Chapter 3, note 49). See also Mary Brunton's clear concern for their dangers in *Discipline*, vol. I, running through chapters 5–9, with the duplicitous Miss Arnold exclaiming: 'At a subscription masquerade, indeed, one might meet with low people, but at Lady St Edmunds' there will be none but the best company in town' (p. 48). Hannah More also took a dim view of them – *Coelebs in Search of a Wife*, p. 220; whereas Fanny Burney's experience of one in 1770 seems to have been largely positive. Frances Burney, *Journals and Letters*, edited by Peter Sabor and Lars E. Troide (London: Penguin, 2001), 10 January 1770, pp. 10–13.

[34] Inchbald, *A Simple Story*, II, viii, pp. 151–160 (notably a prominent character in Burney's masquerade – and clearly a popular choice!); Holcroft, *Hugh Trevor*, I, xvi, p. 90. 'Guttling' being to eat or drink voraciously and noisily.

[35] Wollstonecraft, *A Vindication*, pp. 89, 255, esp. 94.

dazzling object to another, and leaves me but an indistinct crowded recollection of the various beauties.'[36] It was returned to in Wollstonecraft's *Maria*, when she described George Venables almost casual seduction of Maria: 'Without any fixed design, as I am now convinced, he continued to single me out at the dance, press my hand at parting, and utter expressions of unmeaning passion, to which I gave a meaning naturally suggested by the romantic turn of my thoughts.'[37] Alderson/ Opie was similarly critical of the way in which such entertainments trained women to live in the public gaze, with Adeline's mother being humiliated when she finds herself ignored in the fashion spots of the metropolis, when she had been so feted in her provincial setting.[38] And Inchbald's *Nature and Art* had a satirical appreciation in the depiction of the wife of Lord Bendham and of the adjustment women make to the demands of their surroundings: 'The wife of this illustrious peer, as well as himself, took her hue, like the chameleon, from surrounding objects: her manners were not governed by her mind but were solely directed by external circumstances. At court, humble, resigned, patient, attentive: at balls, masquerades, gaming-tables, and routs, gay, sprightly, and flippant; at her country seat, reserved, austere, arrogant, and gloomy.'[39]

Godwin does not discuss dancing in his *Enquiry* (apart from dismissing monarchs trained 'only to dance and eat'[40]), although one suspects that the activity would have been consigned to the flames with concerts, as involving a restraint on the free play of mind.[41] He gave a briskly dismissive account of the acquisition of such accomplishments in *Caleb Williams*, when he described Miss Emily Melville in the following terms: 'Her accomplishments were chiefly of the customary and superficial kind, dancing and music.'[42] Holcroft, in his *Hugh Trevor*, reflected that: 'since I have had the honour to become a philosopher, I have begun to doubt whether, hereafter, when the world shall be wiser, the art of tumbling may not possibly supersede the art of dancing?'[43] Godwin's

---

[36] Elizabeth Fenwick, *Secresy: Or, The Ruin on the Rock* [c. 1796] (Ontario Canada: Broadview Press Ltd., 1998), p. 212. Although the master analyst is Stendhal: 'The ideal breeding ground for love is the boredom of solitude, with the occasional long-awaited ball; wise mothers are guided accordingly.' Stendhal, *Love*, translated by Gilbert and Suzanne Sale (London: Penguin, 1975), p. 61.

[37] Wollstonecraft, *Wrongs of Woman*, p. 115.   [38] Opie, *Adeline Mowbray*, p. 16.

[39] Inchbald, *Nature and Art*, chapter XIX, para 3.

[40] Godwin, *Enquiry*, V, viii, p. 238 – a point that dramatically misjudges the significance of dance (and food) in the seventeenth and eighteenth century French court.

[41] Ibid., VIII, vi, pp. 443–444.

[42] Godwin, 'Things As They Are, or The Adventures of Caleb Williams' (1794), in Mark Philp (ed.), Collected Novels and Memoirs of William Godwin (London: Pickering & Chatto, 1992), v. ii, p. 47.

[43] Holcroft, *Hugh Trevor*, p. 9.

position was not far from that of Hannah More, who thought that the effort of acquiring the bare competence in the musical arts that was within the reach of most was largely a waste of time:

Almost any ornamental acquirement is a good thing, when it is not the best thing a woman has; and talents are admirable when not made to stand proxy/for virtues ... I know several ladies who, excelling most of their sex in the art of music, but excelling them also in prudence and piety, find little leisure or temptation, amidst the delights and duties of a large family, for the exercise of this charming talent; they regret that so much of their own youth was wasted in acquiring an art which can be turned to so little account in married life ...[44]

Fanny Burney's novels, in contrast, recur again and again to balls and dances. This is clearly in part a means of multiplying the obstacles to her heroines engaging in frank, face-to-face discussion with the objects of their affections, leaving those earnest young men in despair. Moreover, Burney saw that society can judge young women harshly and we can see some affinity between her sympathy and concern for them and that of the literary radicals. In *Camilla*, the heroine and Indiana are required to dance the first dance (and their first dances in public) at a ball and are under intense scrutiny:

Indiana and Camilla, in this public essay, acquitted themselves with all the merits, and all the faults common to a first exhibition. The spectators on such occasions, though never equally observant, are never afterwards so lenient. Whatever fails is attributed to modesty, more winning than the utmost success of excellence. Timidity solicits that mercy which pride is most gratified to grant; the blushes of juvenile shame atone for the deficiencies which cause them; and awkwardness itself, in the unfounded terrors of youth, is perhaps more interesting than grace.[45]

Nonetheless, for Burney it is a social trial that has to be borne, being a requirement and necessary consequence of a person's social position and of her entrance into wider society.

In contrast, the Jacobin novel was almost wholly critical (with the exception of Mary Robinson for whom balls are a common element in her fiction – betraying her very different personal history), lamenting the extent to which young women were subjected to the predatory or at best

---

[44] More, *Strictures on the Modern System of Female Education*, v. 1, p. 108.
[45] Frances Burney, *Camilla* (1796), edited by Edward and Linda Bloom (Oxford: Oxford University Press, 1972), II, ii, p. 62. The heightened – and disturbing – experience of dance is also indicated in Burney's *Cecilia* (1782), edited by Peter Sabor and Margaret Anne Doody (Oxford: Oxford University Press, 1988), III, v, p. 1, while in *The Wanderer, or Female Difficulties* (London: Longman, Hurst, Rees, Orme, and Brown, 1814) part of the interest that people show in Juliet Granvill arises from her knowledge of the latest French dances.

critical gaze of others and the extent to which this de-centres them, leaving them a prey to flattery and feelings that they barely comprehend. There could be some sympathy for young heroines, but the man of fashion garnered no such tolerance:

> He, likewise, had his opinions, but their pliability rendered them convenient to himself, and accommodating to his friends. He had courage to sustain fatigue and hardship, when, not his country, but vanity demanded the exertion. It was glorious to boast of having travelled two hundred miles in eight and forty hours, and sat up three nights, to be present, on two succeeding evenings, at a ball in distant counties.[46]

The dominant impression created by these views, however, is that many of these literary radicals had little experience of that of which they spoke, that their balls were imagined and that they had scant sense of the pleasures of dancing, being sensitive only to its moral risks. Few were prepared to share Maria Edgeworth's sense that one might readily be cured of the glitter and the glue, as Belinda becomes relatively early on in the novel:

> 'Is it possible', thought she, 'that I have spent two hours by myself in a library without being tired of my existence? – How different are my feelings now from what they would have been in the same circumstances six months ago! – I should then have thought the loss of a birthnight ball a mighty trial of temper. It is singular, that my having spent a winter with one of the most dissipated women in England should have sobered my mind so completely. If I had never seen the utmost extent of the pleasures of the world, as they are called, my imagination might have misled me to the end of my life; but now I can judge from my own experience, and I am convinced that the life of a fine lady would never make me happy'.[47]

8.3   Background Noise

For the literary radicals, the target was the fashionable world; but they gave little attention to the sheer ubiquity of the 'slight' accomplishments of dancing and music and they were largely uninterested in the more quotidian world outside the *bon ton*. Yet, as More's critical comments demonstrate, most parents with any pretensions to gentility tried to ensure that their children (especially their female children) would acquire some competence in music, singing and dancing. The Somerset parson William Holland refers frequently in his diary to 'Margaret (his daughter)

---

[46] Hays, *Memoirs of Emma Courtney*, chapter VII.
[47] Maria Edgeworth, *Belinda* (1801), edited by Kathryn J. Kirkpatrick (Oxford: Oxford University Press, 1994), p. 126.

at her music'. On her fourteenth birthday in November 1799 she was joined for the afternoon and evening by the two Miss Lewises from Stowey:

The young ones had a dance in the afternoon, minuets first and then the Steps and Reel and I myself sung for them. Margaret dances a very good Minuet indeed. Miss Dodwell a most excellent dancer, so neat and nimble in her steps. Miss Lewis sung and played on the Harpsichord very prettily. Edward Selleck and his wife Esther supped here and they and the servants staid at the door to look on. Esther [had] nursed Margaret and was delighted with the exhibition. The servants had a treat of rum and water in the kitchen. The youngsters were in good spirits, danced themselves quite fatigued and were glad at last to go to bed.[48]

Margaret's birthday dancing was a very restricted social encounter, albeit with a chance to demonstrate one's mastery of lessons to her parents and to put on a display for the visitors and the servants. A great deal of dancing must have taken place in such settings – relatively small, intimate and in the company of friends. In the metropolis, as Eliza Soane's experience suggests, one might find similar occasions in the houses of others. But both provincial and London balls were very much larger spectacles, with more adult purposes and with very much higher stakes. This does not mean that they were open to all and sundry. Dancing at Almack's was a very narrow and élite experience, with close control exercised over the sale of tickets and admission. Assembly rooms in London that were devoted to more open middle-class entertainment developed only in the 1830s and 1840s. Before that dances usually involved men and women who were relatively clearly situated in relation to each other, although provincial balls could be sizable and more socially mixed.[49] This meant that on many occasions those with whom one engaged were familiar. At the same time, the tunes and their naming, the forms of dances, the dress codes (with officers wearing their uniforms) and the formalities of meetings and encounters would have provided reference points for wider events and associations for people who had only indirect connections to them.

The identification with the dance and its music, as in Holland's informal setting in the vicarage, would also draw in its bystanders. These

---

[48] William Holland, *Paupers and Pig Killers: The Diary of William Holland, a Somerset Parson, 1799–1818*, edited by Jack Ayers (Stroud, Gloucestershire: Alan Sutton Publishing Ltd., 1984), pp. 19–20.

[49] Oakes, *Oakes Diaries*, v. 1. See entries for Yarmouth on 19, 24, 26 August 1791 (pp. 273–274) and Bury St Edmunds on 12 October 1792 (p. 285) indicating up to eighty couples dancing. The greater social mixing does not, it must be emphasised, indicate that there were not very substantial barriers between the different sectors of society appearing at such events.

might include those past their youth who were nonetheless also likely to be 'engaged' in the dance, even when sat on the side lines – perhaps especially on more formal, élite occasions. Mothers might be anxious about the young people in their party, concerned about the proprieties of social space, attracted by opportunities for social recognition for oneself or one's progeny (or concerned about either oneself or ones children being slighted) – all these factors adding to the intensity of the experience. Holland himself exhibited this when the family attended a Christmas Ball in 1815: 'There my wife and I saw our children both dance at the same time and they made a good figure.'[50] These observers were unlikely to have been immune to the music or to knowledge of their titles, nor would they have been unmoved – foot-tappers, hummers and those nodding and swaying in the audience in time with the music would all be implicated, their bodies brought into motion by the music and the movement of others and by their semi-conscious memory of their own past engagements.

The potential for the subliminal pleasures of a certain sort of physicality to break out in ways that were not entirely under a person's control should also be recognised. Amelia Alderson's mother died when she was young and she was perceived by contemporaries to lack a certain restraint. Nonetheless, she was an excellent singer and had been taught to dance at Mr Christian's Dancing and French School in Norwich. After her marriage to Opie, she recalled an incident when they were showing a friend around the Dutch church in Norwich that captures some of this complex mix of habituated bodily movement bumping up against social conventions:

I, finding myself somewhat cold, began to hop and dance upon the spot where I stood. Suddenly, my eyes chanced to fall upon the pavement below, and I started at beholding the well-known name of 'Christian', graved upon the slab; I stopped in dismay, shocked to find that I had actually been dancing upon the grave of my old master – he who first taught me to dance.[51]

The involuntary submission to music that might take people out of themselves is also clear in more domestic cases. Sharon Turner was allowed to accompany Watt's daughter and several of her friends in taking a boat ride to visit Pope's house at Twickenham. They left early one summer morning in a company of eight, with violins and voices serenading the party as they were rowed up-river with the flow of the tide. At the end of the day, as they rowed back, Turner asked them to play Handel's Minuet in Ariadne, which he was then learning:

[50] Holland, *Diary of William Holland*, p. 267.   [51] Brightwell, *Memorials*, p. 29.

They gave such an expression to its pathetic melody, that the English words which had been applied to it came into my remembrance & I was irresistibly impelled to recite or chant them, for I do not sing, aloud to the notes of the air, continuing to repeat them after the Violins had ceased – 'How is it possible, how can I forbear, When so many charms all around you you wear' – I was then reclining below her [Watt's daughter] as he sat on the Prow. I did not mean visibly to address them to her, tho my feelings did & were the cause of my reciting them as to myself, but these became so excited that I cd not avoid at last looking up to her as I repeated them. She instantly tapped me on my head with her fan & bade me be quiet while the other ladies burst into a laugh & called me the Knight of the Woeful Countenance. I felt that I was deviating from the momentary impulse into a relaxation of my usual self command & was glad that their jokes recalled it & drew me into that general hilarity with all, which was the most safe & proper.[52]

Turner was not then in a position to propose and could make no declaration, even as they were both well aware of their mutual attraction. In this instance, however, he was undone by the music.

Other musical engagements, in other contexts, could mobilise the body in equally unwitting and overwhelming ways. Consider Dickens' description of the 'Carmagnole' in *A Tale of Two Cities*: 'No fight could have been half so terrible as this dance. It was so emphatically a fallen sport – a something, once innocent, delivered over to all devilry – a healthy pastime changed into a means of angering the blood, bewildering the senses, and steeling the heart.'[53] Dickens grasps that it is the dance itself that directs the bodies of those engaged – and by mobilising and controlling the body it also unleashes deeper, more irrational forces. His representation is worth recalling since it catches something profound about the way that music can marshal the body and move it through space and time in ways that are partly intentional, partly habitual, partly interactive and partly involuntary. This sense of incomplete self-mastery and the taking over of the body by movement is something that reform-minded novelists recognised in highlighting the dangers of the dance or by having heroines, such as Mary Hays's Emma Courtney, remain unexposed to dancing in the name of more reasonable and rational use of the faculties.

8.4   Loyal Bodies

From 1794, and thereafter through the 1800s, loyalist songs and loyalist themes and commemoration were hegemonic in many parts of Britain,

---

[52] Sharon Turner, 'My Autobiography', 9 July 1794: BL Add ms 81089, fols 367–368.
[53] Charles Dickens, *Tale of Two Cities*, edited by A. Saunders (Oxford: Oxford University Press, 1988), III, v, pp. 267–268.

especially southern England and Wales. Very few radical songs, save in association with Ireland around 1797–1798 (where they were often brutally suppressed), can be found in this period.[54] In contrast, in London and much more widely, the performances in public gardens, concerts and assemblies and the collective behaviour of crowds at theatres and entertainments included a range of musical forms that invoked a loyalism in relation to the conflict with France and the associated struggle in Britain over the issue of reform and the war. We might see such 'loyalist performances' as rammed down people's throats – and it is true that some of the songs of Loyalist and Volunteer Associations were rather laboured. But that was not a perspective that the vast majority of contemporaries would have taken of their activities – and if they did, they tended to distance themselves as far as was possible from the more sociable events (as did William Upcott, who, as we have seen, got through his volunteer training as fast as he could and absented himself from the associated activities).[55] For most, part of the attraction of the Volunteers and the associations was precisely the collective activities of singing and playing together – generating a musical and vocal expression of association that matched their movement together in marching and drilling, mirroring and reproducing the emotional identification. Moreover, references to events in musical titles and their implicit re-commemoration in each replaying of a song or tune ensured that the association with the components of the geo-political military status quo seeped into the background of entertainments and 'excitements' – the concert, the theatre, the Gardens, the dance. These entertainments helped create a backdrop that was painted with a particular narrative, which was rehearsed emotionally and bodily by members of the social élite and a wide range of the middling sort in the metropolis and other urban settings. They would have been reinforced in country dances, when hearing the singing of those who re-performed what they heard, in the humming of refrains linked to particular signifiers, in the whistling of tunes in the street that recreated some element of the experience of the felt solidarities of collective experience in a Dibdin entertainment or,

[54] That is, new songs – while there seems to be an outpouring of loyalist songs. There were songs linked to the Irish Rebellion, but these seem not to be widely reproduced in England (and were the target of repression). And while the Marseilles and Ca Ira might be a resource, the impression from collections of songs and music in the period is that these were overwhelmed by songs with loyalist themes.

[55] Diary of William Upcott, BL Add ms 32558, fol 41r–v: 'Many who are in the same squad with myself appeared highly pleased with their new occupation, and to be thought the name of the Volunteer were never absent from their honourable post, at the appointed hour.' See Jensen's discussion of Joseph Mayett and Robert Butler in *Napoleon and British Song*, p. 67.

again, in the bodily memory and its invocation through repetition of moves from a dance. All this involves the involuntary evoking of the memorialisation embedded in the music and dance of the period.

8.5   Calling the Tune

Erica Buurman has recently drawn attention to how much printed dance music in London had titles commemorating aspects of the Revolutionary and Napoleonic Wars and their culmination in the battle of Waterloo.[56] She draws on a range of collections published between 1795 and 1819 and shows that, in addition to strongly commemorative tunes, especially in relation to Waterloo, titles also served as a 'more impassive commentary' that brought the political and military context into the social and cultural life of the nation.

We can extend this picture by examining some of the manuscript collections made in the period. For example, Joshua Gibbons, a paper-maker in Lincolnshire, who developed a local reputation for contributing music to balls, feasts and various rustic entertainments, compiled a collection of tunes from the early 1820s. It is striking for the number of titles involving reference to the events and personages of the Revolution-ary and Napoleonic Wars – 'Battle of the Nile'; 'Battle of Trafalgar'; 'Brunswick Waltz'; 'Conquering Hero'; 'Copenhagen Waltz'; 'Down with the French'; 'Duke of Wellington'; 'Duke of York's March' (and Quickstep); 'Grand March in the Siege of Vallencienes [*sic*]'; and so on.[57] It is worth comparing these tunes with the collection of Joshua Jackson, the North Yorkshire corn dealer and local musician.[58] The start date (1798) is clear, but the closing dating is more uncertain, with the editors suggesting 1820 on the grounds that dances that became popular around that time – the polka, quadrille, and waltz – are not included. Strikingly, Jackson's collection is relatively free of reference to military events of the Revolutionary and Napoleonic Wars, in contrast to the Gibbons manuscript. The compendious digital curating work of the *Village Music Project* allows us to see that, in fact, such variation was quite common.[59] Many of the extant collections made by individual musicians around the beginning of the nineteenth century involved rather less

[56] Buurman and Jensen, 'Dancing the "Waterloo Waltz"', pp. 208–232.
[57] Joshua Gibbons, *Lincolnshire Collections Vol. 1: The Joshua Gibbons Manuscript*, edited by Peter D. Sumner (Rochdale: Dave Mallinson Publications, 1997).
[58] Joshua Jackson, *Tunes, Songs and Dances from the 1798 Manuscript of Joshua Jackson*, edited by G. Bowen, L. Bowen, R. Shepherd, and R. Shepherd, 2 vols. (Yorkshire: Bowen and Shepherd, 1998 and 2011).
[59] village-music-project.org.uk (accessed 29 July 2019).

reference to current or recent events than did Gibbons' or than did the printed editions of music from London. In the latter case, the purpose of such publications was to sell topical referenced dance tunes to a fashionable and predominantly metropolitan clientele. In the case of the manuscript collections, it seems likely that individuals compiled material from across a longer period and with wider interests as a set of 'tools of the trade' with which to work and entertain and the political inflections of those 'tools', in their titles and past associations of tunes, would be likely influenced by a mix of the material they encountered, personal preferences and the salience of the tunes for, and the demand from, the audiences for whom they characteristically performed.

The contents of manuscript collections suggest that many of the 'topically' titled tunes of the printed sources were relatively ephemeral and did not transfer to private collections or became lost or reworked for other purposes, probably losing their nominal connection with the events of the wars. Individual musicians who made collections clearly had their preferences and prejudices and were probably powerfully influenced by their immediate context: the 'Carlisle MS'[60] (c.1812), for example, is distinctive in having, alongside many locally named tunes, a number named after events in the Peninsular War – 'The Spanish Patriots 1810'; 'Morgiana in Spain'; 'Morgiana in Ld. Wellington's Camp';[61] and 'General Graham's Waltz' (Graham being a commander under Wellington in Spain). One of the collections with the most topical tunes is Richard Hughes's 1823 MS (from Shropshire) of 170 tunes, which includes: 'Wellington's Victory'; 'Blucher's March'; 'The Walls of Madrid Waltz'; two tunes for 'Lord Wellington'; 'Waterloo'; 'Lord Nelson's Hornpipe'; 'Lord Nelson's Victory'; 'General Blucher'; 'Lord Hill's Quickstep'; 'Farewell Nelson'; 'Says Bonney I'll invade you!'; 'Admiral Mitchell's Hornpipe'; 'Fourth Dragoon March' (another reference to the Peninsular War); 'The Waterloo Dance'; 'Lord Moira's Strathspey'; and 'Lady Nelson's Reel', making up some 10 per cent of the music transcribed. This is a much higher level of contemporary reference than in most collections. Moreover, in some Northern collections, such as the Irwin collection of 108 tunes from Lancashire (1823), we can see rather different preferences, with 'Bonny crossing the Alps'; 'Young Napoleon's Waltz'; 'Napoleon's March'; 'Buonaparte's Coronation March'; a 'Loyalist Hornpipe'; two tunes referencing Queen Caroline; and one 'Billy Pitt'. These two lists suggest different interests

---

[60] This MS, purchased in Carlisle, formed part of the Frank Kidson Collection. It was transcribed by Anne Geddes Gilchrist; the original MS has since disappeared.
[61] The Morgiana tunes are spin offs from Sheridan's *Ali Baba and the Forty Thieves*.

and (probably) political outlook and they should alert us that collectors and performers drew on a range of sources influenced in part by their sympathies and those of their audiences – but nonetheless embedding contemporary reference in their repertoires.

The more challenging question is whether it mattered that a dance tune had this sort of title? It is certainly difficult to believe that the steps of a dance and its title bore much intrinsic connection. The steps to 'Waterloo', for example, are described as 'Change sides and back again – first couple lead down the middle – up again – pousette at top' ('pousette' being 'two couples pass around each other to places'). For 'French Liberty': 'Two ladies join hands and pass between their partners – the two gentlemen do the same – half figure your own sides – lead up on couple and set – back to back – turn your partner – pousette at top'.[62] In neither case does the title seem to be expressed in the movement.

It is also probable that many titles had only a rather loose connection to their tunes. Just as ballads might appropriate and re-title tunes, so it seems likely that there were earlier incarnations of at least some of the tunes listed by titles referencing the wars. Those titles that developed a stronger link would be those that, for some conjunction of reasons, embedded themselves in people's social and cultural environment, encoding a deeper set of memories and associations that would wholly or partly be recalled by playing the tune, executing the dance or hearing snatches being sung in the streets or hummed in the kitchen. For such embedded tunes, the playing of a snatch of notes would conjure up a range of associations – just as the phrase 'Boney was a warrior' can, even today, summon for many a chain of association that cannot help but culminate in 'went to St Helena' and 'broke his heart and died'! This might be equally true of dance music and its naming. By implicit or explicit reference to military victories, Napoleon's flight or the structure of the constitutional order in the 'Prince of Wales March' or 'Quickstep towards the Throne' tunes and their names could act as a link between the dance and the wider political world. Because dance was an exceptional entertainment, a heightened experience and an encounter with those in one's wider social circles, the calling of a tune when a dance was announced would, if popular and repeated, serve to link the title's contemporary reference to a set of subjective experiences, movements and emotions. As such, the title would gain significance in association with the physical, social and emotional experience of the dance while simultaneously linking those feelings and memories to the wider political context.

---

[62] Chivers, *Modern Dancing Master*, pp. 44, 49.

8.6   Soundscape

In Karl Philipp Moritz's novel *Anton Reiser* (1785), sound is an iterated theme. Moritz comments that, for the first time, as he began his residence in Erfurt, Reiser found the sound of the bells bringing 'all his memories of the past gradually ... to life'. Moritz writes:

This continual recurrence of sensory impressions seems to be the main thing that keeps people under control and confines them to a small area. – One gradually feels more and more irresistibly attracted by the very monotony of the circle in which one turns, one becomes attracted to the old and flees from the new. It becomes a sort of crime to step out of these surroundings, which become, so to speak, our second body, enfolding the first.[63]

We might link that insight to another. In the 1960s the sociologist Frank Parkin wrote a seminal piece on working-class conservatism in which he argued that (even for a self-confessed Marxist) the puzzle should be not why there are working-class conservatives, but how anyone comes to be other.[64] His grounds for framing the question in this way included the daily reproduction of experiences and messages that confirmed the status quo, its 'given-ness' and hence its legitimacy, in the press, in other media and in the daily lives of most people. To develop a form of oppositional class consciousness and to challenge that hegemony one needed insulation from that dominating set of messages and some submersion in more intensive and exclusive forms of experience with different associations and meanings that could provide the platform for a different take on the political and social order. People living in working-class areas, using the same services – public telephones, NHS doctors, public transport, council housing – sharing the same experiences at work and in relation to management, enjoying the same forms of social activity in working men's clubs or popular activities such as football or the dogs would have found contexts where their identities as part of a particular collective were more consistently reinforced and where there was space for the articulation and sharing of these experiences and for the development, through union and party-political activity, of a common set of aspirations and concerns – and these would enable a counter-hegemonic culture to develop.

We might ask similar questions about the 1790s. In some respects there was a loyalist hegemony: the radicals found it hard to compete with

---

[63] Karl Philipp Moritz, *Anton Reiser*, translated and edited by R. Robinson (Harmondsworth: Penguin Books, 1997), pp. 316–317.

[64] Frank Parkin, 'Working Class Conservatives: A Theory of Political Deviance', *British Journal of Sociology* 18 (1967), 278–290.

the weight of loyalist publications, the mobilisation for war and its dominance of the narrative of events, the lighting of windows, and the smashing of those unlit in response to victories. The regular bringing together of people with fasts, balls, concerts, assemblies and drilling and marching to mark events served both to inject a degree of entertainment into people's lives and consistently to underline the sanctity of the status quo and the apostasy of those who espoused 'French principles' or failed to join in.

George Canning gives us some of the flavour of people's reception of news of Howe's victory at the Opera:

We had not been there above half an hour when we perceived a degree of bustle and hurry in the lower boxes – presently the Opera stopped – people stood up, some knowing, but the greater part wondering, for what reason – and Boringdon came prancing into the box where I was with the news of Lord Howe's victory. I never saw a finer or more affecting spectacle than the almost electric and universal sensation that seemed to pervade every part of the House – the transport and triumph which burst forth as soon as their astonishment had a little subsided. The effect to an impartial observer was not a little heightened by the contrast between the feelings *generally* apparent and that discoverable in one or two boxes [containing Foxite Whigs].[65]

And in Bury St Edmunds, Oakes recorded on 18 June: '*This evening very unexpectedly* the town was illuminated on acc[oun]t of the Victory gaind over the French Fleet the 1st of June never hav[in]g any rejoicing in the Town on the Acc[oun]t. It was pretty general considering the short Notice – Ringing of Bells – fir[in]g of Guns &ca. All was not over before 2 O'Clock in the Morning.'[66]

The King's birthday was another such event that, while part of the regular calendar, often took heightened significance in the period: In 1798 Abigail Gawthern's Nottingham diary on June 4 recorded:

Our good and gracious king's birthday; the Infantry fired 3 vollies in the Market Place; the Yeomanry did the broad sword exercise and the barrack soldiers, the 3rd or the King's Own fired three most excellent vollies. I never saw the Market Place so full of people (excepting at an election) and most of them extremely loyal; many bonfires and guns firing all day.

Later that year, the battle of the Nile provided another event to celebrate:

Oct 3 The mail coach came in with blue ribbons and flags, and the Infantry fired in the Market Place on Lord Nelson's victory

---

[65] Canning, *Letter Journal*, p. 121.
[66] Oakes, *Oakes Diaries*, p. 301, see p. 369 for the celebration of the Nile.

Oct 8 We went to the assembly in honour of Sir Horatio Nelson's victory; a full room; Captain Watson, an officer quartered in this town, was seized with apoplexy and taken out of the room in a chair and taken to his lodgings in Friar's Lane; he was seized when we were gone to tea; Mrs Watson and her sister had both been dancing. Captain W. died in about an hour afterwards; the assembly broke up immediately upon hearing that he was dead, which was about one o'clock.

Oct 23 A general illumination, only a partial one the night before ...; the mayor issues bills to order everyone to illuminate at 7 o'clock; it began to rain hard but I and Anna went into the Market Place which was lighted up beautifully, especially the Exchange: Mr Evans etc., walked with us, we got completely wet; the candles were ordered by the mayor to be put out at 10 o'clock.[67]

What might be difficult to avoid in a provincial town could perhaps be ignored in the metropolis. Godwin's diary is ruthlessly silent in relation to such events, as is Holcroft's. Yet Godwin was at the theatre on both 2 and 4 October and it is difficult to believe he would not have encountered an enthusiastic salute to Nelson, in which he may well have been forced to participate.

Under such circumstances, what might have developed and sustained unconventional and critical views? One feature that marks our period, in contrast to Parkin's, is the relative weakness of the national political culture. People lived their lives, I have been arguing, in groups and communities that could provide alternative activities, readings and responses, where they were inclined. The emerging national narrative that Linda Colley in particular has encouraged us to recognise[68] was still one that might be contested. However, to build the resources for sustaining that contestation required both relative insulation from the dominant narrative or a powerful counter-narrative, together with iterated reinforcement from occasions in which an alternative reading might be sustained – not just occasional opportunities for conversations between individuals such as Godwin had when he sat at home with Cooper on 10 June 1794 and talked of 'taste' instead of joining in the celebrations.[69]

[67] Gawthern, Diary of Abigail Gawthern, pp. 74–75.

[68] Linda Colley, Britons: Forging the Nation 1707–1837 (New Haven, CT: Yale University Press, 1992).

[69] In contrast, Robert Owen's socialism in the 1840s clearly recognised the importance of such occasions. In February 1840, the Owenites organised an event to celebrate the Queen's wedding, to lecture the attendees on marriage and divorce and to have a Ball, whose dances were to include the 'Promenade, Contre Danse, Victoria Quadrilles, the Caledonians, the Pickwicks, the Lanciers and the Queen's Own, – A Spanish Waltz, Circular Waltz, the Mescolances, &c.' National Archive HO 44/38. See also Harold Silver, Robert Owen on Education (Cambridge: Cambridge University Press, 1969), for Owen's own account (p. 62) and the fuller account of his son, Robert Dale Owen (pp. 162–164), whose own collection of tunes is also available on the Village Music Project website.

That said, it seems likely that different regions developed and expressed a variety of sentiments and could harbour many resisting the more general political narrative produced in Westminster and St James. The considerable differences in the names of tunes collected in different places – such as between the Carlisle MS and the Irwin MS in the *Village Music Project* – suggest that the political associations of the tunes were markedly different. Nonetheless, while they reference very different aspects of the narrative of the Revolutionary and Napoleonic Wars, it remains the case that a more oppositional perspective would have been working against a deeper tide of custom and practice, expectation and assumption and commemoration and celebration that would have made a more radical narrative hard to develop and sustain, especially once put under pressure.

Similarly, theatre was a further site for contention and display throughout this period. Gillian Russell has drawn attention to the range of riots at theatres recorded throughout the towns of England during the war and it is clear that they often provided a forum for confrontation: for the military to champion the status quo or reformers to resist it, albeit in relatively well worn rituals, especially in towns with well-known reformist traditions.[70] In such cases, the patterns of local action could provide a framework of meaning that a more reformist culture needed if it was to stand up against the more traditional loyalties. That said, the war and its accompanying mobilisation ensured that they often faced confrontation with members of the armed forces, although that could take place along a number of different axes: between for example, loyalists and reformer; or equally between military and civilian, or between central forces and local traditions, or outsiders and residents, or army and navy (that is, there were various dimensions that could fuel the script for the contestation, with the theatre providing a public space which such groups sought to control or contest). In these confrontations, theatrical riotousness might be entirely orthogonal to the content of the play being staged; on other occasions a speech, or sentiment, or character in the play might be seized on and accorded meanings that were trumpeted or objected to by sections of the audience. It is not possible to do justice here to the complexities of such activities and those who have grappled with them are certainly better qualified to do so, but it is worth standing back a little and reflecting that many of the literary radicals were committed to the theatre, as players, playwrights and as members of the audience – to a much greater extent than they were to concert life or dancing. Moreover

---

[70] Russell, *Theatres of War*, pp. 108–109.

(as we have seen) some (like Godwin) saw in the theatre the prospect of engaging and transforming an audience's political understanding, in a way they do not seem to have thought possible in relation to music, dancing and singing. That it was a potentially profitable trade for a playwright is clearly one consideration; but the preference also speaks in part to the sovereignty of words and ideas in reform literature that drove the intellectualism with which they approached issues of reform and fuelled their suspicion of the less reflective components of sound and mobility.[71] Of course, it is also entirely plausible to think that, at least in Godwin's case, it was his intellectualism (rather than his politics) that lost him his audience's attention.[72]

For most people, the church and the singing of psalms or hymns probably provided the most common musical experience in the later Georgian period. Most of Holland's music was experienced in church or from military bands, once his daughter stopped playing (to characteristic parental disappointment) and his aural world was most commonly referenced through comments on the church bells, which rang on almost all occasions from battles to weddings and for announcements of all kinds. Hymn singing too was a physical experience, in the vocal actions but equally in the awareness of one's membership of a body and of a sound larger than oneself. Being part of an audience for religious songs could be physically moving: Holland records the fine melodious singing of the neighbours and workmen gathered in his kitchen on Christmas Day 1799 and of 'our Church musicians who had serenaded the Family this cold morning at five o'clock'.[73] Not every Christmas was so successful – in 1801 'the Singers at the window tuned forth a most dismal ditty, half drunk too with the most wretched voices'.[74]

As with theatre conflicts, this too points to the occasional fragility of the (in this case musical) hegemony. In the journal of John Skinner, another Somerset Rector, working in a mining area of the county, the church choir developed a degree of collective identity that challenged their spiritual director's authority. On one occasion, being ruled too drunk to be permitted 'to chaunt the service' after the first lesson, they clapped their hats on their heads and left the church in the middle of the

---

[71] In addition to Russell, see Marc Baer, *Theatre and Disorder in Late Georgian London* (Oxford: Clarendon Press, 1992); Jane Moody (ed.), *British Theatre: 1730–1830* (Cambridge: Cambridge University Press, 2007) and her *Illegitimate Theatre in London 1770–1840* (Cambridge: Cambridge University Press, 2000).

[72] For his plays see William Godwin, *The Plays of William Godwin*, edited by David O'Shaughnessy (London: Pickering & Chatto, 2010) and O'Shaughnessy's monograph *William Godwin and the Theatre*.

[73] Holland, *Diary of William Holland*, p. 23.   [74] Ibid., 61.

service. Their resistance was temporary, but relations remained strained –
Skinner wanted a girls' choir, but he found himself forced to stick with
his vocal male choir because their introduction of a large number of
instruments into the church had made them very popular with the
congregation.[75]

Music, the church and politics were welded together. In May 1800,
Holland delivered a sermon for the loyalist association, remembering:
'They marched in great order and parade with Colours flying, drums
beating and a band of Musick. After Church they returned in the same
order and parade and we all dined at the Rose and Crown. An excellent
dinner, a great many Loyal Toasts drunk after dinner and the musick
played of God Save the King, and Rule Britannia.'[76] In this world there
were many moments of quiet – Holland's son was forbidden his drum on
Sundays – but we can appreciate Moritz's point about sound becoming
part of the background to people's lives. Sometimes it came to the
foreground – at Christmas and in public ceremonies – but in many cases
it was a largely taken-for-granted framer of experience. Occasionally it
expressed a very personal response to events. Holland's shock over
Nelson's death issued, a few days after the news, in the following entry:
'I have been busy writing my Song on the Victory of Lord Nelson, and
I have sent one off to Mr Northey and one to Mr Ruscomb Poole.' On
the official day of thanksgiving for 'Lord Nelson's Glorious Victory' he
adorned the church gate with laurel and set the pattern with his own
family, and then with all those attending church, of wearing laurel in their
hats: 'Our Bells were ringing all this day and illuminations ordered at this
House ... the Town was very lively and on the top of Castle Hill was a
Glorious Bonfire and Music.' In the evening they had supper at the
Globe Inn:

At length a song was called for and Mr Northey blabbed that I had prepared one.
On this I was called on. I did not relish singing a song of my own making and
declined it much. At last I began and it took very much indeed, several bursts of
applause at each Stanza and when I had finished they all rose up with Glasses in
their Hands drinking my Health and clapping for some minutes so that I began to
feel myself a little awkward.[77]

Loyalist associations attempted to insist on the unquestionability of this
status quo, but there was such local variation in recruitment practices
and connections with the wider community that communities (such as
Norwich) might simply resist involvement if they had strong traditions of

[75] John Skinner, *Journal of a Somerset Rector 1803–1834*, edited by H. Coombs and
P. Coombs (Oxford: Oxford University Press, 1971), pp. 200–202, 398.
[76] Holland, *Diary of William Holland*, p. 35.   [77] Ibid., pp. 33, 121, 123–124.

opposition – just as the Revd Skinner's mining community showed some capacity for getting their own way. Nonetheless, in the last decade of the eighteenth and the first of the nineteenth century, most musical occasions largely confirmed the status quo and it is difficult to identify areas of common musical and physical experience that would have reinforced more reformist aspirations and identities. As such, the sounds, music and disciplined movement of the complex, hierarchical culture of the Georgian world played an important part in integrating people into their communities in a variety of subtle, if partly negotiated ways. In consequence, resistances were more fragmented, less communally solidaristic and more individualistic than they became after the first quarter of the nineteenth century. Their fragility encouraged more satirical (or cynical or parodic) and reactive, but less programmatic responses. That much contention took this form speaks to the socially, bodily and emotionally embedded character of a basic acceptance of the status quo, against which it was possible to react or resist only imperfectly. One might sing 'To the just Guillotine' to the tune of 'Bob shave a Kin', as against the usual lines,[78] or interrupt women singers performing loyal songs in Covent Garden,[79] or excuse oneself from the dance, stay away from Dibdin's entertainments or barrack in the theatre, but such resistance was occasional and took place against a wider sense that the status quo breathed a certain inevitability.[80] Congregating at dinners, in conversational coteries, or in other private spaces might have allowed a person to give free rein to his sentiments, but for many these individual effusions of the mind remained only half articulated rather than the expression of collective commitments. And they became rarer over the last decade of the eighteenth century as the boundaries of the private were (as we have

[78] See Edmund and Ruth Frow, *Citizen Guillotine* (Preston: E and R Frow, 1996), p. 9: 'Citizen Guillotine, a new shaving machine'.

[79] Association for the Preservation of Liberty and Property Against Republicans and Levellers, BL Add ms 16923, fol 127r–v.

[80] At least until after the end of the war. On 20 September 1819, at a dinner in Birmingham for T. J. Wooler, '... the people having a band, Mr Edmunds made some observations tending to induce them to play the national anthem of "God save the King"; but Mr. Johnston, observing that the late thanks of the Crown to the Yeomanry _____, having identified it with all the late atrocities in Manchester, it would be despicable hypocrisy to pretend any respect for such a song under existing circumstances, and the people seemed happy in being relieved from the task'. *Inverness Courier*, 30 September 1819 (BL Newspaper Archive). What is, perhaps, more surprising, is how much the use of the phrase National Anthem increased and how rarely such opposition was recorded. Another instance of Birmingham's resistance is mentioned in the *Public Ledger and Daily Advertiser* on 3 November 1819 in a theatre (where the radicals were overpowered). Manchester similarly recorded opposition at the end of September and were reported in several London papers.

seen) increasingly invaded. The consequence, I am suggesting, was that radical commitments became both more costly and practically more difficult actively to live.

Until the Gagging Acts of 1795 there were political dinners in London in which music and song could play an oppositional role. Shortly before the arrest of leading radicals on charges of treason, Turner managed to satisfy his curiosity about the political associations by securing himself a seat at the Society for Constitutional Information dinner on 2 May 1794, where he contrived to be sat opposite John Horne Tooke:

There were 402 persons present of all ranks & ages, partly members, partly visitors, a fine band of music played the Marseillaise Hymn – Ca Ira – & several other French Patriotic tunes which the company applauded ... When they began to have Songs & Glees of their own Kind from the professional singers who were there, somebody called on Mr H. Tooke for a song. He said he was no musician, but to shew his congeniality with the spirit of the meeting, he wd attempt a short one. He then sang in his way a Jacobin parody on God Save the King to the old tune – of which these 3 lines are a specimen

> O George! when wilt thou rise
> Open thy stupid eyes
> And see thy fall[81]

These occasions became increasingly rare, especially after the Two Acts. But we might also ask how far their collective singing expressed their sense of opposition without necessarily doing much to develop it.[82] Just as Tooke's speech on the occasion, in which he expressed himself happy to die for the cause, was somewhat at odds with his subsequent suggestion in his later trial that he was by no means committed to go all the way in his radical commitments, so too might the collective voicing of opposition through songs and toasts have more the character of expressive flourish and the frisson of transgression than of practical commitment. In the new urban centres of the North in the period after Waterloo, other collective spaces developed that people like Samuel Bamford were immersed in and could draw on, but there is not much evidence that these were available on any scale in the last decade of the eighteenth century and, for many of the participants, such occasions would have gone against the grain of daily experience.[83]

---

[81] Turner, 'Autobiography', 2 May 1794, BL Add ms 81089, fols 347–348.

[82] In contrast with the developing practices of artisanal radicalism in the local meetings of the London Corresponding Society in 1792–1794, which did seem to offer a space for alternative thinking before they were suppressed.

[83] See Katrina Navickas, *Protest and the Politics of Space and Place 1789–1848* (Manchester: Manchester University Press, 2016).

I have noted earlier John Galt's wry satire of both the loyalist Provost and the ardent enthusiasts for the French Revolution, with the Provost suggesting that the 'weavers and shoemakers, who, by the nature of sitting long in one posture, are apt to become subject to the flatulence of theoretical opinions'.[84] Galt's comment follows the understanding of the period in ascribing the orientation of the mind to the posture of the body, which gives further ground for us to be attentive to the way people moved around and located themselves physically: the proprieties of motion in reception rooms, the disciplined allowance of expression in playing music or singing, the rigours of polite intercourse and the rituals of greeting and not greeting in public spaces. The streets of cities could be more rambunctious and unpredictable and as such offered opportunities for transgression, riot, popular justice and momentary collective activity (which also surface repeatedly in Dickens's fiction). But these were episodic and uncertain resources – crowds could parade Horne Tooke in triumph from his acquittal at his Treason Trial in 1794, others might smash the windows of those failing to illuminate them to celebrate a naval victory. But for men and women from the middling orders – whether Upcott, Turner, his father-in-law William Watts, or the literary radicals in London – the resources for radical solidarity and commitment were more private, more particular and increasingly pressured.

8.7   Concluding Note

A reflective account of the music, dance and song of this period considers the disciplining of the body and emotions, understands these phenomena less as chosen pastimes and more as practices through which individuals develop capacities, movements and emotions in an inseparable mix of the physical, affective, mental and memorial. This mix plays a formative role in identity and locks that identity into a range of signifiers and prompts that evoke a wider identification with the established order. Elite groups associated with the Whigs might have cultivated an oppositional and occasionally transgressive political culture, but they were also deeply implicated in the institutions and procedures of society and government and few questioned that basic framework. Among the more middling orders, there was some experimentation with different ways of being, including a degree of sexual experimentation, an alternative sociability and new forms of self-presentation – with cut hair, the abandonment of wigs, new codes of dress and a culture of long-distance walking. But it is

---

[84] John Galt, *The Provost* (1822), edited by Ian A. Gordon (Oxford: Oxford University Press, 1973), p. 57.

difficult to identify opportunities for immersive activities that carried a fully embodied radical experience, in contrast to the wealth of experiences that confirmed the status quo, in theatre, dance, church services, public entertainments, military parades and exercises, each of which could involve a range of intellectual, sensory and bodily experience and could be framed so as to summon components of distinct identities and to evoke elements of a narrative of exceptionalism and national destiny.

To examine the culture of music, dance and song in these ways offers us a way to see the contentious politics of the period as set against a wider set of deep-seated cultural practices – as I was doing earlier in relation to the practises and expectations of sociability and deliberation. It also gives cultural history its proper place as a fully engaged element within a wider political and social history that takes bodies, movement, vocalisations, laughter and sentiment as forms through which people experience their lives and that shape their identities and conceptions of their interests, in ways which gives the status quo considerable implicit weight. In the polarising world of political contention in the years of war against France, this deeper cultural background facilitated the preservation of the status quo and the marginalisation and targeted repression of those who stood against it. Literary radicals might have sought to resist its attractions and imperatives – and could avoid engagement – but in doing so they also cut themselves off from a range of physical and emotional experience and from pleasures and excitements that they insisted on belittling but where their doing so necessarily increased both their sense of and their actual isolation. The high moral ground can become short of its necessary collective oxygen!

Conclusion
Life during Wartime

Although I have dealt separately with the dimensions of language and the understanding of politics, the practices that surrounded disagreement and their apparent collapse at the end of the 1790s, the character of sociability and the radical aspiration for egalitarian forms of friendship and exchange, and the place of sound, movement and conduct in relation to the entertainments and dances that formed a rather underexplored part of the background to society in the period, I have also tried to make the case for their connections with each other. My interest is in the way in which key elements of radical society and culture ran into challenges from the more taken for granted and quotidian aspects of people's lives and the society and culture in which they were embedded and with how its members responded to these challenges – not as isolated obstacles, but as interconnected parts of the fabric within which they acted, debated, socialised and (in the full range of senses of the term) 'moved'. They practiced deliberation, sociability, friendship, disagreement and love not as discrete elements, but as components in a field constructed by conventions and practices that framed the possibilities for and the consequences of their actions. For those who accepted the deliberative challenges of radical circles, change was something they saw both as the subject of conversation and as its inevitable outcome. And sociability formed an integral part of this set of practices. I have suggested that they often overestimated their hand. Indeed, they failed to see it as quite that (as a particular practice in a wider field). Rather, they saw deliberation as a more universal practice that would eventually draw others under its sway. They also overestimated the reach of their circles, operating in silos more than is recognised and setting themselves apart from some of the wider forms of sociality that they condemned as frivolous or dangerous to independent judgement and the development of mind.

In emphasising the importance of people's 'little platoons' I am not claiming exclusiveness for the various circles I have discussed in this book. Indeed, the fact that there are connections between them supports my case both about the kind of culture that many literary radicals aspired to and for the limits of possibility that existed. Godwin met the Ayrtons occasionally before 1820 (usually through Charles Lamb or Thomas Alsager) and then visited them and saw them regularly for several years and maintained contact with them for the rest of his life. Similarly, he was in touch with Soane in 1820, to try and arrange a placement for his son William to train as an architect and he had some dealings with the younger Soane who married the daughter of James Boaden, a friend of Godwin, biographer of Inchbald, etc. We are not, then, dealing with seven degrees of separation, but with cores that have peripheries that touch many other people, and that, on occasion, may provide the kind of weak ties that Granovetter understands as facilitating exchange of information and the development of trust. But we need to understand both the pull of the core for many people and the attraction (especially for men – more rarely for women – who were intellectually committed to equality and to the march of progress) of turning some of these weak ties into strong, disinterested friendships, in which the pursuit of knowledge, the exchange of ideas and the discussion of 'politicks' met their imagined ideal of something close to an instantiation of the *vita contemplativa*: something that was an end in itself, as a form of individual self-development, but something that they believed would also contribute to the further development of knowledge and the progress of society.[1]

More than most, Godwin made major efforts to maintain and, in many cases, reconnect with people with whom he was associated in the 1790s – for example, he wrote to Inchbald in February 1805 to congratulate her on her new play, *To Marry or not to Marry*, in which Kemble played the lover (suggesting a lack of audience memory to the scandal of the green room and Miss De Camp), and to draw her attention to the publication of his *Fleetwood* on the same day; he became reacquainted with Maria Reveley, then Gisborne, in 1820; Sarah Elwes was re-introduced into his domestic circle after 1811 until her death; a rapprochement was effected with James Mackintosh in the late eighteen teens; he held on to a connection with Coleridge long after most others in Coleridge's circle had decamped or rejected him[2]; and for all his being bowed beneath the pressure of work, he

---

[1] Aristotle saw 'contemplation' as an active, deliberative life, not as the solipsistic navel gazing it is now usually assumed to be.

[2] Although Coleridge played a major role in this: In Henry Crabbe Robinson's diary for 30 March 1811 he reports 'C[oleridge] spoke feelingly of Godwin & the unjust treatment he has met with … C spoke with severity of those who were once extravag^t admirers of G. & afterw^s when his fame declined became his most angry opponents … C sd there was more in G after all that he was once willing to admit, tho' not so much as his enthusiasts fancied. He had declaimed agt G openly but visited him notwithstandg he cd not approve even of Wordsworth's feelings & language respect^g G.' I owe the reference to Tim

continued to forge new friendships throughout his life, not just with young men seeking his guidance (of which there were several), but with new communities of acquaintance, such as that around John Martin the artist at the beginning of the 1830s, or, perhaps more oddly, with the Countess of Blessington and the Count d'Orsay in the early 1830s. Given Godwin's penury, we might think these relationships had a weightier slice of interestedness than those of the last decade of the eighteenth century, but that does not mean they were not also representative of his perseverance with a set of deliberative ambitions that testify eloquently to a sense of what he felt he had lost at the turn of the century.

That Godwin turned to the arts and to a corner of fashionable society (the Count d'Orsay was a contender for the best – or most extravagantly – dressed man in Britain) points to a widening of his (and his friends') tolerance for the *bon ton* that was absent in the 1790s. Like his turn to drama, and Holcroft's experiments in the buying and selling of paintings, this suggests their growing appreciation of the value of the wider social and cultural world (not wholly divorced from their interests) as a sphere for the expression and development of human talents that was somewhat more sequestered from the world of politics, but was nonetheless important in the development of abilities, making progress in understanding and in the refinement of experience. Godwin's initial concern about the potential prosecution of *Caleb Williams* and his withdrawal of the Preface to the first edition in May 1794 shows clearly that he feared his tale would be taken as a challenge to the status quo. 'It is but of late that the inestimable importance of political principles has been adequately apprehended. It is now known to philosophers that the spirit and character of the government intrudes itself into every rank of society.'[3] That sense of the extended politicisation of the intellectual and social world was much less evident in the opening two decades of the nineteenth century. When challenges were laid down, as in the prosecutions of Hone's parodies and satires, the government often proved unable to win convictions (in contrast to their pursuit of Luddites and in their conflicts with weavers in the North). In London, Richard Carlile and his family were less fortunate (like Hone, he was accused of blasphemy – for reprinting Paine's *Age of Reason*, Hone was charged for his parodies of scripture),[4] but they too helped mark what was becoming a shifting and gradually expanding (if still insecure) boundary of politics, between a wider cultural sphere in

---

Whelan's Crabbe Robinson project, www.crabbrobinson.co.uk/, and to the transcription that he provided.
[3] Godwin, *Caleb Williams*, v. iii, p. 279.
[4] See Michael Lobban's 'From Seditious Libel to Unlawful Assembly'.

which political allusion and religious controversy was tolerated and the direct challenges through satire to the religious and political status quo by the radical press (although the situation was additionally complicated by the activities of spies and *agents provocateurs* (such as William Franklin, alias Forbes and Fletcher).[5] This was certainly not a one-way street towards an ever-expanding tolerance. Moments of political tension could narrow the boundaries and generate prosecutions of texts that at other times might be ignored. But, in many respects, the struggle increasingly moved out of the realm of publication and into that of the formal limits of legitimate political organisation, the representation of interests and the negotiation over different forms of political expression.

I have set out a picture of the conduct of those who were a part of London's literary and philosophical radical culture in the 1790s that has dealt less than is common with their political associations and literary works and more with the dynamics of their social circles and with the clashes between their intellectual commitments and their more emotional lives and between their deliberative aspirations and the obstacles which their hierarchically ordered society created for egalitarian exchange. Their aspirations for a radical deliberative conduct rested on mutual recognition as equals, but this turned out to be a rarer and more complicated achievement than they initially imagined. And while it clearly sometimes took off in men's relationships with each other, where friendships distinct from interests and family connections could develop, it was more difficult for women to achieve this with each other and still more difficult to achieve it across the sexes. It was not just that some people turned down the invitation – that was common enough, as we have seen, even among men. It was also that, in many cases, those issuing such invitations experienced a confusion of motives and responses when they attempted to breach convention – in Godwin's case, for example, this occurred in respect of emotion and sex and with respect to money (as we saw in his relationship with Burdett – although it subsequently affected pretty much everyone he met in the last thirty-five years of his life).[6] Negotiating relations of equality, in a world that was deeply unequal and hierarchical in many of its aspects and sharply divided on

---

[5] See Hone, *For the Cause of Truth*, pp. 319–354; Robert Poole, *Peterloo: The English Uprising* (Oxford: Oxford University Press, 2019), pp. 52–182; Gilmartin, *Print Politics*.

[6] See especially Don Locke's biography of Godwin, *A Fantasy of Reason*. There is a tendency not to take seriously Godwin's commitment to disinterestedness with respect to money in-hand and his expectation of the same from his associates. But, again, this is an area in which the aspirations clashed with the practices and hierarchies of the period, in many cases leading Godwin into behaviour that was indistinguishable from that of a fawning and grasping supplicant.

gender lines proved to be a major challenge, not least because deliberative relations were often subverted by interests or by emotion and sexual attraction. And part of the point of seeing this is to underline that intellectual commitments and social practices often operated in tension with each other, sometimes opening possibilities, sometimes subverting aspirations. Theory and practice and their relationship is never just a question of either theory or practice.

At the same time, while we can see many of the intellectual reformers as positing something like an open public sphere in the manner of their discourse and in their conduct, in reality this was only one of many spheres. Many of the people with whom they associated relied in large parts of their lives on familial and business or professional interests – Canning, for example, regretted that his and Bobus Smith's circles no longer overlapped – '… our different ways of life throw us very wide from each other, without any fault in either of us. He is special pleading, and I attending the House of Commons – and either of these occupations accounts for by far the greater part of the day.'[7] Again, this restriction by familial relations and professional interests seems to have been especially true for women. But it reflects a wider truth about how relatively thin the common intellectual and social culture of London was, with many people's deeper commitments and more deliberative relationships often operating in rather narrow silos and with most people still relying heavily on older bases (of interest, profession and family) for their contacts, their social life and to get their business done. Even if there is something to be said for London as a meeting place for the able and disconnected, such relationships were generally patterned after professional and commercial connections and we should not confuse deliberative enclaves with a wider, open, deliberative public sphere. And that also means that we cannot take for granted that people's discussions revolved around a shared sense of current topics or a common set of deliberative conventions and procedures. Sharon Turner clearly found Holcroft a shock as a fellow deliberator in comparison to William Watts, despite the latter's fierce republicanism. William Upcott had little sense of the reformers or their aspirations in London, even while being very skeptical of the need for the measures employed by the government to command his obedience. Many literary radicals, perhaps especially Godwin, Holcroft and their closest associates, but certainly not uniquely, invested considerable energy in deliberation and discussion. They sought to engage and develop the minds of their younger acolytes and they often forged strong

[7] Canning, *Letter Journal*, p. 197.

intellectual bonds with people and friendships in which they aspired to the disinterested pursuit of truth. Nonetheless, these were often relatively restricted in their inclusiveness and in many cases the bonds proved fragile, as the openness of communication in private space was increasingly targeted by loyalist spies and informers and the conditions for trust began to evaporate.

If we recognise the case for seeing London society as made up of multiple 'little platoons' we can also better understand the government's response. Against one multiplicity were ranged other multiplicities, linked differentially to government, finance and banking, commerce, the navy and military and, in the course of the two decades, in the form of the loyalist associations and the Volunteer movement. In the face of the practice of open communication in private by critics of the status quo, we see a developing scramble in the government and loyalist circles to establish an alternative consensus (and to try and establish how widely it might be shared or be imposed) that had to be forged and publicly proselytised for through pamphlets, associations, newspapers, Royal Proclamations and parliamentary measures against sedition.[8] If the radicals sought to make a claim for private space, the loyalists' denial of that privilege meant that their own insistence on loyal subscription was to be understood as actively political in character. By 1803, this did indeed become 'platoonised', through the organisation of the volunteers and their express encoding of the hierarchies of the status quo in the manner of their organisation and conduct.[9]

At the same time, it is abundantly clear that the government did not have the full measure of exactly what was going on. Their social and intellectual experience barely brushed against that of metropolitan and philosophical radicals – Canning went to Tooke's trial (and expressly sought out Dundas to talk to him about his neighbour) to get a sense of what kind of person he was. Those in office relied on 'informations' sent in, spies reports, returns from local magistrates, their own perusal of the press and pamphlets and on second-hand reports. Being similarly marshalled in groups of their own that were orientated to support the government, they were often without much sense of where in practice the central risks lay and their conduct seems in many respects to have relied on conjuring traditional images of fidelity to the king through loyal addresses and in response to Royal Proclamations (while seeing unrest

---

[8] The pressures of war and their effects are often understated in the literature on the wider society of the period – Jenny Uglow's popular history *In these Times* is an exception to this.

[9] Although this could raise problems, as Katrina Navickas has shown in *Loyalism and Radicalism in Lancashire 1789–1815* (Oxford: Oxford University Press, 2009).

over food shortages and military impositions as essentially non-political in character – even if it was something that needed a political response).

There is no doubt that the experience of the Gordon Riots in 1780 had given London a scare about the potential for popular action to spiral out of control (an example they then re-experienced in their reading of the revolution in Paris) and this doubtless intensified the government's concerns as it saw a new generation of organisations calling for change. Many coupled this anxiety with a degree of hauteur towards those who dared to imagine that they had a legitimate role in holding the government of Britain to account for its actions to a wider public. Moreover, surface indications tended to be taken as symptomatic of deeper purposes: floes were read as icebergs – superficially slight, but masking threatening, sub-marine forces that put government and, following the declaration of war, the country and its security at risk. As government measures became more pressing, it is not difficult to see that reformers in turn became anxious that what they had initially seen as mild intransigence was looking more like evidence of a systematic plot against the liberties of free-born Englishmen. It is not clear that Canning really believed in the Treason Trials. He was impressed by Horne Tooke, but not by Justice Eyre, whom he saw as bending over backward to afford Tooke a stage for his performance. But his more telling comment was in relation to the meeting at St George's Field on 29 June 1795.

> Boringdon had been there and gave us an account of what had passed. Nothing very formidable. Very little mention among them of the *scarcity*, which after all is the most dangerous and deplorable evil under which we labour at present, and may, if not timely provided against, produce very calamitous consequences. The members of the Privy Council are meeting about it every day.[10]

In Canning's view, it was not politics but economics that was the challenge – not ideas, but stomachs. And while this was in part a touchstone of faith in the docility of a well-fed people and the danger of hungry crowds, it also points to what he took to be the government's most serious challenge – albeit one that irresponsible agitation might dramatically exacerbate.

The deliberative literary culture of the early 1790s survived into the second half of the decade, despite the emigration of some more closely associated with challenging the government and the prosecution and more than occasional imprisonment of others. Whether it was exactly a 'reign of terror' is debatable, but it was often deeply invasive and brutally

---

[10] Canning, *Letter Journal*, p. 283 (on Tooke see p. 148 and p. 155). The outcome of Hardy and Thelwall's trials were not worth mentioning.

callous and insouciant towards the livelihoods (and sometimes the lives) of those the government and loyalists targeted. Nonetheless, in the literary circles in which Godwin moved there remained a sense of sharing in a disinterested pursuit of truth through debate and discussion well into 1797 and 1798. For Godwin, the collapse came very much around the time of the publication of his *Memoirs of the Author of the Vindication of the Rights of Woman* (1798) – a major misjudgement on his part, not least in laying open her private world to an increasingly hostile and anxious Anglican and Tory élite. Indeed, in many respects, because his publication delivered up the details of her life to a public as a vindication it was consequently seen as an explicitly political statement and his enemies reacted accordingly, using the *Memoirs* as a means to tar other women writers with the brush of infidelity, immorality and Gallicism. Moreover, as we have seen, several of Godwin's friends responded by abandoning him and did so by themselves taking to the public pulpit. Moreover, some of his opponents brought to their task a line of sexual innuendo and a rhetoric of immorality that had been a staple part of the machinery used throughout the eighteenth century to undermine women who assumed public roles and they used his account of Wollstonecraft to ramp up that rhetoric. In so far as there was novelty it arose in turning the snipers away from aristocratic women and actresses to a more middling -order set of literary targets. And Godwin's complaint about Parr's use of the pulpit failed to acknowledge (because he failed to see) that his *Memoirs* had also helped open the path to turning private matters of domestic affection into public controversy.[11]

Through his *Memoirs*, Godwin effectively demonstrated that he was prepared to practice what he preached and insisted on his right to do so. Many of those inspired or impressed by his *Enquiry* could appreciate the power of its arguments, without heading wholly down the road sketched in the final book, toward the equalisation or collective ownership of property, the end of marriage and the development of a life of the *houyhnhnms*. But it was only after the publication of the *Memoirs* that several of his friends, probably already concerned about their association with him, found no difficulty in distancing themselves from someone who had turned out to be willing to put into practice what they had previously been willing only to debate and to speculate about.

Britain was at war from 1793–1815, with a brief hiatus in 1801–1803 during the Peace of Amiens. The war was Canning's central

---

[11] Parr's continuing friendship around the time of Wollstonecraft's death underlines his willingness to ignore the truncated space between the marriage and the birth while it remained essentially private.

Parliamentary concern: his friends could prove recalcitrant on a range of different topics, but the key thing on which he wanted their loyalty was the war. In relation to the rest of those in the metropolis, other than the occasional celebration of a victory or the mourning of a loss, the war does not come down to us as a recurrent concern deeply embedded in the diaries and memoirs of members of the middling and professional orders living in London. Marianne Ayrton and Eliza Soane simply did not mention it. They attended public events that may have had reference to the war, but there was little reflection on that. Godwin largely ignored it after its outbreak and, while Holcroft saw it as a topic of discussion, it was not something that might seriously hamper his planned trip to Europe. Turner's diary/memoir looks very much as if he recorded personal matters to do with his wooing of Mary Watts and his relationship with her father in real time. In contrast, his discussions of military affairs reads as if this was something he substantially expanded or added to at a later stage so as to set the context – where doing so meant doing some additional research to establish exactly what had been going on.[12] And Upcott made something of a crisis out of the threat of enlistment in the militia, but essentially successfully navigated that with the help of a wealthy friend and remained dismissive of the Volunteers whom he joined, and especially of the government's alarm.

This rather surprising silence may be a function of sheer ubiquity – when, surrounded by the activities and members of its forces, there may have been little that stuck out for a domestic audience once it had become a 'new normal'. But it may also be that their understanding of this war was patterned on the many previous wars of the century and that on a day-to-day basis they barely noticed its scale or its increasing intensity or longevity, even as they lit their windows (or resisted doing so), watched parades and the mustering of the militias, attended balls replete with men in uniform and found themselves caught up in the popular celebration of naval and military heroes and successful encounters with the enemy. For some there would have been a sense of dissonance between these occasions and the rising criticism of the war among the extra-parliamentary opposition and its coupling with protest against rising food prices and government intransigence. Those who sided with the critics could avoid at least some of the dissonance, by steering clear of Dibdin's entertainments, avoiding the streets after victories and sticking to circles made up of like-minded friends (and this looks very much as if it is what many literary radicals did). And that strategy could be buttressed by conjuring

---

[12] It is worth comparing his account of the fate of Poland with what was published at the time in newspapers.

up a degree of confidence that they held the moral and intellectual high ground. But that probably worked only in so far as it was experienced in and as a group. As these groups became more threatened and thereby more fragile, so too did that confidence, although the grinding character of the later years of the Napoleonic Wars might have provided some renewal of a basis for solidarity and collective opposition.

I have argued for the existence of close, often loosely interconnected circles, made up of a range of ties of varying strength, but that tended to become reinforced and buttressed by forms of exchange and reciprocity (not least around food and drink, discussion, entertainment and often by lending, borrowing and debt). Moreover, these groups shared sets of practices – with Eliza Soane knowing to whose house she could go to have a dance when her husband was away and with some circles becoming almost debating societies while others seem pared down to intense bilateral deliberative relationship. These practices often had multiple dimensions – intellectual, social, emotional – and because of that they were often subject to fallings out and reconciliations. For most people they provided a sense of rootedness, grounding them and their sense of identity in ways that could subsequently be badly shaken when things came to seem other than anticipated – as when Canning fell out with his old college friend Robert Banks Jenkinson over a practical joke or later when he began to fear that Jenkinson's marriage (which he had done so much to bring off against the opposition of Jenkinson's father) had introduced a new froideur in relation to the group.[13] And there is a similar sense of Mrs Soane's being shaken by the collapse of her friendship with Mrs Wheatley; and for both Godwin and Holcroft by the rupture of their friendship with each other.

That said, the literary radicals gave their priority to intellectual relationships and deliberative exchange, especially in male circles, and they had relatively few collective activities other than discussion. They did not (as far as we can ascertain) go to balls or have dances together; Godwin was not a part of the musical entertainments that Holcroft was involved in with William Shield and others and he rather rarely went to concerts. His theatrical visits, while frequent, were most often undertaken on his own; and his attending of exhibitions and lectures was rarely as a part of a small intimate group, even though he recognised and knew many people who also attended (mostly he went on his own and did not follow up with socialising with those whom he met).[14] He did not holiday with friends or

---

[13] Canning, *Letter Journal*, pp. 109–113, 123–124, 240.
[14] George Dyson accompanied him on a few occasions and John Chandler, the artist, also did, but the vast majority of his exhibition 'activity' was solo.

take trips on the river or engage in many of the formidable array of diversions and activities offered in the capital.[15] Of course, he, and many of his friends, needed to work, and that work was often isolating, but that meant that a great many of his ties were effectively weak – useful when it was not necessary to place too much pressure on them, but vulnerable to the heightened political atmosphere. That vulnerability left him unprepared for the reaction when it came and especially for the public reaction against his ideas by those whom he had thought bound by the stronger ties of engagement in a common deliberative enterprise, like Parr, Mackintosh, Montagu and Pinkerton. Moreover, the stronger ties he tried to form were rooted in his confidence in the inevitability of progress through debate and discussion and in his commitment to deliberative equality. Yet this latter proved an elusive objective for relationships: it is striking that most of his strongest deliberative relationships were with younger men. In these he often faced similar problems to those encountered in his more tutelary relations with women, arising from the difficulty of wholly laying aside claims to authority and a corresponding tendency on their part to be unsure how to negotiate a true equality, which often issued in misunderstanding and resentment. And in pretty much every such relationship (save the earliest with his relatives Webb and Cooper), there was little to provide any more formal delimitation of roles and expectations.

Hume, in his *Treatise*, talks of philosophy as a sea voyage, beset by shoals and risking shipwreck. In many respects, that is an apt metaphor for what Godwin and his interlocutors were doing. Although they brought much more confidence to it initially, their sea of inquiry proved, especially in his relationships with women, to be largely uncharted and distinctly choppy. And while, like Hume, he initially conceived of that sea as a wholly intellectual space, to be explored with absolute candour and an utter fidelity to the truth, it is clear that his encounters in the first half of the decade opened him up to a range of other dimensions of emotional and social interaction that he then had to learn to respond to and come to terms with.[16] We can see evidence of this in his writing and his revisions to his *Enquiry* in the form of an increasing acknowledgement that progress and engagement in deliberation could not be merely an activity for talking heads. In his recognition of a place for feeling he was also

---

[15] At least until after his marriage to Mary Jane Clairmont and once the children were older – see, for example, 13 September 1806 and 3 September 1807.

[16] David Hume, *Treatise of Human Nature* (Edinburgh: A. Miller and A. Kincaid, 1740), I.4.7, para 1. Hume goes on to indicate the importance of our embeddedness in 'the sphere of common life' against which his skepticism seems unwarranted. The contrast is one Godwin seems to have increasingly recognised.

accepting that there was a richer human fabric and array of registers that had to be addressed and that ought to inform his judgement and he sought new means for doing so, although with rather little success.[17]

There have been many examples of radical egalitarian aspirations foundering on gender, class, race and a range of deeply engrained forms of inequality – inequalities that prompted their ambitions but also proved resistant enough to subvert them. I do not say that to make a case for the pointlessness of the ambition. With Godwin and his allies, equality and the exercise of deliberative cooperation was essential to any society that aspired to diminish ignorance, coercion and the exercise of what Paine called 'force and fraud'. The challenge concerned – and concerns – its achievement. Again, this was not because the appetite for it is in some way disordered – as when Tocqueville says that there 'exists in the human heart a depraved taste for equality, which impels the weak to attempt to lower the powerful to their own level and reduces men to prefer equality in slavery to inequality with freedom.'[18] Rather, it is because what we think of as a simple thing, equality, is in fact a complex, finely grained value, interlocked with other values, such as freedom, that we also aspire to realise and that are very much rooted in particular cultures, with specific histories and hierarchies of difference and with distinctive local challenges to the claims for equality *simpliciter*. That complexity and local entrenchment of issues requires a distinctive type of deliberative setting to be instantiated and acknowledged: one that protects the experiment, reduces the particular pressures participants face, works to buttress the weak against the assumptions of the stronger and promotes a healthy degree of tolerance, mutual understanding and forbearance. People (and societies) can be mistaken about whether such conditions exist (or just not recognise their necessity) – indeed, we might see London's middle-class and professional culture in the early 1790s as one such case of mistaken confidence. After an initial optimism, they became increasingly engaged in a struggle against forces that seemed wholly opposed to such principles, so that their own ambitions and relationships came under increasing strain, forcing them to make more simplified and categorical choices, when subtlety and patient deliberation were required. Alderson's *cri de coeur* about the deliberative styles of her Norwich friends and

---

[17] Both in literary terms – as in his theatrical ventures; and in personal terms – he retained his capacity for patient silence (and indeed proved increasingly reticent in society), but he hardly extended his emotional range (as seems clear from his response to his daughter's relationship with Shelley).

[18] Alexis de Tocqueville, *Democracy in America*, v.i, pt, 1, 'Political Consequences of the Social Condition of the Anglo-Americans', edited by Alan Ryan (London: Everyman, 1994), p. 53.

her tribute to Godwin's patient and thoughtful manner capture something elementary about the essentially uncoercive and egalitarian character of disinterestedness in the period – something that Holcroft's manner seems routinely to have violated, at least on Turner's account.

Godwin's own intentions and practice were often sorely tried and he increasingly failed to achieve what he aspired to, especially as debt, censoriousness and intolerance swept over him at the end of the eighteenth century and in the opening years of the next. But we should not blame the victim and we should recognise that he, and at least some of his companions, aspired to something laudable, even if the conditions it required for its realisation were a great deal more demanding than they recognised. As I have argued here, Godwin's own intellectual acknowledgement of people's Burkean embeddedness and the gradual process of change that implied was not accompanied with much recognition of the social and psychological boundedness of himself and his colleagues or by much questioning of the forces, in terms of language, emotion, social expectations and culture, that circumscribed and served to frame – to delimit but also to subvert – his aspirations for a community of free deliberative equality in which the life of the mind would tutor the radical conduct of its members. But getting the balance right between despairing conformity to the status quo and over-optimism in challenging it remains a deep challenge. Deep, above all, because it is not a matter wholly of reason and rationality, so much as a practice of judgement, that calls for some cardinal virtues – not least, moderation, courage, wisdom and justice – that are themselves the product of our education in and by the world. Given his early Platonism, it is plausible to think that Godwin saw himself as aiming for something like this and that he might subsequently have been able to accept that he had underestimated the challenge of developing and consistently displaying these across the whole of one's life and engagements. Nonetheless, he would have probably have doggedly insisted that the objective was the right one and was the only one worthy of our aspirations and of our rationality as human beings, even if the world we inhabit all too frequently undoes us.

Bibliography

Manuscript Collections

Barnsley Record Office and Local Studies Department

SpSt/60644/11 (1809)

Bodleian Library

MS Abinger (see: www.bodley.ox.ac.uk/dept/scwmss/wmss/online/1500-1900/abinger/conspectus.html and www.bodley.ox.ac.uk/dept/scwmss/wmss/online/1500-1900/abinger/abinger.html)
Inchbald Letters: Bod Lib. MS Eng. Misc. e.143

British Library

Assorted Correspondence, BL Add ms 39781 f. 44
Association for the Preservation of Liberty and Property Against Republicans and Levellers, BL Add ms 16923
Diary of Sharon Turner, British Library Add ms 51055; Add ms 60647A; Add ms 60647B; Add ms 81089
Marianne Ayrton's Diary BL Add ms 60372, 60373 and BL Add ms 52351
Thomas Hardy papers BL Add ms 27811
William Upcott Diary, BL Add ms 32,558

The John Soane Museum Archive, London

Details Respecting the Conduct and Connexions of George Soane, c.1835
Diary of Joseph Gandy SM/f.179
SM/4/B/8/6 Mrs Soane's Letters 1813
The Diary of Eliza Soane SM Archives MrsSNB/1 to MrsSNB/8; and transcription Mrs Soane's Notebooks 1804–1813
The Diary of John Soane SM Archives SNB/1 to SNB/223 and Transcription, under the aegis of A. T. Bolton c 1920 vols. 1–17

Lambeth Palace Archives

D675 and D 676, case number 3111
Papers relating to Elwes ecclesiastical divorce: G 155/18; G 155/79; G 153/
    89; E45/100; G155/79; MS Film 104, 105; Process books

London Metropolitan Archive

Papers relating to the Elwes Criminal Conversation case DL/6/662/179/3;
    DL/C/0562/177–179; DL/C/562/177/2

National Archive

Dyson papers: National Archives TS 11473/1582
Godwin's writ of habeas Corpus: National Archive KB 1/32/2
Home Office Papers HO 44/38
Papers relating to the Elwes Appeal: National Archive Del 7/1 High Court of
    Delegates Judgment; DEL 1/670 v. 1 and 2; DEL 5/35; and DEL 6/52
Prob-11-1573-269; PROB 11/1591:129/110–12; 11/1600 113r–4v

Web Resources

British Library Newspaper Archive: www.britishnewspaperarchive.co.uk
Edward Pope: http://edpopehistory.co.uk/
Old Bailey Online: www.oldbaileyonline.org/
Papers of Mary Jane Vial/Clairmont: www1.somerset.gov.uk/archives/, cata-
    logue reference DD\DP 17/11, Papers of Dodson and Pulman, Solicitors
    of Taunton, Lethbridge estate papers (correspondence concerning Mary
    Jane Vial); and the transcriptions at https://sites.google.com/site/maryjanes
    daughter/home
The Village Music Project: www.village-music-project.org.uk
William Godwin, *The Diary of William Godwin*, edited by Victoria Myers,
    David O'Shaughnessy and Mark Philp (Oxford: Oxford Digital Library,
    2010), http://godwindiary.bodleian.ox.ac.uk.

**Primary Sources and Modern Editions
by Original Author**

Anon, [H. Gregg], *The Polite Academy, or School of Behaviour for Young Gentlemen
    and Ladies*, 3rd ed. (London: R. McDonald, Green Arbour Court, for
    Parsons & son, London Circulating Library, 1771).
*A Letter from His Grace the Duke of Portland to Lieutenant Colonel Sharman ...
    With Notes by a Member of the Society for Constitutional Information*, 3rd ed.
    (London: np, 1795; first published August 1783).

An Account of the Trial of Thomas Muir, Esq., Younger of Huntershill, for Sedition, Robertson ed. (Edinburgh: J. Robertson, 1793).

The Measures of Ministry to Prevent a Revolution Are the Certain Means of Bringing It On, 2nd ed. (London: D. I. Eaton, 1794).

The Decline and Fall, Death, Dissection, and Funeral Procession of His Most Contemptible Lowness the London Corresponding Society, &c. (London: George Cawthorn, 1796).

The Juvenile Guide, in a Series of Letters on Various Subjects, Addressed to Young Ladies (London: Parsons & son, London Circulating Library, 1807).

Austen, Jane, *Pride and Prejudice* (1813), edited by R. W. Chapman (Oxford: Oxford University Press, 1923).

Mansfield Park (1814), edited by James Kinsley, new ed. (Oxford: Oxford University Press, 2003).

Emma (1815), edited by James Kinsley, new ed. (Oxford: Oxford University Press, 2003).

Bamford, Samuel, *Passages in the Life of a Radical: Autobiography* (1842), edited by Henry Dunckley, vol. ii, reprint (London: Internet Archive, 2014).

Beloe, William, *The Sexagenarian: Or the Recollections of a Literary Life,* 2 vols. (London: F. and C. Rivington, 1817).

Boaden, James, *Memoirs of Mrs Inchbald, Including Her Familiar Correspondence with the Most Distinguished Persons of Her Time. To Which are Added The Massacre, and A Case of Conscience; Now First Published from Her Autograph Copies,* 2 vols. (London: R. Bentley, 1833).

Bowles, John, *Reflections on the Political and Moral State of Society at the Close of the Eighteenth Century,* 2nd ed. (London: Rivington, 1801).

Remarks on Modern Female Manners, as Distinguished by Indifference to Character and Indecency of Dress (London: F. and C. Rivington, 1802).

Brightwell, Celia Lucy, *Memorials of the Life of Amelia Opie, Selected and Arranged from Her Letters, Diaries, and Other Manuscripts,* 2nd ed. (Norwich: Fletcher and Alexander, 1854).

Brunton, Mary, *Discipline: A Novel* (London: Longman, Hurst, Rees, Orme, and Brown, 1814).

Burke, Edmund, *Reflections on the Revolution in France* (1790), edited by Leslie Mitchell, in Paul Langford (general ed.), *The Writings and Speeches of Edmund Burke,* v.viii (Oxford: Clarendon Press, 1989).

Burney, Frances, *The Wanderer, or Female Difficulties* (London: Longman, Hurst, Rees, Orme, and Brown, 1814).

Diary and Letters of Madame D'Arblay, edited by Muriel Masefield (London: G. Routledge & Son, 1931).

Camilla (1796), edited by Edward and Linda Bloom (Oxford: Oxford University Press, 1972).

Cecilia (1782), edited by, Peter Sabor and Margaret Anne Doody (Oxford: Oxford University Press, 1988).

Journals and Letters, edited by Peter Sabor and Lars E. Troide (London: Penguin, 2001).

Evelina (1778), edited by Edward Bloom (Oxford: Oxford University Press, 2002).

Canning, George, *The Letter Journal of George Canning 1793–1795,* edited by Peter Jupp (London: Royal Historical Society, 1991).

Chancellor, E. Beresford, *Memorials of St. James's Street and Chronicles of Almack's* (London: G. Richards Ltd., 1922).

Chivers, G. M. S., *The Modern Dancing Master* (London: published at the author's Salle de danse, 1822).

Dickens, Charles, *Our Mutual Friend*, 2 vols. (London: Chapman and Hall, 1865).
Tale of Two Cities, edited by A. Saunders (Oxford: Oxford University Press, 1988), III, v, 267–268.

Dyer, George, *Poems* (London: J. Johnson, 1792).

Eaton, Daniel Isaac, *Politics for the People or a Salmagundi for Swine*, 2 vols. (London: D. I. Eaton, 1794).

Edgeworth, Maria, *Belinda* (1801), edited by Kathryn J. Kirkpatrick (Oxford: Oxford University Press, 1994).

Farington, Joseph, *The Diary of Joseph Farington*, edited by Kenneth Garlick, Angus Macintyre, Kathryn Cave and Evelyn Newby, 16 vols. (New Haven, CT: Yale University Press, 1978–1998).

Fell, Ralph, *A Tour through the Batavian Republic during the Latter Part of the Year 1800: Containing an Account of the Revolution and Recent Events in That Country* (London: R. Phillips, 1801).
Memoirs of the Public Life of the Late Right Honourable Charles James Fox (London: J. F. Hughes, 1808).

Fenwick, Elizabeth, *Secresy: Or, The Ruin on the Rock* [c. 1796] (Ontario, Canada: Broadview Press Ltd., 1998).

Galt, John, *The Annals of the Parish* (Philadelphia: M. Carey & Sons, 1821).
The Provost (1822), edited by Ian A. Gordon (Oxford: Oxford University Press, 1973).

Gawthern, Abigail, *The Diary of Abigail Gawthern*, edited by Adrian Henstock, *Thoroton Society Record Series XXXIII* for 1978 and 1979 (Nottingham: Thoroton Society, 1980).

Gerrald, Joseph, *A Convention the Only Means of Saving Us from Ruin*, 2nd ed. (London: np, 1794).

Gibbons, Joshua, *Lincolnshire Collections Vol 1: The Joshua Gibbons Manuscript*, edited by Peter D. Sumner (Rochdale: Dave Mallinson Publications, 1997).

Godwin, William, *The Enquirer: Reflections on Education, Manners, and Literature, in a Series of Essays* (London: G. G. and J. Robinson, 1797).
Memoirs of the Author of a Vindication of the Rights of Woman (London: J. Johnson and G. G. and J. Robinson, 1798).
Fleetwood, or the New Man of Feeling, 3 vols. (London: Richard Phillips, 1805).
Collected Novels and Memoirs of William Godwin, edited by Mark Philp, 8 vols. (London: Pickering & Chatto, 1992).
'Things as They Are, or The Adventures of Caleb Williams' (1794), in Mark Philp (ed.), *Collected Novels and Memoirs of William Godwin* (London: Pickering & Chatto, 1992), vol. III.
'Memoirs of the Author of a Vindication of the Rights of Woman' (1798), in Mark Philp (ed.), *Collected Novels and Memoirs of William Godwin* (London: Pickering & Chatto, 1992), vol. I, pp. 87–157.
'St Leon: A Tale of the Sixteenth Century' (1798), in Mark Philp (ed.), *Collected Novels and Memoirs of William Godwin* (London: Pickering & Chatto, 1992), vol. IV.

Political and Philosophical Writings of William Godwin, edited by Mark Philp, 7 vols. (London: Pickering & Chatto, 1993).

The Plays of William Godwin, edited by David O'Shaughnessy (London: Pickering & Chatto, 2010).

The Letters of William Godwin: Volume I: 1778–1797, edited by Pamela Clemit (Oxford: Oxford University Press, 2011).

An Enquiry Concerning Political Justice (1793), edited by Mark Philp (Oxford: Oxford University Press, 2013).

The Letters of William Godwin: Volume II: 1798–1805, edited by Pamela Clemit (Oxford: Oxford University Press, 2014).

Gower, Lord Granville Leveson (first earl Granville): *Private Correspondence, 1781 to 1821*, edited by Countess Castalia Granville (London: J. Murray, 1916).

Gronow, Rees Howell, Captain, *The Reminiscences and Recollections of Captain Gronow* (London: np, 1900).

Hawkins, Laetitia Matilda, *Memoirs, Anecdotes, Facts, and Opinions*, 2 vols. (London: Longman, Hurst, Rees, Orme, Brown, and Green, 1824).

Hays, Mary, *Memoirs of Emma Courtney* (1796), edited by Eleanor Ty (Oxford: Oxford University Press, 1996).

The Victim of Prejudice (London 1799) and *Appeal to the Men of Great Britain on Behalf of Women (1798)*, edited by Eleanor Ty, 2nd ed. (Toronto, Canada: Broadview Press, 1998).

The Correspondence (1779–1843) of Mary Hays, British Novelist, edited by Marilyn L. Brooks (Lampeter, Wales: Mellen Edwin Press, 2004).

Holcroft, Thomas, *Memoirs of the Late Thomas Holcroft, Written by Himself; and Continued to the Time of His Death from His Diary, Notes, and Other Papers* (London: Longman, Brown, Green, and Longmans, 1852).

Anna St Ives (1791), edited by Peter Faulkner (Oxford: Oxford University Press, 1970).

Hugh Trevor (1795), edited by Seamus Deane (Oxford: Oxford University Press, 1978).

Holland, William, *Paupers and Pig Killers: The Diary of William Holland, a Somerset Parson, 1799–1818*, edited by Jack Ayers (Stroud, Gloucestershire: Alan Sutton Publishing Ltd., 1984).

Hume, David, *Treatise of Human Nature* (Edinburgh: A. Miller and A. Kincaid, 1740).

'Of the First Principles of Government', in Eugene F. Miller (ed.), *Essays: Moral, Political and Literary* (Indianapolis, IN: Liberty Classics, 1987).

Hutton, Catherine, *The Miser Married, a Novel in Three Volumes* (London: Longman, Hurst, Rees, Orme, and Brown, 1813).

Welsh Mountaineer, a Novel (London: Longman, Hurst, Rees, Orme, and Brown, 1817).

Oakwood Hall, a Novel (London: Longman, Hurst, Rees, Orme, and Brown, 1819).

Inchbald, Elizabeth, *Nature and Art*, vol. 2 (London: G. G. and J. Robinson, 1797) .

The Diaries of Elizabeth Inchbald, edited by Ben P. Robertson, 3 vols. (London: Pickering & Chatto, 2007).

A Simple Story (1791), edited by J. M. S. Tomkins (Oxford: Oxford University Press, 1998).

Jackson, Joshua, *Tunes, Songs and Dances from the 1798 Manuscript of Joshua Jackson*, edited by G. Bowen, L. Bowen, R. Shepherd and R. Shepherd, 2 vols. (Yorkshire: Bowen and Shepherd, 1998 and 2011).

Lamb, Charles, *The Letters of Charles Lamb*, edited by E. V. Lucas, 3 vols. (London: J. M. Dent & sons & Methuen & Co., Ltd, 1935).

Lequinio, J. M., *Les préjugés détruits* (Paris: De L'Imprimerie Nationale, Et se trouve Chez Desenne, Debray, Libraires, au Jardin de la Révolution, ci-devant le Palais Royal, 1792).

Lister, Anne, *The Secret Diaries of Miss Anne Lister*, edited by Helena Whitbread (London: Virago, 2010).

Mackintosh, James, *Memoirs of the Life of the Rt Hon. Sir James Mackintosh*, 2 vols. (London: Edward Moxton, 1835).

Mackintosh, Robert James (ed.), *Discourse on the Study of the Law of Nature and Nations* (London: np, 1799).

Mathias, Thomas, *The Pursuits of Literature: A Satirical Poem in Dialogue. With Notes. Part the Fourth and Last* (London: T. Becket, 1797).

Montaigne, Michel de, *The Complete Works*, translated by D. Frame (London: Everyman, 2003).

More, Hannah, *Village Politics* (London: np, 1793).

Strictures on the Modern System of Female Education with a View of the Principles and Conduct Prevalent among Women of Rank and Fortune, 2 vols., 3rd ed. (London: T. Cadell, 1799).

Coelebs in Search of a Wife, edited by Patricia Demers (Toronto, Canada: Broadview, 2007).

Moritz, Karl Philipp, *Anton Reiser*, translated and edited by R. Robinson (Harmondsworth: Penguin Books, 1997).

Oakes, James, *The Oakes Diaries I: Business, Politics and the Family in Bury St Edmunds, 1778–1800*, edited by Jane Fiske (Suffolk Record Society), vol. XXXII (Woodbridge, Suffolk: Boydell, 1990).

Opie, Amelia, *The Father and Daughter (1801)* and *Dangers of Coquetry (1790)*, edited by Shelley King and John B. Pierce (Ontario, Canada: Broadview Press, 2003).

Adeline Mowbray (1805), edited by Anne McWhir (Ontario, Canada: Broadview Press, 2010).

Paine, Thomas, 'Rights of Man: Part the Second' (1792), edited by Mark Philp, *Rights of Man, Common Sense, and other Political Writings* (Oxford: Oxford University Press, 1995).

Pigott, Charles, *The Jockey Club* (London: H. D. Symonds, 1792).

The Female Jockey Club (London: np, 1794).

Political Dictionary (London: D. I. Eaton, 1795).

Polwhele, Richard, *The Unsex'd Females: A Poem, Addressed to the Author of The Pursuits of Literature* (London: Cadell and Davies, 1798).

Price, Richard, *The Correspondence of Richard Price: Volume III February 1786– February 1791*, edited by Bernard Peach and D. O. Thomas (Cardiff: University of Wales Press, 1994).

'A Discourse on the Love of Our Country', in *Price, Political Writings* (Cambridge: Cambridge University Press, 2009), pp. 176–196.

Priestley, Joseph, 'Essay on the First Principles of Government and on the Nature of Political, Civil, and Religious Liberty', in Peter Miller (ed.), *Political Writings* (Cambridge: Cambridge University Press, 1993), pp. 1–128.

Radcliffe, Ann, *A Sicilian Romance* (1790), edited by Alison Milbank (Oxford: Oxford University Press, 1993).

The Romance of the Forest (1791), edited by Chloe Chard (Oxford: Oxford University Press, 1999).

Mysteries of Udolpho (1794), edited by Bonamy Dobrée and Terry Castle (Oxford: Oxford University Press, 2008).

The Italian (1797), edited by Nick Groom (Oxford: Oxford University Press, 2017).

Radcliffe, Mary Anne, *The Female Advocate, or an Attempt to Recover the Rights of Women from Male Usurpation* (London: Vernor and Hood, 1799).

Robinson, Mary (pseud Anne Frances Randall), *A Letter to the Women of England* (London, 1799) and *The Natural Daughter* (1799), edited by Sharon M. Selzer (Toronto, Canada: Broadview Press, 2003).

Walsingham, or the Pupil of Nature (1797), edited by Julie A. Shaffer (Toronto, Canada: Broadview Press, 2003).

Rogers, Samuel, *Recollections of the Table Talk of Samuel Rogers to Which Is Added Porsoniana*, edited by W. Sharpe (London: Moxton, 1856).

Skinner, John, *Journal of a Somerset Rector 1803–1834*, edited by H. and P. Coombs (Oxford: Oxford University Press, 1971).

Smith, Charlotte, *Collected Letters of Charlotte Smith*, edited by Judith Phillips Stanton (Bloomington, IN: Indiana University Press, 2003).

Smith, John Thomas, *Nollekens and His Times (1828)* (Oxford: Oxford University Press, 1929).

Spence, Thomas, *Pigs' Meat; or Lessons for the Swinish Multitude* (London: T. Spence, 1795).

Stael, Mme de, *Corinne, or Italy* (1807), edited by S. Raphael (Oxford: Oxford University Press, 1998).

Stendhal, *Love*, translated by Gilbert and Suzanne Sale (London: Penguin, 1975).

Taylor, John, *Records of My Life*, 2 vols. (London: Edward Bull, 1832).

Thelwall, John, *Rights of Nature* (London: H. D. Symonds, 1796).

Thale, Mary (ed.), *Selections from the Papers of the London Corresponding Society: 1792–1799* (Cambridge: Cambridge University Press, 1983).

Thrale, Hester, *Thraliana: The Diary of Mrs Hester Lynch Thrale (Later Mrs Piozzi) 1776–1809*, edited by Katharine C. Balderston (Oxford: Oxford University Press, 2014).

Tocqueville, Alexis de, *Democracy in America*, edited by Alan Ryan (London: Everyman, 1994).

Wardle, Ralph (ed.), *Godwin and Mary: Letters of Mary Wollstonecraft and William Godwin* (Lawrence, KS: University of Kansas, 1967).

Wollstonecraft, Mary, *A Vindication of the Rights of Women* and *A Vindication of the Rights of Men*, edited by Janet Todd (Oxford: Oxford University Press, 1994).

The Collected Letters of Mary Wollstonecraft, edited by Janet Todd (New York: Columbia University Press, 2003).

Mary and The Wrongs of Woman (1798), edited by Gary Kelly (Oxford: Oxford University Press, 2007).

Letters Written in Sweden, Norway, and Denmark (1796), edited by Tonne Brekke and Jon Mee (Oxford: Oxford University Press, 2009).

Wraxhall, Nicholas, *The Historical and Posthumous Memoirs of Sir Nicholas William Wraxall 1772–1784*, edited by Henry B. Wheatley, 5 vols. (London: Bickers & Son, 1884).

Selected Secondary Sources

Aikin-Sneath, Betsy, *Georgian Chronicle: Mrs Barbauld and Her Family* (London: Methuen, 1958).

Alexander, David, *Richard Newton and English Caricature in the 1790s* (Manchester: Manchester University Press, 1998).

Caroline Watson & Female Printmaking in Late Georgian England (Cambridge: The Fitzwilliam Museum, 2014).

Andrew, Donna, *London Debating Societies, 1776–1799* (London: London Record Society, 1994).

Baer, Marc, *Theatre and Disorder in Late Georgian London* (Oxford: Clarendon Press, 1992).

Bailey, Joanne, *Unquiet Lives: Marriage and Marriage Breakdown in England, 1660–1800* (Cambridge: Cambridge University Press, 2003).

Barrell, John, *Imagining the King's Death: Figurative Treason, Fantasies of Regicide, 1793–1796* (Oxford: Oxford University Press, 2000).

The Spirit of Despotism: Invasions of Privacy in the 1790s (Oxford: Oxford University Press, 2006).

Baycroft, T. and David Hopkin (eds.), *Folklore and Nationalism during the Long Nineteenth Century* (Leiden: Brill, 2012).

Bergès, Sandrine, Eileen Hunt Botting and Alan Coffee (eds.), *The Wollstonecraftian Mind* (London: Routledge, 2019).

Binhammer, Katherine, 'The Sex Panic of the 1790s', *Journal of the History of Sexuality* 6(3) (January 1996), 409–434.

Bolton, Arthur T., *The Portrait of Sir John Soane RA: 1753–1837* (London: Butler and Tanner Ltd., 1927).

Brophy, James M., *Popular Culture and the Public Sphere in the Rhineland 1800–1850* (Cambridge: Cambridge University Press, 2007).

Burns, Arthur and Joanna Innes, *Rethinking the Age of Reform: Britain 1780–1830* (Cambridge: Cambridge University Press, 2003).

Buurman, Erica and Oskar Cox Jensen, 'Dancing the "Waterloo Waltz"', in Kate Astbury and Mark Philp (eds.), *Napoleon's Hundred Days and the Politics of Legitimacy* (Basingstoke: Palgrave Macmillan, 2018).

Castle, Terry, *Masquerade and Civilization: The Carnivalesque in English Culture and Fiction* (Stanford, CA: Stanford University Press, 1986).

Chalus, Elaine, *Elite Women English Political Life 1754–1790* (Oxford: Oxford Historical Monograph, 2005).

Chernock, Arianne, *Men and the Making of Modern British Feminism* (Stanford, CA: Stanford University Press, 2010).

Clark, Anna, *Scandal: The Sexual Politics of the British Constitution* (Princeton, NJ: Princeton University Press, 2004).

Clemit, Pamela and Jenny McAuley, 'Sociablity in Godwin's Diary: The Case of John King', *Bodleian Library Record* 24(1) (2011), 51–56.

Cobban, Alfred, *The Debate on the French Revolution 1789–1800* (London: A & C Black, 1950).

Colley, Linda, *Britons: Forging the Nation 1707–1837* (New Haven, CT: Yale University Press, 1992).

Constantine, Mary Ann, '"The Bounds of Female Reach": Catherine Hutton's Fiction and Her Tours in Wales', *Romantic Textualities: Literature and Print Culture, 1780–1840* 22 (2017), 92–105.

Cookson, John, *The Friends of Peace* (Cambridge: Cambridge University Press, 1983).

The British Armed Nation 1793–1815 (Oxford: Oxford University Press, 1997).

Couper, Sarah, 'John Pinkerton', *Oxford Dictionary of National Biography* (2008), https://ezproxy-prd.bodleian.ox.ac.uk:2095/10.1093/ref:odnb/22301.

Darley, Gillian, *John Soane: An Accidental Romantic* (New Haven, CT: Yale University Press, 1999).

Davidoff, Leonora and Hall, Catherine, *Family Fortunes: Men and Women of the English Middle Class 1780–1850*, revised ed. (London: Routledge, 2002).

Davis, Michael T., 'John Horne Tooke', *Oxford Dictionary of National Biography* (2009), https://ezproxy-prd.bodleian.ox.ac.uk:2095/10.1093/ref:odnb/27545.

Davison, Kate, 'Early Modern Social Networks: Antecedents, Opportunities, and Challenges' *American Historical Review* 124(2) (April 2019), 456–482.

Dennant, Paul, 'The Barbarous English Jig': The 'Black Joke' in the Eighteenth and Nineteenth Centuries', *Folk Music Journal* 110(3) (2013), 298–318.

Ditchfield, G. M., 'The Parliamentary Struggle on the Repeal of the Test and Corporation Acts, 1787–1790', *English Historical Review* 89 (1974), 551–577.

Dunbar, R. I. M., 'Neocortex Size as a Constraint on Group Size in Primates', *Journal of Human Evolution* 22(6) (1992), 469–493.

Fitzpatrick, Martin, 'Toleration and Truth', *Enlightenment and Dissent* 1 (1982), 3–31.

'The View from Mount Pleasant: Enlightenment in Late-Eighteenth Century Liverpool', *Oxford University Studies in the Enlightenment* (formerly *SVEC*) 2008(1) (2008), 119–144.

Foreman, Amanda, *Georgiana, Duchess of Devonshire* (London: HarperCollins, 1998).

Fox, Celina, *London: World City* (New Haven, CT: Yale University Press, 2002).

Frow, Edmund and Ruth Frow, *Citizen Guillotine* (Preston: E and R Frow, 1996).

Gambetta, Diego, 'Grandfather's Gossip', *Archives Européennes de Sociologie*, XXXV (1994), 199–223.

Garnai, Amy, *Revolutionary Imaginings in the 1790s: Charlotte Smith, Mary Robinson, Elizabeth Inchbald* (Basingstoke, Hampshire: Palgrave/Macmillan, 2009).

Garrett, Clarke, *Respectable Folly* (Baltimore, MD: Johns Hopkins University Press, 1975).

Gatrell, Vic, *City of Laughter Sex and Satire in Eighteenth Century London* (London: Atlantic Books, 2006).

    The First Bohemians: Life and Art in London's Golden Age (London: Allen Lane, 2013).

Gee, Austin, *The British Volunteer Movement, 1793–1815* (Oxford: Oxford University Press, 2003).

George, M. Dorothy, *Catalogue of Political and Personal Satires Preserved in the Department of Prints and Drawings in the British Museum*, vol. vii (London: The British Museum, 1942).

Gill, Stephen, *William Wordsworth*, Oxford Authors series (Oxford: Oxford University Press, 1984).

Gillaspie, John A., 'Charles Dibdin', *Oxford Dictionary of National Biography* (2014), https://ezproxy-prd.bodleian.ox.ac.uk:2095/10.1093/ref:odnb/7585.

Gilmartin, Kevin, *Print Politics: The Press and Radical Opposition in Early Nineteenth-Century England* (Cambridge: Cambridge University Press, 1996).

    Writing against Revolution: Literary Conservatism in Britain, 1790–1832 (Cambridge: Cambridge University Press, 2007).

    Sociable Places (Cambridge: Cambridge University Press, 2017).

Gleadle, Kathryn, *British Women in the Nineteenth Century* (London: Palgrave, 2001).

    'Revisiting *Family Fortunes*, Reflections on the Twentieth Anniversary of the Publication of L. Davidoff & C. Hall (1987) *Family Fortunes: Men and Women of the English Middle Class, 1780–1850* (London: Hutchinson)', *Women's History Review* 16(5) (2007), 773–782.

    Borderline Citizens: Women, Gender, and Political Culture in Britain, 1815–1867 (Oxford: British Academy/Oxford University Press, 2009).

    'The Juvenile Enlightenment: British Children and Youth during the French Revolution', *Past and Present* 233 (November 2016), 143–184.

Gluckman, Max, 'Gossip and Scandal', *Current Anthropology* 4(3) (June 1963), 307–316.

Goodwin, Albert, *The Friends of Liberty: The English Democratic Movement in the Age of the French Revolution* (London: Hutchinson, 1979).

Gordon, Lyndall, *Vindication: A Life of Mary Wollstonecraft* (London: Virago, 2006).

Graham, Jenny, *The Nation, the Law and the King: Reform Politics in England, 1789–1799* (Lanham, MD: University Press of America, 2000).

Granovetter, Mark, 'The Strength of Weak Ties', *American Journal of Sociology* 78 (1973), 1360–1380.

    Society and Economy: Framework and Principles (Cambridge, MA: Belknap/Harvard University Press, 2017).

Grogan, Claire, 'Mary Wollstonecraft and Hannah More: Politics, Feminism and Modern Critics', *Lumen* 13 (1994), 99–108.

Guest, Harriet, *Small Change: Women, Learning, Patriotism, 1750–1810* (Chicago, IL: Chicago University Press, 2000).

Unbounded Attachment: Sentiment and Politics in the Age of the French Revolution (Oxford: Oxford University Press, 2013).

Gunn, J. A. W., 'Influence, Parties and the Constitution: Changing Attitudes, 1783–1832', *Historical Journal* 17(2) (June 1974), 301–328.

Haakensson, Knud (ed.), *Enlightenment and Religion: Rational Dissent in Eighteenth Century Britain* (Cambridge: Cambridge University Press, 1996).

Habermas, Jurgen, 'The Public Sphere: An Encyclopedia Article', *New German Critique* 3 (1974, orig 1964), 49–55.

The Structural Transformation of the Public Sphere, translated by T. Berger and F. Lawrence (Cambridge: Polity Press, 1989).

'Further reflections on the public sphere', in C. Calhoun (ed.), *Habermas and the Public Sphere* (Cambridge, MA: MIT Press, 1992).

Heard, Kate (ed.), *High Spirits: The Comic Art of Thomas Rowlandson* (London: Royal Collection, 2013).

Hilton, Boyd, *A Mad, Bad, & Dangerous People: England 1783–1846* (Oxford: Clarendon Press, 2006).

Hirschman, A. O., *Rhetoric of Reaction: Perversity, Futility, Jeopardy* (Cambridge, MA: Harvard University Press, 1991).

Hone, J. Ann, *For the Cause of Truth: Radicalism in London 1796–1821* (Oxford: Clarendon Press, 1982).

Hopkin, David, *Voices of the People in Nineteenth-Century France* (Cambridge: Cambridge University Press, 2012).

Horgan, Kate, *The Politics of Songs in Eighteenth Century Britain* (London: Pickering & Chatto, 2014).

Innes, Joanna. 'Networks in British History', *East Asian Journal of British History* 5 (2016), 51–72.

Innes, Joanna and Mark Philp (eds.), *Reimagining Democracy in the Age of Revolutions* (Oxford: Oxford University Press, 2013).

Innes, Joanna and Mark Philp, *Reimagining Democracy in the Mediterranean* (Oxford: Oxford University Press, 2018).

Israel, Jonathan, *Radical Enlightenment* (Oxford: Oxford University Press, 2001).

Jensen, Oskar Cox, *Napoleon and British Song, 1797–1822* (Basingstoke: Palgrave Macmillan, 2015).

Jensen, Oskar Cox, David, Kennerley and Ian Newman (eds.), *Charles Dibdin and Late Georgian Culture* (Oxford: Oxford University Press, 2018).

Johnston, Kenneth, *Unusual Suspects* (Oxford: Oxford University Press, 2013).

Kegan Paul, Charles, *William Godwin: His Friends and Contemporaries*, 2 vols. (London: H. S. King, 1876).

Kerber, Linda, 'Separate Spheres, Female Worlds, Woman's Place: The Rhetoric of Women's History', *Journal of American History* 75(1) (1988), 9–39.

King, Shelley, 'Portrait of a Marriage: John and Amelia Opie and the Sister Arts', *Studies in Eighteenth Century Culture* 40 (2011), 27–33.

Kirk, John, Andrew Noble and Michael Brown, *United Islands? The Languages of Resistance* (London: Pickering & Chatto, 2012).

Lewis, Judith S., *Sacred to Female Patriotism: Gender, Class, and Politics in Late Georgian Britain* (London: Routledge, 2003).

Lloyd, Sarah, 'Amour in the Shrubbery: Reading the Detail of English Adultery Trial Publications of the 1780s', *Eighteenth Century Studies* 39(4) (2006), 421–442.

Lobban, Michael, 'From Seditious Libel to Unlawful Assembly: Peterloo and the Changing Face of Political Crime c1770–1820', *Oxford Journal of Legal Studies* 10(3) (1990), 307–352.

Locke, Don, *A Fantasy of Reason: The Life and Thought of William Godwin* (London: Routledge and Kegan Paul, 1980).

Manvell, Roger, *Elizabeth Inchbald: A Biographical Study* (Lantham, MD: University Press of America, 1987).

McCalman, Iain, 'Feminism and Free Love in an Early Nineteenth Century Radical Movement', *Labour History* 38 (1980), 1–25.

'Newgate in Revolution: Radical Enthusiasm and Romantic Counterculture', *Eighteenth-Century Life* 22 (February 1998), 95–110.

McCormack, Matthew, *Embodying the Militia in Georgian England* (Oxford: Oxford University Press, 2015).

McNeil, Maureen, 'Erasmus Darwin', *Oxford Dictionary of National Biography* (2013), https://ezproxy-prd.bodleian.ox.ac.uk:2095/10.1093/ref:odnb/7177.

Mee, Jon, *Conversable Worlds: Literature, Contention, and Community 1762 to 1830* (Oxford: Oxford University Press, 2011).

Print, Publicity, and Popular Radicalism in the 1790s: The Laurel of Liberty (Cambridge: Cambridge University Press, 2016).

Mellor, Anne, *Mothers of the Nation: Women's Political Writing in England 1780–1830* (Bloomington, IN: Indiana University Press, 2000).

Merry, Sally Engel, 'Rethinking Gossip and Scandal', in Donald Black (ed.), *Toward a General Theory of Social Control*, vol. 1 (New York: Academic Press, Inc., 1984), pp. 271–302.

Moody, Jane (ed.), *Illegitimate Theatre in London 1770–1840* (Cambridge: Cambridge University Press, 2000).

Moody, Jane, *British Theatre: 1730–1830* (Cambridge: Cambridge University Press, 2007).

Myers, Mitzi, '"Reform or Ruin": A Revolution in Female Manners', *Studies in Eighteenth-Century Culture* 11 (1982), 199–216.

Myers, Victoria, 'William Godwin and the *ArsRhetorica*', *Studies in Romanticism* 41(3) (2002), 415–444.

Navickas, Katrina, *Loyalism and Radicalism in Lancashire 1789–1815* (Oxford: Oxford University Press, 2009).

Protest and the Politics of Space and Place 1789–1848 (Manchester: Manchester University Press, 2016).

Neurath, Otto, *Anti-Spengler* (München: Georg D. W. Callwey, Verlagsbuchhandlung, 1921).

Newman, Ian, 'Civilizing Taste: "Sandman Joe", the Bawdy Ballad and Metropolitan Improvement', *Eighteenth-Century Studies* 48(4) (2015), 437–456.

O'Loughlin, Katrina, '"Strolling Roxanas": Sexual Transgression and Social Satire in the Eighteenth Century', in Susan Broomhall (ed.), *Spaces for Feeling: Emotions and Sociabilities in Britain 1650–1850* (London: Routledge, 2015), pp. 112–136.

O'Shaughnessy, David, *William Godwin and the Theatre* (London: Pickering & Chatto, 2010).

'Caleb Williams and the Philomaths: Recalibrating Political Justice for the Nineteenth Century', *Nineteenth-Century Literature* 66(4) (March 2012), 423–448.

Paine, Robert, 'In Search of Friendship: An Exploratory Analysis of Middle-Class Culture' *Man* 4(4) (December 1969), 505–524.

Palmer, Susan, *At Home with the Soanes: Upstairs, Downstairs in 19th Century London* (London: Pimpernel Press, 1997).

Parkin, Frank, 'Working Class Conservatives: A Theory of Political Deviance', *British Journal of Sociology* 18 (1967), 278–290.

Parolin, Christina, 'The "She-Champion of Impiety": Female Radicalism and Political Crime in Early Nineteenth Century England', in *Radical Space: Venues of Popular Politics in London 1790–1845* (Canberra: ANU Press, 2010), pp. 83–103.

Parssinen, T. M., 'Association, Convention and Anti-parliament in British Radical Politics, 1771–1848', *English Historical Review* 88 (1973), 504–533.

Paul, Lissa, *Eliza Fenwick: Early Modern Feminist* (Newark, DW: University of Delaware Press, 2019).

Peterson, Merrill D. and Robert C. Vaughan, *The Virginia Statute for Religious Freedom: Its Evolution and Consequences in American History* (Cambridge: Cambridge University Press, 1988).

Philp, Mark, *Godwin's Political Justice* (London: Duckworth, 1986).

'Democratic Virtues: Between Candour and Preference Falsification', *Enlightenment and Dissent* 19 (2000), 23–44.

'Preaching to the Unconverted', *Enlightenment and Dissent* 28 (2012), 73–88.

Reforming Ideas in Britain: Politics and Language in the Shadow of the French Revolution 1789–1815 (Cambridge, Cambridge University Press, 2014).

'Unconventional Norms', in Kevin Gilmartin (ed.), *Sociable Places* (Cambridge: Cambridge University Press, 2017).

'William Godwin', in Sandrine Bergès, Eileen Hunt Botting and Alan Coffee (eds.), *The Wollstonecraftian Mind* (London: Routledge, 2019), pp. 211–223.

'Candour, Courage and the Calculation of Consequences in Godwin's 1790s' in Eliza O'Brien, Helen Stark and Beatrice Turner (eds.), *Godwin and Fear* (Forthcoming).

Poole, Robert, *Peterloo: The English Uprising* (Oxford: Oxford University Press, 2019).

Porter, Gerald, 'Melody as a Bearer of Radical Ideology', in Eva Guillorel, David Hopkin and William G. Pooley (eds.), *Rhythms of Revolt: European Traditions and Memories of Social Conflict in Oral Culture* (Abingdon: Routledge, 2018), pp. 240–264.

Probert, Rebecca, Julie Shaffer and Joanne Bailey, *A Noble Affair* (Kenilworth: Brandram, 2013).

Rendall, Jane, 'Women and the Public Sphere', *Gender & History* 11 (1999), 475–488.

Richardson, Margaret, 'Learning in the Soane Office', in Neil Bingham (ed.), *The Education of the Architect Proceedings of the 22nd Annual Symposium of the*

Society of Architectural Historians of Great Britain (London: Society of Architectural Historians of Great Britain, 1993).

Rubenhold, Hallie, *Lady Worseley's Whim* (London: Chatto & Windus, 2008).

Russell, Gillian, *The Theatres of War* (Oxford: Clarendon Press, 1995).

Russell, Gillian and Clara Tuite (eds.), *Romantic Sociability: Social Networks and Literary Culture in Britain 1770–1840* (Cambridge: Cambridge University Press, 2006).

Schutte, Kimberly F., Marrying by the Numbers: Marriage Patterns of Aristocratic British Women, 1485–2000, Phd thesis, University of Kansas, 2011.

Women, Rank, and Marriage in the British Aristocracy, 1485–2000: An Open Elite? (London: Palgrave, 2014).

Seed, John, '"A Set of Men Powerful Enough in Many Things": Rational Dissent and Political Opposition in England, 1770–1790', in Knud Haakonssen (ed.), *Enlightenment and Religion: Rational Dissent in Eighteenth Century Britain* (Cambridge: Cambridge University Press, 1996), pp. 140–168.

Setzer, Sharon, 'Original Letters of the Celebrated Mrs Mary Robinson', *Philological Quarterly* 88 (3) (June 2009), 305–336.

Silver, Allan, 'Friendship in Commercial Society: Eighteenth-Century Social Theory and Modern Sociology', *American Journal of Sociology* 95(6) (May 1990), 1474–1504.

Silver, Harold, *Robert Owen on Education* (Cambridge: Cambridge University Press, 1969).

Smith, Olivia, *The Politics of Language 1791–1819* (Oxford: Oxford University Press, 1984).

Spacks, Patricia Meyer, 'In Praise of Gossip', *The Hudson Review* 35(1) (1982), 19–38.

StClair, William, *The Godwins and the Shelleys* (London: Faber and Faber, 1989).

Stafford, William, *English Feminists and their Opponents in the 1790s: Unsex'd and Proper Females* (Manchester: Manchester University Press, 2002).

Staves, Susan, *Married Women's Separate Property in England, 1660–1833* (Cambridge, MA: Harvard University Press, 1990).

Stroud, Dorothy, *Sir John Soane, Architect*, 2nd ed. (London: Giles de la Mare, 1996).

Taylor, Barbara, *Mary Wollstonecraft and the Feminist Imagination* (Cambridge: Cambridge University Press, 2003).

Temperley, Nicholas, *Athlone History of Music in Britain in the Romantic Age 1800–1914*, vol. 5 (London: Athlone Press, 1981).

Thomas, D. O., *The Honest Mind: The Thought and Work of Richard Price* (Oxford: Oxford University Press, 1977).

Thompson, E. P., *The Making of the English Working Class* (Harmondsworth: Penguin, 1963).

Customs in Common (Harmondsworth: Penguin, 1993).

Todd, Janet, *Mary Wollstonecraft: A Revolutionary Life* (New York: Columbia University Press, 2000).

Ty, Eleanor, *Unsex'd Revolutionaries: Five Women Novelists of the 1790s* (Toronto, Canada: University of Toronto Press, 1993).

Uglow, Jenny, *In These Times: Living in Britain through Napoleon's Wars, 1793–1815* (London: Faber and Faber, 2014).

Valladares, Susan, *Staging the Peninsular War: English Theatres 1807–1815* (Basingstoke: Ashgate, 2015).

Vickery, Amanda, 'Golden Age to Separate Spheres? A Review of the Categories and Chronologies of English Women's History', *Historical Journal* 36 (1993), 383–414.

  The Gentleman's Daughter: Women's Lives in Georgian England (London: Yale University Press, 1999).

Wahrman, Dror, *Imagining the Middle Class: The Political Representation of Class in Britain 1780–1840* (Cambridge: Cambridge University Press, 1995).

  The Making of the Modern Self: Identity and Culture in Eighteenth Century England (New Haven, CT: Yale University Press, 2006).

Wardle, Ralph M. (ed.), *Godwin & Mary: Letters of William Godwin and Mary Wollstonecraft* (London: Constable and Co. Ltd., 1967).

Wedd, Annie F. (ed.), *The Fate of the Fenwicks; Letters to Mary Hays (1798–1828)* (London: Methuen, 1927).

Wickwar, William H., *The Struggle or the Freedom of the Press 1819–1832* (London: George Allen & Unwin Ltd, 1928).

Williams, Bernard, *In the Beginning Was the Deed* (Princeton, NJ: Princeton University Press, 2005).

Wykes, David L., '"The Spirit of Persecutors Exemplified" The Priestley Riots and the Victims of the Church and King Mobs', *Unitarian Historical Society, Transactions* 20(1) (1991), 17–39.

Ylivuori, Soile, 'Rethinking Female Chastity and Gentlewoman's Honour in Eighteenth Century England', *Historical Journal* 59(1) (2016), 71–97.

  Women and Politeness in Eighteenth-Century England (London: Routledge, 2018).

Index